BAYONETS

FROM JANZEN'S NOTEBOOK

PUBLISHED IN THE UNITED STATES BY
JERRY L. JANZEN
P.O. BOX 2863
TULSA, OKLAHOMA 74101
U.S.A.

TO NAPOLEON BONAPARTE, WHO SAID "YOU MAY DO ANYTHING WITH BAYO-
NETS EXCEPT SIT ON THEM".

ISBN 0-9618173-0-5

COVER BY CHILTON DESIGN GROUP
PRINTING BY KISSEL PRINTING COMPANY
PHOTOGRAPHY BY LASSITER & SHOEMAKER

ACKNOWLEDGMENTS

THE DOCUMENT WHICH FOLLOWS IS REALLY THE COMPILATION OF MANY PEOPLES EFFORTS AND MERELY UTILIZED MY COLLECTION AS THE FOCAL POINT. THE DRAWINGS FOR THE MOST PART ARE REDUCTIONS OF THOSE IN PAUL KIESLING'S EXCELLENT BOOKS, WITH CONTRIBUTIONS FROM M. H. COLE. THE REMAINDER ARE MY OWN HUMBLE EFFORTS (UTILIZING PIECES FROM DRAWINGS BY KIESLING, COLE, CARTER, WALTER, WALSH, PRIEST AND REILLY), SOME ORIGINAL DRAWINGS BY SHERRY HOVESKELAND AND KATHY ENGHETA AND, FINALLY, A FEW DRAWINGS FROM SOME LONG FORGOTTEN SOURCES. THE NOTES, ON THE OTHER HAND, DOCUMENT MY OWN OBSERVATIONS AND RESEARCH AS WELL AS RESEARCH CONDUCTED BY JACK SCHRADER (WHO WROTE THE BULK OF THE U.S. AND GERMAN SECTIONS), LARRY JOHNSON (WHO CONTRIBUTED HEAVILY TO THE JAPANESE SECTION), AL HARDIN, ANTHONY CARTER, R. D. C. EVANS, JOHN WALTER, M. H. COLE, JOHN WATTS, PETER WHITE AND THE MANY OTHERS WHO HAVE CONTRIBUTED TO THE GENERAL KNOWLEDGE OF BAYONETS. I WANT TO GIVE SPECIAL MENTION TO FREDERICK STEPHENS WHOSE PICTORIAL BOOK ON BAYONETS GOT ME STARTED ON THIS ADDICTIVE AND FASCINATING HOBBY.

THE PREPARATION OF THE BOOK ITSELF WOULD NOT HAVE BEEN POSSIBLE WITHOUT THE TYPING AND PROOFREADING OF ANDREA HOLLAND, THE LAYOUT BY DARLENE JOHNSON, AND SEEMINGLY ENDLESS COPY EFFORTS BY JACKIE SMITH AND VIRGINIA PARKER.

ADDITIONALLY, I OWE A DEBT OF GRATITUDE TO THE FOLLOWING PEOPLE WHO FURNISHED DATA AND PICTURES, ENCOURAGED ME TO CONTINUE, REVIEWED MY DRAFTS AND ARE, IN NO SMALL WAY, RESPONSIBLE FOR THE BOOK:

PHIL STOBER	ROY BRASHEARS
ROD PARKER	BERYL BARNETT
PAT ANTHONY	GARY HENSARLING
JAKE GLICKMAN	JOHN BELLO
HOMER BRETT	MIKE WELSER
FRANK VAN GELDER	JAMES FRASCA
PRUDY MERCER	GREG ENGLEMAN
DICK ORR	NORRIS ROHRER
DUANE SPARKS	"BOB" (BOB'S BASEMENT)
BRIAN CONKLE	ROBERT REILLY
GARY MERCER	FRANK GOW
JAMES B. HUGHES, JR.	JACK BROWN
DAVID SEIBERT	HAROLD KASSEL (DECEASED)
FRANK SMITH	"RED" JACKSON (DECEASED)

THE INDIAN TERRITORY GUN COLLECTORS

JERRY L. JANZEN
TULSA, OKLAHOMA 1987

INTRODUCTION

This book has several objectives, including the documentation of my collection, presentation of the information I have accumulated and, finally, the compilation of a reasonably complete, inexpensive book for the novice collector, partial collector and bayonet-related collector. This effort is in no way a definitive reference work and, in fact, contains only the information which I feel is of interest to my audience. References are included with each bayonet which, coupled with the detailed bibliography, will allow the serious collector to locate all published data on any given piece or country.

The book is organized by country, with the pieces arranged more or less chronologically by date, and a number of factors are important to keep in mind when using this book.

- The references, as noted earlier, are from a variety of authors; however, Kiesling is most prevalent, with Carter used for German ersatz pieces, Hardin and Cole (Book III) for U.S. pieces, and Evans (Evans & Stephens, <u>The Bayonet</u>) on recent pieces.

- The illustrations are not to any scale and were compiled over a number of years. Likewise, my rather erratic printing is the result of pens available at the time, my mood at the time and, lastly, a certain deficiency of artistic ability.

- The reference system utilizes the page number which is in the lower right-hand corner of each page plus an item number which is to the left of each bayonet description.

- Measurements are given only for sockets and other pieces where relevant because the references listed provide more precise data than my ruler.

- The U.S. section is subdivided as to type of bayonet for easier reference.

Any errors and omissions are strictly my responsibility as are any misquotes or erroneous speculations. I hope you profit from this material and would welcome any correspondence.

Country	Page

TROOPS ON PARADE AT FORT RILEY, KANSAS IN 1880. NOTE THE TROWEL
BAYONETS. SEE PAGE 215 FOR DETAILS OF THESE BAYONETS (PICTURE
COURTESY OF THE KANSAS STATE HISTORICAL SOCIETY, TOPEKA).

No. 1. **ARGENTINE MODEL 1875 - REMINGTON.** THESE BAYONETS WERE PRODUCED FOR THE REMINGTON ROLLING BLOCK RIFLE AND WERE RELEASED SOME YEARS AGO. A LARGE NUMBER HAD BEEN MADE INOPERABLE BY EITHER REMOVING THE SPRING OR BREAKING THE SLOT. ONE EXAMPLE IN MY COLLECTION IS STAMPED "RA" (REPUBLIC OF ARGENTINA). ANOTHER HAS A SERIAL NUMBER ONLY. ONE HAS A BRASS-MOUNTED LEATHER SCABBARD AND THE OTHER AN ALL STEEL SCABBARD. THIS BAYONET WAS ALSO UTILIZED BY URUGUAY AND POSSIBLY A NUMBER OF OTHER SOUTH AMERICAN COUNTRIES. IN DISCUSSIONS WITH THE IMPORTER, I WAS TOLD THAT THE LEATHER SCABBARDS WERE ALL OBTAINED FROM ARGENTINA.

NOTE: I HAVE ALSO SEEN ARGENTINE MARKED FRENCH M-1866 (CHASSE-POT) BAYONETS. THE MARK IS NORMALLY ON THE CROSSGUARD AND CONSISTS OF AN "A" IN A CIRCLE WITH A STAR AT THE APEX OF THE "A".

① ARGENTINE M.1875 REMINGTON

WATTS & WHITE PG. #1

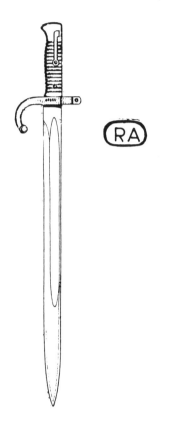

(RA)

SCABBARD TYPES

1985 AD IN SHOTGUN NEWS

No. 1. **ARGENTINE MODEL 1891 - ALLOY GRIPS.** THE MAJORITY OF THESE BAYONETS HAD THE CREST DEFACED, ALTHOUGH A NUMBER OF COMPONENTS FOR THE BAYONETS WERE IMPORTED A FEW YEARS AGO WITH THE CRESTS ON THE BLADES. IT IS MY OPINION THAT SOME BAYONETS AVAILABLE WITH THE CRESTS INTACT WERE PRODUCED FROM THESE COMPONENTS. EXAMPLES OF THIS BAYONET HAVE BEEN NOTED WITH THE ARGENTINE CREST "GROUND" AND THE CREST OF EL SALVADOR EMBOSSED ON THE SCABBARD.

No. 2. **ARGENTINE MODEL 1891 - BRASS GRIPS.** THESE BAYONETS WERE PRODUCED IN COMPARATIVELY FEWER NUMBERS AND WERE UTILIZED BY ARGENTINE NAVY AND/OR POLICE.

* **ARGENTINE MODEL 1891.** I HAVE A SHORTENED EXAMPLE OF THE M-1891 WHICH <u>BAJONETTEN DA TILL NU</u> IDENTIFIES AS POLICE. I TEND TO GO WITH THE VENEZUELAN THEORY NOTED.

No. 3. **ARGENTINE MAUSER MODEL 1909 - WOOD GRIPS.** THESE BAYONETS WERE PRODUCED IN WHAT APPEARS TO HAVE BEEN FEWER NUMBERS THAN THE RIFLES AND ARE RELATIVELY SCARCE. IN ADDITION, ARGENTINA PRODUCED A MODEL 1909 SIDEARM WHICH IS SIMILAR TO THE BAYONET, HOWEVER, HAS ALTERNATELY FACING QUILLONS.

NOTE: ARGENTINA CURRENTLY UTILIZES THE BELGIAN FN FAL KNIFE BAYONET WITH THE TWO-PRONG FLASH SUPPRESSOR (SEE 20-4). EXAMPLES WERE CAPTURED BY THE BRITISH IN THE FALKLANDS. THE ARGENTINE EXAMPLES ALL APPEAR TO HAVE A RATHER COMPLEX WEB BELT FROG WITH A METAL STUD LOOP, U.S. STYLE BELT HOOKS AND A BLACK PLASTIC BLOCK ON THE BACK (TO SLIP ONTO A BELT). THE BRASS SNAP-ON STUDS ARE MARKED "TEMPEX".

① *ARGENTINE M. 1891*
ALLOY GRIPS

KIESLING VOL II #286
WATTS & WHITE PG 2

✳ A SHORTENED VERSION OF 2-1 AND 2-2 ALSO EXISTS WHICH WAS NOT MANUFACTURED WITH THE SERIAL NUMBER ON THE BLADE. I HAVE BEEN TOLD IT WAS USED BY VENEZUELA

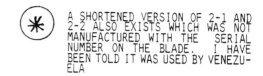

② *ARGENTINE M. 1891*
BRASS GRIPS

KIESLING VOL II #287

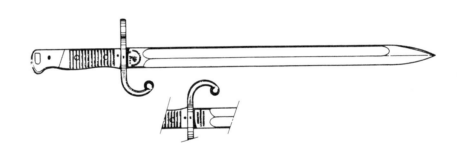

③ *ARGENTINE M. 1909*

KIESLING VOL II #288
WATTS & WHITE PG 2

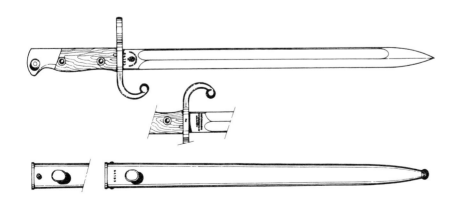

No. 1. SMLE Pattern 1907 - issued in Australia, made in England. The Australian bayonets with hooked quillons are comparatively rare because the Australians apparently removed the quillons at the first opportunity. The piece in my collection is Wilkinson produced, however, the Australians also manufactured the pattern 1907 bayonet with hooked quillon until mid-World War I at Lithgow. The Australian produced pieces have a more squared quillon than the British models.

NOTE: The definitive source on Australian bayonets was authored by I. D. Skennerton and is titled Australian Service Bayonets (see pg. 247).

① S.M.L.E. PATTERN 1907
MFG IN ENGLAND

K. IESLING   VOL. II #320
SKENNERTON   PG #102

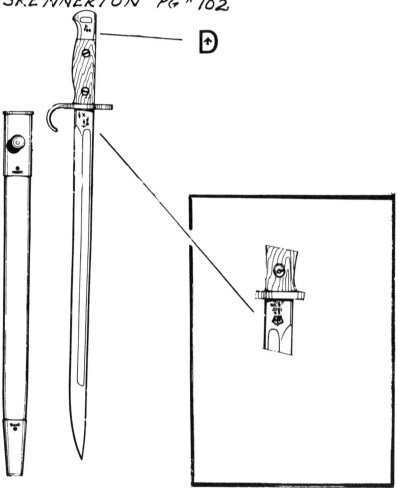

No. 1. SMLE Pattern 1907 "Australia". A number of the earlier bayonets were marked "Australia" on the grips. The World War II scabbard pattern is illustrated (note the early Lithgow proof).

No. 2. SMLE Pattern 1907/1942 "Slaz". Slaz bayonets were marked on the grips and I possess 1942, 1945 and 1955 dates. (The bayonets were refurbished in the 50's for Australian troops in Korea.) The Wood Room was moved from Lithgow to Slazenger in Sydney in 1941 and returned to Lithgow in 1967, hence, the "Slaz" designation during that period.

No. 3. SMLE Pattern 1942 "Slaz". This bayonet is slaz marked, however, has a false edge ground onto the top of the blade which is an official Australian or Indian modification and was performed by 2nd echelon workshops. The No. 2 MK I scabbard pattern is illustrated.

No. 4. SMLE Pattern Bayonet 1907 - issued in Australia, made in England. This bayonet was manufactured in England and is exactly like the one on page 3, with the exception of the quillon being removed.

① SMLE PATTERN 1907 "AUSTRALIA" MARKED

KIESLING VOL II #319

② SMLE PATTERN 1907/1942 "SLAZ" MARKED

KIESLING VOL. II #319
SKENNERTON PAGE 104

③ SMLE PATTERN 1942 FALSE EDGE

SKENNERTON PAGE 51

SLAZ

④ SMLE PATTERN 1907 ISSUED IN AUSTRALIA MFG IN ENGLAND

KIESLING VOL II #318

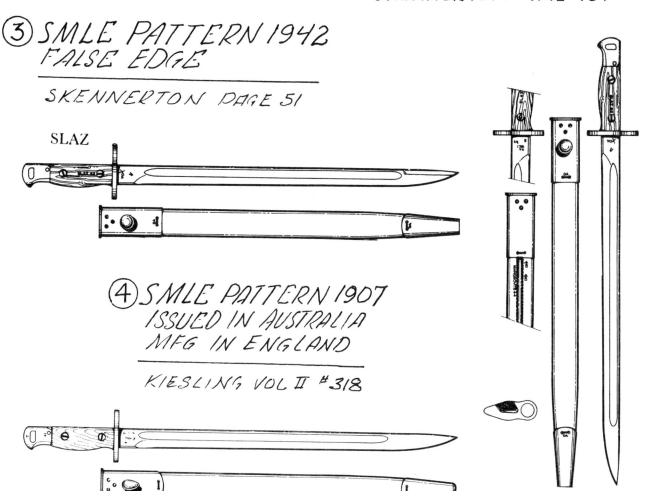

No. 1. EXPERIMENTAL PATTERN 1943 - MACHETTE BAYONET. THESE BAYONETS WERE APPARENTLY PRODUCED IN SMALL QUANTITIES ON AN EXPERIMENTAL BASIS; HOWEVER, BASED ON THE NUMBER I HAVE OBSERVED, I BELIEVE THAT THE QUANTITY WAS MUCH LARGER THAN THE 8000 PRODUCTION INDICATED IN THE LITERATURE. THIS PIECE WAS INITIALLY DESIGNATED "BAYONET PARACHUTIST" AND CHANGED TO "BAYONET MACHETTE MK I" IN 1946.

No. 2. OWEN S.M.G. MK I - 1943. THESE BAYONETS WERE PRODUCED BOTH WITH NEWLY MADE SHORT BLADES AND FROM SMLE P-1907 TYPES WITH THE BLADES SHORTENED.

No. 3. AUSTRALIAN BAYONET L1A2 - 1957. THE L1A2 TYPES PRODUCED BY LITHGOW AND CURRENTLY USED BY AUSTRALIA ARE TOTALLY UNMARKED. THIS BAYONET ALSO FITS THE F1 MACHINE CARBINE.

NOTE: AUSTRALIA CURRENTLY UTILIZES THE STEYR-PRODUCED AUG ASSAULT RIFLE WHICH UTILIZES THE U.S. M16-TYPE, RIFLE-COMPATIBLE BAYONET SERIES.

1. EXPERIMENTAL P.1943 MACHETTE BAYONET

KIESLING VOL I # 156

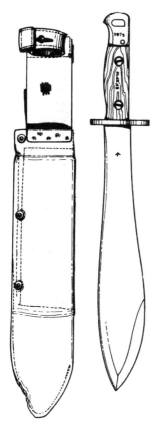

2. OWEN SMG MK I 1943

KIESLING VOL I 125

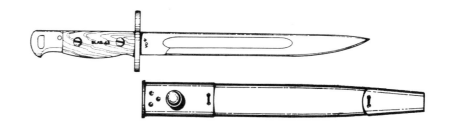

3. BAYONET L1A2

KIESLING VOL IV # 753

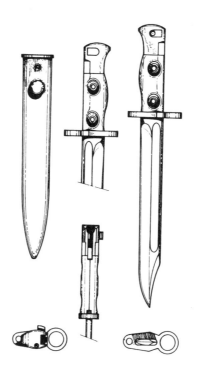

No. 1.   AUSTRIAN MODEL 1849 - AUGUSTIN JAGER CARBINE. A LONG SWORD SOCKET TYPE, THIS BAYONET WAS DESIGNED FOR JAGER UNITS AND COULD ALSO FUNCTION AS A SHORT SWORD. THE SCABBARD IS STEEL-MOUNTED.

*   AUSTRIAN MODEL 1854 - LORENZ JAGER CARBINE. SIMILAR TO NO. 1, HOWEVER, WITH A LORENZ HELICAL-TYPE SLOT AND DESIGNATED THE MODEL 1854.

No. 2.   AUSTRIAN MODEL 1842 - SYSTEM LAUKART. THIS BAYONET UTILIZED THE LAUKART SPRING CATCH AND HAS A MARK (AN ASTERISK IN A CIRCLE) ON THE SHANK SIMILAR TO THE LORENZ MUSKETS USED IN THE U.S. CIVIL WAR, WHICH MAKES ME SPEC-ULATE THAT THIS TYPE WAS ALSO ISSUED.

No. 3.   AUSTRIAN MODEL 1854 - LORENZ MUSKET. THESE BAYONETS ARE VERY COMMON IN THE UNITED STATES DUE TO THE FACT THEY WERE UTILIZED IN GREAT NUMBERS DURING THE CIVIL WAR (APPROXIMATELY 47,000 BY THE CONFEDERACY ALONE).

No. 4.   AUSTRIAN MODEL 1867 - WERNDL CARBINE. THIS BAYONET IS A SPECIAL PIECE ISSUED TO POLICE UNITS AND THE ONE IN MY COLLECTION IS PLATED. IT WAS MADE FOR THE M-1867 WERNDL CARBINE AND THE M-1872 FRUWIRTH GENDARMERIE CARBINE.

① AUSTRIAN M. 1849
KIESLING VOL. II #474

✳ AUSTRIAN M. 1854
KIESLING VOL II #475

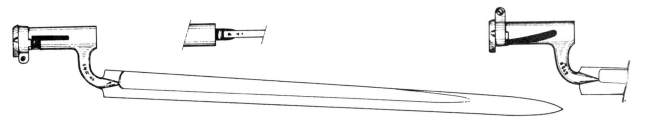

② AUSTRIAN MODEL 1842
SYSTEM LAUKART
KIESLING VOL II #325
WATTS & WHITE #18

④ AUSTRIAN M. 1867
KIESLING VOL II 354

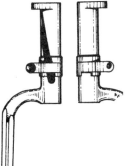

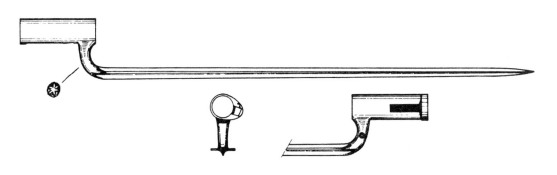

③ AUSTRIAN MODEL 1854
LORENZ MUSKET
KIESLING VOL II #329

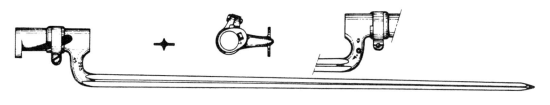

SCABBARD
USED ON
2, 3, 4

No. 1. AUSTRIAN MODEL 1867 - SHORTENED BLADE. THIS IS A SHORT-ENED VERSION OF THE STANDARD AUSTRIAN MODEL 1867 AND IS MUCH MORE COMMON THAN THE FULL-LENGTH VERSIONS. A MODI-FICATION OF THIS PIECE IS SHOWN AS ITEM No. 4.

No. 2. AUSTRIAN MODEL 1870 - SHORTENED BLADE. THIS BAYONET ALSO HAS A SHORTENED BLADE AND IS NOT COMMON IN THE FULL-LENGTH.

No. 3. AUSTRIAN MODEL 1873. THIS BAYONET INCORPORATED THE FIRST USE OF A COIL-SPRING PRESS STUD ARRANGEMENT AND IS ONE OF THE FIRST AUSTRIAN PIECES TO BE PRODUCED IN THIS STANDARD LENGTH.

No. 4. AUSTRIAN MODEL 1867 - BUSHED. MODIFICATION OF No. 1 ABOVE. THE MUZZLE RING HAS BEEN BUSHED DOWN FROM 18.9MM TO 17MM AND THE TOP OF THE SLOT GROUND DOWN PRESUMABLY SO THE BAYONET WILL FIT THE M-1873. THIS MAY HAVE BEEN PRE-WORLD WAR I.

① AUSTRIAN M. 1867 SHORTENED BLADE

KIESLING VOL II #376

④ AUSTRIAN M. 1867 W.W.I MODIFICATION

THE BAYONET PG. 21

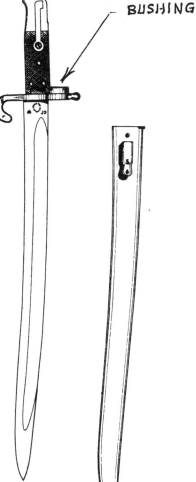

BUSHING

② AUSTRIAN M. 1870 SHORTENED BLADE

KIESLING VOL II #377

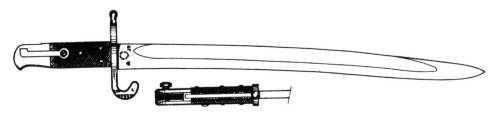

③ AUSTRIAN M. 1873

KIESLING VOL II #381

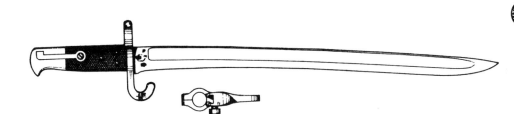

⑦

No. 1. **AUSTRIAN MODEL 1888.** THIS BAYONET WAS THE STANDARD AUSTRIAN INFANTRY BAYONET AND WAS USED AND EXPORTED IN GREAT NUMBERS. THIS PIECE HAS A MUZZLE RING DIAMETER OF 16.3MM, HOWEVER, A MODEL 1886 EXISTS WITH A MUZZLE RING DIAMETER OF 17.5MM WHICH IS <u>VERY</u> RARE. I HAVE ALSO SEEN GERMAN-MANUFACTURED (SIMSON & CO.) EXAMPLES OF THIS BAYONET.

No. 2. **AUSTRIAN MODEL 1888 - NCO BAYONET.** THESE BAYONETS ARE RELATIVELY SCARCE AND MANY I HAVE SEEN WERE SIAMESE ISSUE.

No. 3. **AUSTRIAN CONVERSION 1888/95.** THIS BAYONET IS AN ODDBALL WHICH HAS AN 1888 BLADE AND POMMEL, HOWEVER, WILL FIT THE M-95. I ASSUME THIS WAS A WW I CONVERSION. IT IS HEAVILY BLUED.

No. 4. **AUSTRIAN MODEL 1888/93.** THIS BAYONET IS A TRANSITION PIECE BECAUSE IT RESEMBLES THE M-1895, HOWEVER, WILL NOT FIT THE M-1895 RIFLE.

NOTE: THE BULGARIANS ALSO UTILIZED THE AUSTRIAN M-1888 KNIFE BAYONETS. THESE CAN BE IDENTIFIED BY A SMALL CROWNED "F" STAMPED ON THE CROSSGUARD. THIS WAS THE MARK OF KING FERDINAND OF BULGARIA.

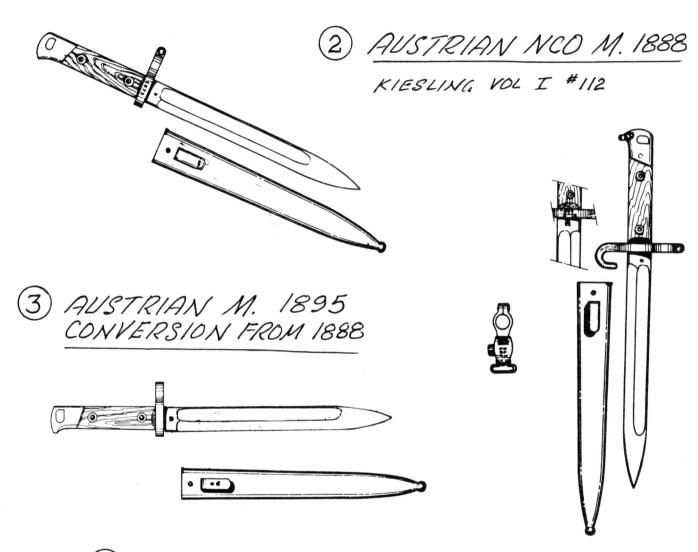

① *AUSTRIAN M. 1888*

KIESLING VOL I # 95
WATTS & WHITE PG 17

② *AUSTRIAN NCO M. 1888*

KIESLING VOL I # 112

③ *AUSTRIAN M. 1895*
CONVERSION FROM 1888

④ *AUSTRIAN M. 1888/93*

KIESLING VOL I # 67

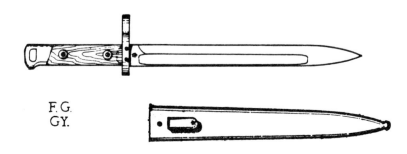

F.G.
GY.

⑧

No. 1. **AUSTRIAN MODEL 1895.** THIS WAS A STANDARD AUSTRIAN INFANTRY BAYONET IN WW I AND WAS OSTENSIBLY MADE IN GREATER NUMBERS THAN ANY OTHER BAYONET. I HAVE BOTH GOVERNMENT-PRODUCED AND CONTRACTOR-PRODUCED EXAMPLES INCLUDING THE L. ZEITLER MANUFACTURED VERSION ILLUSTRATED IN KIESLING VOL. I. No. 69.

No. 2. **AUSTRO-HUNGARIAN MODEL 1895 - SPANNER FASTENED GRIPS.** THIS IS THE STANDARD AUSTRO-HUNGARIAN BAYONET; HOWEVER, THE GRIPS ARE FASTENED WITH SPANNER NUTS - PERHAPS A LATE-WAR MODIFICATION OR, ACCORDING TO WATTS AND WHITE, IT COULD BE A YUGOSLAV MODIFICATION.

No. 3. **AUSTRO-HUNGARIAN MODEL 1895 - CARBINE.** THIS IS ONE VARIATION OF THE CARBINE BAYONET AND HAS THE SIGHT MOUNTED ON TOP OF THE MUZZLE RING. DUE TO THE WEIGHT OF THE BAYONET, THE HARMONICS OF THE BARREL WERE CHANGED AND GAVE A NEW SIGHT PICTURE, WHICH THE SIGHT ON THE MUZZLE RING CORRECTED.

No. 4. **AUSTRO-HUNGARIAN MODEL 1895 - NCO BAYONET.** THIS PIECE IS THE NCO BAYONET AND HAS THE HOOKED QUILLON AND LOOP ON THE POMMEL. I HAVE SEVERAL OF THESE WITH DIFFERENT TYPES OF LOOP (WIRE AND STAMPED METAL), BLADE FULLERS (ROUND AND SQUARE), AND FINISH (BRIGHT AND BLUE). SEE 10-4 FOR ANOTHER VARIATION.

NOTE: MANY OF THE MODEL 1895 BAYONETS WERE REFURBISHED AND SUPPLIED TO THE SUDANESE.

① AUSTRIAN M. 1895
KIESLING VOL. I # 67

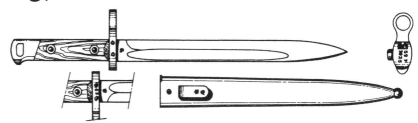

② AUSTRO-HUNGARIAN M. 1895
SPANNER FASTENED GRIPS

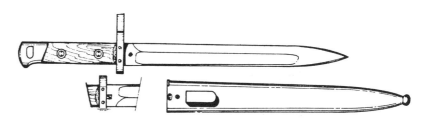

③ AUSTRO-HUNGARIAN M. 1895
CARBINE
KIESLING VOL. I # 74

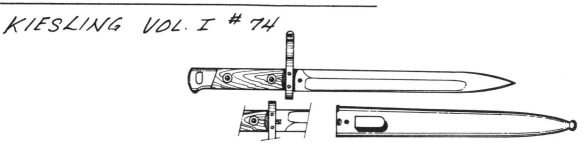

④ AUSTRO-HUNGARIAN M. 1895
CARBINE · NCO
KIESLING VOL I # 76

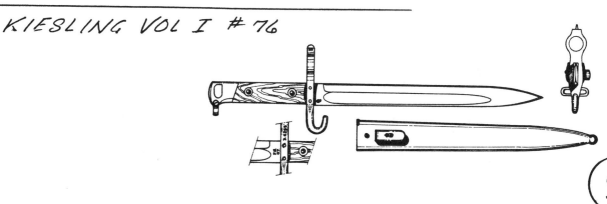

No. 1. AUSTRO-HUNGARIAN MODEL 1895 - CARBINE. THIS BAYONET IS ANOTHER VARIATION OF THE STANDARD CARBINE BAYONET AND HAS A LARGER SIGHT ON THE MUZZLE RING, AS WELL AS A BLADE VARIATION.

No. 2. AUSTRIAN NCO MODEL 1895 - NO HOOK ON CROSSGUARD. THIS BAYONET IS A MIXTURE BETWEEN THE CARBINE BAYONET AND THE NCO, IN THAT IT HAS THE POMMEL LOOP, HOWEVER, DOES NOT HAVE A HOOKED QUILLON.

No. 3. AUSTRIAN NCO MODEL 1895 - NO LOOP ON POMMEL. THIS BAYONET IS A VARIATION WHICH INCORPORATES A HOOKED QUILLON BUT NO LOOP ON THE POMMEL.

No. 4. AUSTRO-HUNGARIAN MODEL 1895 - NCO MODEL. THIS BAYONET IS ANOTHER VARIATION OF NO. 4 ON PAGE 9 AND IS A RELATIVELY COMMON NCO BAYONET.

NOTE: MANY OF THE AUSTRIAN MODEL 1895 NCO BAYONETS WILL BE FOUND WITH A BULLION KNOT ATTACHED TO THE POMMEL LOOP. THIS KNOT FREQUENTLY DISPLAYS THE LETTER "K" WHICH IS THE CYPHER OF EMPEROR KARL.

① *AUSTRO-HUNGARIAN M.1895 CARBINE VARIATION*

KIESLING VOL I # 73

ARMS OF THE
AUSTRO-HUNGARIAN EMPIRE
STAMPED ON M95 BAYONETS.

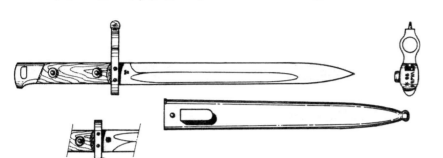

② *AUSTRIAN NCO M.1895 NO HOOK ON CROSS GUARD*

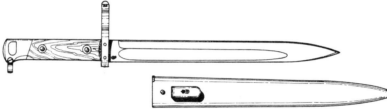

③ *AUSTRIAN NCO M.1895 NO LOOP ON POMMEL*

④ *AUSTRO-HUNGARIAN M.1895 NCO VARIATION*

KIESLING VOL. I #70

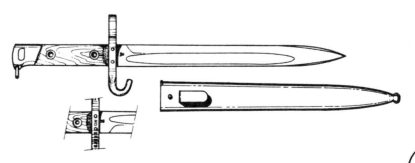

No. 1. AUSTRIAN DRESS MODEL 1895 – NON-FUNCTIONAL PLATED, NCO. THIS BAYONET IS PURELY FOR DRESS. IT IS PLATED AND WILL NOT MOUNT ON A WEAPON. R. D. C. EVANS INDICATES THAT POLICE BAYONETS ARE PLATED.

No. 2. AUSTRIAN MODEL 1888/16 – NO M.R. ADJUSTMENT. THIS BAYONET WAS OBVIOUSLY PRODUCED IN LATE WORLD WAR I FOR THE 88 RIFLE AND LOOKS VERY MUCH LIKE LATER AUSTRIAN EXPORTS.

No. 3. AUSTRIAN "ERSATZ" 1917 – FOR MODEL 1895. THIS IS THE AUSTRIAN EQUIVALENT OF THE GERMAN ERSATZ BAYONET AND COMES IN TWO VARIETIES – THE PIECE PICTURED BEING ONE, AND ANOTHER WITH A SLIGHT HILT VARIATION. AUSTRIAN ERSATZ BAYONETS ARE NOT COMMON AND MUST HAVE BEEN PRODUCED IN FEWER NUMBERS THAN THE GERMAN MODELS.

AUSTRIAN MINIATURES. THE AUSTRIANS ALSO PRODUCED SMALL SCALE BAYONETS FOR LETTER OPENERS AND DESK ORNAMENTS. THE ONE ON THE FAR RIGHT IS A TOY AND ACTUALLY FITS A SMALL RIFLE.

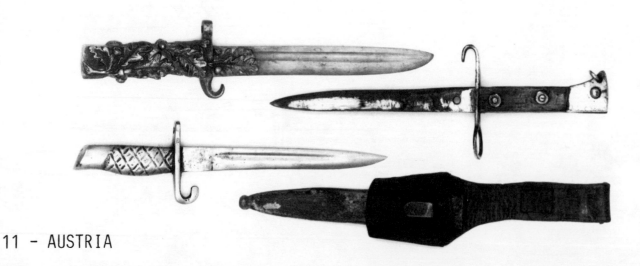

① AUSTRIAN DRESS M. 1895
PLATED, NON-FUNCTIONAL

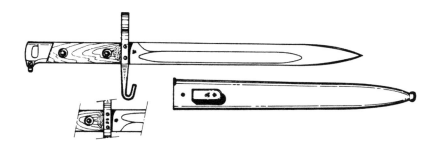

② AUSTRIAN M. 1888/16
W/O MUZZLE RING ADJ.

WATTS & WHITE PG #17

③ AUSTRIAN "ERSATZ" M1917
FOR M. 1895 RIFLE

KIESLING VOL. III #538
WATTS & WHITE PG. #23

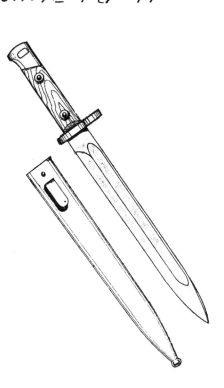

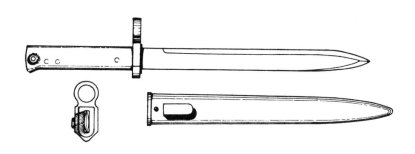

No. 1. **Austrian "Ersatz" 1917 - for Austrian Mannlicher Rifles.** These bayonets are ersatz variants for the Austrian service rifles. The one on the top fits the M-1888 and M-1890 while the version on the bottom fits the M-1895 rifles. A reproduction of the second bayonet exists, which was produced in the mid-1970's and can be distinguished by the twist on the blade being opposite from that pictured.

* Another "Ersatz" variation is illustrated which fits the German M-1871 and M-1871/84 rifles.

No. 2. **Austrian Mosin Nagant - Captured Russian 1891.** This is a Mosin Nagant bayonet which has been fitted with an Austrian scabbard. I have in my collection another piece with a straight slot which was actually produced by the Austrians and is stamped with the Austrian eagle (see 164-1).

No. 3. **Austrian Model 1912 - Export.** This is a Mauser model 98 export (7mm) and was used by Austria early in the first World War. The rifles and bayonets were initially manufactured for Mexico, however, the Mexican versions are marked "RM" (Republic of Mexico).

No. 4. **Austrian Circa 1977.** This is a commercial bayonet made for trials with the Austrian STG 58 assault rifle (FN FAL). It was manufactured by Ludwig Zeitler of Vienna and marked "Zeitler" on the blade. The bayonet is attached to the rifle through the use of an adapter.

NOTE: The current Austrian service rifle is AUG assault rifle produced by Steyr. It utilizes a bayonet similar to the U.S. M7 series (see pages 230-231).

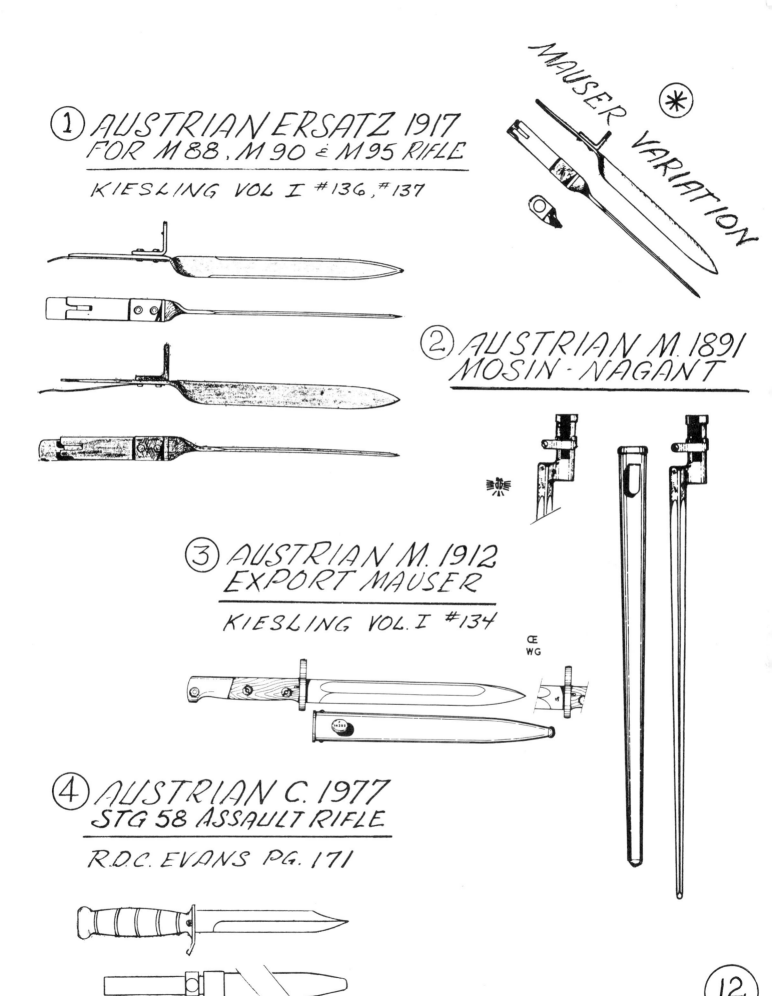

① AUSTRIAN ERSATZ 1917
FOR M88, M90 & M95 RIFLE

KIESLING VOL I #136, #137

※ MAUSER VARIATION

② AUSTRIAN M.1891
MOSIN-NAGANT

③ AUSTRIAN M.1912
EXPORT MAUSER

KIESLING VOL.I #134

ŒWG

④ AUSTRIAN C.1977
STG 58 ASSAULT RIFLE

R.D.C. EVANS PG.171

12

No. 1.   **BAVARIAN MODEL 1858.** THIS BAYONET LOOKS MUCH LIKE THE AUS-
TRIAN BAYONETS, HOWEVER, CAN BE DISTINGUISHED BY THE SQUARED
END ON THE SLOT. R. D. C. EVANS SAYS THIS PIECE WAS FOR THE
MUSTER 2 PODEWILS RIFLE M-1858.

No. 2.   **BAVARIAN MODEL 1858.** THIS BAYONET WAS IDENTIFIED ON A RATHER
SPECULATIVE BASIS AND, DUE TO THE SLOT SHAPE, I ASSUME IT IS
BAVARIAN.

No. 3.   **BAVARIAN MODEL 1869/75 - WERDER.** THIS IS THE STANDARD ISSUE
INFANTRY BAYONET; IT IS AN 1875 MODIFICATION OF THE ORIGINAL
M-1869 WHICH HAS A FINALE ON THE END OF THE QUILLON AND A
HEAVIER BLADE.

No. 4.   **BAVARIAN MODEL 1869 - WERDER.** THIS IS A MODIFIED VERSION OF
THE WERDER M-1869 BAYONET AND ALLOWS THE BAYONET TO BE UTI-
LIZED WITH THE M-1871 PATTERN NOSE CAP USED ON THE M-1869NM
RIFLES. MANY AUTHORS ATTRIBUTE THIS MODIFICATION TO WORLD
WAR I; HOWEVER, JOHN WALTER ON PAGE 31 OF THE GERMAN BAYONET
STATES THAT THE MODIFICATIONS WERE UNDERTAKEN IN 1876 -
1877.

*   I ALSO HAVE A BAYONET IN MY COLLECTION WHICH LOOKS EXACTLY
LIKE NO. 3 ABOVE, HOWEVER, HAS HAD THE CROSSGUARD MOVED
APPROXIMATELY 8MM ABOVE THE BLADE TO ALLOW USE ON THE M-1871
NOSE CAP.

① *BAVARIAN M. 1858*
PODEWILS RIFLE

KIESLING VOL. II #386
WALTER PG. # 33

DIMENSIONS	
BLADE LENGTH	19 11/16"
BLADE WIDTH	27/64"
SOCKET LENGTH	3 3/16"
SOCKET O.D.	26/32"
SOCKET I.D.	43/64"
SHANK LENGTH	1 23/32"

② *BAVARIAN M. 1858*
PODEWILS RIFLE

WALTER PG #33

DIMENSIONS	
BLADE LENGTH	15 1/2"
BLADE WIDTH	23/32"
SOCKET LENGTH	3 3/16"
SOCKET O.D.	26/32"
SOCKET I.D.	43/64"
SHANK LENGTH	1 1/8"

③ *BAVARIAN M. 1869*
WERDER

KIESLING VOL. II #359

④ *BAVARIAN M. 1869*
MODIFIED

KIESLING VOL II #360

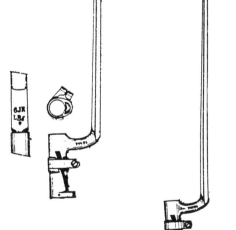

✱ *MODIFICATION*
FOR M. 1871

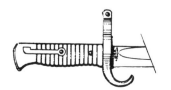

No. 1. BAVARIAN MODEL 1871/84 - SECOND MODEL (L) LUDWIG II.
THIS IS THE GERMAN MODEL 71-84 WITH BAVARIAN MARKINGS.
NOTE THAT THE CROWNED "L" OF LUDWIG II (WHO DIED IN
1886) IS IDENTICAL TO THAT USED BY LUDWIG III WHEN HE
TOOK THE THRONE IN 1914.

No. 2. BAVARIAN MODEL 98/05 - (O) OTTO. THIS IS THE EARLY
MODEL WITH NO FLASHGUARD AND HIGH EARS. IT IS MARKED
WITH THE "O" CYPHER AND DATED "11" (1911). KING OTTO
DIED IN 1913; THUS, THE CROWNED "O" WILL APPEAR ON
BLADES DATED "87" THROUGH "13".

No. 3. BAVARIAN MODEL 98/05 - (L) LUDWIG III. THIS IS THE
STANDARD GERMAN 98/05 WITH BAVARIAN MARKINGS. THE
CROWNED "L" OF LUDWIG III WILL ONLY BE FOUND ON BLADES
DATED "14" THROUGH "18".

No. 4. BAVARIAN MODEL 98/05 - (L) LUDWIG III. THIS IS THE
BAVARIAN MODEL WITH THE SAW BACK "GROUND".

① *BAVARIAN M. 1871/84*
SECOND MODEL

KIESLING VOL. I #123

② *BAVARIAN M. 98/05*
a/A

WALTER PG #63

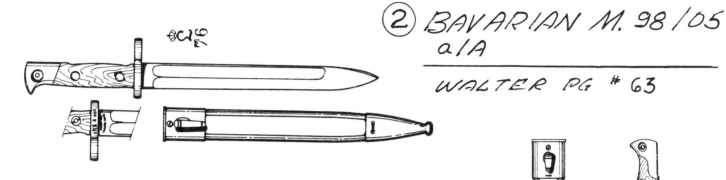

③ *BAVARIAN M. 98/05*
N/A

KIESLING VOL. I #256

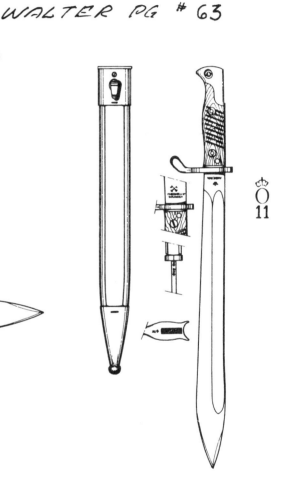

④ *BAVARIAN M. 98/05*
SAW BACK REMOVED

KIESLING VOL. I #258

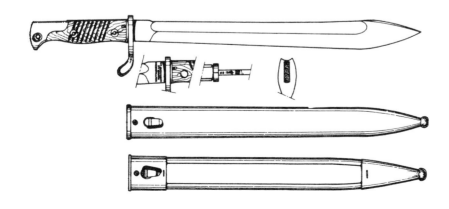

⑭

No. 1. BELGIUM MODEL 1848 - CARBINE. THIS IS A VERY LONG BAYONET FOR THE 17.5MM THOUVENIN CARBINE. THIS PIECE WAS ALSO THOUGHT TO BE UTILIZED ON LATER WEAPONS.

* BELGIUM PISTOL C. 1850. THIS BAYONET IS ON A PISTOL IN MY COLLECTION AND WAS APPARENTLY A COMMON APPENDAGE TO GENTLEMEN'S PISTOLS IN THE 1850'S.

No. 2. BELGIUM PERCUSSION C. 1850. THIS BAYONET WAS IN MY COLLECTION FOR SOME TIME AS A SWISS FEDERAL AND LOOKS A GREAT DEAL LIKE ONE; HOWEVER, IT IS IDENTIFIED BY KIESLING AS BELGIAN.

No. 3. BELGIUM MODEL 1867. FOR ALBINI BRANDLIN - MODEL 1857 AND MODEL 1868, SOUTH AMERICAN EXPORTS. THIS BAYONET WAS EXPORTED TO MANY SOUTH AMERICAN COUNTRIES AND HAS AN EXTREMELY UNUSUAL ZIGZAG SLOT.

No. 4. FLOBERT CADET MODEL 1880 - BOYS MUSKET. THIS BAYONET WAS COMMONLY USED WITH A SMALL CADET RIFLE WHICH WAS SOLD IN LARGE NUMBERS THROUGH THE BANNERMAN CATALOG AND OTHER SOURCES. THE BELGIUM IDENTIFICATION WAS DERIVED FROM THE BELGIUM PROOFMARKS ON THE RIFLE ITSELF. THE BAYONET IS 12" IN LENGTH.

① BELGIUM M.1848

KIESLING VOL. II # 490

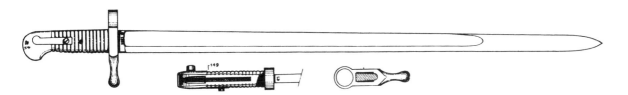

＊ BELGIUM C.1850 PISTOL

KIESLING VOL. II #581

② BELGIUM C.1850 PERCUSSION

KIESLING VOL. II #390

③ BELGIUM M.1867

KIESLING VOL. II #307

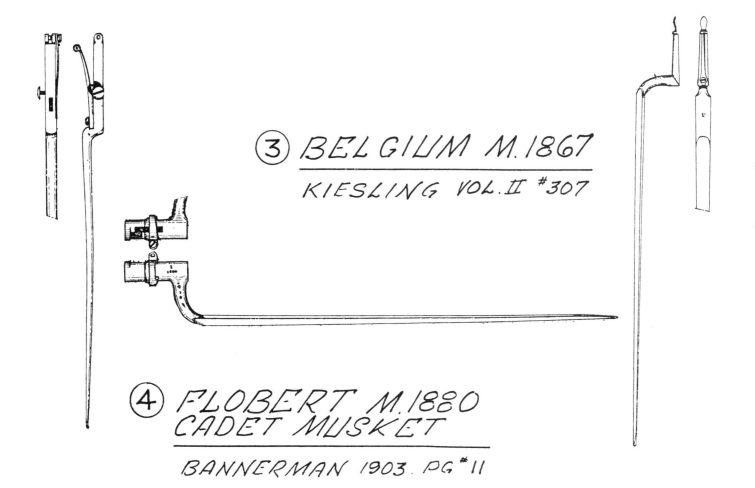

④ FLOBERT M.1880 CADET MUSKET

BANNERMAN 1903. PG #11

No. 1.   BELGIUM MODEL 1882 - GARDE CIVIQUE.   THIS BAYONET FOR THE COMBLAIN RIFLE HAS A T-BACK BLADE VERY SIMILAR TO THE FRENCH GRAS BAYONETS AND THE SCABBARDS APPEAR TO BE INTERCHANGEABLE WITH THE FRENCH.

No. 2.   BELGIUM MODEL 1868 - TERSSEN CARBINE.   THIS BAYONET IS VERY SIMILAR TO THE FRENCH CHASSEPOT, HOWEVER, POSSESSES DIFFERENT BLADE FULLERS AND APPEARS TO BE COMPARATIVELY SCARCE.

No. 3.   BELGIUM MODEL 1868 - ENGINEERS.   THIS BAYONET FOR THE TERSSEN CARBINE IS A WIDELY SOUGHT-AFTER PIONEER VERSION WITH A BLADE VERY COMPARABLE TO THE LARGE GERMAN ENGINEER BAYONETS OF THE SAME PERIOD.

No. 4.   BELGIUM MODEL 1880 - ENGINEERS.   THIS BAYONET FOLLOWED THE CURRENT TREND FOR SMALLER, LIGHTER ENGINEER BAYONETS WHICH WAS PREVALENT IN THE 1880'S AND FITS THE COMBLAIN AND ALBINI SHORT RIFLES.

① BELGIUM M.1882
GARDE CIVIQUE
KIESLING VOL. II #430

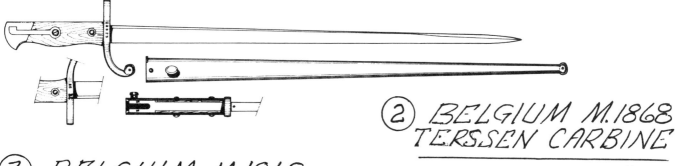

② BELGIUM M.1868
TERSSEN CARBINE
KIESLING VOL II #468

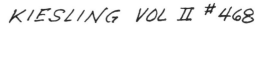

③ BELGIUM M.1868
KIESLING VOL II #384

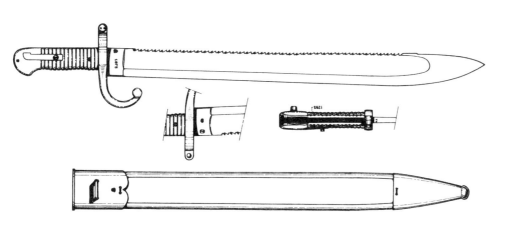

④ BELGIUM M. 1880
KIESLING VOL II #364

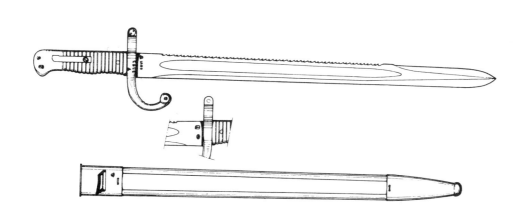

No. 1.   BELGIUM CADET MODEL 1880 - COMBLAIN.   THIS IS A MINIATURE
CADET VERSION OF THE 1880 COMBLAIN AND HAS A ROUNDED TIP.   I
PURCHASED IT SOME YEARS AGO AS A PART OF A SHIPMENT OF COM-
BLAIN BAYONETS FROM BRAZIL, HOWEVER, HAVE CHOSEN TO CLASSIFY
IT AS BELGIAN.

No. 2.   BELGIUM MODEL 1889 - SHORT.   THIS BAYONET IS THE STANDARD
BELGIUM INFANTRY BAYONET AND, FOR SOME REASON, IT IS RELA-
TIVELY SCARCE.

No. 3.   BELGIUM MODEL 1889 - LONG.   THIS IS A UNITED STATES MANUFAC-
TURED BAYONET FOR THE BELGIUM 89 RIFLE AND IS STAMPED
"HOPKINS AND ALLEN" ON THE BLADE.   I HAVE SEEN EXAMPLES WITH-
OUT THE "HOPKINS AND ALLEN" STAMP.

No. 4.   BELGIUM MODEL 1916 - GENDARMERIE.   THIS BAYONET HAS THE T-
BACK BLADE USED BY THE BELGIUM POLICE WITH THE LARGE MUZZLE
RING USED ON THE 1916 RIFLE.   CARTER & WALTER INDICATE THAT
THE BLADES ARE SHORTENED M-1882 GARDE CIVIQUE BAYONET BLADES.

BELGIUM MINIATURE BAYONET.   THESE CRUDE COPIES OF THE M-1889
COME IN A VARIETY OF SIZES AND OFTEN HAVE THE NAME OF A CITY
OR TOWN STAMPED ON THE BLADE:

① BELGIUM M.1880 COMBLAIN CADET

STEPHENS #109

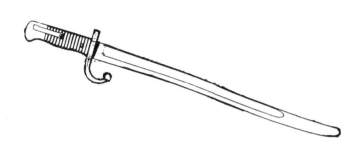

② BELGIUM M.1889 SHORT

KIESLING VOL.I #116

③ BELGIUM M.1889 LONG

KIESLING VOL II #290

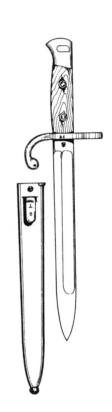

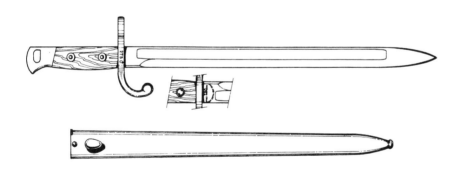

④ BELGIUM M.1916 GENDARMERIE

KIESLING VOL.II #340

No. 1. BELGIUM MODEL 1924 – GENDARMERIE. THIS BAYONET HAS THE T-BLADE SIMILAR TO 17-4; HOWEVER, IT HAS A BUSHED MUZZLE RING TO ALLOW IT TO BE FIXED TO THE 1924 RIFLE.

No. 2. BELGIUM MODEL 1916/24. THIS IS A STANDARD BELGIUM INFANTRY BAYONET AND IS AVAILABLE IN BOTH THE 1916 AND 1924 MUZZLE RING CONFIGURATIONS.

No. 3. BELGIUM MODEL 1924 – SHORT. THESE BAYONETS WERE SHORT-ENED ALONG WITH THE SCABBARDS AND I HAVE TWO BLADE LENGTHS IN MY COLLECTION – ONE IS 13-3/4" AND THE OTHER 12-1/4".

No. 4. BELGIUM MODEL 1916/24 – MUZZLE RING REMOVED. THIS IS THE BELGIUM 1924 BAYONET WITH THE MUZZLE RING REMOVED OSTENSIBLY BY THE GERMANS.

BELGIUM PRESENTATION BAYONET. SEE 19-3.

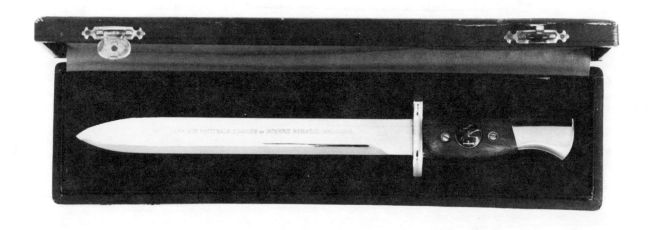

① BELGIUM M. 1924
GENDARMERIE

ERNST VOL. I #9

② BELGIUM M. 1916/24

KIESLING VOL. II #337

③ BELGIUM M. 1924
SHORT

KIESLING VOL. III #608

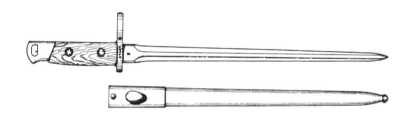

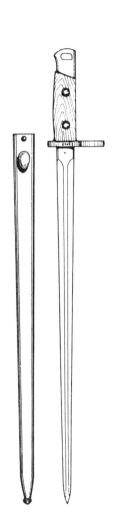

④ BELGIUM M. 1916/24
MUZZLE RING REMOVED

No. 1. BELGIUM F.N. EXPORT MAUSER MODEL 1924/30/34 – SHORT. THIS IS A BELGIUM F.N. EXPORT BAYONET WHICH WAS APPARENTLY USED BY A NUMBER OF SOUTH AMERICAN COUNTRIES AND I POSSESS SEVERAL IN MY COLLECTION WITH UNIDENTIFIED SOUTH AMERICAN MARKS.

No. 2. BELGIUM F.N. EXPORT MAUSER MODEL 1924 – LONG. THIS BAYONET WAS PRODUCED IN LARGE QUANTITIES. IT WAS SHIPPED TO LITHUANIA, YUGOSLAVIA, GREECE AND INDONESIA AS WELL AS VARIOUS SOUTH AMERICAN COUNTRIES. I HAVE A PORTUGUESE-MARKED EXAMPLE IN MY COLLECTION AND THE YUGOSLAVS UTILIZED THIS BAYONET AS A COPY FOR THEIR OWN 98 MAUSER BAYONET. (AN ISRAELI MARKED VERSION IS SHOWN AS 117-1).

No. 3. PRESENTATION BAYONET BY FABRIQUE NATIONALE OF BELGIUM. THIS BAYONET IS A PRESENTATION PIECE WHICH I ASSUME WAS PRESENTED BY THE FACTORY TO COUNTRIES OR AGENTS PURCHASING BAYONETS. THE ONE IN MY COLLECTION IS IN A SMALL, VELVET-LINED CASE WITH AN ENAMELED F.N. SEAL ON THE HANDLE.

No. 4. BELGIUM MODEL 1930. THIS INTERESTING PIECE WAS MANUFACTURED TO SERVE AS PART OF A MOUNT FOR THE BELGIUM VERSION OF THE U.S. BROWNING AUTOMATIC RIFLE. IT WAS DEVELOPED FOR PILOTS OF THE BELGIUM AIR FORCE AND IS A SCARCE BAYONET.

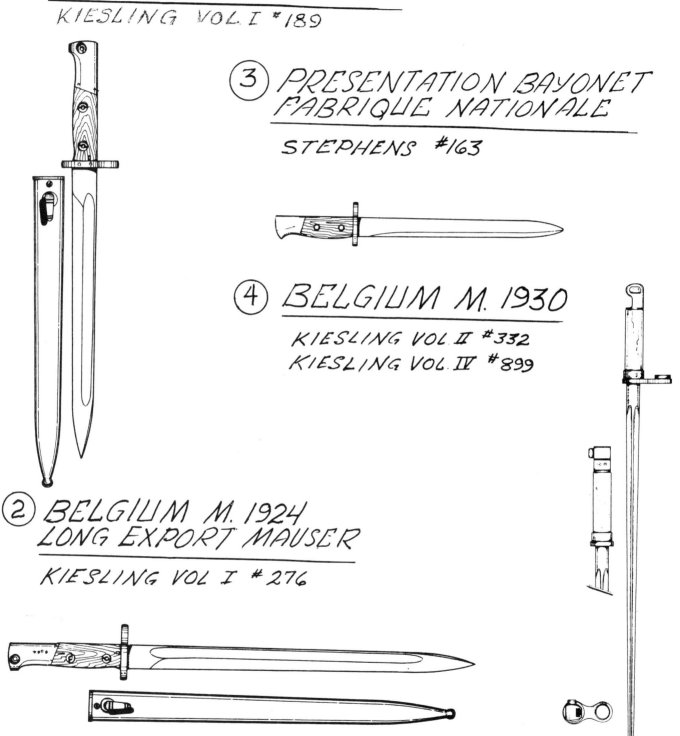

① BELGIUM M. 1924/30/34
SHORT EXPORT MAUSER
KIESLING VOL. I #189

③ PRESENTATION BAYONET
FABRIQUE NATIONALE
STEPHENS #163

④ BELGIUM M. 1930
KIESLING VOL. II #332
KIESLING VOL. IV #899

② BELGIUM M. 1924
LONG EXPORT MAUSER
KIESLING VOL I #276

No. 1.   BELGIUM F.N. EXPORT MODEL 1924/1949 - LONG. THIS BAYONET
IS IDENTICAL TO 19-2 EXCEPT FOR THE MUZZLE-RING DIAMETER
AND WAS UTILIZED ON THE F.N. MODEL 1949 RIFLE. I HAVE A
VENEZUELAN-MARKED PIECE AND A PLATED VERSION IN MY COL-
LECTION.

No. 2.   BELGIUM F.N. EXPORT MODEL 1949 - SHORT. THIS PIECE WAS
A SHORTER VERSION FOR THE MODEL 1949 RIFLE AND APPEARS
TO HAVE BEEN UTILIZED PRIMARILY BY EGYPT (IDENTIFIABLE
BY ARABIC NUMERALS), LUXEMBERG AND VENEZUELA.

No. 3.   BELGIUM F.N. EXPORT FAL MODEL 1953 - 7.62 CAL NATO.
THIS BAYONET IS FOR THE 7.62 CALIBER NATO EXPORT RIFLE
AND IS THE VARIATION WITH THE METAL GRIPS.

No. 4.   BELGIUM F.N. FAL MODEL 1953. THE WOOD-GRIPPED VARIANT
OF THE FAL WAS USED BY THE BELGIANS AND A SLIGHTLY MODI-
FIED VERSION WAS EXPORTED TO ENGLAND, AUSTRALIA AND
CANADA (SEE 27-1) FOR TRIALS.

① BELGIUM M. 1924/49
LONG EXPORT

KIESLING VOL I # 278

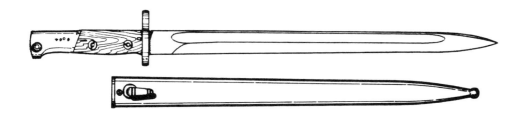

② BELGIUM M. 1949
SHORT EXPORT

KIESLING VOL. I # 81

③ BELGIUM M. 1953
NATO EXPORT

KIESLING VOL IV # 742

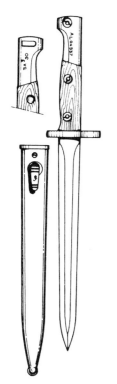

④ BELGIUM M. 1953
F.N. F.A.L.

KIESLING VOL. I # 49

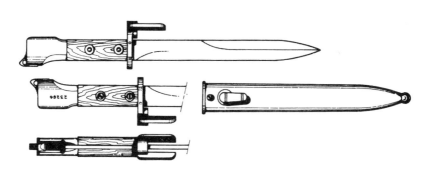

No. 1. **BELGIUM FAL MODEL 1963.** THIS BAYONET IS THE TUBULAR FAL AND IS A VERY HIGH QUALITY BAYONET; THEREFORE, I SUSPECT IT WAS ONE OF THE EARLIER VERSIONS MANUFACTURED.

No. 2. **BELGIUM FAL MODEL 1965.** THIS BAYONET HAS BEEN PRODUCED TO MUCH LESS DEMANDING MANUFACTURING STANDARDS AND HAS A STAMPED RELEASE CATCH. THE ONE IN MY COLLECTION WAS IMPORTED FROM SOUTH AFRICA.

No. 3. **BELGIUM FAL MODEL 1965.** THIS BAYONET IS IDENTICAL TO No. 3 ON PAGE 20 EXCEPT THE PRONG TYPE FLASH HIDERS ARE OMITTED. IT HAS A METAL HANDLE AND RESEMBLES THE UZI BAYONET. THESE ARE KNOWN AS THE TYPE "B" BAYONET AND ISSUED FOR TRIALS IN THE U.S. (THESE ARE SOMEWHAT SCARCE.)

No. 4. **BELGIUM FAL MODEL 1965.** THIS IS IDENTICAL TO THE 20-4, HOWEVER, IT IS PARKERIZED AND HAS RIBBED PLASTIC GRIPS. THE DATE IS SPECULATIVE, HOWEVER, THE BAYONET IS USED BY PORTUGAL.

NOTE: BELGIUM CURRENTLY UTILIZES THE FN FAL FNC ASSAULT RIFLE.

① BELGIUM M. 1963
F.A.L.

KIESLING VOL. I #12

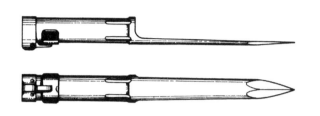

② BELGIUM M. 1965
F.A.L.

KIESLING VOL. IV #744

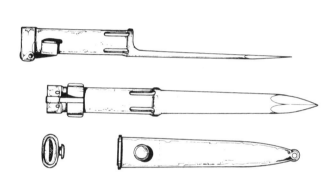

③ BELGIUM M. 1965
F.A.L.

KIESLING VOL. IV #742

④ BELGIUM M. 1965
F.A.L. EXPORT

KIESLING VOL IV #765

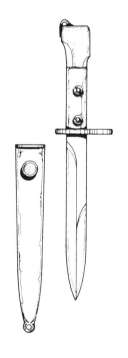

No. 1.   COMBLAIN RIFLE MODEL 1872 - ARTILLERY. THIS BAYONET WAS
         IDENTIFIED BY JIM HUGHES OF DEEP RIVER ARMORY AND LOOKS
         ALMOST LIKE A CADET BAYONET. I ASSUME THESE PIECES WERE
         NOT USED IN GREAT QUANTITY.

No. 2.   COMBLAIN RIFLE MODEL 1880 - INTERNAL SPRING. THIS PIECE
         WAS IMPORTED TO THE U.S. A FEW YEARS AGO BY DEEP RIVER
         ARMORY AND POSSESSES BRAZILIAN AND BELGIUM PROOFMARKS.
         IT HAS THE INTERNAL COIL SPRING.

No. 3.   COMBLAIN RIFLE MODEL 1880 - EXTERNAL SPRING. THIS PIECE
         IS VERY SIMILAR TO ITEM No. 2 ABOVE EXCEPT IT HAS THE
         EXTERNAL SPRING.

No. 4.   BRAZILIAN MODEL 1904 - MAUSER. THIS PIECE IS DEFINITELY
         BRAZILIAN AND HAS A BRAZILIAN COAT OF ARMS STAMPED ON
         THE BLADE. R. D. C. EVANS SAYS IT WAS THE LAST YATA-
         GHAN-BLADED BAYONET PRODUCED.

① COMBLAIN M. 1872

② COMBLAIN M. 1880
KIESLING VOL IV # 980

③ COMBLAIN M.1880
EXTERNAL SPRING

④ BRAZILIAN M. 1904
KIESLING VOL. IV # 905
WATTS & WHITE PG. 475

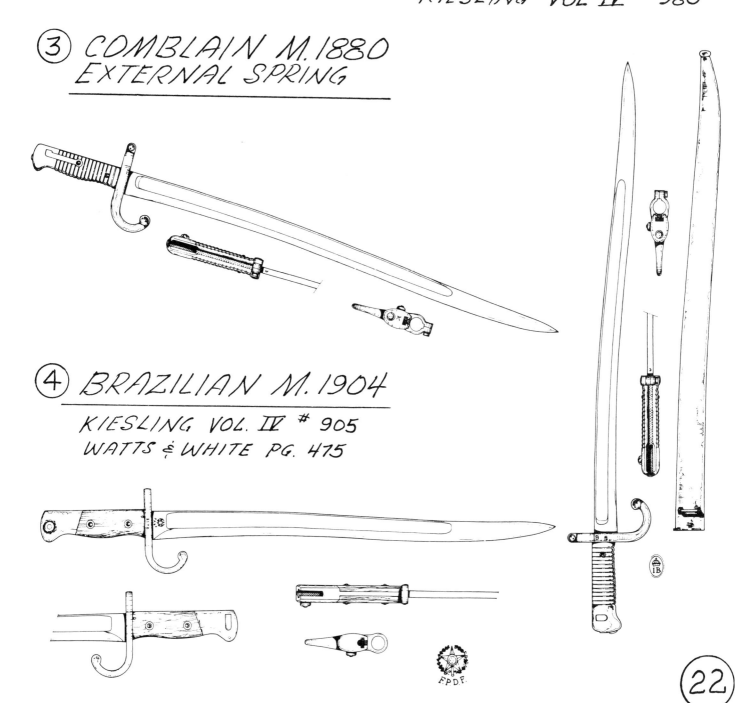

F.P.D.F.

㉒

No. 1. **BRAZILIAN MODEL 1908 - MAUSER.** THIS BAYONET WAS FUR-
NISHED WITH THE GERMAN MANUFACTURED M-1908 RIFLE AND
COMES WITH BOTH A STEEL MOUNTED LEATHER SCABBARD AND A
BRASS MOUNTED LEATHER SCABBARD. THE M-1908 BAYONET WAS
MANUFACTURED BY COPPEL, WEYERSBERG AND SIMPSON. AN
UNMARKED VERSION ALSO EXISTS WITH A BLACK STEEL MOUNTED
LEATHER SCABBARD MARKED "FI" ON THE FROG STUD.

No. 2. **BRAZILIAN MODEL 1934 - MAUSER.** THESE BAYONETS WERE PRO-
DUCED FOR THE MODEL 1908/34 BRAZILIAN RIFLE, A SHORTER
VERSION OF THE M-1908 RIFLE, ACCORDING TO R. D. C.
EVANS.

No. 3. **BRAZILIAN MODEL 1935 - MAUSER.** THIS BAYONET WAS APPAR-
ENTLY MANUFACTURED BY GERMANY FOR BRAZIL AND IS SIMILAR
TO THE COLOMBIAN BAYONETS EXCEPT FOR THE SHORT SLOT. IT
HAS A 11-1/2" (300 MM) BLADE AND AN ALL STEEL SCABBARD.

① BRAZILIAN M. 1908

KIESLING VOL IV #836

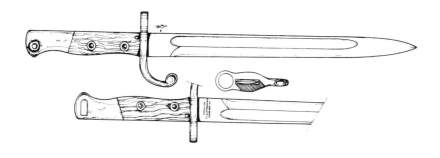

② BRAZILIAN M. 1934

RDC EVANS, GUNS WEAPONS & MIL.

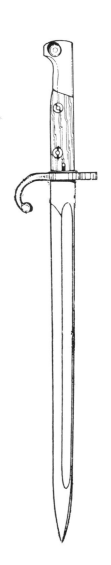

③ BRAZILIAN M. 1935

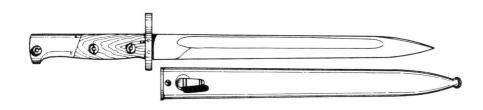

No. 1.   BRAZILIAN MODEL 1924 – MAUSER. THIS BAYONET IS A EURO-
PEAN EXPORT BAYONET UTILIZED BY BRAZIL ON CZECH V2-24
MAUSER RIFLES PURCHASED IN 1931. IT HAS THE TYPICAL
SMALL SERIAL NUMBER ON THE CROSSGUARD.

NOTE: BRAZIL ALSO UTILIZED THE BELGIUM M-1949 SELF-LOADING
RIFLE AND BAYONET. WATTS & WHITE REFER TO THE DOUBLE-
EDGED VERSION OF THE M-1949 (SEE 20-2); HOWEVER, I SUS-
PECT BRAZIL UTILIZED THE LONGER VERSION (20-1).

① *BRAZILIAN M.1924*

KIESLING VOL. I #277
WATTS & WHITE PG. 41

No. 1. **ROSS RIFLE MODEL 1905.** THIS BAYONET WAS THE FIRST BAYO-
NET PRODUCED FOR THE ROSS RIFLE AND WAS ACTUALLY INTRO-
DUCED IN 1908. THE BLADE HAS A "BUTCHER-KNIFE" SHAPE TO
IT.

No. 2. **ROSS RIFLE MODEL 1910.** THIS BAYONET WAS PRODUCED IN
1910 AND THE STEP HAS BEEN TAKEN OUT OF THE CROSSGUARD
FOR MANUFACTURING PURPOSES. (SEE 222-1 FOR THE U.S.
USED AND MARKED VERSION.)

No. 3. **ROSS RIFLE MODEL 1910 MK. II.** THIS BAYONET IS THE ROSS
RIFLE BAYONET WITH THE BLADE SHARPENED. THE CANADIAN
GOVERNMENT ORDERED THE BLADE POINTED IN WORLD WAR I.
KIESLING SAYS THIS POINTING WAS PERFORMED IN ENGLAND;
CARTER & WALTER SAY "THESE BAYONETS WERE MANUFACTURED
WITH POINTED BLADES". (SEE PG. 222 FOR INFORMATION ON
ROSS CONTRACTS.)

NOTE: CANADA UTILIZED THE U.S. M-1855 SOCKET BAYONET (SEE
200-2) ON THEIR CANADIAN RIFLE MUSKET ORDERED FROM
PROVIDENCE TOOL COMPANY. I HAVE AN UNMARKED M-1855 IN
MY COLLECTION WHICH MIGHT HAVE BEEN PART OF THIS CON-
TRACT. ACCORDING TO EDWARD A. HULL IN HIS BOOK PROVI-
DENCE TOOL COMPANY MILITARY ARMS, ONLY 3,000 RIFLE MUS-
KETS WERE DELIVERED TO CANADA.

① ROSS RIFLE M.1905
KIESLING VOL. I #108

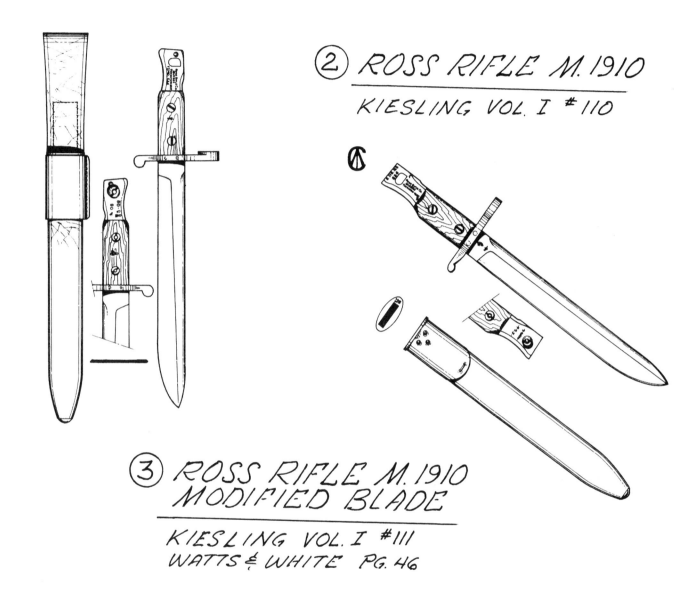

② ROSS RIFLE M.1910
KIESLING VOL. I #110

③ ROSS RIFLE M.1910
MODIFIED BLADE
KIESLING VOL. I #111
WATTS & WHITE PG. 46

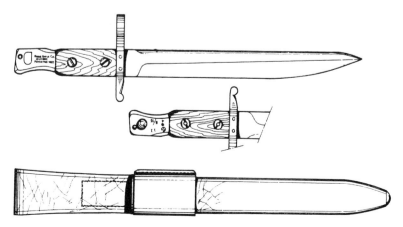

No. 1.   MODIFIED ROSS BAYONET.   THIS PARTICULAR PIECE IS A ROSS BAYONET WHICH HAS BEEN CONVERTED INTO A TRENCH KNIFE. SOME AUTHORS FEEL THIS WAS A COMMERCIAL MODIFICATION; HOWEVER, THE PIECE IN MY COLLECTION HAS A MILITARY OBSOLESCENCE MARK STAMPED ON THE HANDLE, WHICH LEADS ME TO BELIEVE THAT AT LEAST SOME OF THESE WERE MILITARY MODIFICATIONS.

No. 2.   CANADIAN P.1907 MK. I.   THIS BAYONET IS THE STANDARD PATTERN 1907 PRODUCED IN ENGLAND AND ISSUED TO CANADIAN TROOPS (IT IS CANADIAN MARKED).

No. 3.   CANADIAN P.1907 MK. I - SECOND PATTERN.   THIS PIECE IS A CANADIAN MARKED VERSION OF THE P.1907 WITHOUT THE HOOKED QUILLON.

No. 4.   CANADIAN No. 4 MK. II - LONG BRANCH MFG. 1940.   THIS PARTICULAR PIECE WAS PRODUCED BY LONG BRANCH ARSENAL IN CANADA FOR THE No. 4 MARK II RIFLE.

① MODIFIED ROSS BAYONET

KIESLING VOL. III * 513
R. B. MANAREY PG. 50

② CANADIAN P. 1907 MK. I

KIESLING VOL. II #316

③ CANADIAN P. 1907 MK.I SECOND PATTERN

KIESLING VOL. II #318

④ CANADIAN NO.4 MK.II LONG BRANCH

R. B. MANAREY PG. 36

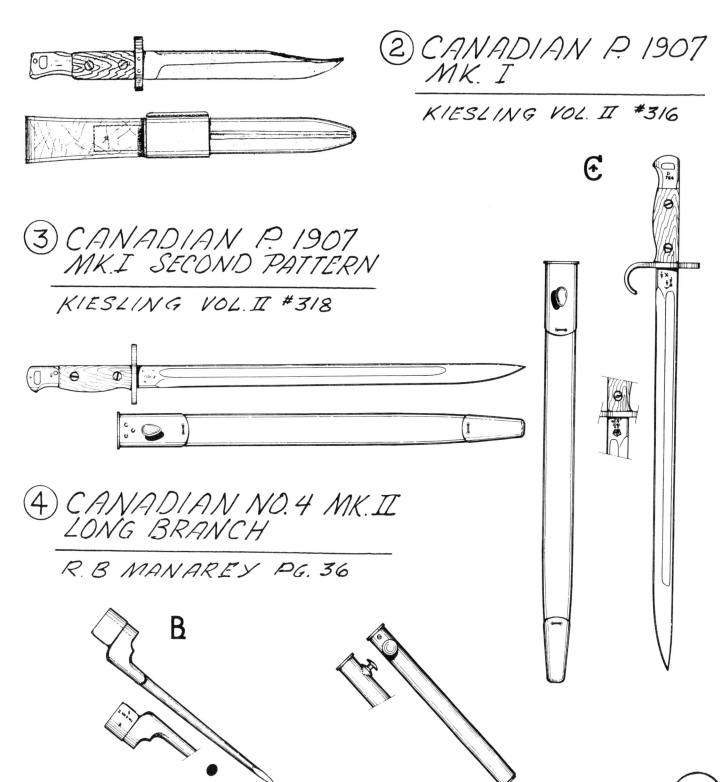

B

C

No. 1. **CANADIAN F.N. F.A.L. - 1954 (EXPERIMENTAL).** THIS PIECE IS THE CANADIAN STAMPED VERSION OF A BAYONET MANUFACTURED IN BELGIUM AS PART OF THE NATO STANDARDIZATION PROGRAM. I HAVE READ THAT ONLY 2,000 WERE SUPPOSEDLY ISSUED AND THEY WERE CARRIED IN THE SCABBARD SHOWN WITH NO. 2 BELOW. THE RIFLES WERE DESIGNATED EX1 OR EX2 BY CANADA.

No. 2. **CANADIAN C1 1957.** THIS IS THE CURRENT CANADIAN ISSUE BAYONET AND IS VERY SIMILAR TO PIECES IN USE BY THE U.K. AND OTHER COMMONWEALTH COUNTRIES. IT IS USED ON THE FN FAL FNC ASSAULT RIFLE.

① CANADIAN F.N. F.A.L. EXPERIMENTAL

KIESLING VOL. I #50

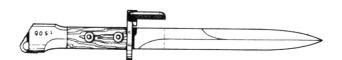

② CANADIAN C1

WATTS & WHITE PG. 46
DEREK COMPLIN

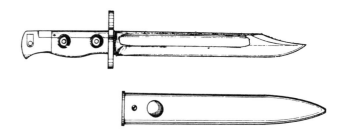

No. 1.   CHILEAN MODEL 1885 - KROPATSCHEK.   THIS BAYONET WAS PRODUCED INITIALLY FOR A FRENCH GRAS AND WAS MODIFIED BY THE CHILEAN GOVERNMENT TO FIT ON THEIR 1885 KROPATSCHEK.

No. 2.   CHILEAN POLICE SIDE ARM - MADE FROM GRAS BAYONET.   THESE PIECES WERE PRODUCED FROM GRAS BAYONETS AND ARE NOT DESIGNED TO FIT A RIFLE.   THEY WERE PROBABLY USED AS A POLICE SIDE ARM.

No. 3.   CHILEAN MODEL 1895 - MAUSER.   THESE BAYONETS WERE IMPORTED TO THE U.S. IN LARGE QUANTITIES IN RECENT YEARS AND APPEAR TO HAVE TWO VERSIONS OF A CREST STAMPED ON THE BLADE; ONE HAS THE FULL CHILEAN CREST, WHILE ANOTHER MERELY A CREST OUTLINE.   THEY CLOSELY RESEMBLE THE MEXICAN 1910 REPLACEMENT BAYONET.

No. 4.   CHILEAN MODEL 1912/1935 - MAUSER.   THESE BAYONETS ARE PROBABLY STEYR EXPORTS AND COME IN TWO BLADE LENGTHS (11" AND 9-1/2").   THE SHORTER BLADE (9-1/2") IS PROBABLY FOR THE M-1912.   THE 11" BLADE IS A RECENT CHILEAN EXPORT AND FITS THE 1935 POLICE CARBINE OF WHICH ONLY 10,000 WERE MADE.

NOTE: CHILE ALSO UTILIZED THE JOHNSON M-1941 RIFLE IN A 7MM VERSION.   THE BAYONET IS IDENTICAL TO THE U.S. VERSION (SEE 205-3) EXCEPT FOR A SERIAL NUMBER ON THE MUZZLE RING AND A UNIQUE "SQUARISH" SCABBARD.

28 - CHILE

① CHILEAN M. 1885

KIESLING VOL IV # 947

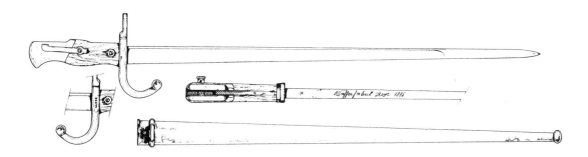

② CHILEAN SIDE ARM POLICE

EVANS & STEPHENS PG. 188

③ CHILEAN M. 1895

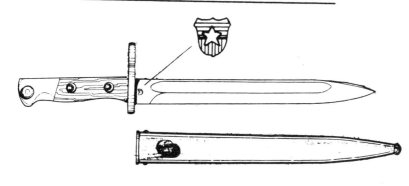

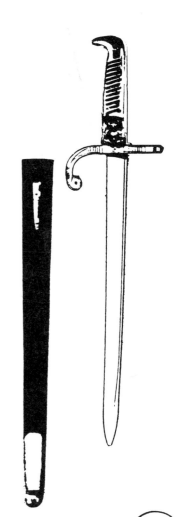

④ CHILEAN M. 1912/35

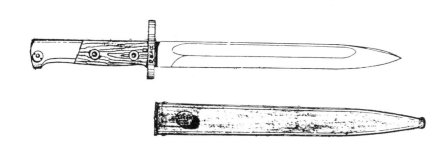

No. 1. **CHINESE MODEL 1907 - HANYANG.** THIS BAYONET IS DOUBLE-EDGED WITH AUSTRIAN CHARACTERISTICS; HOWEVER, IT FITS THE CHINESE COPY OF THE GERMAN MODEL 1888 COMMISSION RIFLE CALLED THE HANYANG.

No. 2. **CHINESE C. 1920 - BELGIUM.** THIS BAYONET IS ONE OF A SERIES OF CHINESE BAYONETS OSTENSIBLY MANUFACTURED BY BELGIUM IN 1920 FOR THE CHINESE AND COME IN TWO VERSIONS. THE ONE IN MY COLLECTION HAS AN ALL METAL HANDLE; HOWEVER, I HAVE SEEN A SIMILAR BAYONET WITH RUDIMENTARY WOODEN GRIPS.

No. 3. **CHINESE C. 1920 - BELGIUM.** THIS BAYONET IS ANOTHER BELGIUM EXPORT WHICH WAS USED BY THE CHINESE. IT IS MANUFACTURED FROM A SOCKET BAYONET BLADE. IT HAS BEEN FREQUENTLY MISREPRESENTED AS A GERMAN ERSATZ, HOWEVER, HAS A FULL MUZZLE RING UNLIKE THE GERMAN PIECES.

No. 4. **CHINESE C. 1935 - TYPE 79.** THIS BAYONET IS A COPY OF THE GERMAN MODEL 84/98 AND WAS EITHER IMPORTED OR MANUFACTURED IN CHINA TO FIT THEIR COPY OF THE GERMAN 8MM MAUSER. IT WAS PRODUCED UNDER THE CHIANG KAI SHEK REGIME AND ENDED UP IN USE BY THE PEOPLES REPUBLIC OF CHINA AS THE "TYPE 79" IN KOREA.

NOTE: THE MANCHURIAN MAUSER MANUFACTURED AT MUKDEN UTILIZED A SHORT BAR TYPE OF BAYONET LUG INDICATING THAT A BAYONET WITH A MUZZLE RING WOULD HAVE BEEN EMPLOYED.

① CHINESE M. 1907
WATTS & WHITE PG. 48

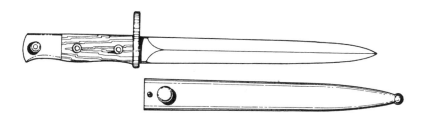

② CHINESE C. 1920
BELGIUM MFG.
KIESLING VOL IV #854
WATTS & WHITE PG. 50

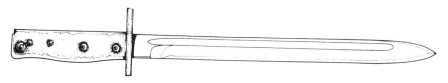

③ CHINESE C. 1920
BELGIUM MFG.
KIESLING VOL II #311

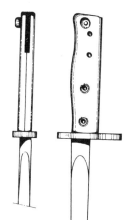

④ CHINESE C. 1935

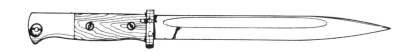

No. 1.   CHINESE TYPE 53 - CARBINE.   THIS IS A FOLDING BAYONET WHICH FITS ON THE TYPE 53 CARBINE AND IS IDENTICAL TO THE RUSSIAN M-1944 MOSIN NAGANT.   I HAVE LOOKED AT BOTH RUSSIAN AND CHINESE VERSIONS AND SEE NO DIFFERENCE.

No. 2.   CHINESE TYPE 56 - CARBINE.   THIS IS ALSO A FOLDING BAYONET FOR THE CHINESE COPY OF THE RUSSIAN DESIGNED SKS. THE BLADE IS A DULL SILVER WITH THREE DEEP FULLERS.

No. 3.   CHINESE TYPE 56 - CARBINE.   THIS IS A BLADE-TYPE FOLDING BAYONET THAT ALSO FITS THE TYPE 56 CARBINE.   THERE IS A SIMILAR VERSION FOR THE TYPE 56 ASSAULT RIFLE.

No. 4.   CHINESE TYPE 56 - ASSAULT RIFLE.   THIS IS A SPIKE BAYONET WHICH FOLDED UNDER THE BARREL OF THE KALASHNIKOV ASSAULT RIFLE AND IS PRODUCED IN TWO DISTINCT MANUFACTURING PATTERNS.   KIESLING DESIGNATES THIS BAYONET AS AN AK47.

NOTE: A T-68 SPIKE BAYONET ALSO EXISTS WHICH IS THE SAME OVERALL LENGTH OF THE SKS, HOWEVER, HAS GROOVES BETWEEN THE CRUCIFORM BLADE WHICH ARE 2 OR 3 TIMES AS DEEP AS THE SKS.   THE MUZZLE ATTACHMENT APPEARS TO BE A COMBINATION OF THE SKS AND "CHICOM" SPIKE.

① CHINESE TYPE 53
KIESLING VOL. I #128

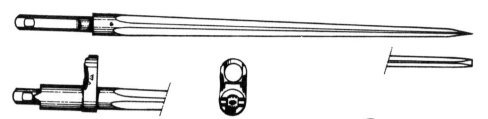

② CHINESE TYPE 56
SKS CARBINE
KIESLING VOL III #559

③ CHINESE TYPE 56
SKS CARBINE
KIESLING VOL. I #45

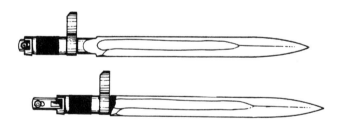

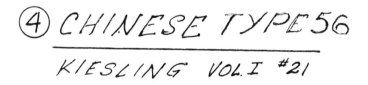

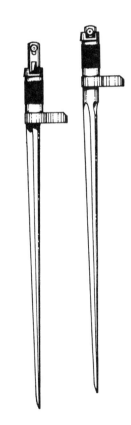

④ CHINESE TYPE 56
KIESLING VOL. I #21

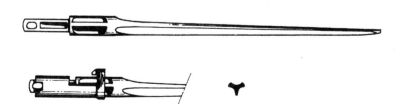

No. 1. CHINESE MAUSER MODEL 1924 - BELGIUM MFG. THIS IS A STANDARD BELGIUM 1924 BAYONET WHICH WAS APPARENTLY EXPORTED TO THE CHINESE AND HAS BEEN BLUED AND FITTED WITH A LEATHER CHINESE SCABBARD WITH AN INTEGRAL FROG.

No. 2. CHINESE MAUSER MODEL 1924 - BRITISH BLADE. THIS IS A SIMILAR BAYONET TO NO. 1 ABOVE; HOWEVER, THE MAUSER-TYPE HANDLE HAS BEEN FITTED WITH A BRITISH P-1907 BLADE.

No. 3. CHINESE MAUSER MODEL 1924 - ARISAKA BLADE. THIS IS A SIMILAR PIECE TO THE PREVIOUS TWO BAYONETS; HOWEVER, THE HANDLE HAS BEEN FITTED WITH A JAPANESE ARISAKA BLADE. THIS PIECE IS FINISHED IN DARK BLUE AS ARE THE PREVIOUS TWO BAYONETS.

No. 4. CHINESE AKS 56-1. THESE BAYONETS WERE EXPORTED IN LARGE QUANTITIES IN THE 1984-85 TIME PERIOD WITH A CHINESE MANUFACTURED COPY OF THE RUSSIAN AKM. IT IS A COPY OF THE RUSSIAN AKM BAYONET <u>WITHOUT</u> THE SAW BACK. THE HANDLE AND SCABBARD IS MOLDED PLASTIC AND COMES IN BOTH A BLACK AND REDDISH BROWN COLOR.

NOTE: IN ADDITION TO THE MAUSER SERIES, THE CHINESE ALSO UTILIZED JAPANESE T-30 BAYONETS, CZECH VZ24 MAUSER BAYONETS, GERMAN MODEL 84/98 BAYONETS AND PROBABLY MANY OTHERS. TAIWAN IS CURRENTLY USING A TYPE 65 ASSAULT RIFLE OF THEIR OWN MANUFACTURE (5.56 X 45 CALIBER).

① *CHINESE M. 1924*
BELGIUM MFG.

② *CHINESE M. 1924*
BRITISH BLADE

③ *CHINESE M. 1924*
ARISAKA BLADE

EVANS & STEPHENS PG. 150

④ *CHINESE AKS*

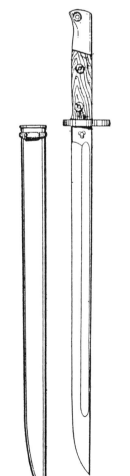

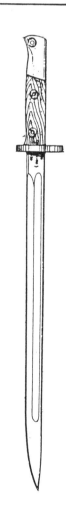

③¹

No. 1.   COLOMBIAN MODEL 1924/30 - MAUSER. THIS BAYONET WAS PART OF THE FAMOUS COLOMBIAN CONTRACT AND WAS AVAILABLE IN LARGE QUANTITIES IN THE SURPLUS STORES FOR THE LAST TWENTY YEARS.

No. 2.   COLOMBIAN MODEL 1935 - MAUSER. THIS BAYONET IS IDENTIFIED AS COLOMBIAN BECAUSE IT HAS THE LETTERS "R DE C" ON THE CROSSGUARD; HOWEVER, IT HAS A SHORT BAR ATTACHMENT UNLIKE No. 1 ABOVE, SO THIS MAY BE AN INCORRECT IDENTIFICATION. THE "R DE C" COULD STAND FOR REPUBLIC OF COLOMBIA OR CHILE OR ANY NUMBER OF THINGS (SEE PHOTOGRAPH).

NOTE: COLOMBIA CURRENTLY UTILIZES THE BELGIAN-PRODUCED SAFN ASSAULT RIFLE.

① *COLOMBIAN M. 1924/30*

WATTS & WHITE PG. 41

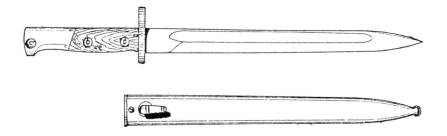

② *COLOMBIAN M. 1935*

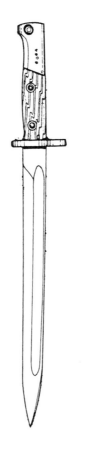

No. 1. Czechoslovakian Model 1918/22. This is the Czechoslovakian manufactured version of the Austrian M-1895 Mannlicher (it is marked "CSZ" and some have the Czech lion). These might be Austrian manufactured because the Czechoslovakian Republic was created in 1918 and Mannlicher M-1895 rifles from the old Austro-Hungarian empire were utilized.

No. 2. Czechoslovakian VZ-23 - Long with muzzle ring. This is the long Czechoslovakian VZ23 bayonet and is identified by Carter as pattern 98/22. These bayonets were utilized by Lithuania, Iran and South America. They are easily identified by the reversed cutting edge. Rare Belgian-manufactured examples of this model also exist.

No. 3. Czechoslovakian VZ-24 - Short with muzzle ring. This bayonet is the short version of No. 2 above and I have in my collection several variations, including bright finishes, parkerized finishes, and blue finishes. All have the reversed cutting edge. I assume that these bayonets were exported to various South American countries.

No. 4. Czechoslovakian VZ-24 - Cutting edge normal. This bayonet is an interesting variation of No. 3. above in that the blade is in the normal position; i.e., flat edge facing the muzzle ring.

① CZECH. M. 1895

KIESLING VOL. I # 78

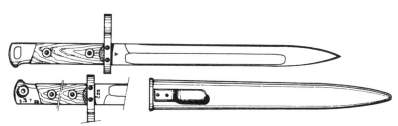

② CZECH VZ 23
LONG

KIESLING VOL. II #309
WATTS & WHITE PG. 53

③ CZECH VZ 24
SHORT

KIESLING VOL. I #193

ČSZ

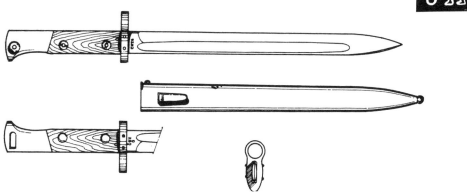

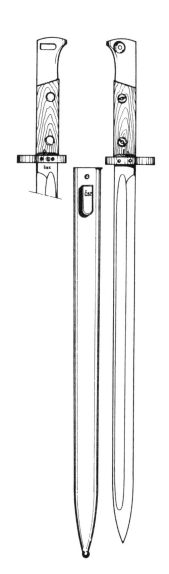

④ CZECH VZ 24
CUTTING EDGE NORMAL

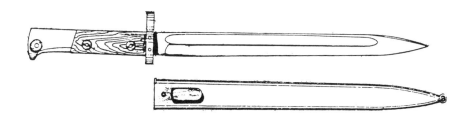

㉝

No. 1.   CZECHOSLOVAKIAN MODEL 1924/30 - EXPORT. THIS BAYONET WAS EXPORTED IN LARGE QUANTITIES. I HAVE TWO VARIATIONS IN MY COLLECTION - ONE WITH SCREW BOLTS AND THE SECOND WITH THE FASTENERS WHICH MUST BE REMOVED BY A SPANNER WRENCH (PROBABLY BELGIAN OR YUGOSLAVIAN).

No. 2.   CZECHOSLOVAKIAN EXPORT - IRISH MAUSER. THIS PIECE IS ANOTHER CZECH EXPORT AND HAS BEEN IDENTIFIED AS IRISH. COULD BE! THE FROG STUD ON THE SCABBARD IS IN THE FORM OF A "T" INSTEAD OF THE "L" TYPE COMMON ON OTHER CZECH SCABBARDS.

No. 3.   CZECHOSLOVAKIAN VZ-33 - CARBINE. THIS IS THE VZ-33 BAYONET WITH THE SHORT BLADE, WHICH WAS OSTENSIBLY USED BY THE FINANCIAL GUARDS AND POLICE. IT HAS A SHORT BAR ATTACHMENT AND IS A VERY WELL MADE PIECE. 30,000 OF THESE BAYONETS WERE PRODUCED BETWEEN 1933 AND 1938, ACCORDING TO R. D. C. EVANS.

① *CZECH M. 1924/30*
EXPORT

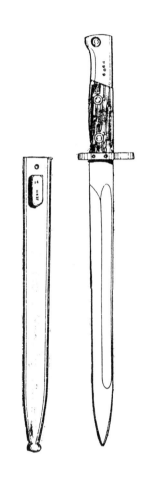

② *CZECH EXPORT*

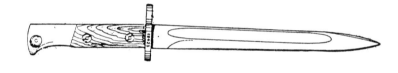

③ *CZECH VZ 33*
KIESLING VOL. I #77

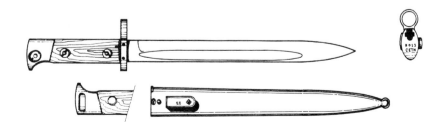

No. 1. CZECHOSLOVAKIAN VZ-24 - GERMAN MODIFIED. THIS BAYONET IS A CZECHOSLOVAKIAN BAYONET WHICH WAS MODIFIED BY THE GERMANS. THIS PIECE HAS THE MUZZLE RING GROUND OFF LEAVING HIGH EARS.

No. 2. CZECHOSLOVAKIAN VZ-24 - GERMAN MODIFIED. THIS BAYONET HAS THE MUZZLE RING GROUND OFF; HOWEVER, IT IS GROUND FLUSH. THESE WERE ALSO MANUFACTURED WITHOUT THE MUZZLE RING UNDER GERMAN OCCUPATION.

No. 3. CZECHOSLOVAKIAN VZ-24 - GERMAN MODIFIED. THIS PARTICULAR BAYONET HAS THE MUZZLE RING GROUND OFF LEAVING VERY HIGH EARS, ALMOST ONE-FOURTH THE BOTTOM PORTION OF THE MUZZLE RING REMAINS.

No. 4. CZECHOSLOVAKIAN NCO SIDE ARM. THIS WEAPON IS IDENTICAL TO THE VZ-24 BAYONETS, HOWEVER, IT HAS A LONG SOLID (UNSLOTTED) POMMEL AND IS APPARENTLY A SIDE ARM ONLY.

No. 5. CZECHOSLOVAKIAN VZ-58. THIS IS THE CURRENT CZECH BAYONET AND COMES IN FOUR VARIATIONS THAT I AM AWARE OF, INCLUDING WOOD AND FIBER HANDLE MATERIAL (THE PIECE ILLUSTRATED IS REDDISH FIBER) AND WITH THE HANDLES FITTED TO THE TANG OR WITH A PORTION OF THE TANG EXPOSED, AS ILLUSTRATED. THESE WERE VERY SCARCE UNTIL RECENTLY (1984) RELEASED.

① CZECH VZ 24
HIGH EARS
KIESLING VOL. I #195

② CZECH VZ 24
GROUND FLUSH
KIESLING VOL. I #197

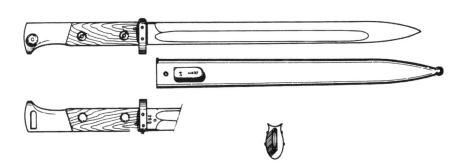

③ CZECH VZ 24
VERY HIGH EARS
KIESLING VOL I #196

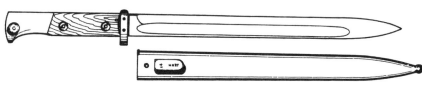

⑤ CZECH VZ 58
KIESLING VOL. IV #740

④ CZECH SIDE ARM
NCO

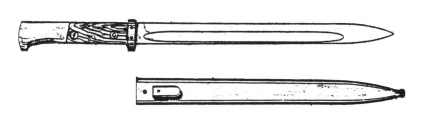

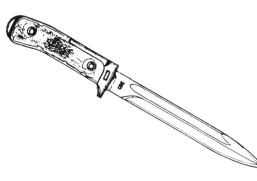

No. 1.   DANISH MODEL 1769. I IDENTIFIED THIS BAYONET AS DANISH DIRECTLY FROM THE KIESLING'S BOOKS AND MUST CONFESS IT WAS SOMEWHAT OF A GUESS; HOWEVER, THE DIMENSIONS ARE PRECISELY THOSE IN KIESLING.

No. 2.   DANISH MODEL 1854 - WITH KYHL'S LOCKING SPRING. THIS BAYONET WAS PRODUCED FOR THE DANISH REBELS BY THE GERMANS AND POSSESSES AN INTERESTING LOCKING ARRANGEMENT WHICH WAS APPARENTLY VERY EFFECTIVE.

No. 3.   DANISH MODEL 1867 - REMINGTON. THIS BAYONET IS A GERMAN MANUFACTURED SABER TYPE FOR THE FIRST DANISH ROLLING BLOCK RIFLE PRODUCED BY REMINGTON AND IS A WELL MADE BAYONET WITH A STEEL-MOUNTED LEATHER SCABBARD.

No. 4.   DANISH MODEL 1867 - REMINGTON. THIS BAYONET IS A LATER VERSION OF NO. 3 ABOVE AND HAS THE INTERNAL SPRING LOCKING MECHANISM.

① DANISH M. 1769
KIESLING VOL. IV #802

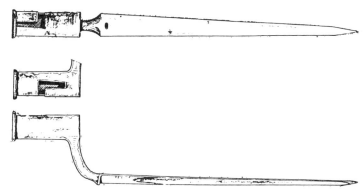

② DANISH M. 1854
KIESLING VOL. II #333

③ DANISH M. 1867
FIRST MODEL
KIESLING VOL II #442

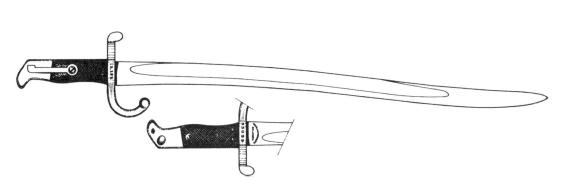

④ DANISH M. 1867
SECOND MODEL
KIESLING VOL. IV #967

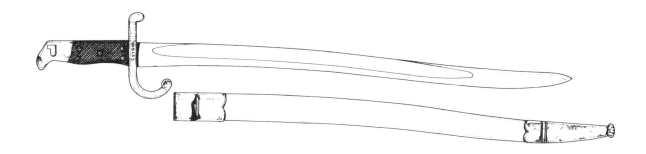

No. 1. DANISH MODEL 1889 - KRAG JORGENSEN. THIS IS THE DANISH KRAG RIFLE BAYONET AND THE GRIPS ON THIS PARTICULAR PATTERN ARE CHECKERED LEATHER. THESE PATTERNS WERE PRODUCED BY BOTH W. K. & C. AND ALEX COPPEL IN GERMANY AND SLIGHT MANUFACTURING VARIATIONS EXIST.

No. 2. DANISH MODEL 1889 - KRAG JORGENSEN. THIS BAYONET IS THE WOODEN HANDLED VARIATION OF No. 1 ABOVE AND HAS BRASS PINS IN THE GRIPS.

No. 3. DANISH MODEL 1915. THIS BAYONET IS AN EXTREMELY UNUSUAL PIECE AND CONSISTS OF A LONG T-BACK BLADE AND A SINGLE PIECE GRIP CONSTRUCTION. THESE BAYONETS ARE QUITE SCARCE.

No. 4. DANISH MODEL 1915 - MODIFICATION. THIS BAYONET IS AN ERSATZ VERSION OF THE MODEL 1915 AND THE T-BACK BLADE HAS BEEN MODIFIED INTO A BOWIE SHAPE. THIS WAS UNQUESTIONABLY A FIELD MODIFICATION OF SOME TYPE AND HAS PROBABLY NOT BEEN DUPLICATED.

NOTE: THE DANISH ALSO UTILIZED THE U.S. MODEL 1917 BAYONET (223-3) WITH ENFIELD M-1917 RIFLES IN 1953. THESE BAYONETS WERE DESIGNATED BAJONET M-53/17.

① DANISH M.1889

KIESLING VOL. I #58

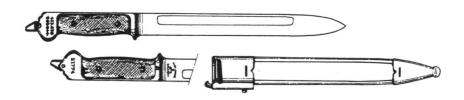

② DANISH M.1889

KIESLING VOL. I #57

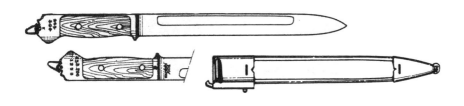

④ DANISH M.1915
MODIFICATION

③ DANISH M.1915

KIESLING VOL II #327

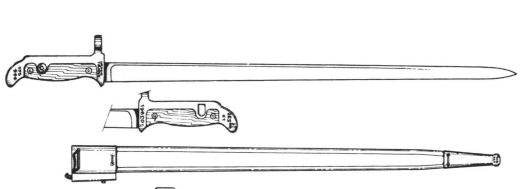

No. 1. **Danish Model 1947 - Madsen.** The Danish Madsen rifle and bayonet were developed for the export trade in the late 40's and apparently was not successful; however, the bayonet is beautifully made and is relatively common.

No. 2. **Danish Model 1967 - HMAK.** This bayonet is part of the G-3 family and is current issue for the Danish forces. It has a bright double-edge blade.

NOTE: Denmark utilized the U.S. Garand rifle (as the GM50) and copies of the U.S. M5 bayonet (see 229-1). According to R. D. C. Evans, these were marked with a crown over HTK M/62 on the pommel.

① *DANISH M.1947*
MADSEN

KIESLING VOL. I #55

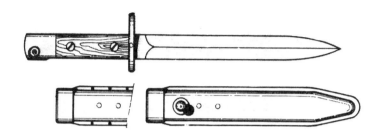

② *DANISH M.1967*
HMAK

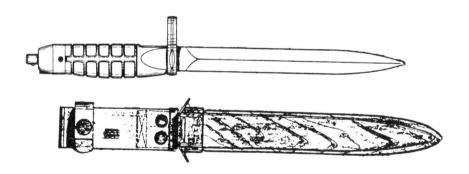

No. 1. EGYPTIAN MODEL 1867 – REMINGTON.   THIS IS THE BAYONET ISSUED WITH THE EGYPTIAN REMINGTON ROLLING BLOCK AND CLOSELY RESEMBLES THE FRENCH CHASSEPOT WITH THE MAJOR DIFFERENCE BEING THE CONNECTING LUG SLOT.   ALL PIECES OF THIS TYPE HAVE BEEN CALLED EGYPTIAN REMINGTONS; HOWEVER, BASED ON MARKS I HAVE SEEN ON THE BAYONETS, I SUSPECT THEY WERE UTILIZED BY OTHER COUNTRIES. (110,000 OF THESE RIFLES AND BAYONETS WERE DIVERTED TO FRANCE BY REMINGTON FOR USE IN THE FRANCO PRUSSIAN WAR.) ONE VERSION IN LARRY JOHNSON'S COLLECTION WHICH DOES POSSESS EGYPTIAN MARKS HAS THE INITIALS "EPCH" IN ADDITION TO THE ARABIC MARKS. CARTER IDENTIFIES THIS PIECE AS THE M-1870.

No. 2. EGYPTIAN MODEL 1876-80.   THIS IS AN EGYPTIAN MODIFICATION OF THE OLD REMINGTON SABER BAYONETS TO ALLOW USE ON THE SNYDER CONVERSION OF THE TWO BAND ENFIELD RIFLE. IT IS A VERY INTERESTING PIECE IN THAT THE GROOVES ON THE HANDLE ARE HAND MACHINED AND GO AROUND THE BACK OF THE HANDLE. THESE HAVE BEEN IDENTIFIED AS "CONFEDERATE" BY SOME DEALERS.

No. 3. EGYPTIAN MODEL 1914 – POLICE.   THIS PIECE IS ANOTHER EGYPTIAN MODIFICATION OF THEIR OLD REMINGTON BAYONETS, HOWEVER, THIS TIME FOR THE .303 MARTINI ENFIELD RIFLES. THE BAYONET RETAINS THE REMINGTON HANDLE AND INCORPORATES A NEW CROSSGUARD. THE SCABBARD IS ALL STEEL.

No. 4. EGYPTIAN MODEL 1914 – POLICE VARIATION. THIS BAYONET IS ANOTHER VARIATION FOR THE MARTINI ENFIELD MODIFICATION AND IS STAMPED "EPOL", WHICH CARTER SPECULATES IS FOR EGYPTIAN POLICE.

① EGYPTIAN M.1867

CARTER & WALTER PG. 50

② EGYPTIAN M.1876/80

J. A. CARTER, GUNS REVIEW 9/81

KIESLING VOL IV #971

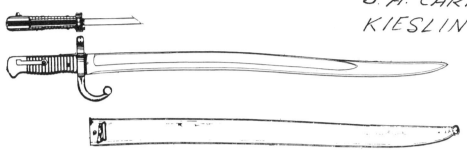

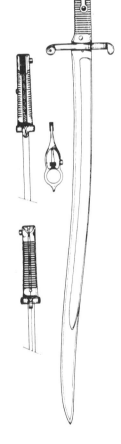

③ EGYPTIAN M.1914 POLICE

J.A. CARTER, GUNS REVIEW 9/81

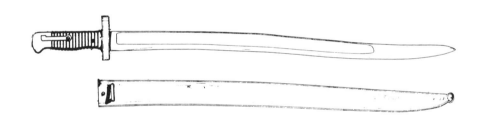

④ EGYPTIAN M.1914

J. A. CARTER, GUNS REVIEW 9/81

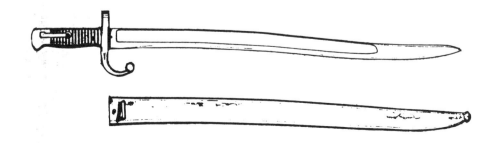

No. 1.   EGYPTIAN HAKIM CIRCA 1950. THIS BAYONET IS VERY UNUSUAL
AND WAS PRODUCED IN EGYPT FOR THE 7.92 HAKIM RIFLE
(BASED ON THE LJUNGMAN M42). THE STRONG RESEMBLANCE TO
THE SWEDISH MODEL 1896 BAYONET IS BECAUSE THE PLANT
WHICH MANUFACTURED THE RIFLE AND PRESUMABLY THE BAYONETS
WAS ESTABLISHED IN THE 1949/50 TIME FRAME WITH THE HELP
OF SWEDISH TECHNICIANS. IT IS THEREFORE POSSIBLE THE
BAYONETS WERE PRODUCED USING SWEDISH PARTS OR SURPLUS
BAYONETS.

No. 2.   EGYPTIAN F.N. MODEL 1949. THIS PIECE IS IDENTICAL TO
No. 2 ON PAGE 20 AND WAS ISSUED TO EGYPTIAN FORCES
ENGAGED IN THE SUEZ CANAL CONFLICT. THE PIECE IN MY
COLLECTION HAS AN ARABIC SERIAL NUMBER ON THE SIDE OF
THE HILT. THE SIMILARITY OF THIS BAYONET TO 40-1 MAY BE
INTENTIONAL AND REFLECT THE PREFERENCE OF KING FAROUK'S
GENERALS.

① EGYPTIAN C. 1950 HAKIM

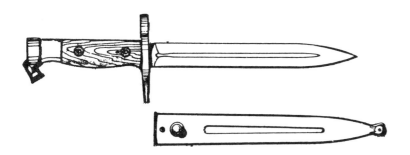

② EGYPTIAN M. 1949

KIESLING VOL. I #81

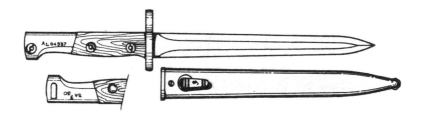

No. 1. PLUG BAYONET - SCHNITZLER & KIRSCHBAUM OF SOLINGEN, GERMANY. THIS IS AN EARLY PLUG BAYONET WITH AN ENGRAVED BLADE. THE BLADE HAS THE LETTERS "S & K" ENGRAVED ON THE RICASSO WITH BATTLE MOTIFS ON THE FACE OF THE BLADE. THE INCLUSION AS ENGLISH IS PURE SPECULATION. (IF PRODUCED BY S & K, IT WAS MANUFACTURED AFTER 1811.)

No. 2. ENGLISH PLUG BAYONET - CIRCA 1680-1700. THIS BAYONET IS DEFINITELY ENGLISH AS I HAVE NOTED IDENTICAL SPECIMENS IN THE TOWER OF LONDON AND IT IS PROBABLY ONE OF THE FIRST "QUASI STANDARDIZED" BAYONETS IN EXISTENCE.

No. 3. ENGLISH PLUG BAYONET - CIRCA 1680. THIS BAYONET IS IDENTIFIED AS ENGLISH ONLY BECAUSE OF THE HANDLE FORM (WHERE THE GERMAN FORM WAS FAVORED BY ENGLAND). IT HAS A TRIANGULAR SHAPED BLADE, IS WELL MARKED AND WOULD BE A GOOD ARMOR PIERCING WEAPON. AS WITH THE PREVIOUS PIECES, IT IS VERY WELL MADE.

No. 4. EARLY PLUG BAYONET - HUNTING. THIS PLUG BAYONET HAS GERMAN CHARACTERISTICS (ONION-SHAPED HANDLE) WITH A BRASS CROSSGUARD (EMBELLISHED WITH HUNTING SCENES, HOUNDS, BOARS, ETC.). I HAVE SEEN SEVERAL IDENTICAL PIECES AND SUSPECT THESE WERE PRODUCED IN SOME QUANTITY.

① EARLY PLUG BAYONET

② PLUG BAYONET C. 1680/1700

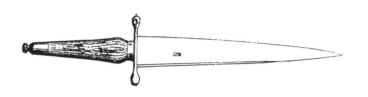

③ PLUG BAYONET C. 1680/90

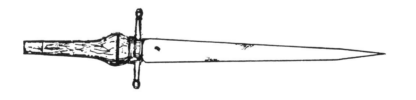

④ EARLY PLUG BAYONET

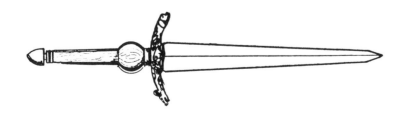

No. 1. SOCKET BAYONET CIRCA 1750. THIS PIECE IS TYPICALLY CALLED A BROWN BESS AND IS "L" MORTISED TO ENGAGE A TOP-MOUNTED BARREL STUD. THE COLLAR IS BRAISED TO THE REAR OF THE SOCKET, NOT ONLY STRENGTHENING THE PIECE BUT ALSO PROVIDING A BRIDGE OVER THE PRIMARY SLOT. THESE WEAPONS VARY IN SIZE, ALTHOUGH THE BRITISH WERE CERTAINLY CLOSEST TO A STANDARDIZED SOCKET BAYONET FOR THE PERIOD.

No. 2. SOCKET BAYONET PATTERN 1750. ANOTHER MORE STANDARDIZED VARIATION OF THE BROWN BESS. I HAVE THREE PIECES; ONE MARKED T. GILL, ONE MARKED JOHN GILL, AND ONE MARKED OSBORN. THESE MAKERS ARE DISCUSSED AT LENGTH IN WILKINSON LATHAM'S BOOK.

No. 3. ENGLISH FUSIL CIRCA 1800. THIS IS AN INTERESTING BAYONET THAT IN MANY WAYS RESEMBLES THE SHAPE OF A SCOTTISH DIRK, HOWEVER, WAS OSTENSIBLY FOUND IN A BUTT COMPARTMENT OF AN ENGLISH OFFICER'S FUSIL. IT IS A VERY WELL MADE PIECE AND COULD ACTUALLY BE PART OF SOME TYPE OF POLE ARM.

No. 4. FERGUSON TYPE SOCKET PATTERN 1777. THIS PIECE IS ANOTHER VARIATION OF THE BROWN BESS BAYONET, HOWEVER, HAS A COMPLETELY FLAT SPADE-TYPE BLADE WHICH RESEMBLES A FERGUSON RIFLE BAYONET. THE L-MORTIS SLOT ON THIS EXAMPLE IS NOT CONFIGURED EXACTLY LIKE THE FERGUSON BAYONET PICTURE IN WILKINSON LATHAM'S BOOK.

① SOCKET BAYONET C. 1750

KIESLING VOL. II #310

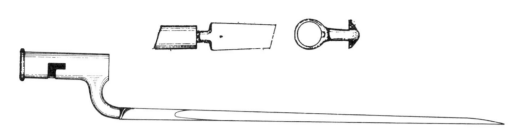

DIMENSIONS	
BLADE LENGTH	17"
BLADE WIDTH	1 1/4"
SOCKET LENGTH	4"
SOCKET O.D.	1 3/64"
SOCKET I.D.	15/16"
SHANK LENGTH	1

② SOCKET BAYONET P. 1750

KIESLING VOL. II #310

DIMENSIONS	
BLADE LENGTH	16 3/4"
BLADE WIDTH	1"
SOCKET LENGTH	4"
SOCKET O.D.	1 1/16"
SOCKET I.D.	15/16"
SHANK LENGTH	1"

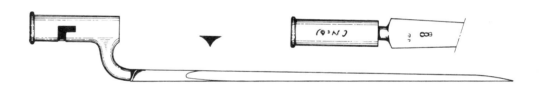

③ ENGLISH FUSIL C. 1800

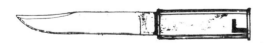

④ FERGUSON TYPE P. 1777

DIMENSIONS	
BLADE LENGTH	25"
BLADE WIDTH	1 1/2"
SOCKET LENGTH	4"
SOCKET O.D.	1"
SOCKET I.D.	7/8"
SHANK LENGTH	1 1/16"

No. 1. **VOLUNTEER BAYONET CIRCA 1795.** THIS PIECE HAS A SABRE-TYPE BLADE MOUNTED TO A COLLARED L-MORTISED SOCKET OF VERY LARGE DIMENSIONS AND IS ONE OF THE MANY VARIATIONS USED BY VOLUNTEER COMPANIES OF THAT ERA.

No. 2. **EAST INDIA PATTERN 1844.** THIS BAYONET IS VERY SIMILARLY CONFIGURED TO THE BROWN BESS; HOWEVER, IT HAS A SPRING ATTACHMENT TO HOLD THE ARM FIRMLY TO THE STUD. I HAVE TWO VARIATIONS WHICH ARE NOTED; ONE WITH A SHORT L-MORTISED SLOT AND THE OTHER WITH A LONG L-MORTISED SLOT. MANY OF THE BAYONETS OF THIS CONFIGURATION ARE MARKED WITH THE EAST INDIAN COMPANY LOGO.

No. 3. **PATTERN 1839.** THIS BAYONET IS A STEP IN THE EVOLUTION OF SOCKET BAYONETS IN THE BRITISH ARMY WHERE A SPRING WAS ADDED TO THE RIFLE TO FASTEN THE BAYONET AND IS A MUCH MORE STANDARDIZED ARM THAN THE BROWN BESS TYPE OF BAYONETS PREVIOUSLY ILLUSTRATED.

NOTE: THE DEFINITIVE SOURCE OF INFORMATION ON THE "BROWN BESS" IS A BOOK AUTHORED BY GRAHAM PRIEST TITLED THE BROWN BESS BAYONET 1720-1860 PUBLISHED IN ENGLAND BY THARSTON PRESS (SEE BIBLIOGRAPHY, PG. 247).

① VOLUNTEER C. 1795
KIESLING VOL. III #696

DIMENSIONS	
BLADE LENGTH	22 2/3"
BLADE WIDTH	1 1/2"
SOCKET LENGTH	4"
SOCKET O.D.	1 3/64"
SOCKET I.D.	15/16"
SHANK LENGTH	7/8"

② EAST INDIA P. 1844
KIESLING VOL. I #248

DIMENSIONS	
BLADE LENGTH	15 - 15 1/4"
BLADE WIDTH	1 1/8 - 1 1/4"
SOCKET LENGTH	4"
SOCKET O.D.	1 - 1 1/16"
SOCKET I.D.	7/16 - 15/16"
SHANK LENGTH	7/8 - 1"

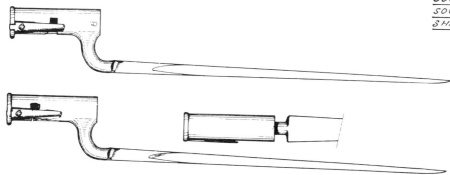

③ ENGLISH P. 1839
KIESLING VOL. I #250

DIMENSIONS	
BLADE LENGTH	17"
BLADE WIDTH	1 1/32"
SOCKET LENGTH	3"
SOCKET O.D.	1 1/32"
SOCKET I.D.	31/32"
SHANK LENGTH	1"

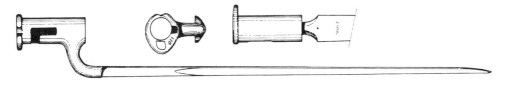

43

No. 1. PATTERN 1842 – SERGEANTS OF THE LINE. THIS IS ANOTHER IN THE CONTINUING EVOLUTION OF BRITISH SOCKET PATTERNS AND HAS A VERY UNUSUAL COLLAR CONFIGURATION, WHICH IS ILLUSTRATED. THIS ALSO UTILIZED LOVEL'S SPRING CATCH.

No. 2. PATTERN 1842. THIS ARM IS VERY SIMILAR TO No. 1 ABOVE, HOWEVER, IS OF LARGER PROPORTIONS AND WAS USED BY LINE INFANTRY.

No. 3. PATTERN 1843 – SAPPERS AND MINERS. THIS BAYONET HAS A HEAVY SABRE BLADE ATTACHED TO AN L-MORTISED SOCKET OF LARGE DIMENSIONS. IT IS OBVIOUSLY A TOOL-TYPE WEAPON, POSSIBLY USED BY SAPPERS OR ENGINEERS OF THAT PERIOD.

No. 4. PATTERN 1844 – LAND. THIS BAYONET IS VERY SIMILAR TO THE EAST INDIA PATTERNS DESCRIBED ON THE PREVIOUS PAGE AND IS EQUIPPED WITH A SPRING CATCH; HOWEVER, THIS PIECE IS BRITISH MARKED. THE INDIAN TROOPS RECEIVED THE OBSO-LETE WEAPONS FROM THE BRITISH ARMY, ESPECIALLY AFTER THE SEPOY REBELLION. THE REASON WAS TO MAKE SURE THAT, IN THE EVENT OF ANY NATIVE UPRISINGS, THE QUALITY OF ARMS WOULD BE INFERIOR. THE INDIANS FREQUENTLY MODIFIED THESE BAYONETS TO FIT MORE MODERN ARMS AND THIS MAY BE AN EXAMPLE OF SUCH A MODIFICATION.

① *ENGLISH P. 1842*
SERGEANTS

LATHAM PG. 18

DIMENSIONS	
BLADE LENGTH	15"
BLADE WIDTH	1 5/32"
SOCKET LENGTH	3"
SOCKET O.D.	1 1/32"
SOCKET I.D.	15/16"
SHANK LENGTH	1"

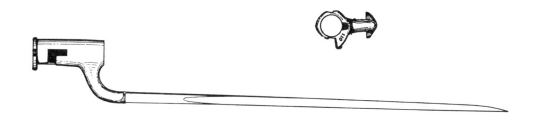

④ *ENGLISH P. 1844*
LAND

KIESLING VOL. I #248
LATHAM PG 46

② *ENGLISH P. 1842*

KIESLING VOL. II #298

DIMENSIONS	
BLADE LENGTH	17 1/4"
BLADE WIDTH	1 3/16"
SOCKET LENGTH	3 1/8"
SOCKET O.D.	1 1/8
SOCKET I.D.	31/32"
SHANK LENGTH	1 1/8"

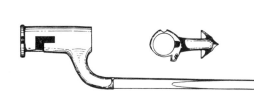

DIMENSIONS	
BLADE LENGTH	15"
BLADE WIDTH	1 5/16"
SOCKET LENGTH	4"
SOCKET O.D.	1 1/16"
SOCKET I.D.	15/16"
SHANK LENGTH	1"

③ *ENGLISH P. 1843*
SAPPERS & MINERS

HUGHES PART 2 # 250

DIMENSIONS	
BLADE LENGTH	22 1/4"
BLADE WIDTH	2"
SOCKET LENGTH	4"
SOCKET O.D.	1 1/16"
SOCKET I.D.	31/32"
SHANK LENGTH	3/4"

No. 1.   **East India Company - Circa 1845 - Sword Socket.** This is an unusual and interesting piece with a socket bayonet configured into a short sword through the addition of a stirrup grip. It would appear that this would be a very difficult weapon to use as a sword.

No. 2.   **Pattern 1853 - Enfield Socket.** This bayonet is the first pattern of the most prolific socket bayonet produced by the British Empire and is the first bayonet equipped with a locking ring which the British finally adapted from French designs. This is a very well made piece and was used in large quantities by both sides during the U.S. Civil War.

No. 3.   **Pattern 1853 - Enfield Socket.** This bayonet is the same as No. 2, however, the tip has been clipped so that the piece can be used for training purposes. (It might also be a movie prop, as the condition is "mint".)

① EAST INDIA C. 1845 SWORD SOCKET

KIESLING VOL. IV #972
WATTS & WHITE #734

DIMENSIONS	
BLADE LENGTH	22 1/4"
BLADE WIDTH	1 3/16"
SOCKET LENGTH	4 39/64"
SOCKET O.D.	1 1/16"
SOCKET I.D.	15/16"

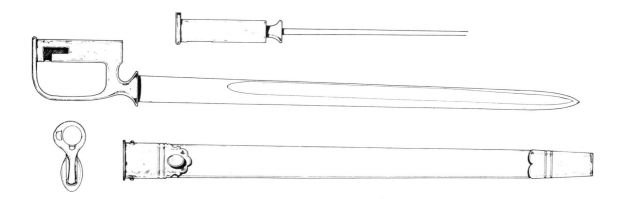

② ENGLISH P. 1853 FIRST PATTERN

KIESLING VOL. I #274
LATHAM PG. 62-63

DIMENSIONS	
BLADE LENGTH	17 7/8"
BLADE WIDTH	13/16"
SOCKET LENGTH	3"
SOCKET O.D.	15/16"
SOCKET I.D.	25/32"
SHANK LENGTH	1"

③ ENGLISH P. 1853 CLIPPED

KIESLING VOL. I #274

DIMENSIONS	
BLADE LENGTH	17"
BLADE WIDTH	13/16"
SOCKET LENGTH	3"
SOCKET O.D.	15/16"
SOCKET I.D.	25/32"
SHANK LENGTH	1"

No. 1.   PATTERN 1853 - ENFIELD.   THIS BAYONET HAS A STANDARD 1853 ENFIELD SOCKET WITH A SLIT DOWN THE TOP OF THE SOCKET AND A LONGER SCREW PLACED IN THE LOCKING RING SUCH THAT THE ARM CAN BE FITTED ONTO A LARGER DIAMETER BARREL.   THIS MODIFICATION IS SOMEWHAT COMMON, AS I HAVE SEEN SEVERAL OF THESE PIECES AND MAY HAVE BEEN PERFORMED IN INDIA OR EVEN DURING THE U.S. CIVIL WAR.

No. 2.   PATTERN 1853/58 - ENFIELD.   THIS IS THE SECOND-PATTERN BAYONET AND I HAVE TWO VARIATIONS - ONE ENGLISH MANUFAC- TURED AND THE SECOND INDIAN MANUFACTURED.   THE DIFFER- ENCES BETWEEN THE SECOND AND FIRST PATTERN ARE SLIGHT WITH THE MOST APPARENT BEING SLIGHTLY DIFFERENT BLADE FLUTES AND A DIFFERENT BLADE FORGING PATTERN, POSSIBLY FOR MANUFACTURING PURPOSES.

No. 3.   PATTERN 1853/1876 - MARTINI HENRY.   THIS PARTICULAR PIECE IS A STANDARD M-1853 BAYONET WHICH HAS BEEN BUSHED TO FIT THE MARTINI HENRY RIFLE.   THIS MODIFICATION IS QUITE COMMON AND THESE BAYONETS APPEAR TO BE MORE NUMER- OUS THAN ORIGINAL 1853s.

No. 4.   PATTERN 1867 - SNYDER.   THIS BAYONET IS VERY SIMILAR TO THE ENFIELD PATTERNS AND IS IDENTIFIED AS A "SNYDER" BECAUSE THIS PARTICULAR PIECE WAS FOUND ON A .577 CAL. SNYDER RIFLE.

① ENGLISH P. 1853 MODIFIED

KIESLING VOL. IV #880

DIMENSIONS	
BLADE LENGTH	17 7/8"
BLADE WIDTH	13/16"
SOCKET LENGTH	3 "
SOCKET O. D.	1 1/8" ±
SOCKET I. D.	1" ±
SHANK LENGTH	1"

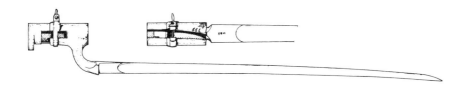

② ENGLISH P. 1853/58 SECOND PATTERN

KIESLING VOL. I #275

DIMENSIONS	
BLADE LENGTH	17 7/8"
BLADE WIDTH	13/16
SOCKET LENGTH	3 3/32"
SOCKET O. D.	29/32"
SOCKET I. D.	23/32"
SHANK LENGTH	7/8"

③ ENGLISH P. 1853/76 BUSHED

LATHAM PG 62-63

DIMENSIONS	
BLADE LENGTH	17 7/8"
BLADE WIDTH	13/16"
SOCKET LENGTH	3 3/32"
SOCKET O. D.	13/16"
SOCKET I. D.	25/32"
SHANK LENGTH	7/8

④ ENGLISH P. 1867 SNYDER RIFLE

DIMENSIONS	
BLADE LENGTH	17 7/8"
BLADE WIDTH	13/16"
SOCKET LENGTH	3 3/32"
SOCKET O. D.	15/16
SOCKET I. D.	25/32
SHANK LENGTH	7/8"

No. 1. **PATTERN 1876 - MARTINI HENRY.** THIS BAYONET WAS MANU-FACTURED FOR THE MARTINI HENRY RIFLE AND HAS A LONG BLADE (22"). THE MUZZLE RING DIAMETER IS 17.9MM.

No. 2. **PATTERN 1876 - MARTINI METFORD.** THIS ARM IS THE STANDARD 1876 PATTERN, HOWEVER, IT HAS BEEN BUSHED FOR THE MARTINI-METFORD RIFLE.

No. 3. **PATTERN 1895 - MARTINI ENFIELD.** THIS BAYONET WAS MANU-FACTURED FOR THE M-1895 RIFLE AND HAS A COLLAR BRIDGE TO THE SIDE OF THE ARM. IT IS ALSO A LONG PATTERN (22" BLADE) AND HAS A SMALLER MUZZLE RING DIAMETER (17.8MM).

① ENGLISH P. 1876 MARTINI HENRY

KIESLING VOL II #405
HUGHES PART 2 #254

DIMENSIONS	
BLADE LENGTH	22"
BLADE WIDTH	13/16"
SOCKET LENGTH	3"
SOCKET O.D.	29/32"
SOCKET I.D.	23/32"
SHANK LENGTH	7/8"

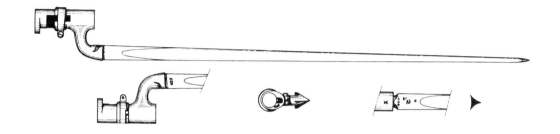

② ENGLISH P. 1876 MARTINI METFORD

KIESLING VOL II #405

DIMENSIONS	
BLADE LENGTH	22"
BLADE WIDTH	13/16"
SOCKET LENGTH	3"
SOCKET O.D.	13/16"
SOCKET I.D.	21/32
SHANK LENGTH	7/8"

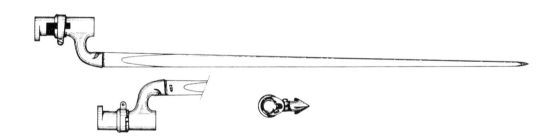

③ ENGLISH P. 1895 MARTINI ENFIELD

KIESLING VOL IV #942
LATHAM PG. 62-63

DIMENSIONS	
BLADE LENGTH	22"
BLADE WIDTH	13/16"
SOCKET LENGTH	3"
SOCKET O.D.	27/32"
SOCKET I.D.	21/32"
SHANK LENGTH	7/8"

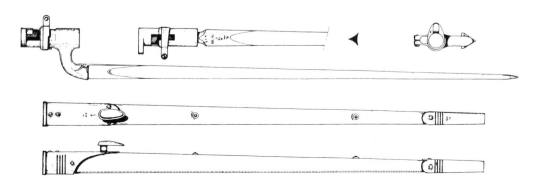

No. 1. **VOLUNTEER PATTERN CIRCA 1795.** THIS IS AN UNUSUAL BAYONET AND IS ONE OF THE VOLUNTEER VARIATIONS. THESE PIECES WERE PRIVATELY PURCHASED EITHER BY THE MEMBERS OR THE OFFICERS OF THE VOLUNTEER REGIMENTS AND ARE TYPICALLY MORE ORNATE THAN REGULAR ARMY PATTERNS. THIS PARTICULAR PIECE HAS A STIRRUP GRIP GUARD AND A VERY UNUSUAL SOCKET ATTACHMENT. I CONSIDER THIS A RARE PIECE. (THESE FIT A SPECIALLY PRODUCED BAKER RIFLE.)

No. 2. **PATTERN 1801 - BAKER RIFLE SECOND PATTERN.** THIS BAYONET IS BRASS HILTED AND DESIGNED TO MOUNT ON THE SIDE OF THE BAKER RIFLE. THERE ARE TWO VARIATIONS OF THIS BAYONET DIFFERING ONLY IN THE SHAPE OF THE GUARD. THE PIECE ILLUSTRATED IS THE SECOND PATTERN. THE FIRST PATTERN WAS PRODUCED FOR ONLY ONE YEAR AND HAS A SQUARE-TYPE KNUCKLE GUARD. REPRODUCTIONS OF THESE BAYONETS HAVE BEEN RECENTLY MADE.

No. 3. **PATTERN 1825 - BAKER RIFLE.** THIS BAYONET IS A MODIFIED VERSION OF THE PATTERN 1801 AND HAS HAD THE HILT TURNED DOWN OR LIGHTENED AND THE ORNAMENTAL EXTENSION REMOVED. THE BLADE APPEARS ORIGINAL.

① *VOLUNTEER C. 1795*

STEPHENS PG. 24

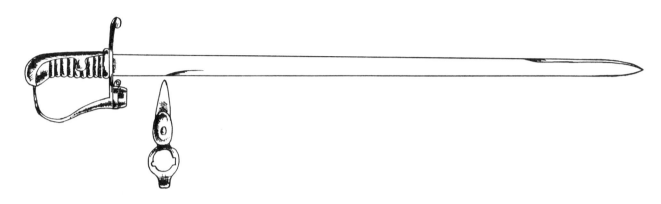

② *ENGLISH P. 1801*
BAKER RIFLE

KIESLING VOL II #440

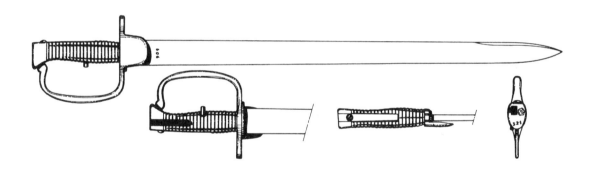

③ *ENGLISH P. 1825*
BAKER RIFLE

WALTER & HUGHES #180

No. 1.   **PATTERN 1837 - BRUNSWICK.**   THIS IS ANOTHER BRASS-HANDLED BAYONET, ONCE AGAIN DESIGNED TO BE MOUNTED ON THE SIDE OF THE RIFLE. THESE BAYONETS ALSO WERE USED EXTENSIVELY DURING THE U.S. CIVIL WAR.

No. 2.   **PATTERN 1848 - BRUNSWICK.**   THIS BAYONET IS IDENTICAL TO NO. 1; HOWEVER, THE ATTACHMENT MECHANISM WAS IMPROVED IN 1847 AND SITS FLUSH WITH THE HANDLE AND ON THE OTHER SIDE.

No. 3.   **VIVIAN CONSTABULARY CARBINE.**   THIS IS AN INTERESTING BAYONET WITH A LOCKING ARRANGEMENT VERY SIMILAR TO THE EARLY BRUNSWICK. WHEN PURCHASED, I FELT IT WAS A BAYONET DESIGNED FOR SOME TYPE OF CARBINE BUT LATER FOUND IT IS NEWLY MANUFACTURED IN INDIA AND HAS BEEN ARTIFICIALLY AGED.

No. 4.   **PATTERN 1855 - LANCASTER.**   THIS IS A BEAUTIFULLY PROPORTIONED BAYONET WITH A PIPE BACK BLADE AND A BRASS POMMEL AND CROSSGUARD. THESE PIECES WERE ALSO MANUFACTURED WITH STEEL POMMELS AND CROSSGUARDS FOR VARIOUS VOLUNTEER UNITS. (IT HAS A 24" BLADE.)

① *ENGLISH P. 1837*
BRUNSWICK

KIESLING VOL. II #434

② *ENGLISH P. 1848*
BRUNSWICK

LATHAM PG. 52

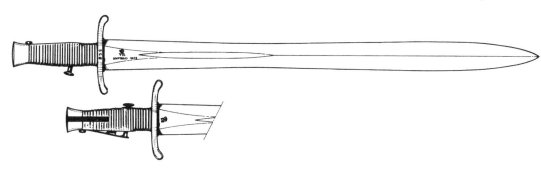

③ *VIVIAN CARBINE*

④ *ENGLISH P. 1855*
LANCASTER

KIESLING VOL. II #489

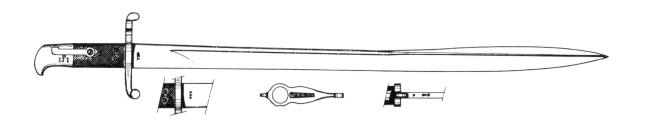

49

No. 1.   **PATTERN 1856 – ENFIELD.**   THIS BAYONET WAS MANUFACTURED IN VAST QUANTITIES AND USED EXTENSIVELY BY BRITISH COLONIAL TROOPS, BY BOTH SIDES IN THE U.S. CIVIL WAR AND BY JAPAN.   I POSSESS TWO PIECES – ONE A SERVICE MODEL BAYONET AND THE OTHER A PLATED BAYONET WITH CADET MARK-INGS, APPARENTLY USED BY AN OFFICERS' TRAINING SCHOOL IN ENGLAND.   THIS PARTICULAR PIECE IS DESIGNED FOR THE BAR-ON-THE-BARREL RIFLE AND HAS THE MUZZLE RING ALMOST FLUSH WITH THE HANDLE.

No. 2.   **PATTERN 1856/60 – ENFIELD.**   THIS BAYONET IS IDENTICAL TO No. 1, HOWEVER, IS DESIGNED FOR THE RIFLE WITH THE LUG AND SHORT BAR ATTACHMENT.

No. 3.   **PATTERN 1858 – SHORT RIFLE.**   THIS IS ANOTHER VARIATION OF THE 1856 PATTERN AND IS DESIGNED FOR THE SHORT RIFLE WHICH HAS THE BAR ON THE BAND.   AS YOU CAN SEE FROM THE ILLUSTRATION, THE MUZZLE RING IS SOME DISTANCE FROM THE HANDLE.

NOTE: THERE ARE TWO SCABBARD TYPES FOR THIS SERIES OF BAYO-NETS; THE MOST COMMON IS STEEL-MOUNTED LEATHER.   THE SECOND TYPE IS ALL STEEL (ARTILLERY ISSUE?).

① ENGLISH P. 1856

KIESLING VOL II #479
LATHAM PG. 14-15

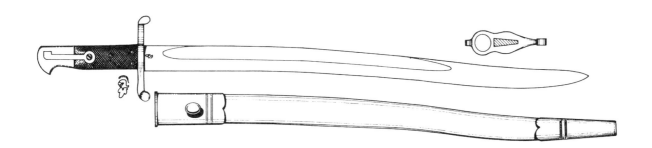

② ENGLISH P. 1856/60

WATTS & WHITE #753

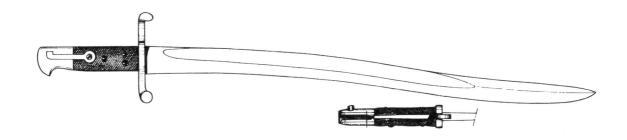

③ ENGLISH P. 1858
SHORT RIFLE

KIESLING VOL II # 478
LATHAM PG. 23

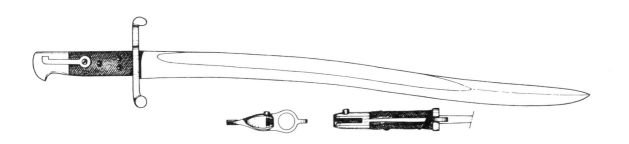

No. 1. **PATTERN 1863 - WHITWORTH.** THIS BAYONET HAS THE GENERAL CONFIGURATION OF THE PREVIOUS ENFIELD SABRE BAYONET TYPES, HOWEVER, HAS A VERY INTERESTING CIRCULAR MORTISE LOCK. THESE PIECES ARE SCARCE.

No. 2. **PATTERN 1873 - MARTINI HENRY.** THIS IS A MODIFICATION TO THE PATTERN 1856 AND HAS MODIFICATIONS BOTH TO THE SLOT AND THE MUZZLE RING.

No. 3. **PATTERN 1860 - JACOBS.** THIS BAYONET IS A VERY INTERESTING AND BEAUTIFUL WEAPON. IT WAS DESIGNED TO BE USED WITH A DOUBLE-BARREL RIFLE AND WAS PRODUCED IN TWO VARIATIONS - ONE WITH A FULL BASKET AND ONE WITH A HALF BASKET. THE ARM WAS USED BY VOLUNTEER COMPANIES AND IS MUCH MORE FUNCTIONAL AS A SWORD THAN AS A BAYONET.

① ENGLISH P. 1863 WHITWORTH

WATTS & WHITE #767

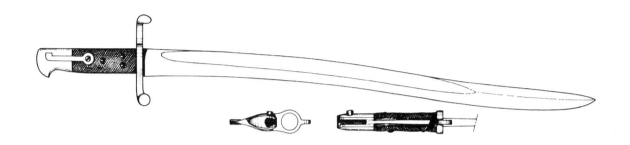

② ENGLISH P. 1873 MARTINI HENRY

KIESLING VOL II #480
WATTS & WHITE #753

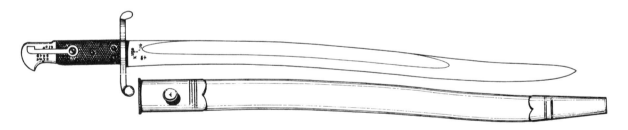

③ ENGLISH P. 1860 JACOBS

KIESLING VOL. IV #1014
WATTS & WHITE #763

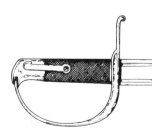

No. 1. **PATTERN 1858 - NAVAL CUTLASS.** THIS BAYONET IS THE FIRST PATTERN OF THE NAVY CUTLASS BAYONET. IT HAS RIBBED WOOD GRIPS WHICH WERE ORIGINALLY COVERED WITH LEATHER (THE LEATHER IS GONE ON THE EXAMPLE IN MY COLLECTION). THE HEAVY CURVED BLADE IS 26-3/4" LONG. THIS IS A RARE BAYONET.

No. 2. **PATTERN 1859 - NAVAL CUTLASS.** THIS IS THE LEATHER-GRIPPED VERSION OF THE CUTLASS BAYONET AND WAS APPARENTLY TOO HEAVY AND UNWIELDY AS A BAYONET, RESULTING IN MODIFICATION TO THE 1871 VERSION. THESE PIECES HAVE, ONCE AGAIN, BEEN REPRODUCED IN QUANTITY AND MANY OF THE "BOGUS" VERSIONS ARE VERY WELL MADE AND HARD TO DETECT.

No. 3. **PATTERN 1871 - NAVAL CUTLASS.** THIS BAYONET IS A MODIFIED VERSION OF THE CUTLASS PATTERN 1859 AND HAS HAD THE BLADE STRAIGHTENED AND LIGHTENED. THIS PARTICULAR MODIFICATION APPEARS SOMEWHAT SCARCE.

① ENGLISH P. 1858 NAVAL CUTLASS

KIESLING VOL. IV #1013

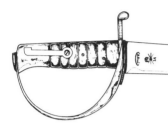

② ENGLISH P. 1859 NAVAL CUTLASS

KIESLING VOL. III #706

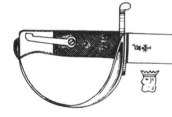

③ ENGLISH P. 1871 NAVAL CUTLASS

KIESLING VOL IV #1010

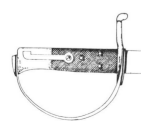

No. 1. **PATTERN 1871 - ELCHO.** ORIGINAL EXAMPLES OF THIS BAYONET ARE VERY EXPENSIVE AND THE SPECIMEN IN MY COLLECTION IS A REPRODUCTION. THE ORIGINAL WAS PRODUCED IN TWO DISTINCT PATTERNS AND WAS USED PRIMARILY BY COLONIAL TROOPS FIGHTING IN TROPICAL AREAS. THESE PIECES ARE QUITE SCARCE, ALTHOUGH REPRODUCTIONS ARE AVAILABLE IN QUANTITY. THE ELCHO BAYONET WAS, IN MY OPINION, NEVER OFFICIALLY ISSUED (EXCEPT FOR TRIALS), HOWEVER, WAS PRIVATELY PURCHASED BY OFFICERS TO REPLACE THEIR SWORDS IN TROPICAL CAMPAIGNS.

No. 2. **PATTERN 1875 - MARTINI HENRY.** THIS PIECE IS A SAWBACK VERSION CLOSELY RESEMBLING THE SABRE MODEL VARIATIONS. THIS BAYONET APPEARS TO BE QUITE SCARCE. NOTE THE GERMAN MAKERS' MARK OF KIRSCHBAUM.

No. 3. **PATTERN 1879 MARK I - MARTINI HENRY.** THIS IS A SAWBACK VERSION WITH A STIRRUP GUARD UTILIZED BY ARTILLERY UNITS. THIS PIECE APPEARS TO BE MUCH MORE COMMON THAN THE PATTERN 1875.

① ENGLISH P. 1871
ELCHO

KIESLING VOL III # 683

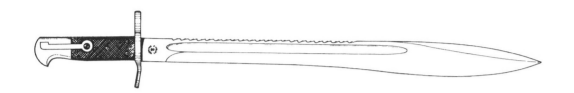

② ENGLISH P. 1875

KIESLING VOL. II # 363

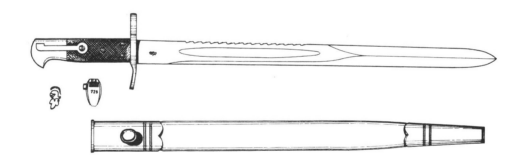

③ ENGLISH P. 1879
MARK I

KIESLING VOL. III # 705

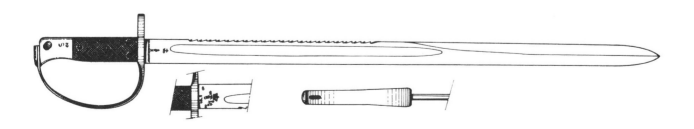

No. 1. **PATTERN 1887 MARK II – MARTINI HENRY.** THIS IS THE SECOND BAYONET OF THIS SERIES AND HAS A FULLERED BLADE AND A BRASS-MOUNTED SCABBARD. (THE FIRST VERSION HAD AN EXTERNAL SPRING.)

No. 2. **PATTERN 1887 MARK III – MARTINI HENRY.** THIS IS THE THIRD VARIATION OF THIS MARTINI HENRY SERIES AND HAS AN UNFULLERED BLADE. THE GRIPS ARE HELD BY TWO LARGE RIVETS, AS IN THE MARK II. THIS BAYONET WAS APPROVED JUNE 22, 1888.

No. 3. **PATTERN 1887 MARK IV – MARTINI HENRY.** THIS ARM IS IDENTICAL TO NO. 1 WITH THE EXCEPTION OF THE GRIP FASTENING METHOD (RIVETS) AND WAS THE LAST BAYONET OF THE SERIES. IT HAS A STEEL-MOUNTED LEATHER SCABBARD AND WAS APPROVED JUNE 1, 1891.

NOTE: THERE IS DISAGREEMENT AMONG THE VARIOUS AUTHORS ON THE DESIGNATION OF M-1887 BAYONETS. MY CONTENTION IS VERY SIMILAR TO THAT EXPRESSED BY WATTS & WHITE.

① ENGLISH P. 1887
MARK II

WATTS & WHITE #793
KIESLING VOL IV #921

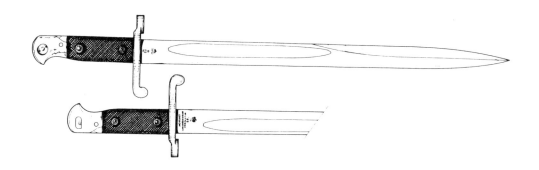

② ENGLISH P.1887
MARK III

KIESLING VOL II #375

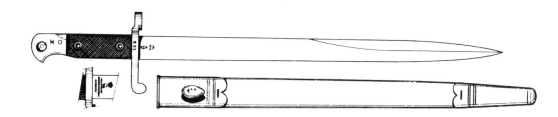

③ ENGLISH P.1887
MARK IV

KIESLING VOL. II #374

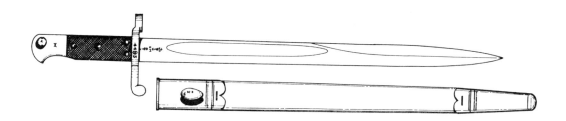

No. 1. **PATTERN 1888 MARK I - LEE METFORD.** THIS BAYONET IS THE FIRST OF THE LEE METFORD PATTERNS AND HAS THE GRIP ATTACHED BY THREE BRASS RIVETS. IT IS A RELATIVELY SCARCE PIECE.

No. 2. **PATTERN 1888 MARK I - LEE METFORD SECOND TYPE.** THIS BAYONET WAS PRODUCED IN LARGE QUANTITIES AND HAS THE GRIPS FASTENED BY TWO BRASS RIVETS WITH AN OIL HOLE ABOVE THE TOP RIVET. INTERESTINGLY ENOUGH, THIS BAYONET WAS SOLD WITH THE MARLIN MODEL 1893 MILITARY MUSKET IN THE UNITED STATES. IN THE 1915 CATALOG, THE MUSKET COMPLETE WITH BAYONET LISTED FOR $23.00.

No. 3. **PATTERN 1888 MARK II - LEE ENFIELD.** THIS BAYONET APPEARS VERY SIMILAR TO THE LEE METFORD TYPES, HOWEVER, HAS THE OIL HOLE IN THE POMMEL AND NO PROVISION FOR A CLEANING ROD.

No. 4. **TRENCH KNIFE BAYONET.** THIS PIECE APPARENTLY RESULTED FROM A MODIFICATION OF THE 1888 BAYONETS DURING THE FIRST OR SECOND WORLD WAR WHICH, IN MY OPINION, WAS DONE IN QUANTITY, AS I HAVE SEEN A NUMBER OF PIECES IDENTICALLY MODIFIED. THERE IS NO INDICATION THIS WAS AN OFFICIAL MODIFICATION.

NOTE: THE REIGN MARK STAMPED ON THE P-1888 SERIES OF BAYONETS IS "VR" FOR VICTORIA REGINA (SEE ILLUSTRATION).

① ENGLISH P. 1888
MARK I

KIESLING VOL. I #174

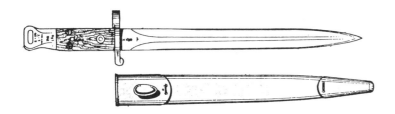

② ENGLISH P. 1888
MARK I, TYPE 2

KIESLING VOL. I #175

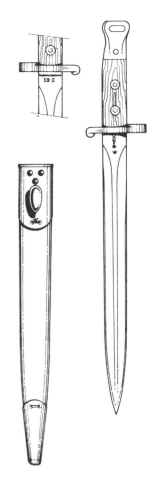

③ ENGLISH P. 1888
MARK II

KIESLING VOL. I #176

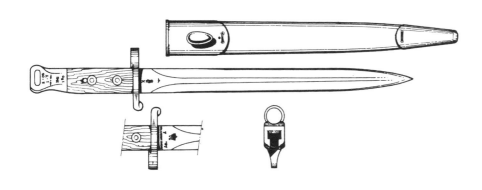

④ TRENCH KNIFE

ERNST VOL. I #18

VR

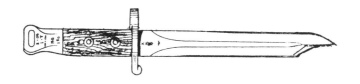

No. 1. **PATTERN 1888 MARK III - LEE ENFIELD.** THIS BAYONET IS OF THE STANDARD 1888 PATTERN, HOWEVER, HAS THE HANDLE FASTENED BY TWO SCREW BOLTS. THE PIECE IS COMPLETELY BLUED, AS ARE THE SCABBARD FITTINGS.

No. 2. **PATTERN 1895 CADET - MARTINI HENRY.** THIS BAYONET HAS BEEN SHORTENED TO 465MM FOR CADET USE. IT WAS USED ON A MODIFIED MARTINI ARTILERY CARBINE AND IS THE FINAL MODIFICATION OF WHAT WAS ONCE A P-1856.

No. 3. **PATTERN 1907 - SMLE.** THIS IS A MODIFICATION OF THE WIDELY UTILIZED PATTERN 1907 BAYONET WHICH HAS BEEN CUT DOWN AND MARKED FOR DRILL PURPOSES. I HAVE TWO SPECIMENS - ONE REMINGTON-MARKED AND ONE SANDERSON-MARKED.

NOTE: MANY OF THE PATTERN 1888 BAYONETS WHICH ARE UNMARKED WERE UTILIZED BY THE VOLUNTEER TRAINING CORPS.

① ENGLISH P. 1888
MARK III, TYPE 2

KIESLING VOL. I #178

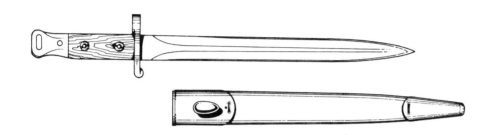

② ENGLISH P. 1895
CADET

KIESLING VOL III #617

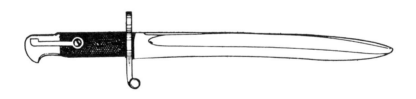

③ ENGLISH P. 1907
MODIFICATION

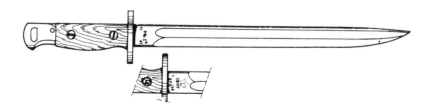

D↑P

56

No. 1.   **PATTERN 1903 - SMLE.**   THIS BAYONET WAS PRODUCED FOR THE .303 SMLE RIFLE IN TWO VARIATIONS - ONE A REHILTED ORIGINAL 1888 BLADE AND THE SECOND WITH A NEWLY MANUFACTURED BLADE WITH A DIFFERENT GRINDING CONFIGURATION (NOTE THE REIGN MARK OF EDWARD VII WHO ONLY REIGNED IN THE PERIOD 1901-1910).

No. 2.   **PATTERN 1907 MARK I LAND - SMLE.**   THIS BAYONET WAS PRODUCED FOR THE ENFIELD RIFLE IN VERY LARGE QUANTITIES AND THE INITIAL MODELS WERE EQUIPPED WITH A HOOKED QUILLON COPIED FROM THE JAPANESE TYPE 30 ARISAKA BAYONETS.   MANY HAD THE QUILLONS SUBSEQUENTLY REMOVED SO THAT THE QUILLON TYPES ARE RELATIVELY SCARCE.

No. 3.   **PATTERN 1907 MARK I - SMLE.**   THIS BAYONET IS THE NON-QUILLON VERSION OF THE MARK I AND WAS PRODUCED BY THE MILLIONS.   I POSSESS PIECES MANUFACTURED BY SANDERSON, REMINGTON AND WILKINSON.   THIS IS THE FIRST PATTERN.

No. 4.   **PATTERN 1907 - SMLE PARADE BAYONET.**   THIS PIECE IS A PARADE OR TRAINING VERSION OF THE STANDARD P-1907 BAYONET AND I POSSESS TWO VERSIONS - ONE WHICH IS PLATED AND A SECOND ONE WITH A ROUNDED TIP MARKED "DP" FOR DRILL PURPOSE.   THE SECOND PATTERN WITH THE OIL CLEANING HOLE IS ILLUSTRATED.

NOTE: THE REIGN MARK STAMPED ON MOST OF THE PATTERN 1907 BAYONETS IS "GR" FOR GEORGIUS REX, AS ILLUSTRATED.

① ENGLISH P. 1903
KIESLING VOL. I #181

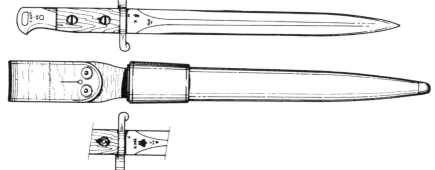

② ENGLISH P. 1907
W/ QUILLON
KIESLING VOL II #316

③ ENGLISH P. 1907
W.O. / QUILLON
KIESLING VOL. II #317

④ ENGLISH P. 1907
PARADE
LATHAM PG. 14

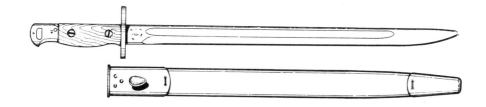

No. 1. **PATTERN 1913 – FOR THE P-14 RIFLE.** THE P-14 RIFLE WAS MADE FOR ENGLAND BY THE U.S. FOR AN EXPERIMENTAL .276 CAL. CARTRIDGE. THE CONTRACT WAS NOT COMPLETE AT THE TIME WORLD WAR I STARTED; HENCE, THE BRITISH REQUESTED THAT THE RIFLES BE RECHAMBERED FOR THE .303 CALIBER CARTRIDGE. THE P-14 RIFLE UTILIZED A BAYONET SIMILAR TO THE PATTERN 1907, THOUGH NOT INTERCHANGE-ABLE. THE PRIMARY DIFFERENCE IS THE MUZZLE RING WHICH SETS MUCH HIGHER, DUE TO THE STUD PLACEMENT ON THE RIFLE. THE BAYONETS WERE MADE BY BOTH REMINGTON AND WINCHESTER AND MANY CONTAIN BOTH BRITISH AND U.S. MARK-INGS, AS THEY WERE USED BY BOTH COUNTRIES DURING BOTH THE FIRST AND SECOND WORLD WARS. THE P-1913 BAYONET IS INTERCHANGEABLE WITH THE U.S. MODEL 1917 (SEE PAGE 223).

* ANOTHER VERSION OF THE P-1913 IS ILLUSTRATED. IT HAS A FALSE EDGE AND IS APPARENTLY AN INDIA PATTERN. IT IS STAMPED MK. I/1.

No. 2. **INDIA PATTERN NO. 1 MARK I*.** THIS BAYONET WAS ACTUALLY THE SECOND OF THE SO-CALLED INDIA PATTERN SERIES AND WAS A SHORTENED 1907 (THE FIRST BEING THE P-1907 BAYONET WITH THE FULL-LENGTH BLADE). IT IS STAMPED NO. 1 MARK I* AND WAS APPARENTLY CARRIED IN A FULL-LENGTH 1907 SCABBARD.

① ENGLISH P. 1913

KIESLING VOL. II # 321

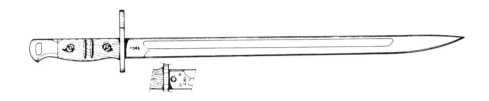

✱ INDIA PATTERN 1913
MK. 1/1

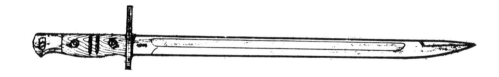

② INDIA PATTERN
NO. 1 MK I *

KIESLING VOL. I #182

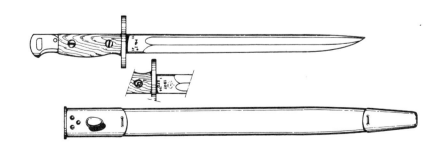

No. 1. INDIA PATTERN No. 1. MARK II. THIS IS THE SECOND OF THE SHORT INDIA PATTERN SERIES AND HAS AN UNFULLERED BLADE WITH A FALSE EDGE.

No. 2. INDIA PATTERN No. 1 MARK II*. THIS IS IDENTICAL TO No. 1 EXCEPT THAT THE BLADE HAS NO FALSE EDGE.

No. 3. INDIA PATTERN No. 1 MARK III. THIS IS THE THIRD MAJOR CHANGE IN THE SHORT INDIA PATTERN SERIES AND HAS A SQUARED POMMEL WHICH, APPARENTLY, WAS THE RESULT OF MANUFACTURING SIMPLIFICATION. THIS PATTERN HAS AN UNFULLERED BLADE WITH A FALSE EDGE. THIS PATTERN WAS ISSUED TO THE DELHI ARMED POLICE AS LATE AS 1985.

No. 4. INDIA PATTERN No. 1 MARK III*. THIS IS IDENTICAL TO No. 3 EXCEPT THAT THE BLADE HAS NO FALSE EDGE. FOR SOME REASON, THIS VARIATION IS RELATIVELY SCARCE.

NOTE: THIS ENTIRE SERIES WAS MANUFACTURED IN INDIA AND CONTAINS MANUFACTURING DESIGNATIONS, SUCH AS: RFI - RIFLE FACTORY ISHAPORE; MIL - METAL INDUSTRIES LAHORE; NWR - NORTH WESTERN RAILWAY. THE SCABBARDS ACTUALLY PRODUCED IN INDIA ARE SIMILAR TO THOSE PRODUCED IN ENGLAND, HOWEVER, HAVE A ROUND FROG STUD. THEY COME IN BOTH SHORT AND LONG VERSIONS. (AN INTERESTING ASPECT OF THE REIGN MARK ON INDIAN PATTERN BAYONETS IS THE ADDITION OF THE LETTER "I", GIVING THE MARK "GRI", GEORGIUS REX IMPERATOR. THIS IS ILLUSTRATED ON THE FAR RIGHT.) SEE PAGE 114 FOR OTHER INDIAN BAYONETS.

① INDIA PATTERN
NO. 1 MK II

KIESLING VOL. I #183

② INDIA PATTERN
NO. 1 MK II *

KIESLING VOL. I #184

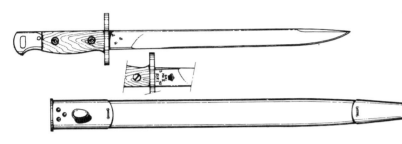

③ INDIA PATTERN
NO. 1 MK III

KIESLING VOL. I #185

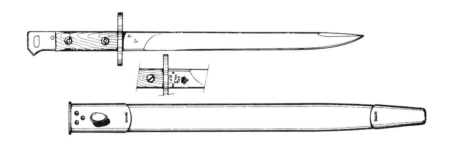

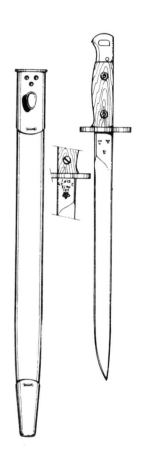

G R I

④ INDIA PATTERN
NO. 1 MK III *

KIESLING VOL. I #186

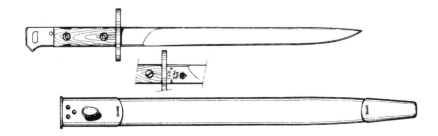

No. 1. **No. 4 Mark I.** This is the first of the "spike" bayonet series and is a very well made piece with a cruciform blade. This particular blade type is relatively scarce.

No. 2. **No. 4 Mark II*.** This variation of the No. 4 "spike" series is cast in one piece with the blade having the cruciform machining eliminated. It is, however, machined to tolerance where the blade enters the socket. The scabbard illustrated was produced in the United States by Beckwith Manufacturing whose trade name was "Victory Plastics" (VP).

No. 3. **No. 4 Mark II.** This variation reflects further manufacturing simplification and is cast in one piece with the majority of machining done on the socket and at the blade tip. I also have the U.S. manufactured version of this bayonet. It can be recognized by an "S" in a square which denotes Savage Arms Corp. A relatively uncommon scabbard variation is illustrated.

No. 4. **Sten Mk. II.** This bayonet is designed for the Sten Mk. II submachine gun. It is very rare and the example in my collection is a replica. It is my understanding that the majority of Sten bayonets were destroyed in Post World War II years.

① ENGLISH NO. 4
MK I

KIESLING VOL. I #2
LATHAM PG 7

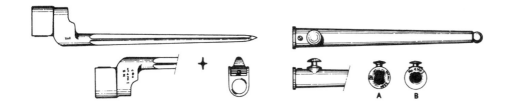

② ENGLISH NO. 4
MK II*

LATHAM PG. 7

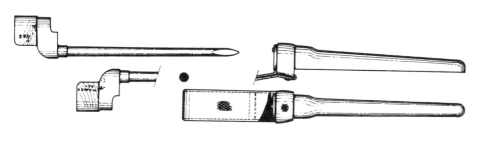

④ ENGLISH STEN
MK II

KIESLING VOL III #512

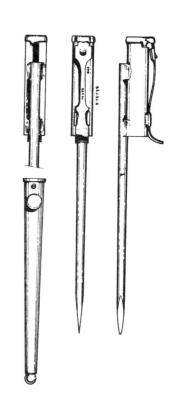

③ ENGLISH NO. 4
MK II

KIESLING VOL. I #3

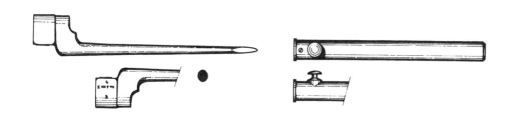

No. 1. **No. 4 Mark II*.** This variation has the blade brazed to the socket with final machining done where the blade connects to the socket. Illustrated is a quite rare scabbard with an integral frog. This scabbard is the MK I (see 60-1).

No. 2. **No. 4 Mark III.** This particular piece is very crudely made with virtually no machine work and reflects the final manufacturing simplification. Illustrated with this particular bayonet is the all plastic scabbard produced in the United States.

No. 3. **Entrenching Tool with Spade and No. 4 Bayonet.** Although not a bayonet, this is a very interesting combination tool produced by the British Army which allowed the bayonet to be used as a digging tool in combination with a spade and ax attachment or, with bayonet attached, it could be used for mine probing.

No. 4. **No. 9 Mark I.** This bayonet, designed for the No. 4 rifle and Sten MK5 SMG, utilized the socket configuration of the spike series, however, is fitted with a blade similar to the jungle carbine. These bayonets were made in great quantity and exist in several variations. The latest date I have noted was 1950.

① ENGLISH NO. 4 MK II *

KIESLING VOL. I #4

② ENGLISH NO. 4 MK III

KIESLING VOL. I #5

③ ENTRENCHING TOOL W/ SPADE

STEPHENS #232

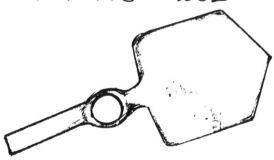

④ ENGLISH NO. 9 MK I

KIESLING VOL. I #8

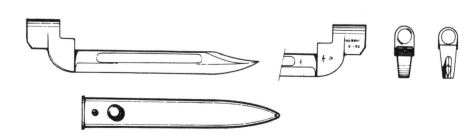

No. 1. **No. 5 Mark I.** The jungle carbine series, of which this is the first, introduces a totally different weapon than previous British designs and actually set the pattern for the bayonet type and style used at the present time. The Mark I is a relatively rare bayonet and has wooden grips fastened by <u>ONE</u> screw bolt in the center of the handle.

No. 2. **No. 5 Mark II.** This bayonet is the most common of the jungle carbine series and is identical to the Mark I, however, the grips are fastened by <u>TWO</u> screw bolts.

No. 3. **No. 7 Mark I - Land.** This is an interesting application of the jungle carbine-type of bayonet to the No. 4 rifle and incorporates a swivel pommel which allows the bayonet to be utilized on the No. 4 rifle. This particular piece has a red handle.

No. 4. **No. 7 Mark I - Land.** This bayonet is identical to No. 3, however, has a black plastic handle.

① ENGLISH NO. 5 MK I

KIESLING VOL. I #33

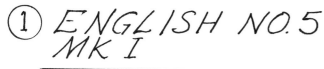

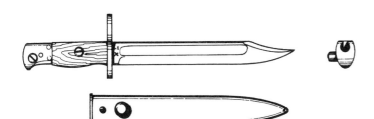

② ENGLISH NO. 5 MK II

KIESLING VOL I #34

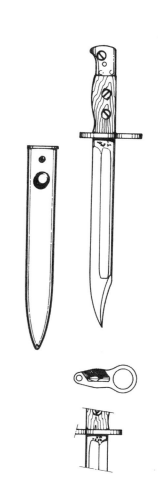

③ ENGLISH NO. 7 MK I

KIESLING VOL. I #44

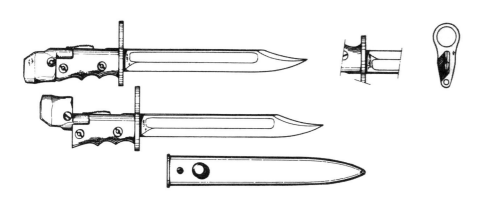

④ ENGLISH NO. 7 MK I

KIESLING VOL I #44

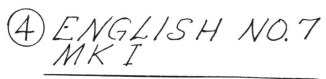

No. 1. **MODEL L1A1.** THIS IS A TRANSITIONAL BAYONET WHICH RETAINS THE WOODEN GRIPS OF THE JUNGLE CARBINE, HOWEVER, HAS A LOCKING ATTACHMENT FOR THE BRITISH FAL RIFLE. I DO NOT POSSESS THE ACTUAL BRITISH STEEL HANDLE ISSUE OF THE L1A1. THESE ARE QUITE RARE BECAUSE MOST WERE CONVERTED TO THE L1A3.

No. 2. **MODEL L1A3.** THIS IS THE CURRENT ISSUE BRITISH BAYONET AND HAS AN ALL METAL HANDLE. IT UTILIZES THE SAME ALL STEEL SCABBARDS INTRODUCED WITH THE JUNGLE CARBINE. THE BAYONETS MODIFIED FROM L1A1s HAVE A SERIAL NUMBER ON THE HANDLE (9600011) WHILE POST-MODIFICATION BAYONETS ARE MARKED L1A396000257.

No. 3. **MODEL L1A3 – SECOND PATTERN.** THIS BAYONET IS IDENTICAL TO No. 2, HOWEVER, HAS THE LATER TYPE SHORT FULLERS (THE FULLER STOPS APPROXIMATELY 1.4" FROM THE CROSSGUARD) AND AN ALL BLACK FINISH.

No. 4. **BAYONET L2 – STERLING S.M.G.** THIS BAYONET IS AN ALL METAL VERSION OF THE No. 5 BAYONET WHICH IS NEWLY MANUFACTURED (BY ENFIELD) FOR THE STERLING. THE WORD "STERLING" WAS ETCHED ON THE BLADE TO PREVENT CONFUSION WITH THE L1 SERIES OF BAYO- NETS. KIESLING ILLUSTRATES A PLASTIC GRIPPED VERSION IN VOL. IV, #751.

NOTE: ON OCTOBER 2, 1985, THE BRITISH ADOPTED A NEW BAYONET: THE L85A1, WHICH IS A SOCKET-TYPE SIMILAR TO 76-2.

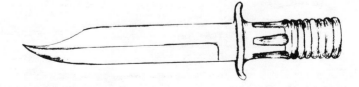

63 - ENGLAND

① ENGLISH L1A1

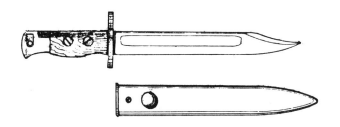

② ENGLISH L1A3
KIESLING VOL I # 38

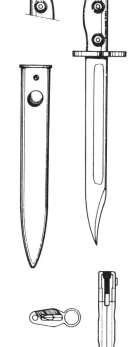

③ ENGLISH L1A3
KIESLING VOL III # 511

④ ENGLISH L2
STERLING S.M.G.

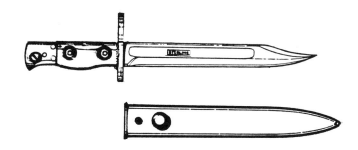

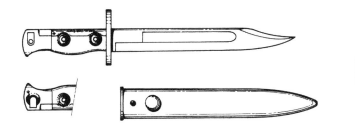

No. 1. **MOSIN NAGANT MODEL 1891/30.** THIS IS THE STANDARD RUSSIAN BAYONET WHICH IS PROBABLY PART OF 300,000 RUSSIAN RIFLES AND BAYONETS PURCHASED BY THE FINNS FROM THE ITALIANS AND EXTENSIVELY MODIFIED. THE BAYONET HAS BEEN REGROUND TO ELIMINATE THE SCREWDRIVER TIP. THE GRINDING RUNS ALL THE WAY TO THE COLLAR. THE FINNS USED THESE RIFLES AND BAYONETS EXTENSIVELY AND PERFORMED NUMEROUS MODIFICATIONS, OF WHICH THIS IS ONLY ONE. THEY ALSO USED QUANTITIES OF THE AUSTRIAN MANUFACTURED M-1891 (STRAIGHT SLOT) BAYONETS, ACCORDING TO R. D. C. EVANS. THE FINNS ISSUED A LEATHER SCABBARD WITH THE M-1891 BAYONETS.

No. 2. **FINNISH MODEL 1927.** THIS BAYONET WAS DESIGNED FOR THE FINNISH NAGANT AND IS HEAVILY BLUED WITH WALNUT GRIPS FASTENED BY TWO RIVETS. IT IS MARKED "SA" DENOTING ARMY USE. THE 1927 DIFFERS FROM THE LATTER BAYONETS IN HAVING A BLADE WITH A CONVEX CUTTING EDGE.

No. 3. **FINNISH MODEL 1928.** THIS IS ANOTHER ARMY VARIATION AND THE GRIPS ARE HELD BY TWO HOLLOW RIVETS.

No. 4. **FINNISH MODEL 1935.** THIS BAYONET IS A MODIFICATION OF THE 1927 AND HAS AN OIL HOLE IN THE POMMEL AND BURLED GRIPS WITH TWO POLISHED RIVETS. THIS PIECE IS COMPLETELY FINISHED BRIGHT. THE "SK" DENOTES "WHITE GUARD", A GROUP DEDICATED TO AN INDEPENDENT FINLAND.

① FINNISH M. 1891/30 MOSIN NAGANT

④ FINNISH M. 1935
KIESLING VOL. I #165

② FINNISH M. 1927
KIESLING VOL. I #163

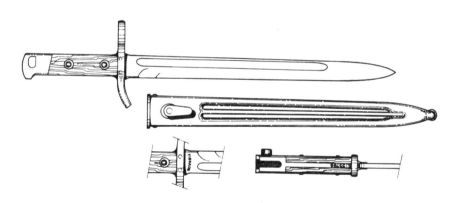

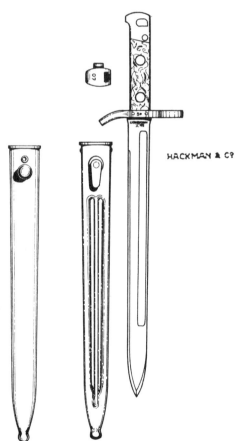

HACKMAN & C?

③ FINNISH M. 1928
KIESLING VOL. IV #829

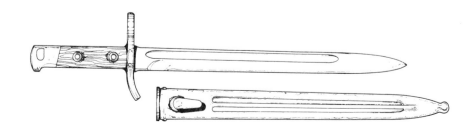

No. 1. **FINNISH MODEL 1928/30/39.** THIS BAYONET IS A HEAVILY MODIFIED MODEL 1927 AND IS APPARENTLY AN OFFICIAL MODIFICATION PERFORMED BY THE FINNS TO FILL SHORTAGES OF THE MODEL 1939. PRIMARY MODIFICATIONS TO THE PIECE ARE A REDUCTION IN CROSSGUARD LENGTH AND EXTENSIVE REWORKING OF THE BLADE SO THAT IT RESEMBLES THE BOWIE POINT OF THE MODEL 1939.

No. 2. **FINNISH MODEL 1939 - MOSIN NAGANT.** THIS IS A BEAUTIFULLY MADE PIECE CLOSELY RESEMBLING A HUNTING KNIFE. IT IS CARRIED IN A GREEN LEATHER SCABBARD AND IS A RELATIVELY SCARCE BAYONET, APPARENTLY BEING ISSUED IN LIMITED NUMBERS. IT WAS MANUFACTURED BY VELJEKSET KULMALA AND CAN BE FOUND WITH OR WITHOUT THE "SKY" MARKINGS.

NOTE: WATTS & WHITE INDICATE THAT THE FINNS ALSO UTILIZED JAPANESE ARISAKA RIFLES AND BAYONETS WHICH HAD BEEN CAPTURED DURING THE RUSSO-JAPANESE WAR.

① FINNISH M. 1928/30/39

BAYONETTEN DA TILL NU #239

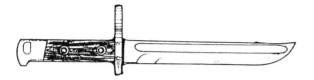

② FINNISH M. 1939

KIESLING VOL. I #19

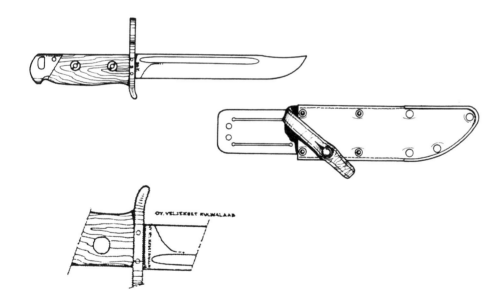

OY. VELJEKSET KULNALAAD

No. 1. **FINNISH CARCANO MODEL 1938.** THIS IS A STANDARD ITALIAN CARCANO FOLDING BAYONET, HOWEVER, THE BACK STRAP IS STAMPED WITH THE "SA" IN A SQUARE DENOTING FINNISH ARMY ISSUE. THE FINNS COPIED THIS PRINCIPLE ON THE FIRST M-1960 ASSAULT RIFLE BAYONET.

No. 2. **FINNISH FENCING MODEL 1960/62.** THIS BAYONET IS ALL RUBBER AND DESIGNED TO FIT ON OLD MOSIN NAGANT RIFLES FOR TRAINING PURPOSES. WATTS & WHITE IDENTIFY THIS AS TRAINING BAYONET C-1966.

No. 3. **FINNISH MODEL 1962.** THIS IS A SHORT KNIFE BAYONET WITH A HEAVILY DARKENED BLADE AND GREEN HANDLE. IT IS CARRIED IN A TRADITIONAL FINNISH HUNTING KNIFE-TYPE SHEATH WHICH IS FINISHED IN DARK GREEN. THE PIECE APPEARS VERY FUNCTIONAL AND ALSO IS AVAILABLE IN A "DRESS" OR PLATED VERSION WHICH IS NOT DESIGNED FOR ATTACHMENT TO A WEAPON.

NOTE: THE "SA" MARKINGS FOUND ON FINNISH RIFLES AND BAYONETS STAND FOR "SVOMEN ARMEIJA" OR "FINNISH ARMY".

① FINNISH M. 1938
CARCANO

KIESLING VOL. I #13

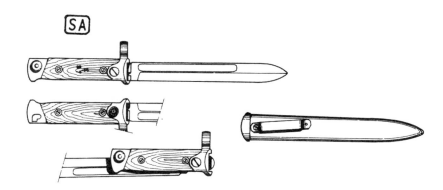

② FINNISH M. 1960/62
FENCING

KIESLING VOL. IV #745

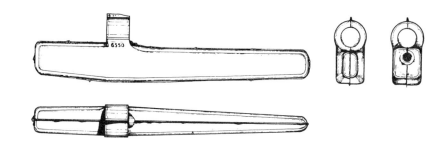

③ FINNISH M. 1962

KIESLING VOL. I #7

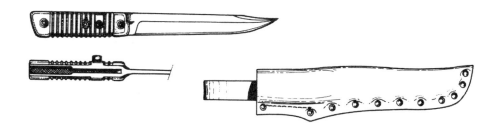

No. 1. **FRENCH MODEL 1771.** THIS SOCKET BAYONET WAS VERY ADVANCED FOR ITS TIME, SINCE IT INCLUDED A LOCKING RING ATTACHMENT. IT WAS UTILIZED EXTENSIVELY IN COLONIAL AMERICA AND IS KNOWN AS THE CHARLEVILLE MUSKET BAYONET. IT IS A RELATIVELY SCARCE PIECE.

No. 2. **FRENCH CIRCA 1790/95.** THIS PIECE IS HANDMADE AND WAS APPARENTLY MADE BY VILLAGE BLACKSMITHS DURING THE FRENCH REVOLUTION. IT IS MARKED "RF" FOR REPUBLIC FRANCE AND, AS ARE ALL BLACKSMITH-PRODUCED WEAPONS, PROBABLY ONE OF A KIND.

No. 3. **FRENCH MODEL 1847N.** THIS SOCKET BAYONET IS DESIGNATED 1847N TO DISTINGUISH IT FROM THE 1822 AND 1822T BAYONETS IN MUCH THE SAME WAY THAT THE BRITISH PUT THE GROOVES IN THE HANDLE OF THE P-1913 TO DISTINGUISH IT FROM THE P-1907.

No. 4. **FRENCH MODEL 1857.** THIS PIECE MAY BE MISIDENTIFIED; HOWEVER, BASED ON MEASUREMENTS AND MY MEAGER KNOWLEDGE OF FRENCH, I THINK IT IS THE M-1857.

NOTE: FRANCE WAS ONE OF THE FIRST COUNTRIES TO USE THE BAYONET AND PRODUCED DESIGNS WHICH WERE WIDELY COPIED.

① FRENCH M.1771

KIESLING VOL III #602

DIMENSIONS	
BLADE LENGTH	14"
BLADE WIDTH	1 1/8"
SOCKET LENGTH	2 3/4"
SOCKET O.D.	1"
SOCKET I.D.	7/8"
SHANK LENGTH	1 1/2"

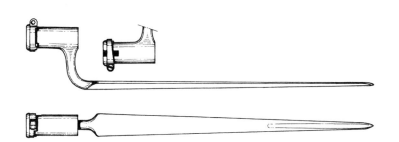

② FRENCH C.1790/95 "R F" MARKED

KIESLING VOL. IV #851

DIMENSIONS	
BLADE LENGTH	13 39/64"
BLADE WIDTH	1 13/64"
SOCKET LENGTH	3 41/64"
SOCKET O.D.	1"
SOCKET I.D.	27/32"

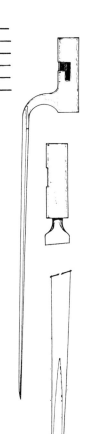

③ FRENCH M.1847 N

PITOUS PG. 58

DIMENSIONS	
BLADE LENGTH	18 1/2"
BLADE WIDTH	59/64"
SOCKET LENGTH	2 11/16"
SOCKET O.D.	15/64"
SOCKET I.D.	7/8
SHANK LENGTH	1 1/4"

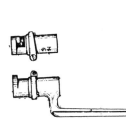

④ FRENCH M.1857

KIESLING VOL I #240

DIMENSIONS	
BLADE LENGTH	16"
BLADE WIDTH	29/32"
SOCKET LENGTH	2 39/64"
SOCKET O.D.	1"
SOCKET I.D.	13/16"
SHANK LENGTH	1 23/64"

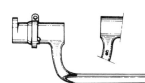

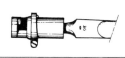

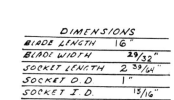

No. 1. **FRENCH MODEL 1840.** THE MODEL 1840 WAS THE FIRST SABER BAYONET USED BY FRANCE AND, IN MANY WAYS, IS THE GRANDFATHER OF AN ENTIRE SERIES OF SABER BAYONETS WHICH WERE COPIED BY EVERY MAJOR COUNTRY IN EUROPE AS WELL AS USED EXTENSIVELY IN THE U.S. CIVIL WAR. THE MODEL 1840 IS A VERY INTERESTING PIECE IN THAT IT HAS BOTH A BRASS HANDLE AND BRASS CROSSGUARD. IT WAS THE BRASS CROSSGUARD WHICH PROVED INADEQUATE IN SERVICE AND WAS SUBSEQUENTLY REPLACED WITH A STEEL CROSSGUARD. THIS PARTICULAR BAYONET WAS ISSUED ONLY TO NONCOMMISSIONED OFFICERS AND WAS CONSIDERED A BADGE OF STATUS (THE OVERALL LENGTH OF THIS BAYONET IS 24.75" AND THE BLADE LENGTH IS 20.25").

No. 2. **FRENCH MODEL AN IX.** THIS PARTICULAR BAYONET IS A SOCKET-TYPE WHICH WAS USED BY THE LINE INFANTRY AND WAS ALSO WIDELY COPIED, INCLUDING THE U.S., WHERE IT WAS DESIGNATED AS U.S. MODEL 1847.

No. 3. **FRENCH MODEL 1842.** THIS BAYONET IS A FURTHER EVOLUTION OF THE FRENCH SABER TYPES AND INCORPORATES A STEEL CROSSGUARD, A REDESIGNED BLADE OF GREATER LENGTH (2.5"), AND A REDESIGNED SPRING CATCH. THESE BAYONETS WERE WIDELY COPIED AND MANY CAN BE FOUND WHICH WERE MANUFACTURED BY GERMAN MAKERS.

No. 4. **FRENCH MODEL 1842/59.** THIS BAYONET IS IDENTICAL TO THE MODEL 1842, EXCEPT THAT THE SPRING CATCH HAS BEEN ELIMINATED AND A RUDIMENTARY PRESS STUD UTILIZED. TO MY KNOWLEDGE, THIS WAS ONE OF THE EARLY INNOVATIONS IN BAYONET DESIGN. FRENCH PRODUCED SABER BAYONETS ARE MARKED ON THE BACK OF THE BLADE, AS SHOWN IN THE ILLUSTRATION, WITH THE DATE AND ARSENAL OF MANUFACTURE (THE OVERALL LENGTH IS 27" AND THE BLADE LENGTH IS APPROXIMATELY 22.8").

① FRENCH M.1840
KIESLING VOL. II #399

② FRENCH M. ANIX
KIESLING VOL. II #345

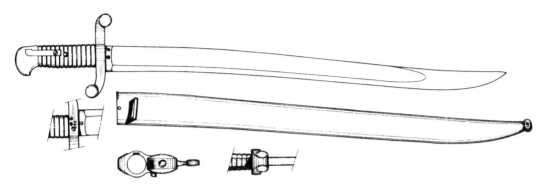

③ FRENCH M.1842
KIESLING VOL. II # 453

DIMENSIONS	
BLADE LENGTH	18"
BLADE WIDTH	59/64"
SOCKET LENGTH	2 43/64"
SOCKET O.D.	1"
SOCKET I.D.	56/64"
SHANK LENGTH	1 13/32"

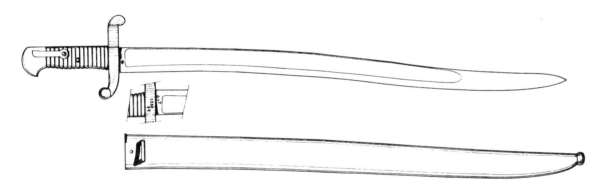

④ FRENCH M.1842/59
KIESLING VOL. II 454

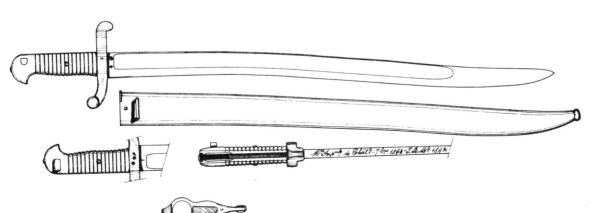

No. 1. FRENCH MODEL 1866-CHASSEPOT. THIS IS THE FINAL EVOLUTION OF THE FRENCH SABER BAYONET AND REFLECTS A CHANGE IN MILITARY THINKING, IN THAT THE CROSSGUARD HAS A HOOKED QUILLON AND THE FRENCH DISCARDED THE PRESS STUD AND RETURNED TO THE SPRING CATCH. THIS PARTICULAR BAYONET WAS MANUFACTURED IN VERY LARGE QUANTITIES BY A NUMBER OF COUNTRIES, AND I HAVE SEEN EXAMPLES WHICH WERE GERMAN MARKED AS WELL AS EXAMPLES WHICH WERE BRITISH (REEVES) MARKED. THE U.S. DESIGNED SEVERAL RIFLES UTILIZING THIS BAYONET INCLUDING THE JOSLYN AND A REMINGTON ROLLING BLOCK.

No. 2. FRENCH MODEL 1866 TRENCH KNIFE. THIS EXAMPLE IS A CONVERSION OF THE PREVIOUSLY DISCUSSED BAYONET WHICH HAS BEEN CONVERTED TO A TRENCH KNIFE, PROBABLY DURING WORLD WAR I.

No. 3. SCOLAIRE MODEL 1866 - CHILD'S BAYONET. THIS PIECE IS A VERY UNIQUE ARM IN THAT IT IS IDENTICAL TO THE FRENCH CHASSEPOT, EXCEPT THAT IT IS APPROXIMATELY TWO-THIRDS OF THE SIZE AND IS NOT EQUIPPED WITH THE SCREW-TIGHTENING DEVICE ON TOP OF THE MUZZLE RING.

① FRENCH M. 1866
KIESLING VOL. II # 460

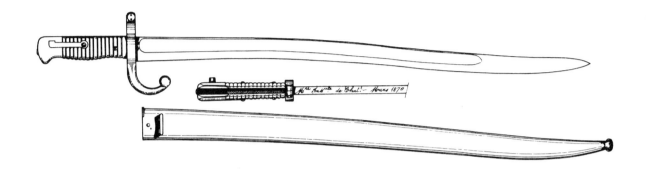

② FRENCH M. 1866
TRENCH KNIFE

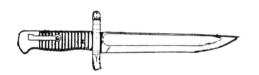

③ FRENCH M. 1866
CHILDS BAYONET
PITOUS PG 73

No. 1. **FRENCH MODEL 1874 - GRAS.** THIS BAYONET WAS PRODUCED FOR THE GRAS RIFLE IN VERY LARGE QUANTITIES. ONCE AGAIN, THIS FRENCH DESIGN MARKED THE BIRTH OF THE T-BACK BLADE WHICH WAS WIDELY COPIED BY OTHER COUNTRIES. IT WAS PRODUCED BY A NUMBER OF FRENCH ARSENALS, AS WELL AS STEYR IN AUSTRIA. AS CAN BE NOTED FROM THE ILLUSTRATION, THE BACK OF THE BLADE IS MARKED WITH THE DATE AND ARSENAL (OVERALL LENGTH 25.3").

No. 2. **FRENCH MODEL 1874 - MODIFIED.** THIS PIECE WAS A STANDARD MODEL 1874 WITH THE BLADE SHORTENED IN A VERY PROFESSIONAL MANNER; PROBABLY A WORLD WAR I MODIFICATION (OVERALL LENGTH 13").

No. 3. **FRENCH MODEL 1878 - KROPATSCHEK.** THIS BAYONET LOOKS A GREAT DEAL LIKE THE FRENCH MODEL 1874; HOWEVER, IT DOES NOT HAVE THE STEP IN THE BACK OF THE HANDLE AND THOSE WHICH I HAVE SEEN WERE MANUFACTURED AT STEYR. THE BAYONET WAS DESIGNED FOR THE KROPATSCHEK RIFLE USED BY THE FRENCH NAVY. THESE PIECES ARE RELATIVELY SCARCE (OVERALL LENGTH 25.25").

① FRENCH M. 1874
KIESLING VOL. II #415

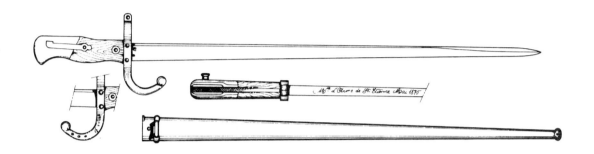

② FRENCH M. 1874
MODIFIED
KIESLING VOL. I #204

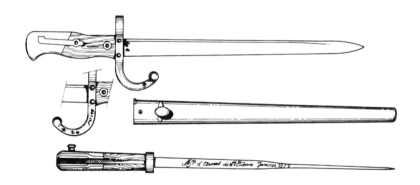

③ FRENCH M. 1878
NAVY
KIESLING VOL II #433

No. 1. FRENCH MODEL 1886 - LEBEL. THESE BAYONETS REFLECTED A REVOLUTION IN DESIGN BY THE FRENCH AND WERE USED FROM 1886 THROUGH WORLD WAR II. THE ORIGINAL MODEL 1886 WAS A LONG BAYONET (25.12" OVERALL LENGTH) WITH A HOOKED QUILLON AND A SILVER-ALLOY HANDLE WHICH WAS PERMANENTLY AFFIXED.

No. 2. FRENCH MODEL 1886/35 - LEBEL. THIS BAYONET IS A SHORTENED VERSION (18" OVERALL LENGTH) OF THE MODEL 1886; HOWEVER, THE HANDLE HAS BEEN MODIFIED TO BE REPLACED BY UTILIZING A THREADED TOP MOUNT. THIS PIECE CONTINUES TO UTILIZE THE SILVER-ALLOY HANDLE.

No. 3. FRENCH MODEL 1886/93/16 - LEBEL. THIS BAYONET IS OF THE ORIGINAL 25.12" LENGTH, HOWEVER, WAS MANUFACTURED WITHOUT THE HOOKED QUILLON AND THE HANDLE IS MADE OF BRASS.

No. 4. FRENCH MODEL 1886/91/16/35 - LEBEL. THIS PIECE IS A SHORTENED VERSION OF NO. 3 WITH THE BRASS HANDLE. THIS WAS THE LAST VERSION OF THE EPEE BAYONET AND WAS MANUFACTURED DURING OR AFTER 1916.

NOTE: THE LEBEL BAYONET WAS VERY POPULAR WITH THE FRENCH INFANTRY, WHO AFFECTIONATELY NAMED IT "ROSALIE".

① FRENCH M. 1886
KIESLING VOL. II #410

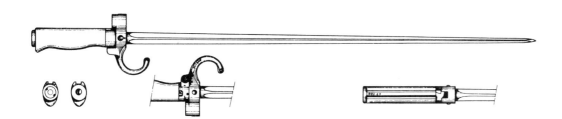

② FRENCH M. 1886/35
KIESLING VOL I # 223

③ FRENCH M. 1886/93/16
KIESLING VOL. II #412

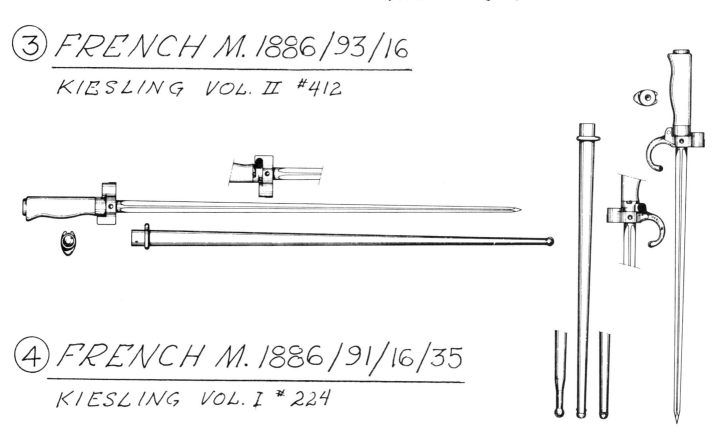

④ FRENCH M. 1886/91/16/35
KIESLING VOL. I # 224

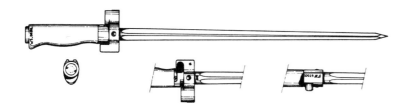

No. 1. FRENCH MODEL 1886/93/16 - LEBEL. THIS BAYONET IS ANOTHER VARIATION WITH A FULL-LENGTH BLADE, NO HOOKED QUILLON AND A SILVER-ALLOY HANDLE, WHICH IS REMOVABLE.

No. 2. FRENCH MODEL 1886/93/16 - LEBEL. THIS BAYONET IS A CROSS BETWEEN THE 1886 AND LATER VERSIONS AND HAS A HOOKED QUILLON AND A REMOVABLE BRASS HANDLE. I HAVE TWO EXAMPLES IN MY COLLECTION, ONE WITH AN 18.25" BLADE AND ONE WITH A 20.25" BLADE. SUCH VARIATIONS WERE COMMON BECAUSE THE BLADES WERE SIMPLY REPOINTED WHEN THEY BROKE IN FIELD USE.

No. 3. FRENCH MODEL 1886/91/16/35 - LEBEL. THIS IS A SHORTENED VERSION OF THE MODEL 1886/93/16, HOWEVER, IT HAS A BLUED STEEL HANDLE MAKING IT A MUCH HEAVIER ARM THAN THOSE PREVIOUSLY DISCUSSED. I ALSO HAVE A FULL LENGTH VERSION WITH THE STEEL HANDLE.

No. 4. FRENCH MODEL 1895 DAUDETEAU. THIS BAYONET WAS PRODUCED FOR THE DAUDETEAU RIFLE. IT IS UNUSUAL IN THAT ITS SILVER-ALLOY HANDLE HAS A SLOT MACHINED IN IT AS CAN BE NOTED IN THE ILLUSTRATION. THIS SLOT IS APPARENTLY FOR CLEANING ROD CLEARANCE. THESE BAYONETS ARE SCARCE.

① FRENCH M. 1886/93/16
KIESLING VOL. II #412

② FRENCH M. 1886/93/16
KIESLING VOL. IV #1020

③ FRENCH M. 1886/91/16/35
KIESLING VOL. I #224 (STEEL)

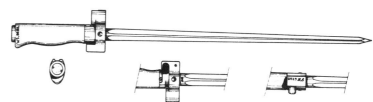

④ FRENCH M. 1895
KIESLING VOL II #413

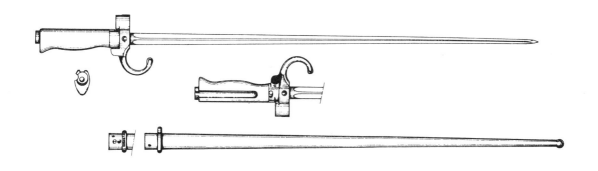

No. 1. **FRENCH MODEL 1892 – FIRST PATTERN.** THESE BAYONETS WERE PRODUCED FOR A SHORT RIFLE, THE M-1892 MANNLICHER BERTHIER. THE RIFLE WAS INTENDED FOR USE BY RAILROAD TROOPS, MOUNTED TROOPS AND TELEGRAPH UNITS. THE FIRST PATTERN IS EQUIPPED WITH HARD, BLACK COMPOSITION GRIPS AFFIXED BY TWO RIVETS. IT IS A BLADE-TYPE BAYONET WITH A HOOKED QUILLON. THE OVERALL LENGTH IS 20.25".

No. 2. **FRENCH MODEL 1892 – FIRST PATTERN.** THIS PIECE IS IDENTICAL TO No. 1, HOWEVER, IT HAS WOODEN GRIPS AFFIXED BY TWO WASHER/RIVETS. THIS MODIFICATION WAS PERFORMED DURING THE FIRST PART OF WORLD WAR I.

No. 3. **FRENCH MODEL 1892 – SECOND PATTERN.** THIS BAYONET IS IDENTICAL TO No. 1, HOWEVER, HAS A MODIFICATION WHICH WAS A FEATURE OF THE SECOND PATTERN CONSISTING OF A LONGER MUZZLE RING, EXTENDING SLIGHTLY BEHIND THE HANDLE.

NOTE: THE M-1892 BAYONETS USED BY THE FRENCH NAVY HAVE AN ANCHOR STAMPED BETWEEN THE CROSSGUARD RIVETS WHILE THOSE ISSUED TO POLISH ARMY UNITS ARE STAMPED "W.Z."92". THE GERMANS ALSO ISSUED CAPTURED M-1892 BAYONETS TO RAILWAY PROTECTION TROOPS DURING WORLD WAR I; HOWEVER, I AM NOT AWARE OF MARKED EXAMPLES.

① FRENCH M. 1892
FIRST PATTERN

KIESLING VOL. I #271

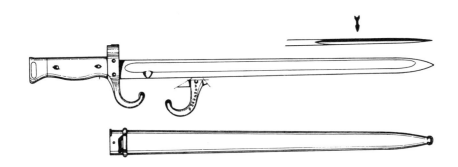

② FRENCH M. 1892
FIRST PATTERN

KIESLING VOL. III #636

③ FRENCH M. 1892
SECOND PATTERN

KIESLING VOL. I #272

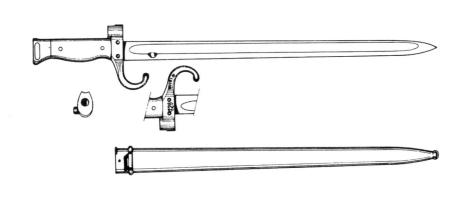

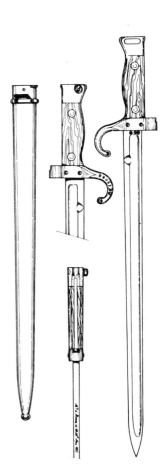

73

No. 1.   FRENCH MODEL 1892 - MODIFIED.   THIS PIECE IS A FIRST MODEL BAYONET, HOWEVER, THE HOOK HAS BEEN REMOVED FROM THE CROSSGUARD AND THE RIVETS IN THE HANDLE HAVE BEEN SMOOTHED OUT.

No. 2.   FRENCH MODEL 1892 - MODIFIED.   THIS PIECE IS IDENTICAL TO NO. 1 EXCEPT THAT IT HAS THE SECOND MODEL MUZZLE RING.   THIS MODIFICATION WAS APPARENTLY DONE DURING THE FIRST WORLD WAR.

No. 3.   FRENCH MODEL 1914 - REMINGTON.   THIS BAYONET WAS PRO-DUCED FOR THE REMINGTON ROLLING BLOCK RIFLE FURNISHED TO FRANCE BY THE UNITED STATES.   THIS IS MERELY A LONG VERSION OF THE REMINGTON BAYONET WHICH CAN BE FOUND IN THE U.S. SECTION AND I HAVE TWO EXAMPLES IN MY COLLEC-TION - ONE MARKED ON THE BLADE "REMINGTON ARMS COMPANY" AND THE SECOND ONE MARKED "UNION METALLIC CARTRIDGE COMPANY".

NOTE: I HAVE ONE MODEL 1892 BAYONET IN MY COLLECTION WHICH HAS THE ARSENAL (MRE DE CHAT 8 BRE 1893) ON THE BACK OF THE BLADE SIMILAR TO THE CHASSEPOT AND GRAS BAYONETS. THIS IS RELATIVELY RARE, HOWEVER, CAN BE FOUND ON ANY OF THE MODEL 1892 SERIES.   THIS PARTICULAR PIECE HAS NO OTHER MARKS.

1 FRENCH M. 1892 MODIFIED

KIESLING VOL. I #273

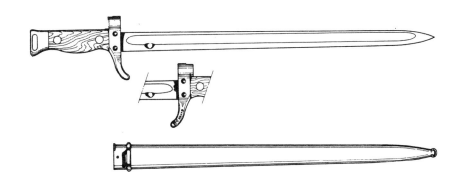

2 FRENCH M. 1892 MODIFIED

KIESLING VOL I #273

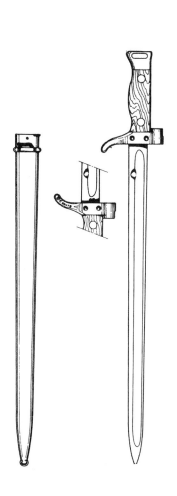

3 FRENCH M. 1914 REMINGTON

KIESLING VOL. II #284

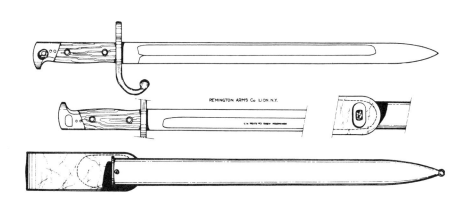

REMINGTON ARMS Co ILION. N.Y.

74

No. 1. FRENCH MODEL 1936 - MAS FIRST VARIATION. THIS BAYONET IS A SPIKE BAYONET WHICH WAS DESIGNED TO FIT UNDER THE BARREL ON THE MAS RIFLES. WHEN NOT IN USE, IT COULD BE REVERSED AND STORED IN THE SAME TUBE. THIS WEAPON TYPICALLY HAS A TWO-DIGIT NUMBER ON THE BACK CAP.

No. 2. FRENCH MODEL 1936 - MAS SECOND VARIATION. THIS PIECE IS IDENTICAL TO THE FIRST VARIATION EXCEPT THAT AN OIL HOLE HAS BEEN DRILLED JUST BEHIND THE CATCH.

No. 3. FRENCH MODEL 1936 - MAS THIRD VARIATION. THIS PIECE IS IDENTICAL TO THE PREVIOUS TWO VARIATIONS EXCEPT THAT IT HAS THE SIMPLIFIED GRINDING PATTERN ON THE FINGER GRIP. THIS BAYONET WAS APPARENTLY ALSO UTILIZED BY THE GERMANS ON THEIR FG 42 ASSAULT RIFLE, ALTHOUGH THOSE FOUND WITH THE RIFLE HAVE BEEN SHORTENED.

No. 4. FRENCH MODEL 1936 - MAS CR 39. THIS BAYONET HAS A SHORTER BLADE (289MM) THAN THE REMAINDER OF THE SERIES AND WAS UTILIZED WITH THE MODEL 1936 CR 39 FOLDING STOCK MAS CARBINE. I HAVE ONE OF THESE WITH A FIVE DIGIT SERIAL NUMBER STAMPED ON THE SHANK AND ONE WITH THE TWO DIGIT NUMBER STAMPED ON THE BACK CAP, AS ON THE FIRST, SECOND AND THIRD VARIATIONS.

① FRENCH M.1936
FIRST VARIATION

KIESLING VOL. I #201

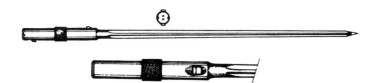

② FRENCH M.1936
SECOND VAR.

KIESLING VOL. I #202

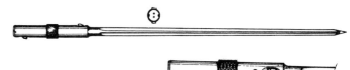

③ FRENCH M.1936
THIRD VARIATION

KIESLING VOL. III #588

④ FRENCH M.1936
CR 39

KIESLING VOL. III #561

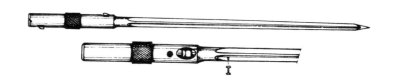

No. 1. **FRENCH MODEL 1956 MAS.** THIS IS A BAYONET FOR THE FRENCH 49/56 MAS RIFLE AND THE DESIGN IS TYPICAL OF THE FRENCH IN THAT IT UTILIZES TWO MUZZLE RINGS - ONE ON THE CROSS-GUARD AND ONE AT THE TOP OF THE HILT. IT HAS A VERY FLAT METAL SCABBARD CONFORMING TO THE BLADE AND IS HEAVILY DARKENED. THERE ARE TWO VARIATIONS OF THIS BAYONET, THE ONLY DIFFERENCE BEING THE LENGTH OF THE FALSE EDGE.

No. 2. **FRENCH MODEL 1982.** THIS IS A CURRENT BAYONET USED BY THE FRENCH FOREIGN LEGION. IT HAS A GREEN TUBULAR HANDLE AND FITS THE SWISS-DESIGNED SIG ASSAULT RIFLES SG 540 AND SG 542. THE PIECE IS 11" IN TOTAL LENGTH WITH A 7-1/8" BLADE. THE SCABBARD IS GREEN PLASTIC. THESE WEAPONS WERE PRODUCED AT NEUHAUSEN-AM RHEINFALLS SWITZERLAND AND UNDER LICENCE AT MANHURIN, MULHOUSE, FRANCE.

① FRENCH M. 1949/56

KIESLING VOL. IV #767

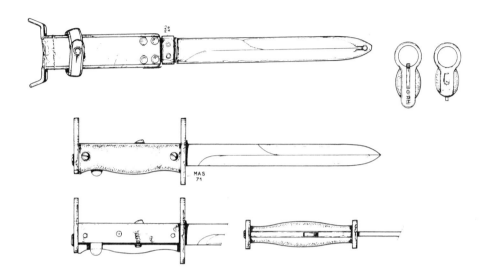

② FRENCH M. 1982
SIG

G. PRIEST GUNS REVIEW 10/86

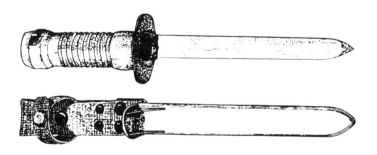

No. 1.   PRUSSIAN MODEL 1809 - SOCKET. THE SOCKET HAS NO FRONT SIGHT SLOT, BUT HAS A REAR NOTCH TO SECURE IT TO THE RAMROD. IT WAS PART OF THE NEW WEAPON DESIGN AND REORGANIZATION OF THE PRUSSIAN ARMY AFTER THE DISASTER AT JENA.

No. 2.   PRUSSIAN MODEL 1839 - SOCKET. THE BLADE OF THIS BAYONET HAS FULLERS EXTENDING THROUGH THE ELBOW, WITH STILL NO SLOT IN SOCKET. IT ALSO HAS THE REAR NOTCH.

No. 3.   PRUSSIAN MODEL 1860 FUSILIER. THIS BAYONET WAS THE GRAND-FATHER OF THE ENTIRE SERIES OF GERMAN BRASS HANDLED BAYONETS AND WAS ISSUED WITH A DISTINCTIVE DREYSE M-1860 RIFLE TO EIGHT ELITE PRUSSIAN FUSILIER REGIMENTS WHICH WERE CREATED IN 1860. THESE PIECES WERE BASED ON EARLY INFANTRY SIDE ARMS AND WERE IN SERVICE FOR OVER A DECADE BEFORE BEING BUSHED AND PASSED TO THE ARTILLERY.

No. 4.   PRUSSIAN MODEL 1865/71 - PIONIERFASCHINENMESSER. THIS BAYO-NET IS A BUSHED VERSION OF THE M-1865 AND IS A MASSIVE WEAPON WITH AN OVERALL LENGTH OF OVER TWO FEET AND WEIGHING APPROXI-MATELY 28 OZ. THE ARM WAS UTILIZED BY PRUSSIAN PIONEERS ON THE M-1871 AND M-1888 MAUSERS AFTER 1874, ACCORDING TO JOHN WALTER. IT WAS INITIALLY ISSUED WITH THE M-1865 DREYSE RIFLE. (AS A NOTE OF INTEREST, A "FASCINE" IS A CYLINDRICAL BUNDLE OF BRUSH WOOD, TIGHTLY BOUND AND PLACED IN A CRADLE; THUS, THIS BAYONET IS A PIONEER TOOL FOR CUTTING BRUSH WOOD.)

① PRUSSIAN M.1809
KIESLING VOL.II #335

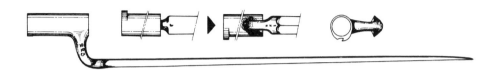

② PRUSSIAN M.1839
KIESLING VOL.II #336

③ PRUSSIAN M.1860 FUSILIER
KIESLING VOL.II #404

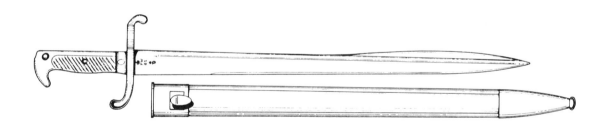

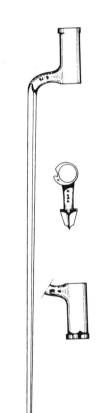

④ PRUSSIAN M.1865/71 FASCHINENMESSER
KIESLING VOL.II #368

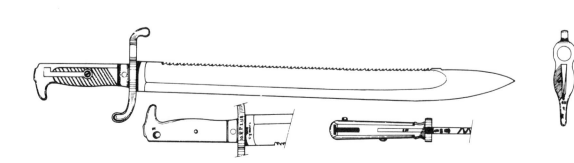

No. 1. MODEL 1871. THIS BAYONET WAS ISSUED IN THE FIRST YEAR OF THE NEW IMPERIAL GERMANY AND WAS USED WITH THE INFANTERIE-GEWEHR MODEL 1871 RIFLE. THE DESIGN IS BASED ON THE FUSILIER MODEL 1860 WITHOUT THE RIB-BACK. IT WAS REISSUED WITH THE COMMISSION RIFLE M-1888.

No. 2. MODEL 1971 - SAWBACK. THIS BAYONET WAS ISSUED TO NCOs ONLY. THE SAWBACK DENOTED RANK. I HAVE TWO DISTINCT PATTERNS OF THIS PIECE DIFFERING IN THE NUMBER OF TEETH. THE PIONEERS HAD THEIR OWN ISSUE, THE MODEL 1871 FASCHINENMESSER (SEE 77-4).

No. 3. MODEL 1871 - HIRSHFANGER. THIS WEAPON WAS DESIGNED FOR A DISTINCTIVE JAGER RIFLE WHICH WAS ISSUED IN 1875-76 AND WAS BASED ON THE M-1865. UNLIKE OTHER GERMAN BAYONETS, IT HAS BLACK LEATHER GRIPS RETAINED BY FIVE RIVETS AND IS VERY SCARCE. I HAVE BOTH ISSUE AND DRESS EXAMPLES. THE DRESS VERSIONS WERE PRIVATELY PURCHASED FOR WALKING OUT (THE PIECE IN MY COLLECTION IS ENGRAVED TO A POMERANIAN JAGER BATTALIAN).

No. 4. MODEL 1871 - CHILD'S BAYONET. THIS IS A VERY INTERESTING SMALL BAYONET WITH A ROUNDED TIP. IT HAS A 71-STYLE HILT AND IS DESIGNED TO FIT A SMALL CADET RIFLE.

① GERMAN M 1871
KIESLING VOL. II #366

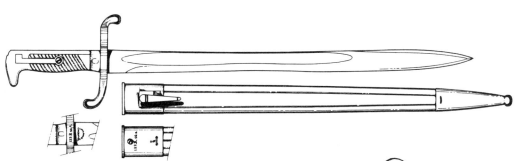

② GERMAN M. 1871
SAW BACK
KIESLING VOL. II #367

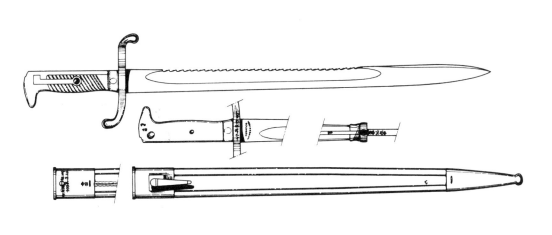

④ GERMAN M. 1871
CHILDS

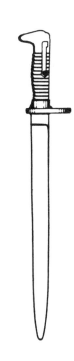

③ GERMAN M. 1871
HIRSHFANGER
KIESLING VOL III #677

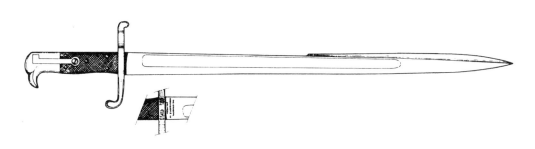

No. 1. MODEL 1871/84 - FIRST MODEL. AFTER THE COMPLETE REDESIGN OF THE MODEL 1871 MAUSER TO A MAGAZINE RIFLE, THE FIRST KNIFE BAYONET FOR THE GERMAN ARMY WAS ISSUED IN 1886 WITH LONG FULLERS. THE SCARCITY OF THE M-71/84 BAYONET IS DUE TO THE SHORT EXISTENCE OF THE RIFLE. THE STEEL-MOUNTED, BLACK LEATHER SCABBARDS FOLLOWED TRADITIONAL DESIGN.

No. 2. MODEL 1871/84 - FIRST MODEL DRESS. HAS BEEN MODIFIED WITHOUT MUZZLE RING. ALL METAL PARTS ARE NICKLE-PLATED, INCLUDING THE SCABBARD MOUNTS. THESE WERE PRIVATE PURCHASE.

No. 3. MODEL 1871/84 - FIRST MODEL. THIS BAYONET HAS SHORTER FULLERS WHICH DO NOT RUN TO THE POINT. THIS IS THOUGHT DUE TO THE MANUFACTURER'S TOOLING AND IS NOT A MODIFICATION. KIESLING IDENTIFIES THIS AS A SECOND MODEL.

No. 4. MODEL 1871/84. THIS IS AN UNUSUAL MODIFICATION IN THAT THE GRIPS ARE STRAIGHT, SLAB-SIDED WITH NO "HUMP" ON THE BACK OF THE GRIP AND THE POMMEL LENGTH HAS BEEN INCREASED.

NOTE: ALTHOUGH I HAVE USED THE TERM "MODEL", THE GERMANS ACTUALLY DESIGNATED THEIR BAYONETS S.G., WHICH WAS THE GERMAN ABBREVIATION OF "SEITENGEWEHR" WHICH, IN ENGLISH, MEANS "SIDE ARM" OR BAYONET.

① GERMAN M. 1871/84
FIRST MODEL

KIESLING VOL. I #121

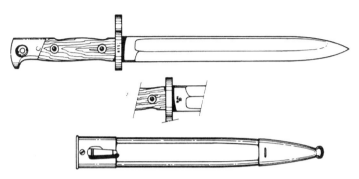

② GERMAN M. 1871/84
FIRST MODEL DRESS

③ GERMAN M. 1871/84
FIRST MODEL

KIESLING VOL. I #123

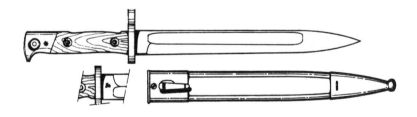

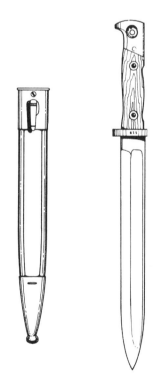

④ GERMAN M. 1871/84
DRESS

BAJONETTEN DA TILL NU #86

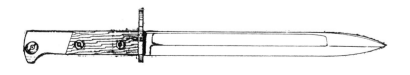

No. 1.   MODEL 1871 - INFANTRY DRESS. A PRIVATE PURCHASE
FOR "WALKING OUT" OFF DUTY. ALSO USED BY INFAN-
TERIE KADETEN IN MILITARY SCHOOLS. THERE ALSO
EXISTS A KADET SAWBACK VERSION. (GERD MAIER
VOL. V, PG. 824). THIS PIECE WAS PRODUCED INTO THE
1900S AND HAS VERY LIGHT "ROLLED-ON" ETCHING ON THE
BLADE.

*   MODEL 1871 - ARTILLERY DRESS. THE WALKING-OUT
VERSION FOR THE ARTILLERY DIFFERS FROM THE INFANTRY
DRESS VERSION IN THAT THE FALSE SPRING IS ON THE
SMOOTH SIDE OF THE HANDLE (OR WAS OMITTED ENTIRELY
BY SOME MANUFACTURERS).

No. 2.   MODEL 1871 - JAGER DRESS. THIS WAS A PRIVATE PUR-
CHASE PIECE FOR A JAGER UNIT. IT WAS ALSO UTILIZED
IN MILITARY SCHOOLS.

No. 3.   MODEL 1871/84 - DRESS (CIRCA 1884). THIS IS
ANOTHER UNUSUAL DRESS BAYONET IN THAT THE UNFUL-
LERED BLADE IS POLISHED BRIGHT AND IS ETCHED. IT
HAS NO BUTTON RELEASE AND WILL NOT FIT A RIFLE.

No. 4.   MODEL 1871/84 - DRESS (CIRCA 1884). THIS VERSION
IS IDENTICAL TO THE PRECEDING BAYONET EXCEPT FOR A
LONGER BLADE. IT IS ALSO POLISHED BRIGHT AND
ETCHED.

① GERMAN M. 1871 INF. DRESS

STEPHENS #88

WATTS & WHITE #382

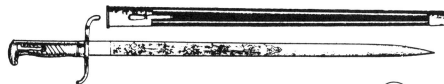

✳ GERMAN M. 1871 ART. DRESS

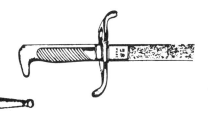

② GERMAN M. 1871 JAGER DRESS

WATTS & WHITE #377

③ GERMAN M. 1871/84 DRESS

WATTS & WHITE #385

④ GERMAN M. 1871/84 DRESS

WATTS & WHITE #385

No. 1. MODEL 1884/98 - FIRST PATTERN. THIS BAYONET WAS CONVERTED FROM THE ORIGINAL MODEL 1871/84, BY REMOVING THE MUZZLE-RING AND REPLACING THE EXISTING "T" SLOT WITH THE MAUSER "T/O" SLOT THAT WAS EXTENDED TO 40 MM. THIS WAS LONG ENOUGH TO SUPPORT THE BAYONET ON THE RIFLE WITHOUT THE MUZZLE-RING. IT HAS A BLACK LEATHER SCABBARD WITH BRIGHT STEEL MOUNTS.

No. 2. MODEL 1884/98 - SECOND PATTERN. THIS WAS THE STANDARD SHORT BAYONET ISSUED IN WW I. MOST WERE FITTED WITH FLASHGUARDS. THEY HAD WOODEN GRIPS, BRIGHT BLADES AND METAL SCABBARDS.

No. 3. MODEL 1884/98 - SECOND PATTERN, SAWBACK. THE SAWBACK AGAIN DENOTES NCO RANK. THE POMMEL MEETS THE GRIPS STRAIGHT ACROSS AND THE BLADE IS SLIGHTLY MODIFIED. FROM THE SECOND PATTERN ON, THE LEATHER SCABBARD WAS REPLACED WITH A METAL ONE. THE MOUTHPIECE AND RETAINER SPRINGS BEING HELD BY A SCREW.

No. 4. MODEL 1884/98 - SECOND PATTERN, WITH SAWBACK REMOVED. DUE TO ALLIED PROPAGANDA AND THE DISCONTINUATION OF WOODEN BARBED-WIRE POSTS, THE GERMAN HIGH COMMAND ORDERED ALL SAWBACKS REMOVED IN 1917. LUCKILY, MANY ESCAPED THIS MODIFICATION.

① GERMAN M.1884/98
FIRST PATTERN

KIESLING VOL. I #139

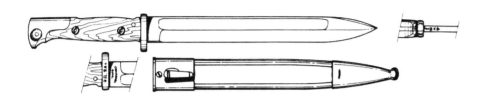

④ GERMAN M.1884/98
SAWBACK REMOVED

KIESLING VOL. III #565

② GERMAN M.1884/98
SECOND PATTERN

WATTS & WHITE #283

③ GERMAN M.1884/98
SAWBACK

KIESLING VOL. I #141

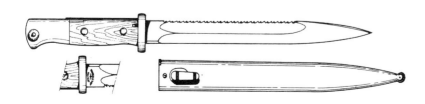

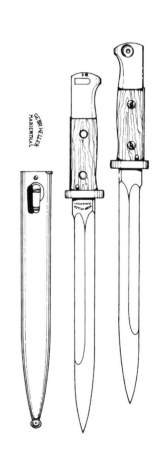

No. 1. **Model 1898a/A.** After years of experimentation with all metal, hollow-tube grips and epee-type blades (see 85-3), the Prussian Gewehr-Prufungs Kommission, with an eye to the French Model 1886 Lebel Bayonet, adopted the Model 1898 a/A rib-backed blade with a <u>one-piece wooden grip</u>. It had a black leather scabbard with bright steel mounts.

No. 2. **Model 1898 n/A.** The fragility of the one-piece grip resulted in a modification in 1902, i.e., the redesigning of a two-piece grip, designated Model 1898 n/A. These were made up to 1914 and had a black leather scabbard with bright steel mounts. These were also available in a nickle-plated private purchase version.

No. 3. **Model 1898 n/A - Saxon.** The so-called "Saxon version" are those models that have flashguards attached. The blade in my collection is Saxon-marked; however, recent research has proven there were non-Saxon marked blades with this addition. The all-metal scabbards were made in small numbers to replace the leather types which were easily broken in trench warfare.

NOTE: The proper placement of the bayonet knot or troddel is illustrated. These devices were used to designate both rank and unit. A complete description of the side arm knots is contained in Appendix 1 of <u>The German Bayonet</u> by John Walter.

① GERMAN M.1898
KIESLING VOL. II #425

② GERMAN M.1898 "NEUER ART"
KIESLING VOL. II #426

③ GERMAN M.1898 W/ FLASHGUARD
KIESLING VOL. II #427

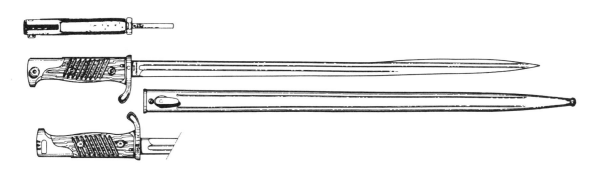

No. 1. **MODEL 1898 A/A - SAWBACK.** THIS IS AN NCO SAW-BACK. ONLY 6 TO 7 PERCENT OF ALL BAYONETS MANUFAC-TURED FOR THE GERMAN MILITARY WERE SAWBACKS AND, AS SUCH, WERE MEANT AS A DISTINCTION OF RANK ONLY AND NOT MEANT TO INFLICT HORRIBLE WOUNDS, AS ALLIED PROPAGANDA SUGGESTED.

No. 2. **MODEL 1898 N/A - SAWBACK.** THIS SAWBACK ALSO DENOTES NCO RANK AND INCORPORATES THE TWO-PIECE GRIPS INTRODUCED IN 1902. IT IS IDENTICAL TO NO. 1 IN ALL OTHER RESPECTS. THE ALL METAL SCABBARD MARKED "FAG" (TRADEMARK OF FRIEDERICH AUGUST GOBEL OF SOLINGEN), IS QUITE SCARCE FOR THIS MODEL.

No. 3. **MODEL 1898 A/A - SHORTENED.** IN KAISERZEIT VOL. IV #4, PG. 15. MR. C. BROWN QUOTES GERHARD SEIFERT SAYING SOME UNITS SHORTENED THESE BAYONETS ON THEIR OWN AUTHORITY FOR TRENCH KNIVES. THERE IS NO OFFI-CIAL DESIGNATION ON THESE SHORTENED BAYONETS.

No. 4. **MODEL 1898 N/A - DRESS.** THIS COULD BE WORN AS A "WALKING OUT" BAYONET AND WAS POSSIBLY ALSO SHORT-ENED FOR CLOSE COMBAT, ALTHOUGH DRESS BAYONETS ARE MUCH WEAKER AND MANY OF THE HANDLE FRAMES ARE MADE OF "POT-METAL". SCABBARD ALSO SHORTENED TO FIT.

① GERMAN M.1898
A/A SAWBACK

KIESLING VOL II #428

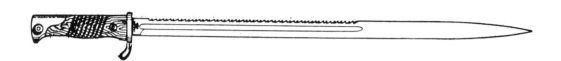

② GERMAN M.1898
N/A SAWBACK

KIESLING VOL II #428

③ GERMAN M.1898
SHORTENED

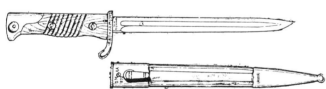
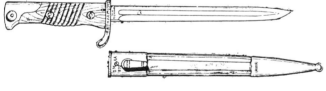

MARK ON
OTHER SIDE
OF SCABBARD.

④ GERMAN M.1898
SHORT DRESS

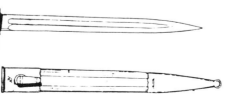

No. 1. **MODEL 1898 - KURZES SAWBACK.** THE KURZES SEITENGEWEHR (KS) WAS ORIGINALLY INTENDED AS A BAYONET FOR MACHINENGEWEHR-ABTEILUNGEN (MACHINE GUN UNITS), BUT WAS ALSO ADOPTED BY THE LUFTSCHIFF, KOLONIAL SCHUTZTRUPPEN AND TELEGRAPHEN UNITS. ISSUE PIECES ARE ALMOST INVARIABLY MARKED "ERFURT" AND HAVE UNIT MARKS ON THE GUARDS. THE MAJORITY WERE PRIVATE PURCHASE. THIS MODEL HAS WOODEN GRIPS AND SCREW-BOLTS. (NOTE THE CYPHER OF KAISER WILHELM II WHO REIGNED FROM 1888 TO 1918.)

No. 2. **MODEL 1898 - KURZES SAWBACK.** IN 1915, ALL OFFICERS WERE REQUIRED TO SEND THEIR SWORDS TO THE REAR DUE TO STATIC TRENCH WARFARE. MOST OFFICERS THEN PRIVATELY PURCHASED THE POPULAR KURZES MODEL, WITH BLACK PAINTED METAL SCABBARDS; HOWEVER, I HAVE BOTH PROOFED AND UNMARKED VARIATIONS.

No. 3. **MODEL 1898 - KURZES.** ANOTHER PRIVATE PURCHASE KURZES WITHOUT SAWBACK WITH GRIPS HELD BY TWO SCREW-BOLTS INSTEAD OF THE MORE COMMON THREE RIVETS. SCABBARD IS BLACK-LACQUERED STEEL.

No. 4. **MODEL 1898 - KURZES DRESS.** THE VARIATION ILLUSTRATED HAS A CARBINE BLADE AND MAY BE OF WORLD WAR II VINTAGE, HOWEVER, THE ENTIRE HANDLE IS KURZES DESIGN. I ALSO HAVE A PLATED DRESS VERSION OF THE STANDARD KURZES SAWBACK.

① GERMAN KS 98
SAWBACK

J. WALTER PG 58

ERFURT

② GERMAN KS 98
SAWBACK

KIESLING VOL. I #133

③ GERMAN KS 98

WATTS & WHITE #263

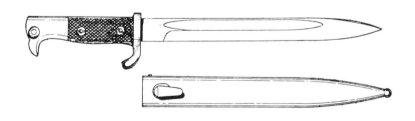

④ GERMAN KS 98
DRESS

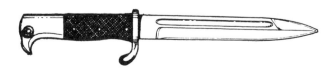

No. 1. MODEL 1898/02. ADOPTED IN 1902, THIS MASSIVE BAYONET WAS ISSUED TO PIONEERS, RAILWAY AND TELEGRAPH TROOPS. DUE TO ITS SIZE, IT HAD A SHORT MILITARY LIFE AND SOON GAVE WAY TO THE HANDIER MODEL 1898/05 SAWBACK. THE PARTIAL MUZZLE-RING IS THE FIRST OF THIS TYPE TO APPEAR ON GERMAN ARMS. THE SCABBARD IS BLACK LEATHER WITH BRIGHT STEEL MOUNTS. SOME SCHOLARS FEEL THAT THIS MODEL WAS, IN FACT, EXPERIMENTAL WITH NO MORE THAN A FEW UNITS ACTUALLY RECEIVING THIS ISSUE.

No. 2. MODEL 1871/98. THIS BAYONET UTILIZED THE BLADE FROM THE PRUSSIAN M-1860 MATED TO THE MAUSER M-1898 HILT AND CROSSGUARD. THIS PIECE WAS USED BY THE FIELD ARTILLERY AND IS QUITE SCARCE. THE SCABBARD IS BRASS-MOUNTED LEATHER (SEE 77-3 FOR THE ORIGINAL BAYONET).

No. 3. MODEL 1895/98 - EXPERIMENTAL. THIS IS A PRUSSIAN BAYONET WHICH WAS MADE IN VERY SMALL NUMBERS BY ERFURT GEWEHRFABRIK IN THE 1895-96 TIME FRAME. THE ONE IN MY COLLECTION IS THE MOST COMMON OF THE FOUR PROTOTYPE VARIATIONS AND HAS A CRUCIFORM BLADE BASED ON THE FRENCH MODEL 1886. THE TUBULAR SCABBARD HAS NO LOCKING SPRING FOR THE BLADE. THIS BAYONET IS EXTREMELY RARE.

① GERMAN M. 1898/02
KIESLING VOL. II #331

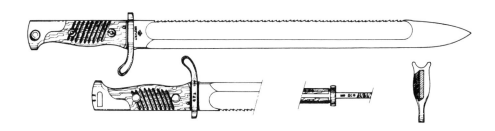

② GERMAN M. 1871/98
KIESLING VOL. II #409

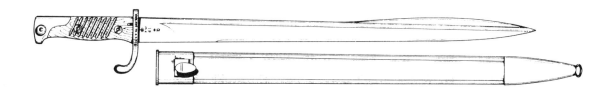

③ GERMAN M. 1895/97
EXPERIMENTAL
KIESLING VOL. II #406, #951
WALTER, T.G.B. PG. 48

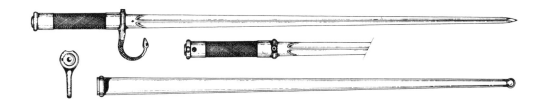

No. 1. **Model 1898/05 N/A.** This bayonet was commonly called the "Butcher blade" due to its uncharacteristic blade shape and probably a touch of Allied propaganda. These eventually made up the majority of all German bayonets issued in WW I. The first models had a black leather scabbard with steel mounts, changing in 1915 to a blued, all steel version. I have both the A/A (no flash guard) and the N/A (flash guard) bayonet as well as an A/A (high ears) converted to an N/A by adding a flash guard. The N/A model is illustrated.

No. 2. **Model 1898/05 N/A - Sawback.** With this sawback model, Germany departed from the former system of denoting rank with sawback bayonets. The Pioneer troops were the only recipients of the sawback version of the M-1898/05.

No. 3. **Model 1898/05 - "Sagerucken abgeschliffen" or Sawback removed.** Allied propaganda caused the recall of all sawbacks which were then ground and reissued, their use unimpaired.

NOTE: Cyphers of the reigning monarchs will be encountered on all German bayonets through 1918. The Bavarian cyphers "O" and "L" were discussed on page 14; the Prussian cypher for Wilhelm II is "W" and noted on page 84-1; however, Saxon marks will also be found. These cyphers will be "GR" for King Georg who reigned from 1902-1904 and the "FA" of King Friedrich August III who reigned from 1904 to 1918.

① GERMAN M. 1898/05

KIESLING VOL. I #256

② GERMAN M. 1898/05
SAWBACK

KIESLING VOL. I #257

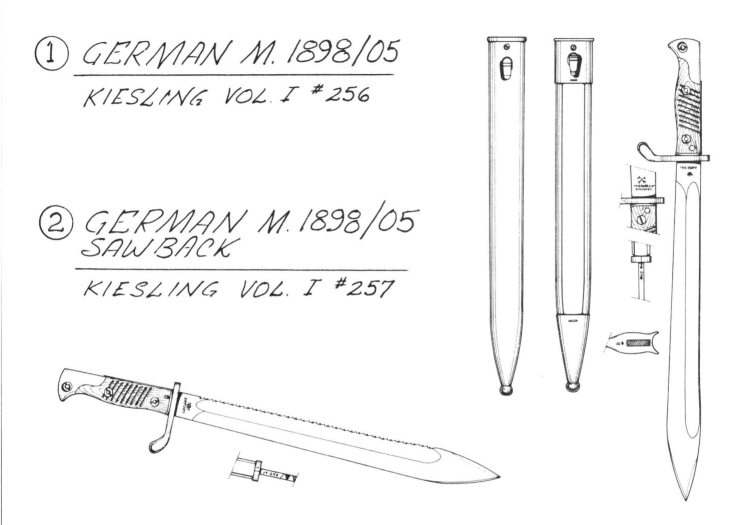

③ GERMAN M. 1898/05
SAWBACK REMOVED

KIESLING VOL. I #258

✳ SAXON ROYAL CYPHERS
GEORG (1902-04)
FRIEDRICH AUGUST III

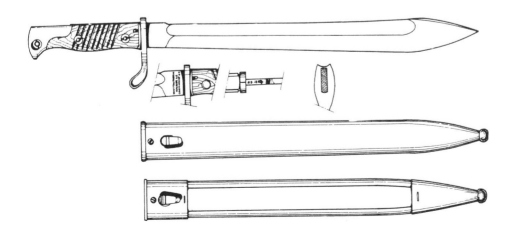

No. 1. **MODEL 1884/98 - DRESS.** THIS PIECE IS A PLATED WALKING-OUT VERSION OF THE 1884/98 WITH CHECKERED WOOD GRIPS.

No. 2. **MODEL 1884/05 - DRESS.** THIS BAYONET IS UNUSUAL IN THAT IT HAS THE 98/05 GRIP/POMMEL BUT AN 84/98 SAWBACK BLADE WITH ALL METAL PARTS NICKLED. I SUSPECT IT WAS MANUFACTURED IN THE 1910 ERA.

No. 3. **MODEL 1907 - HAENEL.** NEVER OFFICIALLY ADOPTED BY GERMANY, THIS BAYONET WAS MADE FOR A CHINESE CONTRACT WHICH WAS NOT ACCEPTED. IT HAS THE "T" TYPE SLOT, NOT THE USUAL MAUSER "T/O" SLOT. THIS MODEL HAS HAD ITS CROSSGUARD MODIFIED.

① GERMAN M.1884/98
DRESS

KIESLING VOL III #564 (CLOSE)

② GERMAN M.1884/98/05
DRESS

WATTS & WHITE #390 (CLOSE)

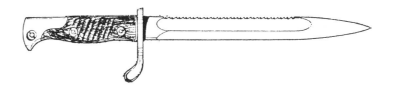

③ GERMAN M.1907
HAENEL

KIESLING VOL IV #826

C.G.H.

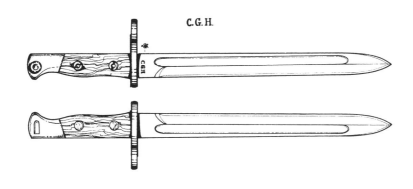

No. 1.   **MODEL 1914.** THIS WAS THOUGHT TO BE ORIGINALLY FOR SOUTH AMERICAN EXPORT AND HAS BEEN MODIFIED TO FIT THE GEWEHR MODEL 1898. THE WOODEN GRIPS ARE HELD BY TWO RIVETS, ALTHOUGH THERE ARE VARIANTS WITH SCREW-BOLTS. IT HAS NO FLASHGUARD FOR FITTING TO THE KAR. 98 RIFLE. ALL PARTS ARE POLISHED BRIGHT. IT HAS THE BELGIUM BAYARD HALLMARK ON THE RICASSO.

No. 2.   **MODEL 1914 – A VARIANT OF THE PRECEDING.** THIS TYPE OF BAYONET WAS THOUGHT ORIGINALLY TO HAVE HAD A FORWARD SWEEPING QUILLON AND HAS A MORE ROUNDED POMMEL.

No. 3.   **MODEL 1914 – SAWBACK.** THIS SAWBACK MODEL WAS MEANT FOR NCOs AND NOT FOR PIONEER TROOPS. I HAVE EXAMPLES OF THIS BAYONET <u>WITH</u> AND <u>WITHOUT</u> A FLASHGUARD.

No. 4.   **MODEL 1914 – GOTTSCHO.** THIS MODEL HAS BEEN CALLED THE "MACHINE-GUNNERS" BAYONET SINCE THE OLD BANNERMAN DAYS. THERE IS NO EVIDENCE TO SUBSTANTIATE THIS ASSERTION. IT HAS AN UNUSUAL CONSTRUCTION AND WAS DESIGNED BY DR. LUCIAN GOTTSCHO IN BERLIN ON OR ABOUT 1915. HE IS PROBABLY THE "G" IN THE VACUUM TUBE LOGO ON THE RICASSO. THIS IS A BAVARIAN-ISSUED WEAPON AND ALSO IS AVAILABLE IN SAWBACK.

① GERMAN M.1914

KIESLING VOL. I #213

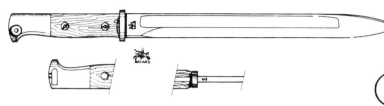

② GERMAN M.1914

KIESLING VOL. I #211

③ GERMAN M.1914 SAWBACK

KIESLING VOL.I #214

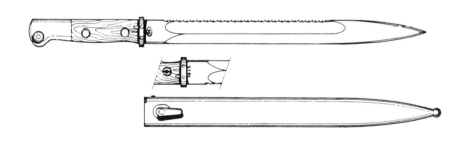

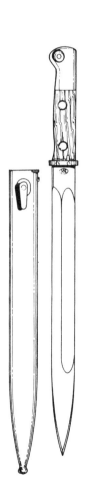

④ GERMAN M.1915

KIESLING VOL. I #249

K.S.

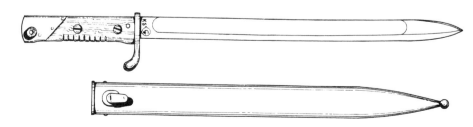

ERSATZ NOTE:

ERSATZ BAYONETS WERE THE DIRECT RESULT OF THE RE-ALLOCATION OF PRIORITIES FOR THE GERMAN WAR EFFORT. HEAVY INDUSTRY WAS NEEDED FOR THE MORE COMPLICATED WEAPONRY OF WAR; THEREFORE, SIMPLIFIED BAYONET PATTERNS THAT COULD BE QUICKLY AND EASILY PRODUCED BY SMALL SHOPS WERE STARTED IN EARLY 1915. THUS, WE FIND THE REASON FOR THE PROLIFERATION OF STYLES AND MODELS. THE TERM "ERSATZ" CAN BE TRANSLATED AS "SUBSTITUTE" AND, ACCORDING TO EVANS, OVER 80 DISTINCT VARIANTS ARE KNOWN.

No. 1. ERSATZ MODEL 1915. THIS IS ONE OF THE BEST MADE OF THE ERSATZ BAYONETS AND MAY BE ONE OF THE RAREST. CHARLES DANGRE LISTS IT FIRST AMONG HIS GREAT STUDY OF ERSATZ BAYONETS. IT IS THE ONLY ERSATZ WITH WOOD IN THE GRIPS.

No. 2. ERSATZ MODEL 1915. THIS IS ANOTHER WELL MADE BAYONET; HOW-EVER, IT WAS MADE TO FIT ONE RIFLE ONLY - THE BELGIAN MODEL 1889. IT HAS AN ALL STEEL HANDLE AND A BELGIAN-MADE BLADE WITH SAWBACK FOR NCOs. THE MAJORITY OF GERMAN TROOPS ISSUED THE M-1889 USED THE BELGIAN 1889 BAYONET. HOWEVER, KEEPING WITH THE GERMAN PRACTICE OF EQUIPPING 6% OF A REGIMENT'S STRENGTH WITH SAWBACK BAYONETS, A SMALL QUANTITY OF THESE WEAPONS WERE PRODUCED.

* BAYONET ADAPTER. THIS ADJUSTABLE SLEEVE WAS USED BY THE GERMANS TO EQUIP CAPTURED FRENCH AND RUSSIAN RIFLES WITH GERMAN BAYONETS.

① *ERSATZ M.1915*

KIESLING VOL. I #207
CARTER PG. 34 # 55

② *ERSATZ M.1915 BELGIAN MAUSER*

KIESLING VOL III #587
CARTER PG. 36 # 58

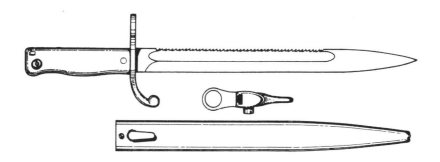

✳ *BAYONET ADAPTER*

BANNERMAN, GEW 98, PG. 19

No. 1.   ERSATZ MODEL 1915 - BAVARIAN. THIS TOO IS A WELL MADE BAYONET IN THE STYLE OF THE BELGIAN MODEL 1889. IT FITS THE MODEL 1898, 1888 AND THE FRENCH MODEL 1886/93 RIFLES, WITH GROOVED STEEL GRIP AND METAL ERSATZ SCABBARD.

No. 2.   ERSATZ MODEL 1915 - BAVARIAN SAWBACK. THIS IS ANOTHER ALL METAL BAYONET IN THE STYLE OF THE 98/05 SAWBACK WITH AN ALL METAL SCABBARD. THESE WERE ISSUED MAINLY TO REAR-ECHELON TROOPS. IT FITS THE M-98, M-88 AND FRENCH LEBEL RIFLES.

No. 3.   ERSATZ MODEL 1915 - BAVARIAN. THIS IS IDENTICAL TO THE PRECEDING WEAPON EXCEPT FOR THE SAWBACK. IT ALSO FITS THE SAME RIFLES. THE OPEN TOP MUZZLE RINGS ON ALMOST ALL ERSATZ BAYONETS WAS AN INGENIOUS METHOD OF ATTACHING THESE PIECES TO DIFFERENT MODEL RIFLES.

No. 4.   ERSATZ MODEL 1917 - BAVARIAN. LATER IN THE WAR, THE WORKMANSHIP SUFFERED AND THE BAYONETS SHOWED IT. THIS BLADE HAS PARALLEL SIDES. THE ERSATZ SCABBARD ALSO SHOWS ROUGH FINISHING.

① ERSATZ M.1915 BAVARIAN

KIESLING VOL.I #172
CARTER PG.30 #45

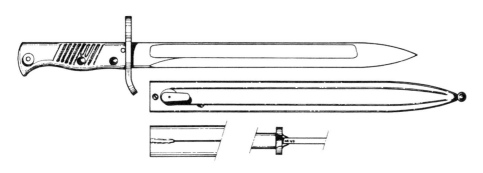

② ERSATZ M.1915 SAWBACK 98/05

KIESLING VOL.I #242
CARTER PG. 28 #42

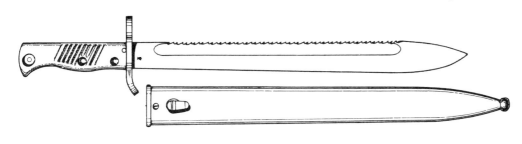

③ ERSATZ M.1915 BUTCHER 98/05

KIESLING VOL.I #241
CARTER PG. 28 #41

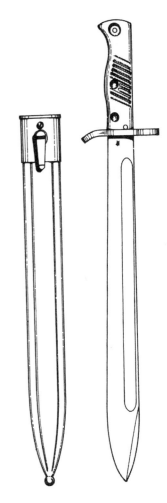

④ ERSATZ M.1915 STRAIGHT 98/05

KIESLING VOL.IV #864
CARTER PG. 30 #43

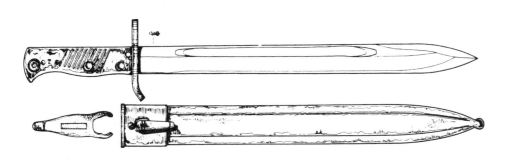

No. 1.   ERSATZ MODEL 1915. THIS BLADE IS UNFULLERED AND IS JUST ANOTHER SHORTCUT TAKEN BY THE GERMANS TO SPEED UP PRODUCTION. THE HILT IS CAST STEEL. IT FITS THE GEW 98 ONLY AND MAY HAVE BEEN USED BY THE POLICE.

No. 2.   ERSATZ MODEL 1916. THIS IS A SLIGHT MODIFICATION OF THE PREVIOUS BAYONET IN THAT IT IS FULLERED AND THE OPEN MUZZLE RING ALLOWS IT TO FIT THE GEW 98, GEW 88 AND THE FRENCH LEBEL. WITH THE ADAPTER SHOWN ON PAGE 89, MOST OF THESE ERSATZ BAYONETS COULD BE AFFIXED TO THE MOSIN-NAGANTS.

No. 3.   ERSATZ MODEL 1916. THIS BAYONET IS OF DIFFERENT CONSTRUCTION THAN THE PRECEDING. IT HAS A RIVETED, TWO-PIECE, SLAB-SIDED GRIP WITH A ONE-PIECE CROSS-GUARD AND IT FITS THE SAME RIFLES AS No. 2.

NOTE: THE DEFINITIVE SOURCE OF INFORMATION ON ERSATZ BAYONETS WAS AUTHORED BY ANTHONY CARTER AND TITLED GERMAN ERSATZ BAYONETS (SEE BIBLIOGRAPHY, PG. 248). THIS BOOK IS REFERENCED IN THE ERSATZ SECTION.

① ERSATZ M. 1915

KIESLING VOL. I #220
CARTER PG. 22 #24

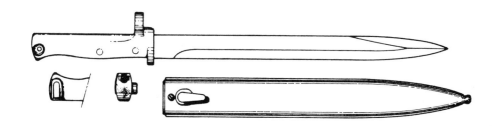

② ERSATZ M. 1916

KIESLING VOL. I #218
CARTER PG 22 #23

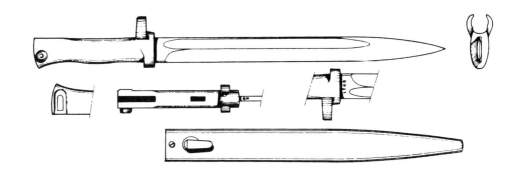

③ ERSATZ M. 1916

KIESLING VOL. I #215
CARTER PG. 16 #9

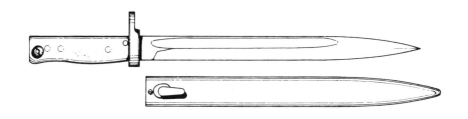

No. 1.   ERSATZ MODEL 1916.   ANOTHER ERSATZ VARIANT WITH THE GUARD AND THE MUZZLE RING SLIGHTLY ROUNDED.   THE FULLERS ARE GROUND INTO THE BLADE AND THE GUARD IS OF ONE-PIECE CONSTRUCTION.

No. 2.   ERSATZ MODEL 1916.   SIMILAR TO NO. 1 BUT THE GUARD IS OF TWO-PIECE CONSTRUCTION AND THE BLADE IS UN-FULLERED.   THE GRIP BUTT HAS A SLIGHT LIP.

No. 3.   ERSATZ MODEL 1916.   THIS IS AN UNUSUAL TYPE WITH SMOOTH SIDED GRIPS AND A SET-BACK MUZZLE RING WHICH IS SELDOM SEEN.   IT FITS THE GEW 98, GEW 88 AND FRENCH LEBEL.

No. 4.   ERSATZ MODEL 1916.   THIS TYPE HAS CAST STEEL GRIPS WITH NINE DIAGONAL GROOVES, SIMULATING THE ISSUE WOOD GRIPS.   THESE ARE VERY WELL MADE AND ARE QUITE SOUGHT AFTER.   THEY FIT THE SAME RIFLES AS ABOVE. I HAVE EXAMPLES WHICH ARE BOTH FULLERED AND UNFUL-LERED AS WELL AS A TURKISH MODIFIED VERSION WHICH IS REDUCED IN LENGTH BY 2-1/2".

① *ERSATZ M.1916*

KIESLING VOL. III #550
CARTER PG. 18 #12

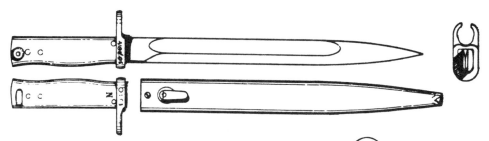

② *ERSATZ M.1916*

KIESLING VOL. I #205
CARTER PG. 28 #39

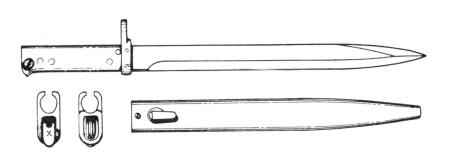

④ *ERSATZ M.1916*

KIESLING VOL III #590
CARTER PG. 32 #49

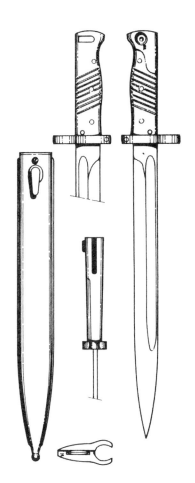

③ *ERSATZ M.1916*

KIESLING VOL I #191
CARTER PG. 26 #34

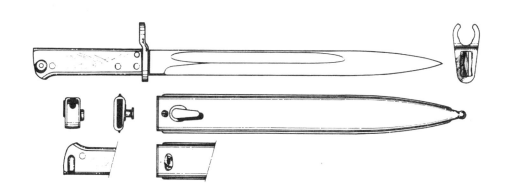

No. 1. **ERSATZ MODEL 1916.** THIS IS ANOTHER UNUSUAL TYPE WITH PRESSED STEEL GRIPS AND WITH GUARD SWEPT BACK. IT IS PROBABLY ONE OF THE MOST EYE APPEALING OF THE ENTIRE ERSATZ GROUP. IT FITS THE SAME RIFLES AS THE PRECEDING PIECES. THE ERSATZ SCABBARD SHOWS A DECLINE IN QUALITY WITH NO BALL FINIAL.

No. 2. **ERSATZ MODEL 1916.** THIS CAST STEEL HANDLE HAS A DOUBLE GUARD CONSTRUCTION AND A FATTER GRIP. THE BLADE IS FULLERED. THIS BAYONET FITS THE GEW 88 AND 98 AS WELL AS THE FRENCH LEBEL RIFLES.

No. 3. **ERSATZ MODEL 1916.** SIMILAR TO NO. 2 BUT WITH SLIGHTLY DIFFERENT GRIPS AND THE BLADE IS UNFULLERED. IT FITS THE GEW 88 AND 98 AS WELL AS THE LEBEL.

No. 4. **ERSATZ MODEL 1917.** THIS UNUSUAL EPEE ERSATZ HAS BEEN FITTED WITH A BRITISH SOCKET BLADE AND IS QUITE SCARCE. THE GRIPS ARE SLAB STEEL HELD BY THREE RIVETS. IT FITS THE GEW 98 AND GEW 88.

① *ERSATZ M. 1916*
KIESLING VOL. I #192
CARTER PG. 30 #47

② *ERSATZ M. 1916*
KIESLING VOL. I #216
CARTER PG. 14 #3

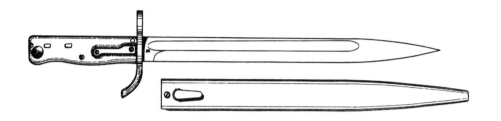

③ *ERSATZ M. 1916*
KIESLING VOL. I #205
CARTER PG. 14 #5

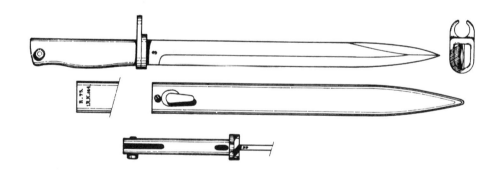

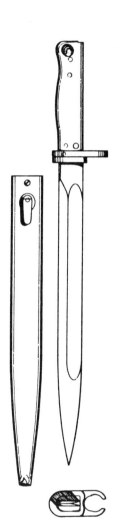

④ *ERSATZ M. 1917*
KIESLING VOL. III #650
CARTER PG. 44 #70

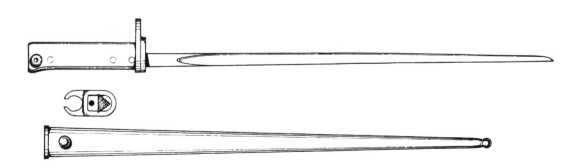

No. 1. **ERSATZ MODEL 1917.** THIS ALL STEEL HILT WITH SEVEN DIAGONAL GROOVES MACHINED INTO IT HAS HAD THE BLADE SHORTENED. HOWEVER, IT WILL STILL FIT A RIFLE. IT FITS THE GEW 98, GEW 88 AND THE FRENCH LEBEL.

No. 2. **ERSATZ MODEL 1917.** THIS SLAB-SIDED, TWO-PIECE CON-STRUCTION ERSATZ HAS HAD ITS MUZZLE RING REMOVED. WHETHER THROUGH DAMAGE OR NECESSITY IS NOT KNOWN. IT HAS A METAL SCABBARD WITHOUT BALL FINIAL. THIS BAYONET WILL ONLY FIT THE GEW 98.

No. 3. **ERSATZ MODEL 1915.** THE BRASS CAST GRIPS ARE QUITE SCARCE AND THIS MODEL WAS SUPPOSEDLY USED BY THE POLICE. IT HAS A SINGLE DIAMETER MUZZLE RING WHICH ALLOWS FOR USE ON THE GEW 98 ONLY. THE BLADE IS UNFULLERED.

No. 4. **ERSATZ MODEL 1917.** THIS IS ANOTHER VARIATION OF 92-3, HOWEVER, IS OF A MORE SIMPLE CONSTRUCTION AND WAS PROBABLY MANUFACTURED LATE IN THE WAR.

① *ERSATZ M.1917*

KIESLING VOL. III #593
CARTER PG. 34 # 53

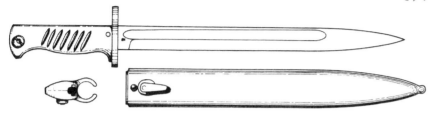

③ *ERSATZ M.1915*
BRASS HANDLE

KIESLING VOL. I # 219
CARTER PG. 22 #21

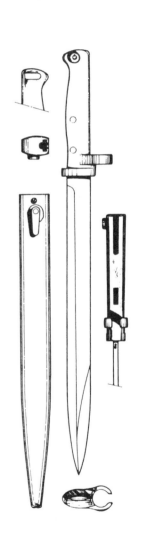

② *ERSATZ M.1917*
M.R. REMOVED

CARTER PG 20 # 18

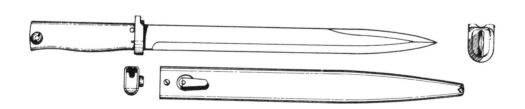

④ *ERSATZ M.1917*

KIESLING VOL III #592
CARTER PG. 26 # 36

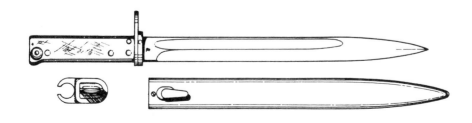

No. 1. ERSATZ MODEL 1915/18. THIS UNUSUAL PIECE IS A COMBINATION BAYONET AND TRENCH KNIFE. THESE WERE COMMERCIALLY SOLD BY DEMAG (DEUTSCHE MACHINEN FABRIK AG.) IN DUISBURG. IT IS COMMONLY CALLED THE "CRANK-HANDLE" FOR OBVIOUS REASONS. IT FITS THE GEW 98. THE SCABBARD COMBINES THE FROG WITH IT. (VERY GOOD REPRODUCTIONS OF THIS WEAPON WERE PRODUCED IN LATE 1986.)

No. 2. ERSATZ MODEL 1915/18. THIS IS ANOTHER COMBINATION BAYONET AND TRENCH KNIFE. IT HAS A STRAIGHT, ALL METAL HANDLE PAINTED FIELD GRAY WITH A BLACK ENAMELED SCABBARD. THIS IS A VERY SCARCE PIECE AND WAS OBVIOUSLY MANUFACTURED IN VERY SMALL QUANTITIES.

No. 3. ERSATZ MODEL 1915/18. ANOTHER DEMAG-PRODUCED COMBINATION BAYONET/TRENCH KNIFE WHICH I CONSIDER RARE. IT IS BOWIE-BLADED WITH THE HANDLE OF STAMPED METAL CONSTRUCTION AND THIN WOOD GRIPS AFFIXED BY RIVETS. THE EXAMPLE IN MY COLLECTION HAS AN EXTENDED CROSSGUARD. OTHER REFERENCE WORKS SHOW THIS PIECE WITHOUT THE CROSSGUARD AND CARTER REFERENCES AN EXAMPLE WITH A REVERSED CROSSGUARD. I SUSPECT THESE GUARDS WERE EASILY BROKEN AND THE CONFIGURATION ILLUSTRATED IS ORIGINAL. (THE CONDITION OF THE PIECE IN MY COLLECTION IS VERY GOOD.)

No. 4. TRENCH KNIFE-BAYONET COMBINATION. THESE WERE COMMERCIALLY SOLD AND USUALLY CARRIED BY OFFICERS. I HAVE SEVERAL VARIATIONS, SOME I SUSPECT WERE MANUFACTURED AFTER WW I. THE COMBINATION FROG-SCABBARD IS SIMILAR TO THE PRECEDING PIECE. PROPERLY MADE, IT FITS THE GEW 98.

① ERSATZ M. 1915/18

KIESLING VOL I #8
CARTER PG 12 #1

② ERSATZ M. 1915/18

KIESLING VOL. I #9
CARTER PG 12 #2

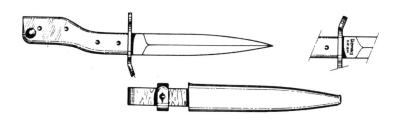

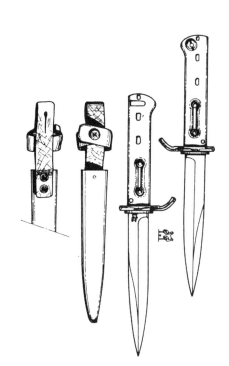

③ ERSATZ M. 1915/18

KIESLING VOL. IV #732

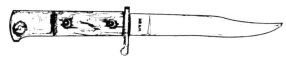

DEMAG
DUISBURG

D.R.G.M.

④ TRENCH KNIFE · BAYONET COMBINATION

KIESLING VOL. III #502

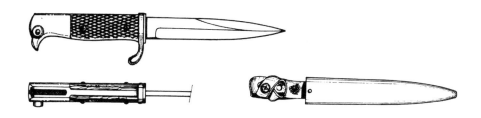

95

No. 1. GREEK MODEL 1903 - CONVERSION. THE GERMANS REHILTED THIS BLADE TO FIT THE GEW 98 AND DESIGNATED IT AS A M-1914 BAYONET. IT WAS USED PRIMARILY BY THE BAVARIANS AND ISSUED EARLY IN THE WAR. THE SCABBARD APPEARS SIMILAR TO THE GEW 98, WITH BLACK LEATHER BODY AND STEEL MOUNTS.

No. 2. FRENCH MODEL 1874 - GRAS CONVERSION. A NEW HILT AND CROSSGUARD ALLOW THIS FORMER FRENCH BAYONET TO FIT THE GEW 98. MUCH WORK WAS REQUIRED TO ADAPT THIS BLADE WHICH IS PROBABLY WHY SO FEW ARE SEEN (DANGRE LISTS ELEVEN SEPARATE CHANGES). THE SCABBARD IS FRENCH ARMY ISSUE.

No. 3. FRENCH MODEL 1874 - GRAS CONVERSION. A SOLID BRASS-CAST GRIP AND NEW CROSSGUARD HAVE BEEN ADDED TO THIS BLADE. LATER, DUE TO THE SCARCITY OF MOST METALS, THESE BAYONETS WERE RECALLED FOR THEIR BRASS CONTENT. THESE FIT THE GEW 98 AND GEW 88.

No. 4. BELGIAN MODEL 1882 - CONVERSION. THIS BELGIAN BAYONET HAS BEEN EXTENSIVELY MODIFIED FOR CONVERSION USING A MINIMUM OF SEVEN STEPS. IT WAS USED ON THE EASTERN FRONT FOR A SHORT WHILE IN 1917. IT HAS THE ORIGINAL BELGIAN SCABBARD AND FITS GEW 1898 RIFLE.

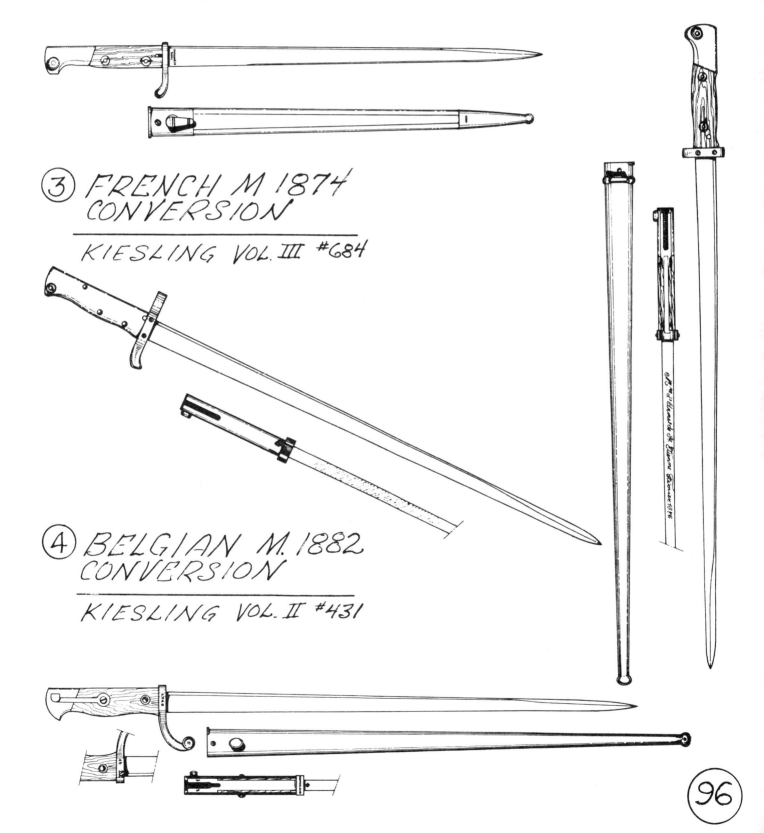

① *GREEK M.1903 CONVERSION*

KIESLING VOL.II #303

② *FRENCH M.1874 CONVERSION*

KIESLING VOL.III #686

③ *FRENCH M 1874 CONVERSION*

KIESLING VOL.III #684

④ *BELGIAN M.1882 CONVERSION*

KIESLING VOL.II #431

No. 1. **FRENCH MODEL 1866 – CHASSEPOT CONVERSION.** FOLLOWING THE FRANCO-PRUSSIAN WAR, ENORMOUS NUMBERS OF THESE BAYONETS WERE CLAIMED AS WAR REPARATIONS BY THE GERMANS. DURING WW I, COUNTLESS VARIATIONS WERE MADE OF THIS PIECE. THIS PARTICULAR CONVERSION FITS THE OLD MODEL PRUSSIAN CARBINE. THE SCABBARD HAS BEEN MODIFIED BY REPLACING THE FROG STUD.

No. 2. **FRENCH MODEL 1866 – CHASSEPOT CONVERSION.** THIS IS AN UNUSUAL CONVERSION IN THAT THE MUZZLE RING TOP HAS BEEN REMOVED, ALLOWING IT TO FIT THE GEW 88. THE POMMEL HAS BEEN NOTCHED TO FIT. THIS PIECE WAS ISSUED TO THE LANDSTURM AND IS CONSIDERED QUITE SCARCE.

No. 3. **AUSTRIAN MODEL 1895.** THIS BAYONET WAS MANUFACTURED BY ERNST BUSCH COMPANY IN GERMANY IN 1917, VERY POSSIBLY FOR GERMAN TROOPS UTILIZING THE AUSTRIAN '95 STRAIGHT-PULL RIFLE ON THE EASTERN AND ITALIAN FRONTS DURING WW I. IT IS STAMPED "W/17" ON THE BACK OF THE BLADE. THE SCABBARD IS OF AUSTRIAN MAKE.

① FRENCH M. 1866 CONVERSION

KIESLING VOL. II #463

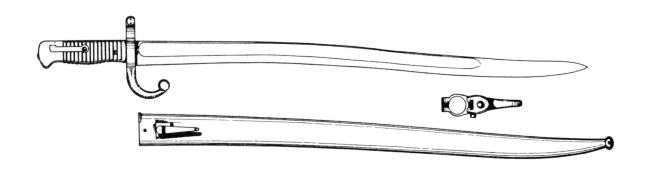

② FRENCH M. 1866 CONVERSION

KIESLING VOL II #461

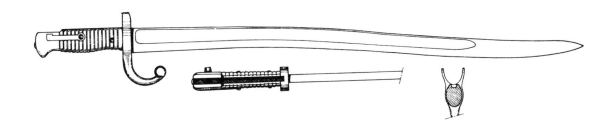

③ AUSTRIAN M. 1895 GERMAN ISSUE

WALTER PG. 82

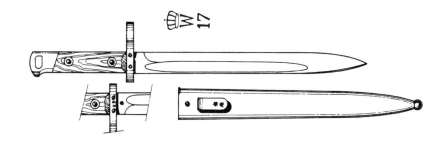

No. 1. ELABORATE DRESS BAYONET - POST WORLD WAR I. THE POMMEL HAS BEEN CHASED INTO AN EAGLE'S HEAD AND THE BLADE ETCHED AND BLUE PANELED. THE EAGLE HAS RED STONES INSET IN THE EYES. THESE ARE QUITE SCARCE.

No. 2. EXPORT MODEL 1884/98. OBVIOUSLY MADE FOR EXPORT WITH THE ADDITION OF A MUZZLE RING WHICH THE GERMANS HAD DONE AWAY WITH FOR THEIR OWN RIFLES. IT DOES NOT HAVE A FLASH GUARD. THESE FIT THE CZECH. VZ 24, SHORT RIFLE, AMONG OTHERS.

No. 3. "SNEAK" MODEL 1884/98. ANOTHER IDENTICAL TO THE ABOVE EXCEPT FOR THE ABSENCE OF THE MUZZLE RING, WHICH WAS REMOVED AND NOT MANUFACTURED THIS WAY. THIS MODEL ALSO HAS NO FLASHGUARD. THE GERMANS FOUND THAT NOT ONLY DID THE FLASHGUARD PREVENT MUZZLE FLASH BURNS TO THE GRIP BUT IT ALSO PROTECTED THE GRIPS FROM SPLITTING WHEN USED AS A HAMMER. THE "SNEAK" MODELS WERE WEAPONS WHICH WERE SUPPOSEDLY FOR EXPORT OR COMMERCIAL SALES, HOWEVER, WERE MARKED AND USED BY THE GERMAN-ARMED FORCES.

① GERMAN M. 1920 DRESS

WATTS & WHITE #391

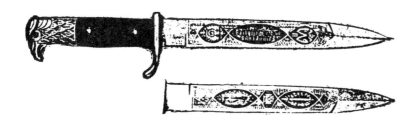

② GERMAN M. 84/98 EXPORT

KIESLING VOL IV #814
WALTER PG. 88

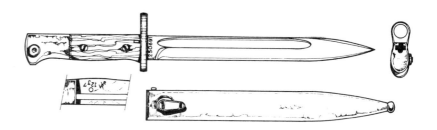

③ GERMAN M. 84/98 "SNEAK" MFG

KIESLING VOL. IV #815
WALTER PG. 88

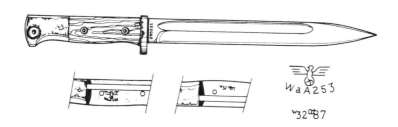

WaA253

ᵂ32°87

No. 1. **MODEL 1884/98 - REICHWEHR.** THE J. R., "1920" AND WEIMAR EAGLE SHOWS THIS TO BE A REICHSWEHR CONVERSION TO THE M-84/98 2ND PATTERN BAYONET USED BETWEEN WW I AND WW II BY THE WEIMAR MILITARY AND POSSIBLY THE POLIZEI. THEY ARE ALMOST ALWAYS FOUND WITH ALL METAL PARTS BLUED, AS IS THE METAL SCABBARD.

No. 2. **MODEL 1898/05 N/A - REICHWEHR.** THESE BAYONETS WERE BLUED AND STAMPED "1920" ON THE CROSSGUARD. APPARENTLY ONLY PLAIN OR "GROUND" MODELS WERE REISSUED TO THE REICHWEHR AND I HAVE BOTH. SOME OF THE ISSUED PIECES WERE RENDERED NONFUNCTIONAL BY CUTTING A NOTCH IN THE POMMEL.

NOTE: THE BAYONETS USED BY THE WEIMAR WILL BE ENCOUNTERED WITH A DATA (GENERALLY "1920" OR "1921") STAMPED ON THE CROSSGUARD. THESE DATES SHOW THEY HAVE BEEN INVENTORIED UNDER THE TERMS OF THE VERSAILLES TREATY.

① GERMAN M. 1884/98 REICHWEHR

WALTER PG. 88·89
WELSER PG. 4 #9

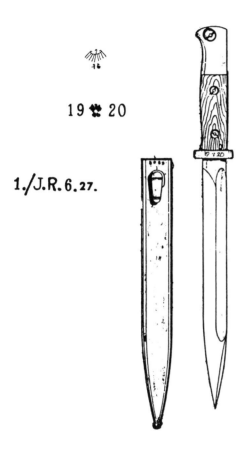

19 ✿ 20

1./J.R.6.27.

② GERMAN M. 1898/05 REICHWEHR

WELSER PG. 3 #5

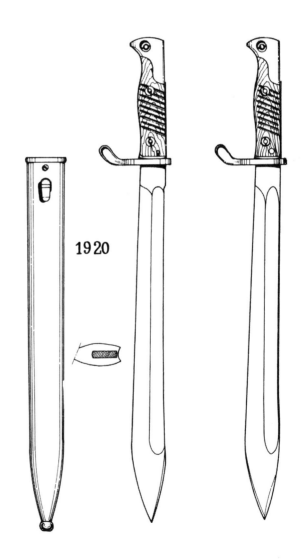

1920

No. 1. MODEL 1884/98 – 3RD PATTERN. THIS BAYONET WAS MANUFACTURED IN IMMENSE NUMBERS, ORIGINALLY IN "S" CODES, THEN WITH THE ACTUAL MANUFACTURER NAMES AND, FINALLY, WITH A LETTER CODE. THE EARLY BLADES WERE MADE WITH WOODEN GRIPS. THE BLUED STEEL SCABBARD HAD MATCHING CODE AND SERIAL NUMBERS ORIGINALLY, BUT FEW ARE STILL FOUND TOGETHER.

No. 2. MODEL 1884/98 – 3RD PATTERN. THIS IS IDENTICAL TO No. 1 EXCEPT FOR THE GRIP MATERIAL WHICH WAS A PETROLEUM-BASED COMPOSITION, CHOCOLATE BROWN ORIGINALLY, BUT LATER IN THE WAR BECOMING REDDER AND, FINALLY, ORANGE IN COLOR. THEY BOTH FIT THE KAR 98K AND, IN CASES WHERE STILL ISSUED, THE KAR 98A2.

No. 3. MODEL 1884/98 – 3RD PATTERN LATE WAR. IDENTICAL TO No. 2 EXCEPT THE GRIPS ARE ATTACHED WITH RIVETS. I HAVE SEEN ONLY FOUR MANUFACTURERS WHO USE THIS MEANS OF GRIP ATTACHMENT ("SGX", "CUL", "CVL" AND "ASW"). THE MAJORITY OF THESE PIECES HAVE A PHOSPHATE FINISH.

No. 4. CZECH VZ-24 – CONVERSION. THIS PIECE HAS GERMAN STAMPS ON BOTH THE BLADE AND SCABBARD. IT WAS CONVERTED IN CZECHOSLOVAKIA UNDER THE GERMAN OCCUPATION BECAUSE THE PROOF IS SIMPLY AN EAGLE AND SWASTICA.

① GERMAN M. 1884/98
WOOD GRIPS

KIESLING VOL. I #142

② GERMAN M. 1884/98
COMPOSITION GRIPS

KIESLING VOL. I #143

③ GERMAN M. 1884/98
RIVETED GRIPS

WELSER PG. 9 #14

④ CZECH. VZ·24
GERMAN MARKED

KIESLING VOL. I #196
WELSER PG. 16 #18

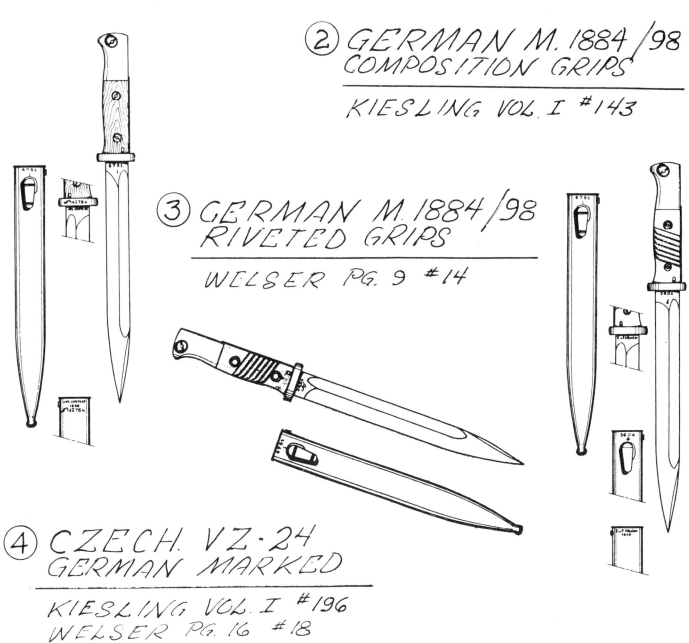

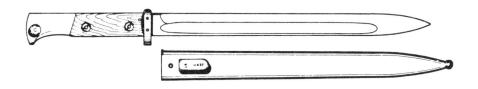

No. 1. MODEL 1898/05/40. DUE TO THE CONTINUING INCREASE OF MEN INTO THE WEHRMACHT AND LUFTWAFFE, 1940 SAW THE REFURBISHING AND USE OF THE M-98/05S. THE BLADES AND SCABBARDS WERE REFURBISHED AND, IN MOST CASES, THE ORIGINAL MARKS WERE UNTOUCHED. THESE WERE PRINCIPALLY ISSUED TO THE LUFTWAFFE AND REAR ECHELON PERSONNEL. THE BUTT OF THIS BAYONET HAS THE LUFTWAFFE EAGLE COMBINED WITH THE LETTERS "L.S." STAMPED ON IT.

No. 2. POLISH WZ1924 - CONVERSION. GERMANY UTILIZED THE POLISH WZ 24 BY REMOVING THE MUZZLE RING, BLUEING ALL METAL PARTS AND, IN SOME CASES, ADDING FLASHGUARDS TO THE GRIPS.

No. 3. MODEL 1942 - SEITENGEWEHR. THE GERMANS HAVE ALWAYS EXPERIMENTED WITH MULTI-USAGE BAYONETS AND IN 1942 CAME UP WITH THIS EXPERIMENTAL TOOL/BAYONET COMBINATION WITH COMPOSITION GRIPS. THE TOOLS WERE STORED WITHIN THE GRIP. THE SCABBARD, AT FIRST, WAS A COMBINATION OF PRESSED PAPER AND METAL; LATER TYPES OF THIN STEEL. THE SG 42 IS ONE OF THE RAREST GERMAN BAYONETS.

No. 4. MODEL 1942 - FALLSCHIRMJAGERGEWEHR. THIS IS COMMONLY KNOWN AS THE FG 42 AND THE PIECE IN MY COLLECTION IS THE FINAL MODEL OF THE THREE SPIKE BAYONETS USED ON THIS SPECIAL PARATROOP RIFLE OF WHICH ONLY 10,000 WERE MADE.

① GERMAN M. 1898/05/40
LUFTWAFFE ISSUE

CARTER PG. 56

L. S.

② POLISH WZ 1924
CONVERSION

WELSER PG 17 #21

③ GERMAN M. 1942
SG 42

KIESLING VOL. IV #754

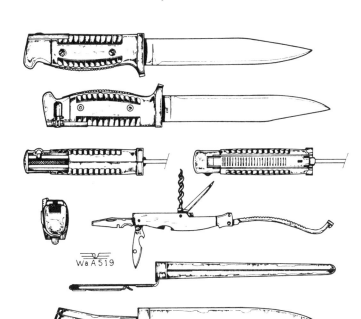

WaA519

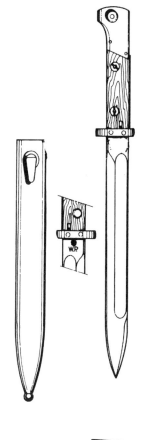

WaA 883

④ GERMAN M. 1942
FG 42

WELSER PG. 21 #30
WALTER PG. 94

No. 1. POLIZEI SEITENGEWEHR – 1920-1934. THIS IS THE STANDARD WEIMARIAN POLICE BAYONET AND HAS THE EAGLE OF THE WEIMAR REPUBLIC EMBLEM ON THE STAG GRIPS. MOST OF THESE WERE CONVERTED BY THE NAZIS. THIS PIECE IS FUNCTIONAL AS A BAYONET.

No. 2. POLIZEI SEITENGEWEHR – 1920-1940. THESE BAYONETS WERE MADE FROM 98/05S AND WERE ELABORATELY CHASED ON THE POMMEL AND GUARD. STAG GRIPS AND A CLAM-SHELL LANGUET WERE ADDED AND ALL METAL PARTS NICKLE PLATED. THESE ARE QUITE SCARCE. THE SCABBARDS ARE LEATHER WITH PLATED METAL MOUNTS. THE COLORS WERE BLACK OR BROWN FOR URBAN OR RURAL POLICE. THESE BAYONETS HAD THE WEIMER EMBLEM REPLACED BY THE NAZI POLICE VERSION. I HAVE BOTH LONG AND SHORT VER-SIONS AND CONSIDER THE LONG VARIATION RARE.

No. 3. POLIZEI SEITENGEWEHR – 1939-1945. THE CLAMSHELLS WERE REMOVED BY THE NAZIS AND THEIR OWN EMBLEM SUBSTITUTED FOR THE WEIMAR EAGLE ON THE GRIPS. MOST OF THESE WERE MEANT TO BE WORN AS A SIDE ARM ONLY AND NEVER MEANT FOR ATTACHMENT TO A RIFLE. I HAVE TWO EXAMPLES – ONE SLOTTED FOR A RIFLE AND ONE UNSLOTTED.

① GERMAN M. 1920/34 WEIMAR POLICE

KIESLING VOL IV #1040

② GERMAN M. 1920/40 CLAMSHELL POLICE

KIESLING VOL IV #1039

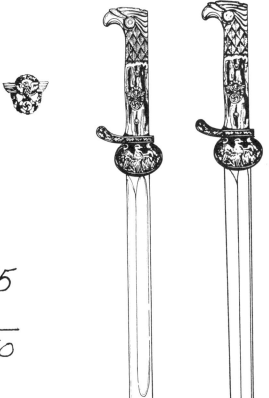

③ GERMAN M. 1939/45 NAZI POLICE

KIESLING VOL IV #1040

No. 1. DRESS BAYONET. ALL WHO COULD AFFORD "DRESS" OR "WALKING OUT" BAYONETS WERE ALLOWED TO PURCHASE AND WEAR THEM OFF DUTY. THIS IS A VERY EARLY (KURZES) VERSION WITH THE GRIPS HELD BY THREE RIVETS AND A POLISHED BLADE.

No. 2. DRESS BAYONET. THIS IS THE MOST COMMON VERSION WITH ALL METAL PARTS PLATED AND THE GRIPS HELD BY TWO RIVETS. THEY FIT A METAL, BLACK-LACQUERED SCABBARD. THE MOST COMMON BLADE LENGTH WAS TEN INCHES. LENGTH MAY HAVE SIGNIFICANCE AS TO RANK. I HAVE EXAMPLES OF THIS BAYONET WHICH ARE BOTH FUNCTIONAL AND NONFUNCTIONAL.

No. 3. DRESS BAYONET. THIS WAS A SHORTER VERSION OF No. 2. THE REASON FOR THE DIFFERENT LENGTHS IS NOT REALLY KNOWN BUT A SHORT BLADE ALLOWED ONE TO SIT MORE COMFORTABLY.

No. 4. DRESS BAYONET. A THIRD VARIANT IS THE "CARBINE BLADE" STYLE. SOLINGEN HAD A BLADE FOR EVERY TASTE AND EVERY POCKET BOOK.

① GERMAN M. 1930
DRESS

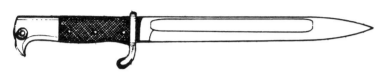

② GERMAN M. 1938
DRESS · LONG

KIESLING VOL IV #1034

③ GERMAN M. 1939
DRESS - SHORT

KIESLING VOL IV #1037

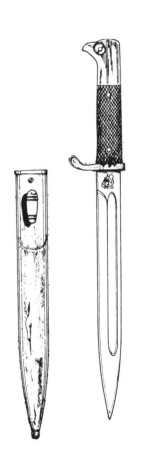

④ GERMAN M. 1940
DRESS - CARBINE

WALTER & HUGHES #164

No. 1. **DRESS BAYONET.** THE SCARCEST OF THE DRESS BAYONETS ARE THOSE WITH THE VARIOUS WORKER ORDERS OR "FRONTS". THIS EXAMPLE HAS THE "DEUTSCHE ARBEIT FRONTE" EMBLEM ON THE GRIP.

No. 2. **DRESS BAYONET.** SOME MANUFACTURERS PREFERRED A DIFFERENT MEANS OF ATTACHING THE GRIPS. THE SCREW-BOLTS IN THIS VARIANT ALLOWED THE GRIPS TO BE MORE EASILY REPLACED IF BROKEN.

NOTE: THE TRODDEL, OR BAYONET KNOT, WAS IMPROVED AND USED BY THE THIRD REICH (SEE ILLUSTRATION ON THE RIGHT). A COMPLETE DESCRIPTION OF THESE KNOTS CAN BE FOUND IN T. M. JOHNSON'S BOOK <u>COLLECTING THE EDGED WEAPONS OF THE THIRD REICH</u> (SEE BIBLIOGRAPHY PG. 251).

① GERMAN DRESS
D.A.F.

KIESLING VOL IV #1035

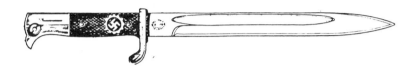

② GERMAN DRESS
SCREW BOLTS

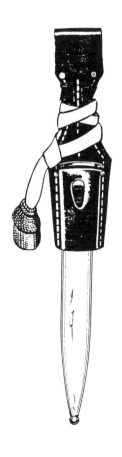

No. 1. DRESS BAYONET. ANOTHER VARIANT DRESS SHORT BAYO-
NET, CIRCA 1936. IT HAS STAGHORN GRIPS WITH A
"CARBINE-TYPE" BLADE.

No. 2. DRESS BAYONET. MANY MANUFACTURERS OFFERED ETCHED
DRESS BLADES OF THE VARIOUS REGIMENTS OR UNITS FOR
THE SOLDIERS OR FOR PRESENTATION BY LOVED ONES.
THE ILLUSTRATED PIECE IS ENGRAVED TO A FLAK REGI-
MENT. THE ONE IN MY COLLECTION IS ENGRAVED TO THE
41ST INFANTRY REGIMENT.

No. 3. DRESS BAYONET. THROUGHOUT GERMAN HISTORY, AWARDS
HAVE BEEN MADE WITH EDGED WEAPONS. THIS IS A
"SCHUTZEN" AWARD FOR A TOP MARKSMAN. THE AWARD AND
DATE ARE ETCHED INTO THE BLADE. THE GRIPS ARE OF
STAG HORN AND THE CROSSGUARD DOES NOT HAVE THE
UPSWEPT QUILLON.

No. 4. DRESS BAYONET. THIS IS ANOTHER DRESS VARIANT WHERE
THE BLADE HAS AIRPLANES ETCHED INTO ONE SIDE AND
THE VERY COMMON INSCRIPTION - "ZUR ERINNERUNG AN
MEINE DIENSTZEIT" (IN MEMORY OF MY SERVICE TIME)
ETCHED ON THE OTHER. THESE ENGRAVING PATTERNS WERE
AVAILABLE IN THE VARIOUS COMPANY CATALOGS AND WERE
SELECTED BY NUMBER.

① GERMAN DRESS
STAGHORN GRIPS

KIESLING VOL. IV #1037

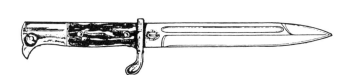

② GERMAN DRESS
ENGRAVED BLADE

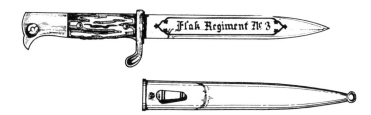

Flak Regiment Nr 3

③ GERMAN AWARD
MARKSMANSHIP

STEPHENS PG 96 #201

④ GERMAN DRESS
ENGRAVED BLADE

Zur Erinnerung an meine Dienstzeit

No. 1. FIREMAN'S DRESS DAGGER - SAWBACK. THE FIREMAN'S DAGGER IS NOT A TRUE BAYONET, BUT SINCE THEY WERE WORN IN THE SAME MANNER AS A DRESS BAYONET, THEY ARE INCLUDED HERE. THE SHORT SAWBACK BLADE IS QUITE SCARCE. FIREMAN DAGGERS ARE THE ONLY NAZI SIDE ARM TO HAVE THE "S" SHAPED GUARD.

No. 2. FIREMAN'S DRESS DAGGER. THIS IS A MORE COMMON FIREMAN'S DRESS DAGGER WITHOUT THE SAWBACK. THE GRIPS ARE CHECKERED COMPOSITION HELD BY TWO RIVETS. ALL METAL PARTS ARE NICKEL PLATED. THE SCABBARD IS BLACK-LACQUERED STEEL.

MANUFACTURER'S NOTE:

NUMEROUS FIRMS MANUFACTURED THE EDGED WEAPONS WHOSE WEAR WAS PROMOTED BY THE NAZIS. THE MAKERS REPRESENTED IN MY COLLECTION INCLUDE THE LARGE PRODUCERS, SUCH AS COPPEL & EICKHORN, AND SOME LESS KNOWN FIRMS, SUCH AS ANTON WINGEN AND ROBERT KLAAS. I WOULD SPECULATE, BASED ON MY OBSERVATION, THAT BETWEEN 80 AND 100 TRADEMARKS EXIST (MANY ARE VARIATIONS OF THE SAME MAKER, SUCH AS EICKHORN, WHICH HAS FOUR DIFFERENT TRADEMARKS REPRESENTED IN MY COLLECTION).

① GERMAN DRESS FIRE DEPT.-SAW

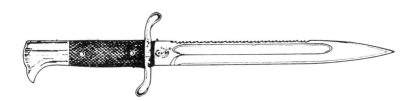

② GERMAN DRESS FIRE DEPT.-PLAIN

KIESLING VOL. IV #1030

TYPICAL GERMAN TRADEMARKS

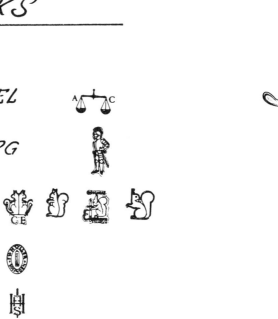

ALEXANDER COPPEL

WILHELM CLAUBERG

CARL EICKHORN

F. W. HÖLLER

E & F HÖRSTER

ROBERT KLASS

LAUTERJUNG

ERNST PACK

WEYERSBERG, KIRSCHBAUM

106

No. 1.   **MINIATURE BAYONETS.**   THESE WERE PRODUCED AFTER WW I AS EXPORT ITEMS.   THEY WERE PROBABLY USED AS LETTER OPENERS, DESK ORNAMENTS OR SALES SAMPLES.

ONE IS ENGRAVED "IN MEMORY OF MY SERVICE TIME", IN GERMAN;

ONE IS MARKED "MADE IN JAPAN";

ONE IS A COMMON EXAGGERATED FACSIMILE OF THE WORLD WAR II GERMAN DRESS BAYONETS;

ONE IS A RECENT REPLICA OF THE M1884 WITH SQUARE FULLERS;

ONE IS A VERY ACCURATE REPLICA OF A MODEL 1884/98 BAYONET WITH A WORKING CATCH WHICH IS MARKED "BERG-FELD & HOPPE" ON ONE SIDE AND "DR. FRANZ GILLIAN" ON THE OTHER.

① GERMAN MINATURES

STEPHENS BK. I #126
R. D. C. EVANS PGS. 226.227

No. 1. MODEL G3 - RHEINMETALL. THIS IS A VERY EARLY EXAM-
PLE OF THE G3 BAYONET SERIES AND WAS MANUFACTURED
BY RHEINMETALL WHO ALSO HELD THE DISTINCTION OF
BEING THE SECOND GERMAN MANUFACTURER OF THE G3
RIFLE. THIS IS PROBABLY THE RAREST OF THE G3
SERIES.

No. 2. MODEL G3 - HECKLER AND KOCH. THIS POST-WW II BAYO-
NET WAS MADE FOR USE WITH THE G3 ASSAULT RIFLE.
ATTACHMENT IS BY A SMALL STUD IN THE POMMEL. THE
SCABBARD IS A COPY OF THE U.S. M8 A1 AND HAS A
WOOD-PATTERN ON THE PLASTIC BODY.

No. 3. MODEL AG3-L - HECKLER AND KOCH. ANOTHER G3, BUT
WITH A LONG DOUBLE-EDGED BLADE FOR EXPORT, CIRCA
1980. THE SCABBARD IS IDENTICAL TO No. 1 EXCEPT
THAT IT IS LONGER.

No. 4. EAST GERMAN AKM. THIS IS A GERMAN VERSION OF THE
RUSSIAN AVTOMATA KALASHNIKOVA MODIFICATSIONNIYA.
IT IS A COMBINATION OF THE RUSSIAN OLD AND NEW
PATTERNS AND IS BLACK IN COLOR.

① GERMAN G-3
RHEINMETALL
KIESLING VOL. I #63

② GERMAN G-3
H & K - SHORT
KIESLING VOL I #42

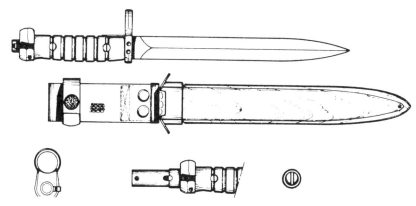

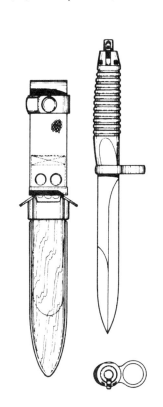

③ GERMAN AG3·L
H & K - LONG
RDC EVANS PG. 176

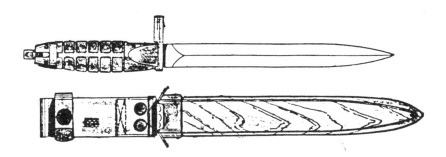

④ EAST GERMAN AKM
RDC EVANS PG. 163

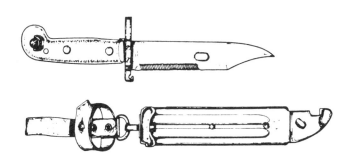

No. 1. **STONER EXPORT BAYONET - KCB-70M1.** THE STONER MODEL 63 ASSAULT RIFLE WAS EXPORTED, PRIMARILY TO THE NETHERLANDS, WHERE IT BECAME THEIR MODEL KCB-70-M1. THE BAYONET WAS A JOINT PROJECT OF EICKHORN AND THE DUTCH FIRM OF "NWM". THE WIRE-CUTTER BLADE IS USED IN CONJUNCTION WITH THE SCABBARD. THIS BAYONET WAS ALSO DESIGNED FOR THE COLT M16 RIFLE AND GIVEN EICKHORN'S NUMBER CE 9110. THE MARK IS THE EICKHORN "SQUIRREL" ABOVE THE "NWM" OF NEDERLANDSE WAPEN MUNITIEFABRIEK.

No. 2. **STONER EXPORT BAYONET - KCB-77CO.** THIS STONER VARIANT LACKS THE WIRE CUTTER CAPABILITY. CIRCA 1980. THE DUTCH CLASSIFICATION IS KCB-70. THE SCABBARD IS IDENTICAL TO No. 1 SAVE FOR THE WIRE CUTTER, HEAVY-DUTY BODY AND ATTACHMENT.

No. 3. **STONER EXPORT BAYONET - KCB-77LM1.** THIS VARIANT IS CIRCA 1977 AND IS KNOWN TO THE DUTCH AS KCB-70 LONG. IT HAS THE WIRE CUTTER CAPABILITY IN USE WITH THE SCABBARD.

NOTE: THESE BAYONETS WERE ALSO PRODUCED FOR THE BELGIAN FN AND GERMAN G-3 RIFLES.

① *GERMAN STONER*
   KCB · 70M · 1

KIESLING, VOL I # 36
RDC EVANS PG. 173

② *GERMAN STONER*
   KCB · 77CO

RDC EVANS PG. 173

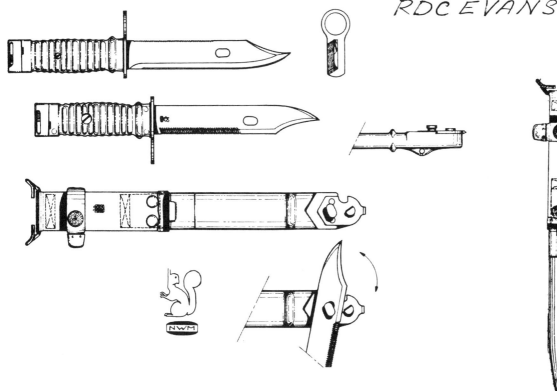

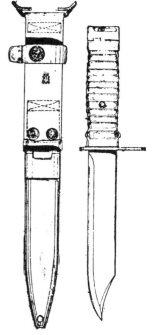

③ *GERMAN STONER*
   KCB · 77 LM1

RDC EVANS PG. 173

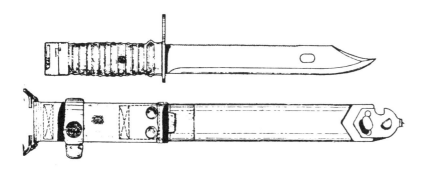

109

No. 1. **C. Eickhorn U.S. M7.** This bayonet was assembled from parts available at the Carl Eickhorn factory at the time of its bankruptcy in 1976. It has a double-edged blade with center ridge and fits both the AR15 and the M16.

No. 2. **A. Eickhorn U.S. M7-L.** This is another double-edged version made with black-checkered, plastic grips. It was manufactured by A. Eickhorn and fits the U.S. M16. The scabbard is also based on the U.S. M8 A1 and has the wood-style plastic body.

No. 3. **A. Eickhorn U.S. M7-S.** This is an unusual wire-cutter bayonet based on the U.S. M7 blade, made circa 1980. The scabbard has the wire hooks for the U.S. ammo belt.

No. 4. **A. Eickhorn U.S. M7.** This is the standard U.S. M7 made for export by Eickhorn circa 1980. The scabbard is the regulation M8A1.

NOTE: These bayonets are also discussed in the U.S. Section, page 232.

① GERMAN EXPORT
FOR U.S. AR·15, M·16
RDC EVANS   PG. 174

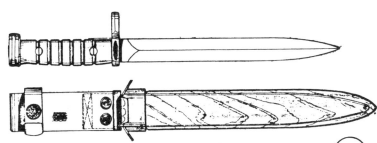

③ GERMAN EXPORT
FOR U.S. M·16

② GERMAN EXPORT
FOR U.S. M·16
RDC EVANS   PG. 175

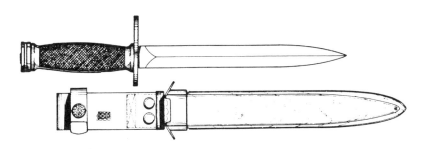

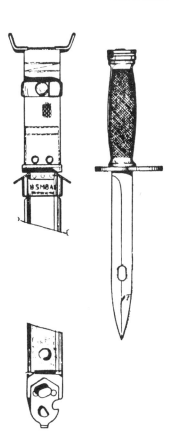

④ GERMAN EXPORT
FOR U.S. M·16
RDC EVANS   PG. 175

No. 1. **GREEK MODEL 1874 - GRAS.** THIS BAYONET IS IDENTICAL TO THE FRENCH 1974 GRAS EXCEPT THAT THE MAKER, ON THE BACK OF THE BLADE, IS "WAFFENFABRIK STEYR". THE DATE IS ALSO ENGRAVED WITH THE MAKER. ALL PIECES SO STAMPED ARE GREEK ISSUE; THE FRENCH ISSUE ARE MARKED "USINE DE STEYR" AND A DATE. IN ADDITION, THERE IS THE TYPICAL GREEK SERIAL NUMBER ON THE CROSSGUARD (CARTER & WALTER NOTE THAT THIS BAYONET WAS ALSO USED WITH THE GREEK MYLONAS' RIFLE).

No. 2. **GREEK MODEL 1874/03 - MANNLICHER.** THIS BAYONET IS A MODIFICATION OF THE GRAS BAYONET WHICH WOULD ALLOW THE PIECE TO FIT A GREEK MODEL 1903 MANNLICHER RIFLE. IN THIS PARTICULAR MODIFICATION, THE HOOK ON THE CROSSGUARD IS RETAINED; HOWEVER, THE MUZZLE RING HAS BEEN REDUCED AND EXTENDED TO FIT THE 1903 AND THE BACK OF THE BRASS POMMEL HAS BEEN GROUND AWAY, AS SHOWN IN THE ILLUSTRATION.

No. 3. **GREEK MODEL 1874/03 - MANNLICHER.** THIS PIECE IS ANOTHER MODIFICATION OF THE GRAS BAYONET TO FIT THE MODEL 1903 AND IS VERY SIMILAR TO No. 2, EXCEPT THAT IN THIS MODIFICATION, THE HOOK HAS BEEN REMOVED FROM THE CROSSGUARD. THESE PIECES APPEAR TO BE MORE COMMON THAN THE MODIFICATIONS WITH THE HOOK.

① GREEK M. 1874
GRAS
KIESLING VOL. III #415

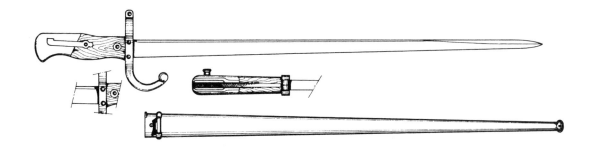

② GREEK M 1874/03
KIESLING VOL IV #945

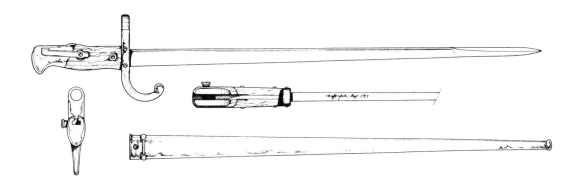

③ GREEK M 1874/03
KIESLING VOL IV #946

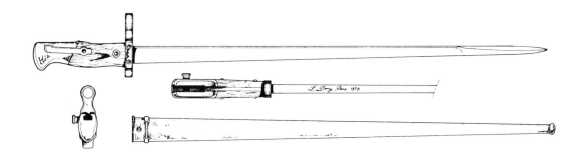

No. 1. **Greek Model 1903.** This bayonet is a conversion of a Greek Gras bayonet and remnants of the maker marking remain on the back of the blade and hilt. A new pommel and very specially shaped handles were fitted on the old Gras blades. These pieces are very easy to spot because of the wide tang on the back of the hilt. I do not know whether this predates or postdates the newly made 1903.

No. 2. **Greek Model 1903.** This is the newly made Model 1903 bayonet and has a slightly different pommel and lighter blade. In addition, the Greek marking of St. George and the Dragon is stamped on the pommel, as shown in the illustration. It appears these bayonets were made by three different manufacturers, although the most common has a star stamp.

No. 3. **Greek Model 1895/03.** This bayonet very closely resembles the Austrian Model 1895 and I possess two, both with the St. George and Dragon stamp; however, one of the pieces has an "anchor" stamped on the crossguard, which I assume designates Greek Navy issue.

① GREEK M. 1903
GRAS BLADE
KIESLING VOL III #635

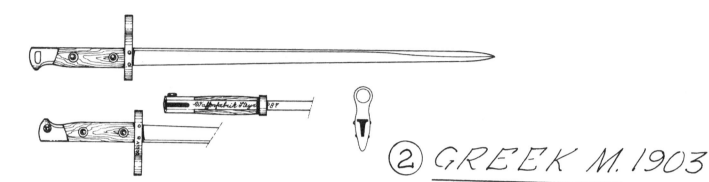

③ GREEK M. 1895
KIESLING VOL I #80

② GREEK M. 1903
KIESLING VOL I #270

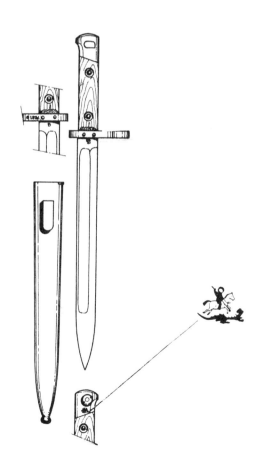

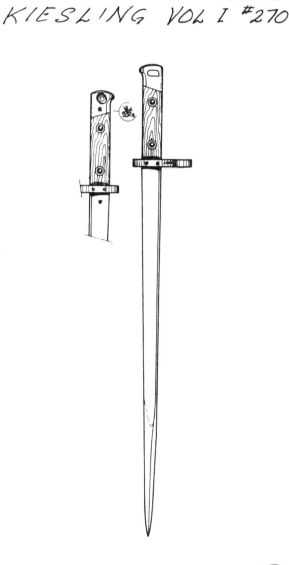

No. 1. HUNGARIAN MODEL 1895 - GENDARMERIE. THIS IS A VERY INTERESTING BAYONET UTILIZING THE AUSTRIAN M-1895 SERIES HILT COUPLED WITH THE BLADE OF AN OLD AUSTRIAN SOCKET BAYONET (KIESLING SAYS THE M-1854 LORENZ). THE HUNGARIAN CREST STAMPED ON THE BLADE IS THE ONLY INDICATION OF HUNGARIAN USE WHICH, BASED ON THE NUMBER ENCOUNTERED, MUST HAVE BEEN VERY LIMITED.

No. 2. HUNGARIAN MODEL 1935 - SERIES. THIS IS A VERY UNIQUE SERIES OF BAYONETS PRODUCED BY HUNGARY FOR THE MANNLICHER RIFLE MODEL 1935. THESE PIECES INCORPORATE THE LOCKING SYSTEM OF THE FRENCH LEBEL BAYONET WITH A WOOD GRIP AND 338MM DOUBLE-EDGED BLADE. I HAVE FOUR DISTINCT TYPES AS ILLUSTRATED. THE INFANTRY VERSION IS ON THE FAR LEFT; THE INFANTRY NCO VERSION, NEXT, INCORPORATES THE AUSTRIAN-STYLE SMALL HOOKED QUILLON AND LOOP ATTACHMENT. THIRD, THE CAVALRY VERSION WHICH COPIES THE AUSTRIAN "SIGHT ON THE CROSSGUARD" CONCEPT; AND FINALLY, ON THE FAR RIGHT, THE CAVALRY NCO VERSION WITH THE SIGHT, SMALL QUILLON AND LOOP ATTACHMENT. THESE WERE OBVIOUSLY PRODUCED IN SMALL QUANTITIES AND ARE SCARCE.

NOTE: HUNGARY CURRENTLY UTILIZES ITS OWN VERSION OF THE RUSSIAN M-1968 (SEE 167-3). THE ONLY REAL DIFFERENCE IS THE PLASTIC GRIPS WHICH ARE OF A CHOCOLATE BROWN COLOR.

① HUNGARIAN M.1895
GENDARMERIE

KIESLING VOL. III #653

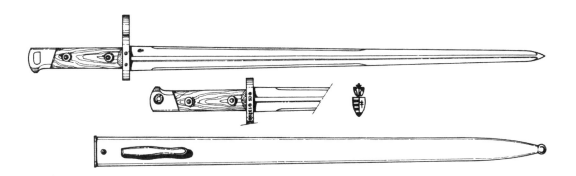

② HUNGARIAN M.1935, SERIES

KIESLING VOL I #233, 234, 235, 236

INFANTRY   INFANTRY NCO   CAVALRY   CAVALRY NCO

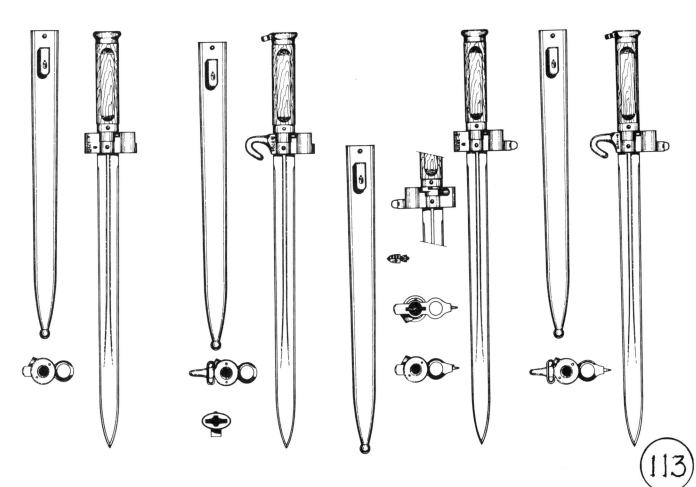

No. 1 and 2.

      Indo-Persian Matchlock Bayonets. These particular bayonets are assumed to be of Indian or Persian origin and were attached to the remnants of some very ancient matchlocks. They are handmade pieces of the period and, interestingly enough, reflect some innovations by the craftsmen of the time which were later copied by European armies.

No. 3.   **Indian Manufactured Pattern 1903.** This bayonet is identical to the British manufactured Pattern 1903s, however, it is "RFI" marked on the butt of the pommel which means that Indian arsenals were producing regulation bayonets prior to World War I.

No. 4.   **Indian Manufactured No. 5. Mark II.** This piece is identical to the British jungle carbine bayonet, however, it is "RFI" marked and has beautiful rosewood grips. It has a 7-13/16" blade and is completely blued. It may have been manufactured for the Sterling submachine gun.

No. 5.   **Indian Pattern L3A3.** This bayonet is an interesting variation of the L3A3 series in that it is identical to the British L3A3, except that it has a 9-7/8" blade and is marked "RFI 65" to "RFI 76". These bayonets were released to the U.S. market in 1984. They have a steel scabbard identical to the other "L" series bayonets, only longer.

Note: See page 59 for Commonwealth bayonets produced in India.

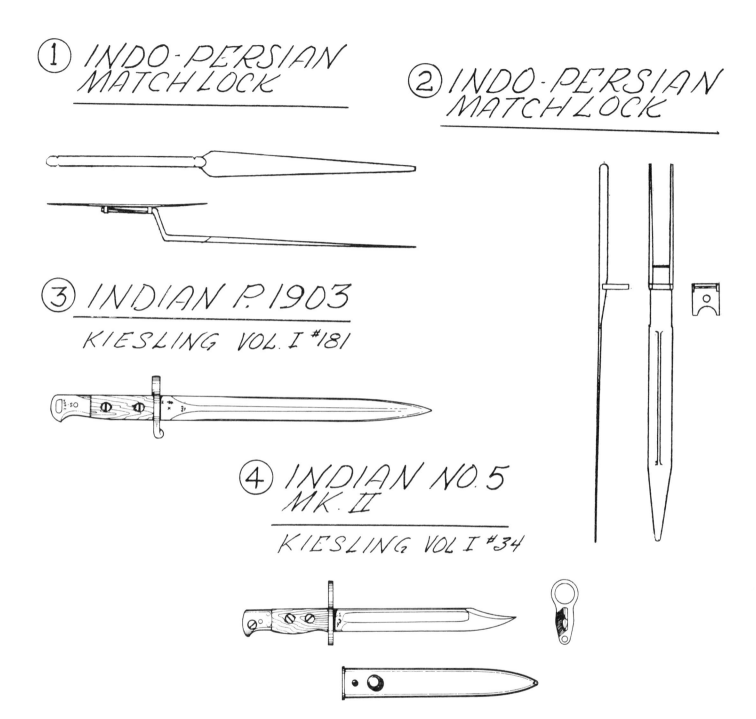

① *INDO-PERSIAN MATCHLOCK*

② *INDO-PERSIAN MATCHLOCK*

③ *INDIAN P. 1903*

KIESLING VOL. I #181

④ *INDIAN NO. 5 MK. II*

KIESLING VOL I #34

⑤ *INDIAN L3A3*

No. 1.   AUSTRIAN MODEL 1904. THIS BAYONET IS IDENTICAL TO
          THE ROMANIAN MANNLICHER; HOWEVER, IT HAS LONG BEEN
          HELD THAT THESE PIECES WERE SHIPPED TO IRELAND
          ALONG WITH MANNLICHER RIFLES DURING THE EARLY 1900
          IRISH REBELLIONS. HENCE, MANY COLLECTORS CALL THIS
          BAYONET THE "IRISH MANNLICHER".

NOTE: R. D. C. EVANS, IN AN ARTICLE IN GUN, WEAPONS &
          MILITARIA, ILLUSTRATED A FRENCH M-1874 GRAS WHICH
          WAS IRISH MARKED "FOR GOD AND ULSTER" (SEE ILLUS-
          TRATION). THESE WEAPONS WERE APPARENTLY ALTERED BY
          THE ULSTER VOLUNTEER FORCE TO FIT BOTH GERMAN
          MAUSER AND ITALIAN VETTERLI RIFLES (SEE 70-1).
          J. A. CARTER ALSO DISCUSSED THESE BAYONETS IN THE
          APRIL 1978 GUNS REVIEW.

① AUSTRIAN M. 1904
IRISH MANNLICHER

KIESLING VOL. III #545

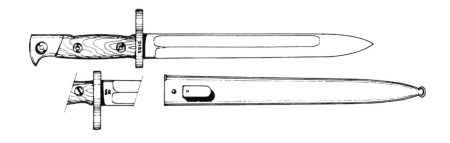

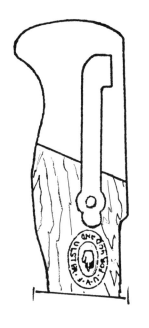

SEE NOTE

No. 1.   ISRAELI CONVERSION 1949. THIS BAYONET IS AN EXAM-
PLE OF ISRAELI CONVERSIONS OF GERMAN 84/98 BAYONETS
TO APPARENTLY FIT THE MAUSER RIFLES USED DURING THE
ISRAELI WAR FOR INDEPENDENCE. IT IS INTERESTING
THAT THE ISRAELIES ADDED A CROSSGUARD WITH A FULL
MUZZLE RING TO THE BAYONETS. THIS PARTICULAR VARI-
ATION UTILIZES THE WOOD-GRIP VERSION OF THE GERMAN
84/98.

No. 2.   ISRAELI CONVERSION 1949. THIS BAYONET IS THE THIRD
MODEL 84/98 WITH THE PLASTIC HANDLE WHICH HAS BEEN
MODIFIED BY ADDING A CROSSGUARD WITH A FULL MUZZLE
RING. ISRAELI MARKS ARE PROMINENT ON BOTH THE
BAYONET AND SCABBARD.

No. 3.   ISRAELI MODEL 1949. THIS IS A NEWLY MADE BAYONET
WHICH HAS BEEN PATTERNED AFTER THE GERMAN MODEL
84/98S, HOWEVER, HAS A MUCH CRUDER FINISH. IT IS
HEAVILY BLUED AND COVERED WITH ISRAELI MARKINGS,
INCLUDING THE STAR OF DAVID.

① *ISRAELI M. 1949 CONVERSION*

KIESLING VOL. I #145

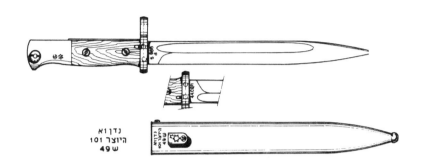

נדן1א
היוצר 101
ש 49

② *ISRAELI M. 1949 CONVERSION*

KIESLING VOL. I #144

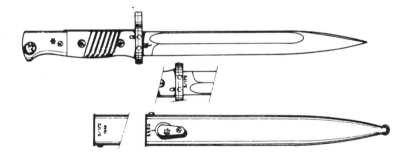

③ *ISRAELI M. 1949 NEW MFG.*

KIESLING VOL I #146

כידון1א
ויוצר 101
ש 49

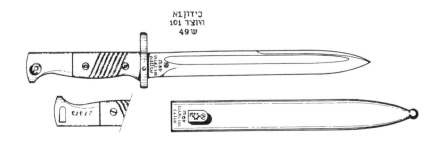

No. 1. **ISRAELI MODEL 1949?.** THIS IS AN ISRAELI ISSUED BELGIUM MODEL 98 EXPORT BAYONET, IDENTIFIED BECAUSE OF THE ISRAELI MARKINGS. IT HAS A DARK BLUE FINISH SIMILAR TO THE PIECES ON PAGE 116.

No. 2. **ISRAELI UZI SUBMACHINE GUN 1952.** THIS IS AN ALL METAL BAYONET FOR THE FN PRODUCED, ISRAELI DESIGNED UZI SUBMACHINE GUN. IT IS 280MM IN OVERALL LENGTH AND HAS A CONVENTIONAL COIL SPRING CATCH UNLIKE THE BELGIAN PRODUCED SERIES OF FN FAL BAYONET. ISRAEL NO LONGER ISSUES A BAYONET WITH THE UZI.

NOTE: THE CURRENT GALIL 5.56MM ASSAULT RIFLE UTILIZES A ONE-PIECE TUBULAR BAYONET SIMILAR TO THOSE ILLUS-TRATED ON PAGE 21 AS ITEMS 1 AND 2. HOWEVER, R.D.C. EVANS ON PAGE 168 OF <u>THE BAYONET, AN EVOLU-TION AND HISTORY</u> STATES THAT THE GALIL HAS BEEN PICTURED IN MILITARY LITERATURE WITH EICKHORN BAYO-NETS ATTACHED BY MEANS OF APPROPRIATE ADAPTERS. THESE BAYONETS ARE ILLUSTRATED ON PAGE 110.

① ISRAELI M.1949 BELGIUM EXPORT

KIESLING VOL I #277

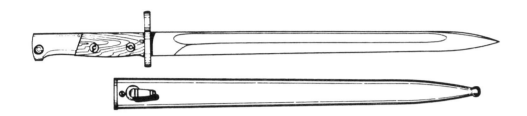

② ISRAELI UZI SUB·MACHINE GUN

KIESLING VOL IV #739

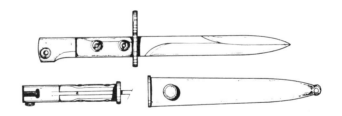

No. 1. PIEDMONT MODEL 1844 - ARTILLERY. THIS BAYONET IS VERY SIMILAR TO THE BRITISH BRUNSWICK WITH A BRASS HANDLE AND DOUBLE-EDGED BLADE. IT IS AN INTERESTING PIECE BECAUSE IT IS ASSOCIATED WITH THE TURBULENT HISTORY OF PREUNIFICATION ITALY. THESE WEAPONS WERE FIRST PRODUCED UNDER THE REIGN OF CHARLES ALBERT, KING OF PIEDONT-SARDINA AND USED IN HIS STRUGGLE WITH AUSTRIA TO UNIFY ITALY. ALTHOUGH INITIALLY ISSUED WITH AN ARTILLERY CARBINE, ACCORDING TO CARTER, THEY WERE MANUFACTURED FOR AT LEAST 22 YEARS AND WHEN THE CARBINES WERE CONVERTED IN 1871 TO THE CARCANO SYSTEM, WERE ISSUED TO THE RESERVES UNTIL 1890, SO WERE USED FOR ALMOST 50 YEARS.

No. 2. ITALIAN M-1870 - VETTERLI CARBINE. THIS SOCKET BAYONET WAS DESIGNED TO FIT UNDER THE BARREL OF THE VV70 CARBINE WHEN NOT IN USE. THIS CARBINE WAS USED PRIMARILY BY THE CARABINERI AND CAVALRY UNITS. IT IS A RELATIVELY SCARCE PIECE AND IS OFTEN FOUND ATTACHED TO THE GUN. KIESLING IDENTIFIES THIS AS A MODEL 1871.

① PIEDMONT M.1844 ARTILLERY

KIESLING VOL II #346

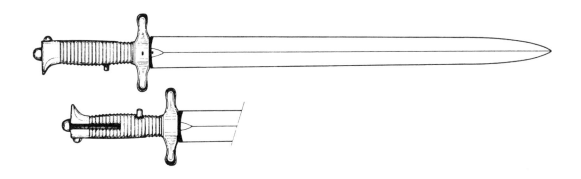

② ITALIAN M.1870 CARABINERI

KIESLING VOL II #883

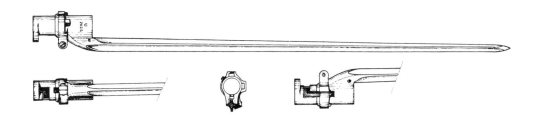

No. 1. **ITALIAN MODEL 1870 – VETTERLI TYPE V.** THIS BAYONET IS THE FIRST OF THE VV70 BAYONET SERIES AND HAS A BRASS HANDLE VERY CLOSELY RESEMBLING THE FRENCH CHASSEPOT BAYONETS. IT IS EQUIPPED WITH A CROSS-GUARD WHICH, ALTHOUGH SIMILAR TO THE REMAINDER OF THE SERIES, IS MORE ORNAMENTAL WITH A SMALL CURL ON THE FRONT SIDE OF THE GUARD AND A TIGHTENING SCREW ON TOP OF THE MUZZLE RING. THE BLADE HAS A VERY LONG FULLER, AS CAN BE SEEN IN THE ILLUSTRATION. THESE PIECES ARE RARE.

No. 2. **ITALIAN MODEL 1870 T.S. – TRUPPE SPECIALI.** THIS PIECE HAS A SHORT CRUCIFORM BLADE AND IS KNOWN AS A "TRUPPE SPECIAL" OR SPECIAL TROOP BAYONET. IT WAS USED IN THE ITALIAN COLONIES AND HAS A HILT IDENTICAL TO THE M-1871 SWORD BAYONET SERIES. THIS BAYONET IS RARE AND MUST HAVE BEEN PRODUCED IN LIMITED QUANTITIES. KIESLING AND CARTER BOTH DESIGNATE THIS A MODEL 1871.

NOTE: THE EARLIER VERSIONS OF THE MODEL 1870/71 SWORD BAYONET SERIES CAN BE FOUND WITH A NOTCH CUT OUT ON THE INSIDE OF THE MUZZLE RING. EARLY VETTERLI RIFLES HAD A REAR STUD FOR THE BAYONET SLOT <u>AND</u> A FRONTAL STUD TO ENGAGE WITH THE NOTCH ON THE MUZZLE RING. THE FRONTAL STUD ON THE RIFLE WAS DISCONTINUED AND LATER BAYONETS WERE MADE WITHOUT THE NOTCH ON THE MUZZLE RING.

① ITALIAN M. 1870 TYPE V

WATTS & WHITE #427

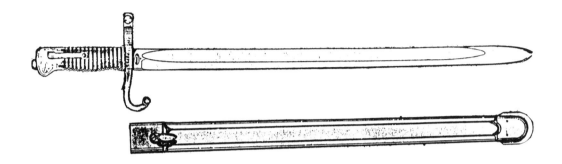

② ITALIAN M. 1870/71 T.S. TRUPPE SPECIALI

KIESLING VOL. III # 576

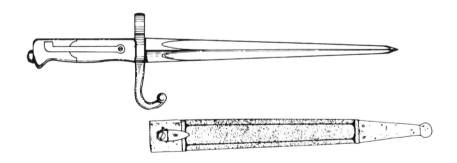

No. 1.   ITALIAN MODEL 1871 - VETTERLI VITALI.   THIS IS THE SECOND
MODEL OF THE VV70 SERIES AND IS FOUND WITH BLACK OR BROWN
COMPOSITION GRIPS, A LONG OR SHORT SPRING AND A MUCH MORE
REFINED BLADE FORM THAN THE EARLIER TYPE V.   THE VERSION WITH
THE SHORT SPRING IS DESIGNATED AS A "TYPE Z".

No. 2.   ITALIAN MODEL 1871/87 - VETTERLI VITALI TYPE U.   THIS PIECE
IS A FURTHER REFINEMENT IN THE VV70 SERIES AND WAS MANUFAC-
TURED WITHOUT THE RETAINING NUT ON THE TOP OF THE HILT.   FOR
SOME REASON, THESE PIECES ARE QUITE RARE.   THE SHORT PRESS
STUD SPRING IS ILLUSTRATED ON NO. 2, HOWEVER, IT IS ASSUMED
THAT THE LONG SPRING COULD ALSO BE FOUND ON THIS MODEL.   THE
"TYPE T" SCABBARD IS ILLUSTRATED.   (THE MARK OF "TORRE
ANNUZIATA" OR THE TORINO ARSENAL AT TURIN IS SHOWN BESIDE
NO. 2 AND IS COMMON ON THIS SERIES.)

No. 3.   ITALIAN MODEL 1871 - SHORTENED WITH QUILLON.   LITTLE IS KNOWN
ABOUT THIS PARTICULAR MODIFICATION EXCEPT THAT THE BLADES
WERE SHORTENED FROM THE ORIGINAL 20-1/4" TO APPROXIMATELY
12", AND THE QUILLON WAS LEFT INTACT.   THESE PIECES ARE ALSO
FOUND WITH A BUSHED MUZZLE RING.

No. 4.   ITALIAN MODEL 1871 - SHORTENED WITHOUT QUILLON.   KIESLING
SAYS THESE BAYONETS WERE FURNISHED TO PARTICIPANTS IN THE
SPANISH CIVIL WAR SOMETIME IN THE 1936/38 TIME FRAME.   THE
WEAPONS THEY WERE USED ON IS A MYSTERY.

① ITALIAN M. 1871
KIESLING VOL II #407

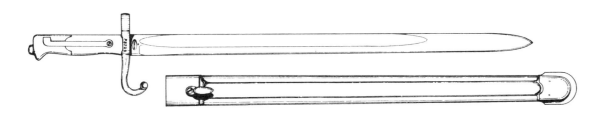

② ITALIAN M 1871/87
TYPE U

TA

KIESLING VOL II #408

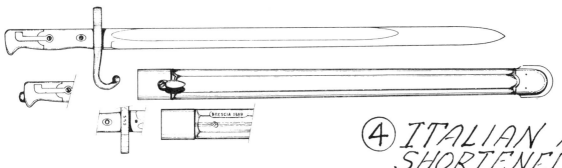

④ ITALIAN M 1871
SHORTENED TO 12"

KIESLING VOL III #598

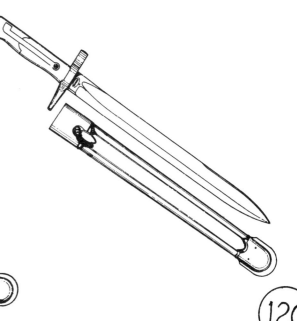

③ ITALIAN M 1871
SHORTENED TO 12"

WATTS & WHITE #440

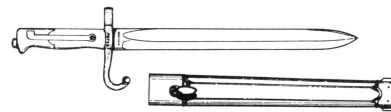

120

No. 1. ITALIAN MODEL 1871/87/1916. A FURTHER MODIFICATION OF THE VV70 SERIES BAYONETS WAS THE MODEL 1871/87/1916 WHEREIN THE ORIGINAL BLADES WERE SHORTENED TO A LITTLE OVER 9" AND THE HOOKED QUILLON REMOVED. THESE PIECES VARY IN CONFIGURATION, INCLUDING BOTH SHORT AND LONG SPRINGS, BRIGHT AND BLUE FINISHES, AND SLIGHTLY DIFFERENT MUZZLE RING CONFIGURATIONS (SOME HAVE A SLOT IN THE RING).

No. 2. ITALIAN MODEL 1871/87/1916. THIS PIECE IS IDENTICAL TO No. 1 EXCEPT THAT THE COMPOSITION GRIPS HAVE BEEN REPLACED BY WOOD GRIPS. THIS MODIFICATION WAS APPARENTLY PERFORMED DURING WORLD WAR I.

No. 3. ITALIAN MODEL 1871/87/1916. THIS PIECE IS IDENTICAL TO No. 2 EXCEPT THE PRESS STUD IS FITTED WITH A LONG SPRING (MODIFICATION OF THE M-1871 TYPE Z).

No. 4. ITALIAN MODEL 1871/87/1916 - ETCHED. THIS ARM IS IDENTICAL TO No. 1 EXCEPT FOR CRUDE ETCHING ON THE BLADE AND SCABBARD MOUNTS. IT IS POSSIBLE THIS VARIATION WAS MANUFACTURED FOR THE SPANISH FASCIST PARTY. I KNOW THAT A NUMBER OF THESE BAYONETS EXIST, SO THE WORK WAS DONE IN SOME QUANTITY.

① ITALIAN M. 1871/87/16
KIESLING VOL. I #82

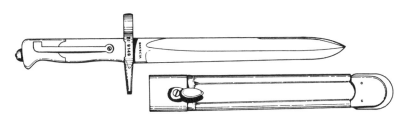

② ITALIAN M. 1871/87/16
SHORT SPRING, WOOD GRIPS
KIESLING VOL IV #800

③ ITALIAN M. 1871/87/16
LONG SPRING, WOOD GRIPS

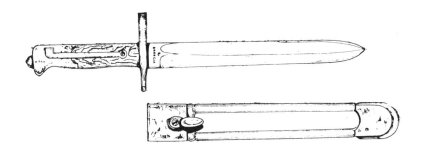

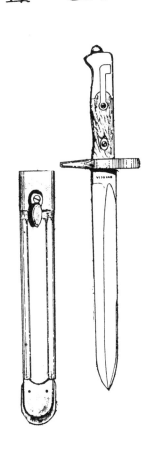

④ ITALIAN M. 1871/87/16
ETCHED BLADE
KIESLING VOL. I #83

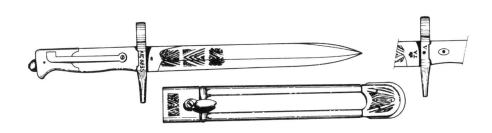

No. 1. ITALIAN MODEL 1891 - CARCANO CARBINE. THIS BAYONET IS THE EARLY VERSION OF THE FOLDING BAYONET USED ON THE M-1891 CAVALRY CARBINES. ON THIS VERSION, THE FORESIGHT IS AFFIXED TO THE BARREL AND THE BAYONET FIXTURE IS ATTACHED BY MEANS OF A SCREW THROUGH THE BACK OF THE FORESIGHT. A SHORT VERSION OF THIS BAYONET WAS UTILIZED ON THE BERETTA 1918/30 SEMI-AUTOMATIC CARBINE.

No. 2. ITALIAN MODEL 1891 - CARCANO CARBINE. THIS IS A LATER EXAMPLE OF THE FOLDING BAYONETS UTILIZED ON THE CARCANO CARBINES AND THIS VERSION UTILIZES A PRESS STUD AND IS PROBABLY THE MOST COMMON FOLDING BAYONET ENCOUNTERED ON THESE WEAPONS.

No. 3. ITALIAN MOSCHETTO "BALILLA" 1891. THIS IS ANOTHER INTERESTING VARIATION OF A FOLDING BAYONET USED ON THE CHILDREN'S CARBINE AND IS ENTIRELY FABRICATED OF BRASS. IT IS APPROXIMATELY THREE-FOURTHS OF THE SIZE OF THE REGULAR CARBINE BAYONET. I ALSO HAVE THE CHILDREN'S BAYONET FABRICATED FROM STEEL WHICH IS SLIGHTLY LONGER.

① ITALIAN M. 1891
FOLDING

KIESLING VOL. III #555

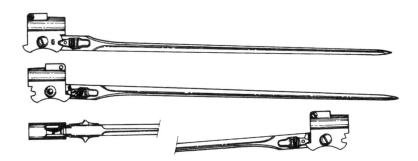

② ITALIAN M. 1891
FOLDING

KIESLING VOL. I #113

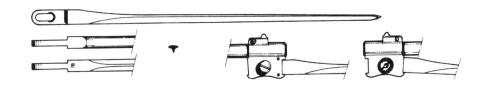

③ ITALIAN M. 1891
CHILDS CARBINE

KIESLING VOL. IV #738

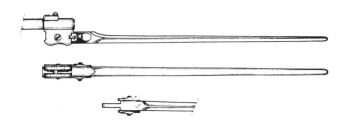

No. 1. **ITALIAN MODEL 1891 - CARCANO.** THIS WAS THE STANDARD ITALIAN BAYONET DURING BOTH WORLD WARS AND WAS MANUFACTURED BY THE MILLIONS. I HAVE IN MY COLLECTION SIX DISTINCT VARIATIONS, INCLUDING DIFFERENT BLADE FULLER FORMS, DIFFERENT TYPES OF LOCKING SLOTS, DIFFERENT FINISHES, AND EVEN SLIGHTLY DIFFERENT SHAPES. THREE OF THE FOUR SCABBARDS UTILIZED WITH THIS AND THE FOLLOWING THREE BAYONETS ARE ILLUSTRATED, WITH THE SMOOTH BLUED VERSION BEING THE MOST SCARCE (THE FOURTH IS BRASS-MOUNTED LEATHER).

No. 2. **ITALIAN MODEL 1891/97 - CARCANO T.S.** THIS BAYONET IS IDENTICAL TO No. 1 WITH THE EXCEPTION OF A VERY UNUSUAL HORIZONTAL SLOT AND A TOP-MOUNTED RELEASE. I POSSESS TWO VARIATIONS OF THIS BAYONET AND HAVE ALSO OWNED ONE OF THE RIFLES. THIS WAS A VERY POOR LOCKING INNOVATION ALTHOUGH YUGOSLAVIA APPARENTLY ALSO UTILIZED THIS RIFLE AND BAYONET.

No. 3. **ITALIAN MODEL 1871/87/16 - VETTERLI VITALI.** THIS LOOKS LIKE A VARIATION OF THE M-1891 SERIES DESCRIBED ABOVE, HOWEVER, WAS ACTUALLY MADE IN LATE WW I TO FIT OBSOLETE VV70 WEAPONS. THIS BAYONET CAN BE FOUND WITH BOTH THE SHORT AND LONG SPRING.

① ITALIAN M.1891 CARCANO

KIESLING VOL. I #160

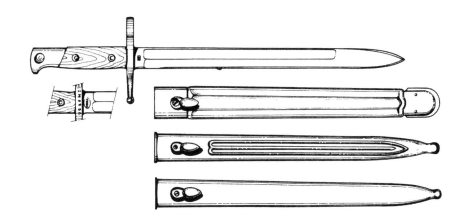

② ITALIAN M.1891/97 T.S.

KIESLING VOL. I #171

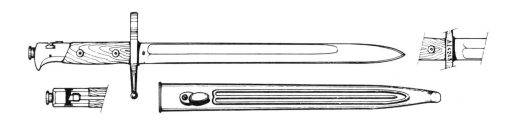

③ ITALIAN M 1871/87/16 BRASS GRIPS

KIESLING VOL. I # 162

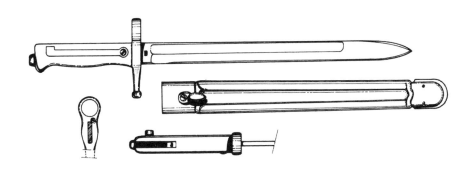

123

No. 1. **ITALIAN MODEL 87/91/15 - VETTERLI.** THIS BAYONET IS MOST UNUSUAL. IT IS THE STANDARD MODEL 91 CARCANO BAYONET FITTED WITH A VV70 CROSSGUARD WHICH HAD TO HAVE BEEN MANUFACTURED SPECIFICALLY FOR THE PIECE. THE POMMEL, WHILE BEING OF THE CARCANO STYLE, HAS A VV70 SLOT. THE MODIFICATION IS VERY WELL DONE AND SUGGESTS THAT THESE BAYONETS WERE PRODUCED IN QUANTITY.

No. 2. **ITALIAN MODEL 1891 - ERSATZ.** THIS IS AN ITALIAN-MANUFACTURED REPLACEMENT BAYONET PRODUCED DURING WORLD WAR I AND UTILIZES THE TIP OF A VV70 BLADE WITH AN ALL STEEL HANDLE AND A VERY UNUSUAL SPRING-TYPE LOCKING DEVICE. THESE BAYONETS ARE RARE.

* **ITALIAN MODEL 1891 - WOOD REPLICA.** THIS IS AN UNUSUAL PIECE AND I HAVE NO CLUE TO ITS SOURCE OR USE.

① *ITALIAN M. 87/91/15*
KIESLING VOL. III #580

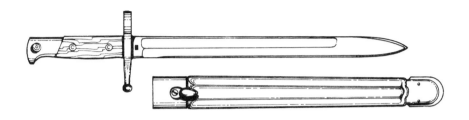

② *ITALIAN M. 1891 ERSATZ*
KIESLING VOL III #500

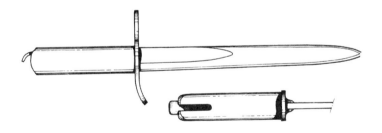

✳ *ITALIAN M. 1891 WOOD REPLICA*

No. 1., No. 2. and No. 3.

ITALIAN MODEL 1938 - MANNLICHER CARCANO. THESE COMPRISE THE MOST COMMON SERIES OF BAYONETS PRODUCED FOR THE MODEL 1938 RIFLE. THE THREE VARIATIONS INCLUDE THE FOLDING BAYONET No. 1, THE NONFOLDING BAYONET WHICH HAS BEEN MODIFIED BY ADDING A NEW CROSSGUARD TO THE FOLDING VERSION DESIGNATED AS No. 2, AND THE VERSION WHICH HAS BEEN PRODUCED AS A NONFOLDING BAYONET DESIGNATED BY No. 3. THESE PIECES ARE COMMON AND COULD BE FOUND IN VIRTUALLY ANY SURPLUS STORE UNTIL APPROXIMATELY THE LAST FIVE YEARS. THIS RIFLE AND BAYONET WAS ALSO USED BY FINLAND. THESE CAN BE IDENTIFIED BY "SA" IN A SQUARE (SEE 66-1).

① ITALIAN M. 1938 FOLDING

KIESLING VOL. I #13

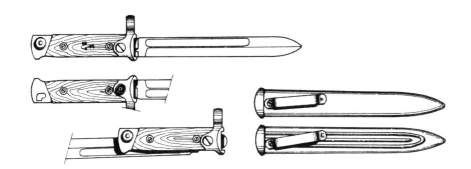

③ ITALIAN M. 1938 FIXED

KIESLING VOL. I #15

② ITALIAN M. 1938 FIXED FOLDING

KIESLING VOL. I # 14

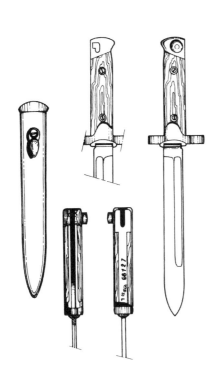

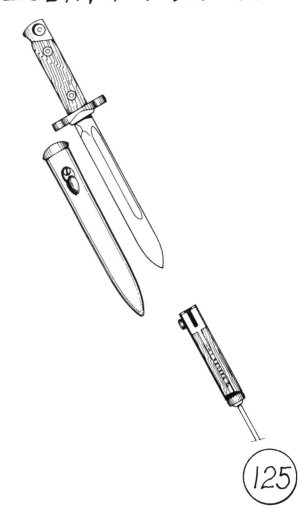

No. 1 AND No. 2.

ITALIAN MODEL 1938 - MANNLICHER CARCANO. THIS BAYONET IS THE MORE UNUSUAL LATCH-LOCK VERSION AND I POSSESS TWO VARIATIONS. ONE IS A FOLDING BAYONET WITH A LATCH LOCK, DESIGNATED No. 1, AND THE OTHER IS A FIXED FOLDING BAYONET WITH A LATCH LOCK DESIGNATED No. 2. THE LATCH LOCK WAS NOT ONLY DIFFICULT TO OPERATE AND FRAGILE BUT WAS ALSO VERY EXPENSIVE TO MANUFACTURE; THEREFORE, THESE BAYONETS ARE RELATIVELY SCARCE.

* ITALIAN TRENCH KNIVES. ITALY UTILIZED OBSOLETE BAYONETS IN THE MANUFACTURE OF TRENCH KNIVES, AS ILLUSTRATED IN THE PHOTOGRAPH. THE MOST INTERESTING (AND COMMON) VARIATION WAS MANUFACTURED FROM THE PIECES REMAINING WHEN THE M-1871 BAYONETS WERE SHORTENED TO THE MODEL 1871/87/16. THE SCABBARD FOR THIS KNIFE WAS ALSO FABRICATED FROM SCABBARD MATERIAL SURPLUSED AS A RESULT OF THIS MODIFICATION. THE SECOND PIECE ILLUSTRATED IS THE ITALIAN MODEL 1938 BAYONET WITH THE GRIPS AND POMMEL REPLACED BY LEATHER WASHERS (THIS MAY NOT BE AN ITALIAN MODIFICATION).

① ITALIAN M. 1938
LATCH LOCK - FOLDING

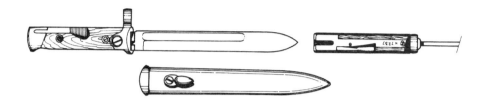

② ITALIAN M. 1938
LATCH LOCK - FIXED

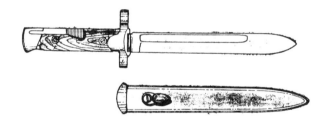

✳ ITALIAN TRENCH KNIVES

No. 1. **ITALIAN MODEL 1938A - BERETTA.** THIS BAYONET WAS PRODUCED FOR THE BERETTA SUBMACHINE GUN AND DIFFERS FROM THE RIFLE MODELS IN THAT THE MUZZLE RING HAS BEEN REPLACED BY AN ATTACHMENT LUG. THESE ARE ALSO RELATIVELY SCARCE; HOWEVER, A BRASS HILTED VERSION EXISTS, WHICH IS RARE.

No. 2. **ITALIAN MODEL 1938A - BERETTA.** THIS IS A VARIATION OF THE BERETTA SUBMACHINE GUN BAYONET AND IS EQUIPPED WITH A LATCH LOCK. THIS BAYONET, HOWEVER, HAS NOTICEABLY DIFFERENT DIMENSIONS AND WAS OBVIOUSLY MANUFACTURED MORE RECENTLY. THE MOST UNUSUAL ASPECT OF THIS PIECE IS THAT THE TOP OF THE HANDLE HAS BEEN MODIFIED TO AID IN UNFOLDING THE BLADE.

① ITALIAN M 1938 A BERETTA SMG

KIESLING VOL I # 43

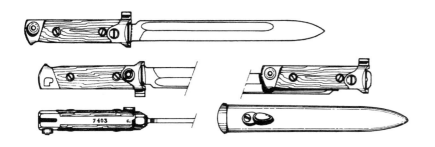

② ITALIAN M. 1938 A BERETTA SMG

KIESLING VOL. III # 514

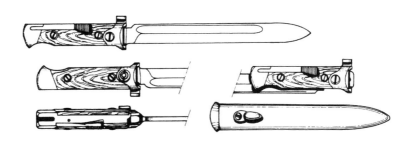

No. 1.   **ITALIAN M1 - GARAND.**   THIS IS THE STANDARD U.S. M-1 GARAND BAYONET; HOWEVER, IT UTILIZES A SCABBARD WHICH IS A COMBINATION OF THE M-91 CARCANO SCABBARD AND THE U.S. GARAND BAYONET SCABBARD. THIS COMBINATION CAN BE NOTED IN THE ILLUSTRATION AND WAS PROBABLY AN ECONOMY MEASURE TO ALLOW THE ITALIANS TO UTILIZE THE U.S. WEB BELTS. THERE ARE NO MARKINGS ON THE BAYONET DIFFERENT FROM THE U.S. MODELS.

No. 2.   **ITALIAN BM59 - BERETTA.**   THIS BAYONET IS A VARIATION OF THE UNITED STATES M1 CARBINE SERIES; HOWEVER, IT HAS A HARD PLASTIC HANDLE AND WAS PRODUCED FOR THE ITALIAN BM59 MARK ITAL RIFLES. DIMENSIONALLY, IT IS IDENTICAL TO THE U.S. CARBINE BAYONETS AND UTILIZES THE SAME TYPE OF SCABBARD. THIS BAYONET IS CURRENTLY USED ON BERETTA ASSAULT RIFLES; THE 5.56MM AR70 AND SC70, FIRST PRODUCED IN 1970 AND NOW USED BY ITALIAN SPECIAL TROOPS.

① ITALIAN M-1 GARAND

KIESLING VOL I #90

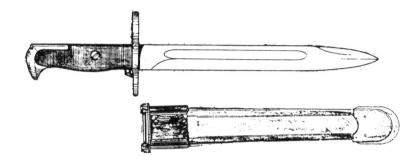

② ITALIAN BM-59 BERETTA

RDC EVANS PG. 161

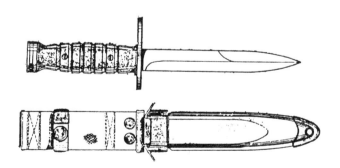

No. 1. THIS IS AN ITEM ADVERTISED IN THE EARLY BANNERMAN CATALOGS AND CONSISTS OF A U.S. MODEL 1873 BAYONET CONVERTED TO FUNCTION AS A CANDLE HOLDER. THE BENDING OF THE BAYONET IS VERY WELL PERFORMED AND THE "BLUE" IS UNHARMED. THE WALL HANGER CONSISTS OF A PLATED BALL MACHINED TO CONFORM WITH THE BLADE SHAPE.

No. 2. THIS ITEM WAS ADVERTISED IN THE 1911 ALFA CATALOG AS A FIREPLACE POKER. IT CONSISTS OF A BELGIUM MODEL 1867 ALBINI BRANDLIN SOCKET BAYONET FITTED WITH A POLISHED WOOD HANDLE. THESE MAY NOT HAVE BEEN BIG SELLERS BECAUSE I HAVE NOTED VERY FEW FOR SALE AT GUN OR ANTIQUE SHOWS.

No. 3. THIS IS A BRASS CANDLE HOLDER, SUPPOSEDLY DESIGNED TO FIT IN THE END OF A U.S. M.1855 SOCKET BAYONET, THUS ALLOWING SOLDIERS TO INSERT THE BAYONET INTO THE GROUND OR A TREE AND HAVE CANDLELIGHT. I SUSPECT THIS INNOVATION WAS SHORT LIVED BECAUSE THIS WOULD BE A BULKY ITEM FOR THE TYPICAL CIVIL WAR INFANTRYMAN.

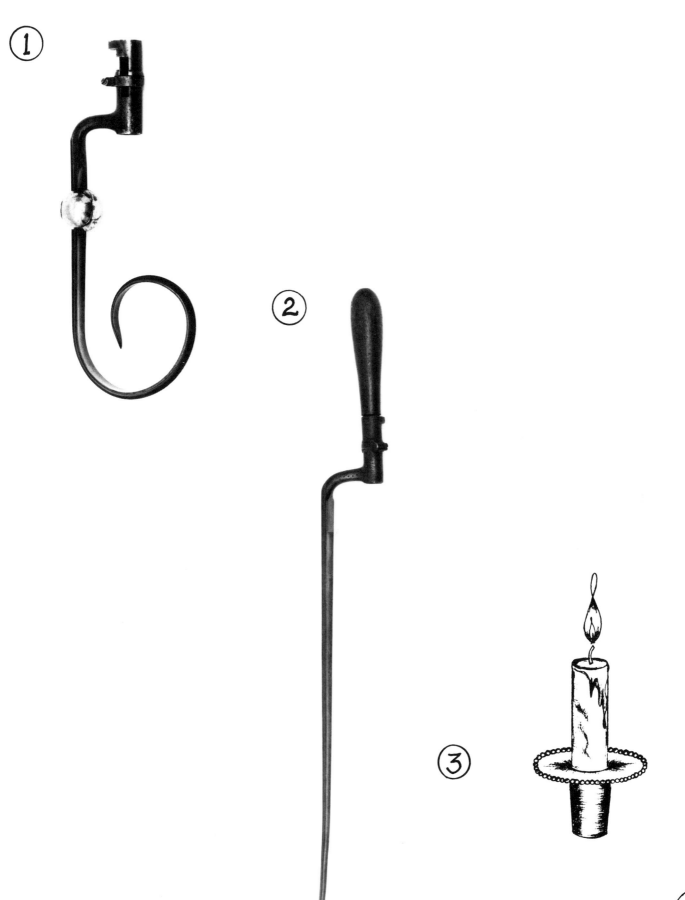

① ② ③

129

No. 1.   JAPANESE PATTERN 1856 - BRITISH ENFIELD PATTERN 1856. THIS BAYONET WAS MANUFACTURED IN GERMANY AND HAS JAPANESE CHARACTERS (NUMBERS) STAMPED ON THE CROSSGUARD. THESE BAYONETS WERE EXPORTED WITH THE RIFLES TO JAPAN IN THE 1860-1870 PERIOD. THE LENGTH IS 27-3/4" AND THERE IS NO MUM.

No. 2.   JAPANESE PATTERN 1856 - COPY OF BRITISH ENFIELD. THIS IS A JAPANESE-MANUFACTURED ENFIELD SABRE BAYONET FOR THEIR COPY OF THE BRITISH PATTERN 1856 MUSKET; 1870-1880 PERIOD. THE ROYAL CHRYSANTHEMUM (MUM) IS ON THE RIGHT CROSSGUARD AND BLADE. THIS BAYONET HAS BEEN SHORTENED TO 16-5/8" AND THE TIP REPOINTED TO A MORE CHARACTERISTIC JAPANESE SHAPE.

NOTE: ALTHOUGH THE ENFIELD WAS THE STANDARD INFANTRY ARM IN 1871, THE JAPANESE UTILIZED SNYDERS AND MARTINIS FROM ENGLAND, DREYSES AND M.1871 MAUSERS FROM PRUSSIA, ALLUMETTES AND CHASSEPOTS FROM FRANCE, ALBINIS FROM BELGIUM AND EVEN MODEL 66 AND 73 WINCHESTERS FROM THE UNITED STATES.

① JAPANESE P. 1856
BRITISH PATTERN

KIESLING VOL. II #479

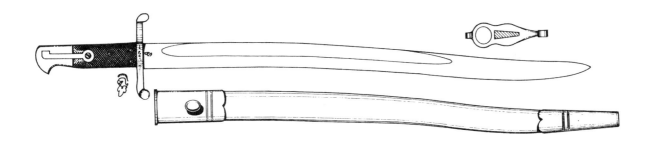

② JAPANESE P. 1856
JAPANESE COPY

WATTS & WHITE PG. 202

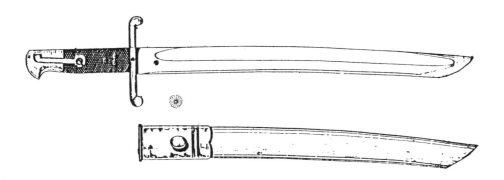

No. 1. **JAPANESE TYPE 13 MURATA 1880.** THE FIRST BAYONET TO BE DEVELOPED IN JAPAN, THIS BAYONET IS FOR JAPAN'S FIRST RIFLE, THE TYPE 13, 11MM SINGLE-SHOT MURATA. THE MUM IS ON THE RIGHT CROSSGUARD. LENGTH IS 28-1/4". THIS PIECE REFLECTS STRONG INFLUENCE FROM THE ITALIAN VV70 (PAGE 120) SERIES OF BAYONETS.

No. 2. **JAPANESE TYPE 13 MURATA 1880 - SHORTENED.** THIS BAYONET IS IDENTICAL TO THE TYPE 13 ABOVE, EXCEPT THAT IT HAS BEEN SHORTENED TO 16". JACK SCHRADER HAS AN EXAMPLE IN HIS COLLECTION WHICH HAS BEEN SHORTENED TO 11" AND HAS THE TIP ROUNDED. I HAVE ALSO SEEN THESE WITH CHECKERED WOOD GRIPS. THIS BAYONET HAS BEEN CALLED A TYPE 16 BY SOME COLLECTORS.

① JAPANESE TYPE 13
MURATA, 1880

KIESLING VOL. IV # 999

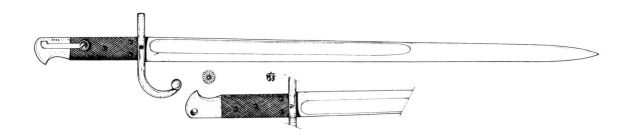

② JAPANESE TYPE 13
SHORTENED

KIESLING VOL IV # 889

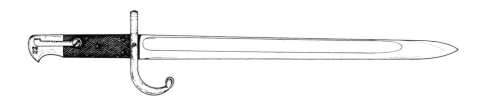

No. 1. JAPANESE TYPE 18 MURATA 1885. THIS BAYONET IS FOR THE TYPE 18, 11MM SINGLE-SHOT MURATA RIFLE. THE MUM IS ON THE RIGHT CROSSGUARD. I HAVE TWO VERSIONS OF THIS; ONE WITH THE MUM, AND ONE WITHOUT. THIS PIECE STRONGLY RESEMBLES THE TURKISH M-1887 (PAGE 191-1).

No. 2. JAPANESE TYPE 22 MURATA 1889 - TYPE I. THIS BAYONET IS FOR THE TYPE 22, 8MM TUBULAR FED MURATA RIFLE. REPORTEDLY ABOUT 20,000 OF THESE WITH A VERY SHORT HILT WERE MADE BEFORE BEING REPLACED WITH THE TYPE II BELOW. THE MUM IS ON THE RIGHT CROSSGUARD.

No. 3. JAPANESE TYPE 22 MURATA 1889 - TYPE II. THIS LATER VERSION HAS A REDESIGNED LONGER HILT. THE BLADE IS IDENTICAL TO THE FIRST VERSION, THE MUM IS ON THE RIGHT CROSSGUARD. THIS REDESIGN WAS REPORTEDLY NECESSARY BECAUSE THE HILT ON THE TYPE I WAS TOO SMALL FOR THE HAND.

① JAPANESE TYPE 18
MURATA 1885

KIESLING VOL IV # 907

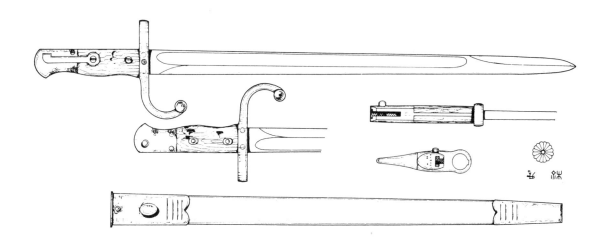

② JAPANESE TYPE 22
MURATA 1889

KIESLING VOL. IV # 784

③ JAPANESE TYPE 22
REDESIGNED HILT

KIESLING VOL. I # 93

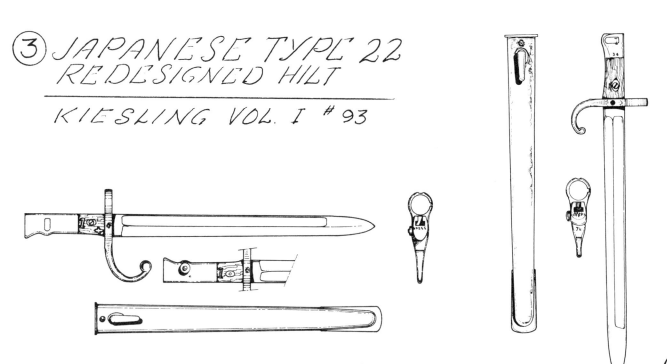

NOTES ON TYPE 30 BAYONETS: THE TYPE 30 SERIES OF BAYONETS WERE INTRODUCED FOR USE WITH THE TYPE 30 ARISAKA RIFLE. THE "30" DESIGNATED THE 30TH YEAR OF THE REIN OF EMPEROR MEIJI AND REPRESENTED THE CALENDAR YEAR 1897. THE RIFLE WAS IMPROVED IN 1905 AND PRODUCED IN SEVERAL VARIATIONS, HOWEVER, THE TYPE 30 BAYONET WAS RETAINED. THE SERIES AVERAGED 20" IN OVERALL LENGTH AND WAS PRODUCED IN 18 DISTINCT MANUFACTURING PATTERNS OF WHICH 12 ARE REPRESENTED IN MY COLLECTION. THESE BASIC TYPES WILL BE PRESENTED ON THE NEXT 4 PAGES FOLLOWED BY THE TYPE 30 TRAINERS AND LATE-WAR TYPES. THE KNOWN ARSENALS ARE SHOWN WITH EACH PIECE, AND IDENTIFIED AND ILLUSTRATED ON THE FACING PAGE.

No. 1. JAPANESE TYPE 30 - ARISAKA. THIS IS THE FIRST MODEL OF THE SERIES AND HAS FULLERS, A HOOK, CONTOUR GRIPS FASTENED BY SCREWS AND A CONTOURED BIRD'S HEAD POMMEL WITH A SERIAL NUMBER ON THE END OF THE POMMEL. THE FIRST VERSIONS HAD THE SERIAL NUMBER ON THE CROSSGUARD, THEN THE BACK STRAP (NUMBERED TO THE RIFLES) AND, FINALLY, THE POMMEL. THESE COME WITH BOTH BRIGHT AND BLUE FINISHED BLADES. THE EARLY TYPE METAL SCABBARD IS ILLUSTRATED.

No. 2. JAPANESE TYPE 30 - ARISAKA. THIS IS AN EARLY MODEL OF THE SERIES AND IS IDENTICAL TO No. 1 ABOVE EXCEPT THAT THE CROSSGUARD IS STRAIGHT WITH NO HOOK. THESE ALSO COME WITH BOTH BRIGHT AND BLUE FINISHED BLADES AND IT IS MY CONTENTION THAT THE HOOK WAS ELIMINATED ON THIS MODEL BECAUSE OF THE PROPENSITY OF THE HOOK TO CATCH VINES AND BRUSH IN JUNGLE CONDITIONS.

JAPANESE ARSENAL MARKS

1. TOKYO ARSENAL PRIOR TO 1936
   KOKURA ARSENAL 1936 – 1945

2. NAGOYA ARSENAL

3. JINSEN ARSENAL

4. MUKDEN ARSENAL

5. NATIONAL DENKI (NATIONAL ELECTRIC)

6. UNKNOWN

7. UNKNOWN COMPANY UNDER KOKURA SUPERVISION

8. NATIONAL DENKI UNDER KOKURA SUPERVISION

9. HOWA JYUKO UNDER NAGOYA SUPERVISION

10. UNKNOWN COMPANY UNDER NAGOYA SUPERVISION

11. TOYADA JIDOSHOKI SEISAKUSHO (TOYADA AUTOMATIC LOOM WORKS) UNDER NAGOYA SUPERVISION

12. UNKNOWN COMPANY UNDER NAGOYA SUPERVISION

① JAPANESE TYPE 30 FIRST PATTERN

KIESLING VOL. I #262

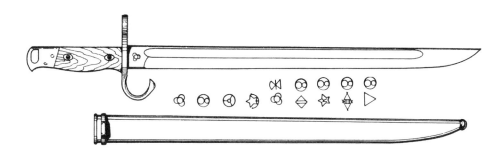

② JAPANESE TYPE 30

KIESLING VOL. I # 263

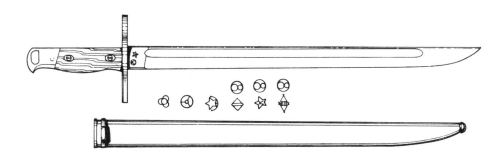

No. 1.   **JAPANESE TYPE 30 - ARISAKA.** THIS IS THE EARLIEST OF THE TYPE 30 SERIES WITH A FLAT BIRD'S HEAD POMMEL, HOOK-TYPE CROSSGUARD AND CONTOUR WRAPAROUND GRIPS FASTENED BY RIVETS. THIS PIECE CAN BE FOUND WITH BRIGHT OR BLUE BLADE. THE SERIAL NUMBER IS STAMPED ON THE END OF THE POMMEL AND FIVE ARSENALS PRODUCED THIS VARIATION. THE LATER TYPE OF METAL SCABBARD IS ILLUSTRATED.

No. 2.   **JAPANESE TYPE 30 - ARISAKA.** THIS IS IDENTICAL TO THE PREVIOUS VERSION EXCEPT THE CROSSGUARD IS STRAIGHT. THIS PIECE CAN ALSO BE FOUND WITH BRIGHT OR BLUED BLADES AND WAS PRODUCED BY TWO ARSENALS. KIESLING STATES THE FLAT BIRD'S HEAD POMMEL/RIVETED GRIP VERSIONS WERE PRODUCED FOR THE TYPE 99 RIFLES, HENCE DESIGNATES THEM AS TYPE 99s.

No. 3.   **JAPANESE TYPE 30 - ARISAKA.** THIS BAYONET RETAINS THE EARLY CONTOUR GRIPS AND POMMEL; HOWEVER, THE BLADE HAS NO FULLERS. THESE WERE PRODUCED BY TWO ARSENALS AND ARE RELATIVELY SCARCE. THE FINISH IS DARK BLUE.

No. 4.   **JAPANESE TYPE 30 - ARISAKA.** THIS PATTERN IS A DISTINCT POINT IN MANUFACTURING DETERIORATION AS WORLD WAR II PROGRESSED. IT RETAINS THE FLAT BIRD'S HEAD POMMEL AND WRAPAROUND GRIPS, FASTENED BY RIVETS, HAS THE STRAIGHT CROSSGUARD, CAN BE FOUND WITH BOTH BRIGHT AND BLUE BLADES, HOWEVER, HAS NO FULLERS ON THE BLADE. THIS PATTERN WAS PRODUCED BY THREE ARSENALS, AS ILLUSTRATED.

① JAPANESE TYPE 30

KIESLING VOL. I # 264

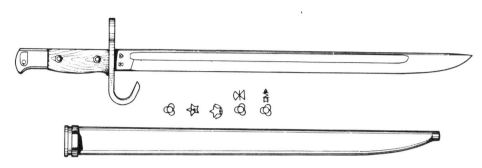

③ JAPANESE TYPE 30

HONEYCUTT PG. 223

② JAPANESE TYPE 30

HONEYCUTT PG. 223

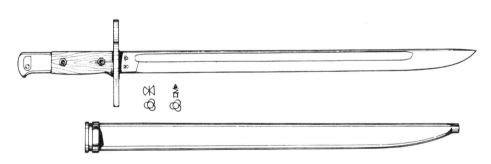

④ JAPANESE TYPE 30

KIESLING VOL. I # 265

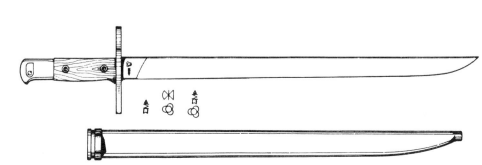

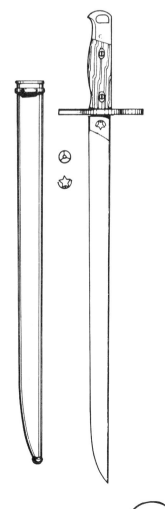

No. 1. JAPANESE TYPE 30 - ARISAKA. THIS VARIATION IS SOMEWHAT OF AN ABERRATION AND IS PROBABLY PRODUCED FROM AVAILABLE PARTS IN THAT IT HAS BOTH THE HOOK CROSSGUARD AND FULLERED BLADE WITH BLUE FINISH, HOWEVER, AT THIS POINT, THE JAPANESE INTRODUCED A MAJOR MANUFACTURING SIMPLIFICATION IN THE FORM OF A RECTANGULAR POMMEL AND CONTOUR WRAPAROUND GRIPS FASTENED BY RIVETS. ONLY JINSEN ARSENAL PRODUCED THIS BAYONET.

No. 2. JAPANESE TYPE 30 - ARISAKA. THIS IS A MORE COMMON VARIATION OF NO. 1 ABOVE AND UTILIZES THE RECTANGULAR POMMEL WITH THE CONTOUR WRAPAROUND GRIPS FASTENED BY RIVETS. IT ALSO HAS A STRAIGHT CROSSGUARD AND BLUE FULLERED BLADE. THE KNOWN ARSENAL MARKS FOUND ON THESE ARE THE TOYADA AUTOMATIC LOOM WORKS UNDER NAGOYA SUPERVISION AND JINSEN.

No. 3. JAPANESE TYPE 30 - ARISAKA. THIS VARIATION IS PRODUCED BY TWO ARSENALS AND INCORPORATES THE FLAT BIRD'S HEAD POMMEL WITH STRAIGHT GRIPS FASTENED BY RIVETS. THE BLADE IS UNFULLERED AND COMES WITH BOTH BRIGHT AND BLUE FINISH. THIS BAYONET HAS ALSO BEEN SEEN WITH A RECTANGULAR CROSSGUARD.

* A VARIATION OF THIS PATTERN WAS PRODUCED FOR THE NAVY T-99 SPECIAL RIFLE AND HAS A DIFFERENT SHAPED STRAIGHT CROSSGUARD AND THE BLADE HAS A FALSE EDGE AS ILLUSTRATED. IT IS FREQUENTLY FOUND WITH THE RUBBERIZED CANVAS SCABBARD. THESE ARE GENERALLY FOUND WITH NO ARSENAL MARKINGS; HOWEVER, A FEW HAVE THE STAR AND ANCHOR MARK.

① JAPANESE TYPE 30
RECTANGULAR POM.

② JAPANESE TYPE 30
HONEYCUTT   PG. 223

③ JAPANESE TYPE 30
KIESLING   VOL. I   #266

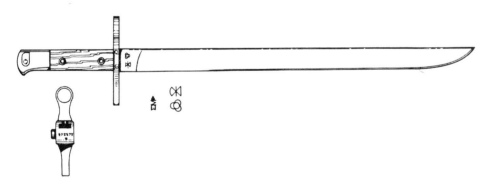

✳ JAPANESE TYPE 30
SPECIAL RIFLE

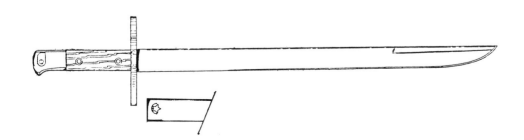

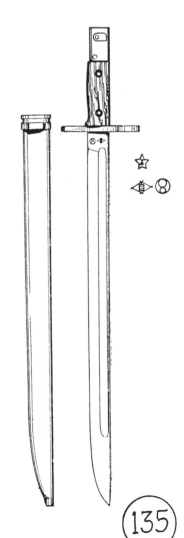

No. 1. JAPANESE TYPE 30 - ARISAKA. THIS IS A LATE-WAR PATTERN INCOR-PORATING A RECTANGULAR POMMEL, CONTOUR WRAPAROUND GRIPS, RIVET FASTENING, STRAIGHT CROSSGUARD AND UNFULLERED BLADE. THIS PIECE HAS A BLUE FINISH AND THE WORKMANSHIP IS CRUDE. THE PIECE ILLUSTRATED IS EQUIPPED WITH A LATE-WAR WOOD SCABBARD.

No. 2. JAPANESE TYPE 30 - ARISAKA. THIS IS A VERY LATE-WAR PATTERN AND HAS VIRTUALLY ALL OF THE MANUFACTURING SIMPLIFICATIONS INCORPORATED. THESE INCLUDE THE BLUE UNFULLERED BLADE, STRAIGHT CROSSGUARD, STRAIGHT GRIPS FASTENED BY RIVETS AND RECTANGULAR POMMEL. TO MY KNOWLEDGE, THIS PIECE WAS PRODUCED BY TWO ARSENALS AND I HAVE ONE EXAMPLE WITH THE SERIAL NUMBER ON THE BACK STRAP.

No. 3. JAPANESE TYPE 30 - ARISAKA. THIS IS ANOTHER VERY LATE MANU-FACTURING PATTERN THAT WAS ONLY PRODUCED BY ONE ARSENAL. IT HAS A BLUE UNFULLERED BLADE, CONTOUR WRAPAROUND GRIPS AND A RECTANGULAR POMMEL. THE UNIQUE FEATURE OF THIS VARIATION IS THE CROSSGUARD WHICH IS FABRICATED OF A RECTANGULAR PIECE OF STEEL. ANOTHER VARIATION EXISTS WITH THE MUZZLE RING SIDE OF THE CROSSGUARD ROUNDED. THIS IS THOUGHT TO BE ONE OF THE LAST ARSENAL-PRODUCED BAYONETS.

① JAPANESE TYPE 30
KIESLING VOL. I #268

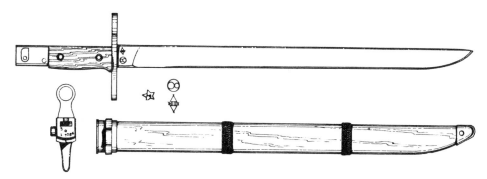

② JAPANESE TYPE 30
KIESLING VOL. III #630

③ JAPANESE TYPE 30
HONEYCUTT PG. 223

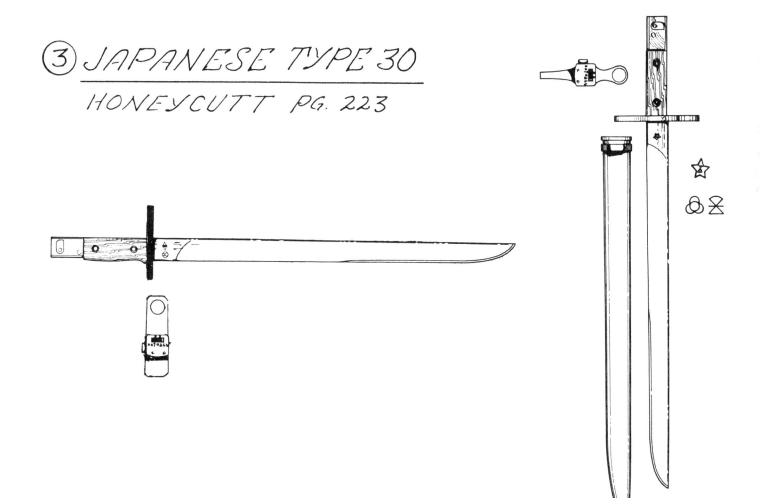

No. 1.   **JAPANESE TYPE 30 - REWORK 1942.** AN EMERGENCY BAYO-
NET WITH A BLADE SIMILAR TO THE DUTCH MODEL 1895
CAVALRY BAYONET. THE BAYONET HAS BEEN DESIGNED TO
FIT THE TYPE 30 ARISAKA RIFLE (IT WILL NOT LOCK ON
THE TYPE 99S). THE BLADE IS STAMPED WITH A
JAPANESE CHARACTER IN A CIRCLE. THE SCABBARD IS A
DUTCH SCABBARD, PROBABLY OBTAINED WHEN THE DUTCH
EAST INDIES WERE OVERRUN IN 1942. THESE BAYONETS
ARE SCARCE.

No. 2.   **JAPANESE TYPE 30 - SHORTENED 1942.** FOR SOME
UNKNOWN REASON, THIS BAYONET HAS BEEN SHORTENED TO
A 9-3/4" BLADE. THE SCABBARD HAS ALSO BEEN SHORT-
ENED. ALL WORK LOOKS PROFESSIONALLY DONE.

No. 3.   **JAPANESE TYPE 100 - SPECIAL PARATROOP MODEL.** THIS
BAYONET WAS DESIGNED DURING THE WAR FOR PARATROOP
USE AS AN ACCESSORY FOR THE TYPE 100 SUBMACHINE GUN
AND IS ALSO REPORTED TO HAVE BEEN USED ON OTHER
PARATROOP RIFLES. THE BLADE IS 7-3/4" LONG AND
THERE IS NO QUILLON OR LOWER CROSSGUARD. IT WAS
PRODUCED BY ONLY ONE ARSENAL (TOYADA AUTOMATIC LOOM
WORKS) WHOSE MARK IS ON THE BACK OF THE HILT.

① JAPANESE TYPE 30
REWORK 1942

KIESLING VOL. III #542

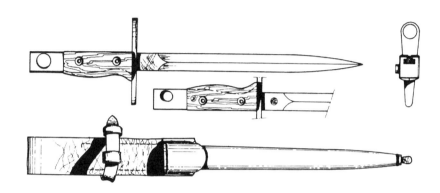

② JAPANESE TYPE 30
SHORTENED 1942

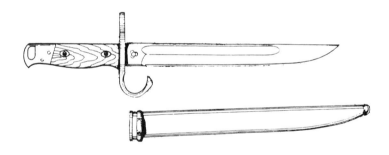

③ JAPANESE TYPE 100
PARATROOP BAYONET

KIESLING VOL. IV # 758

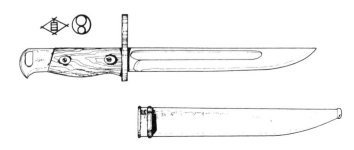

No. 1. **Japanese Type 30 - Training Bayonet.** The Japanese were believers in the training and use of the bayonet; consequently, they produced training bayonets in many variations. Most have a quillon and crude fullers. They have <u>no edge</u> and few are arsenal marked. Two variations are illustrated.

No. 2. **Japanese Type 38 - Child's Trainer.** A scarce bayonet, this fits the children's trainer rifle. The handle is checkered solid metal; the blade is of soft metal and has a dull edge and rounded point. The rifle is a smooth bore Type 38 trainer built on a 7/8 scale. The scabbard is all metal with a ball finial (which is missing on the illustration).

No. 3. and No. 4.

Japanese Type 44 - 1911, Folding Bayonet for Arisaka Carbine. The Type 44 carbine, originally intended for mounted troops, is fitted with a folding bayonet. There are three bayonet variations, all similar except for the housing, which was modified for added strength and improved accuracy of the carbine. The second variation is not illustrated. The mounting screws are quite close, which may have resulted in problems with the stock. This contention is based on the fact that the third variation (also illustrated) has two screws spaced some distance apart. According to Frank Knapp, there were 55000 of the first variation manufactured by Tokyo Arsenal between 1911 and 1923 and only 8000 of the second variation produced (by Kokura). The third and final variation (24500) was manufactured by Kokura and Nagoya.

① *JAPANESE TYPE 30*
TRAINING BAYONETS

② *JAPANESE TYPE 38*
CHILDS TRAINER

KIESLING VOL. I #151

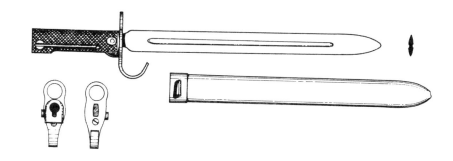

③ *JAPANESE TYPE 44*
FIRST VARIATION

HONEYCUTT PG. 65

④ *JAPANESE TYPE 44*
THIRD VARIATION

KIESLING VOL. I #94

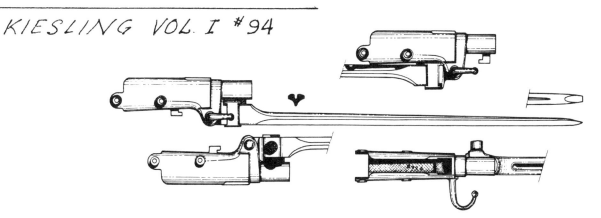

138

No. 1. **JAPANESE POLE BAYONET - MUKDEN.** THIS BAYONET WAS A <u>VERY</u> LAST DITCH WEAPON AND WAS DESIGNED FOR USE WITH A POLE. THERE ARE TWO HOLES IN THE CROSSGUARD, ONE ON EITHER SIDE OF THE HANDLE. THIS BAYONET WAS MADE IN THE MUKDEN ARSENAL IN MANCHURIA AND DIFFERS FROM THE JINSEN-MANUFACTURED POLE BAYONET BELOW. THE BASIC DIFFERENCES ARE THE METAL EXTENSION AT THE END OF THE GRIP AND THE SCABBARD HELD TOGETHER BY STAPLES.

No. 2. **JAPANESE POLE BAYONET - JINSEN.** THIS IS A "POLE BAYONET" MADE LATE IN WORLD WAR II AND WAS INTENDED TO BE LASHED TO A POLE FOR CIVILIAN DEFENSE OF THE HOMELAND. THERE IS NO PROVISION FOR ATTACHMENT TO A RIFLE. THE CROSSGUARD HAS TWO IDENTICAL HOLES, ONE ON EACH SIDE OF THE BLADE. JINSEN ARSENAL MANUFACTURE.

No. 3. **JAPANESE TYPE 30 - MODIFIED ENFIELD.** THIS IS A U.S. M-1917 BAYONET MODIFIED TO FIT THE ARISAKA RIFLE.

No. 4. **JAPANESE S.D.F. 1952 - SELF-DEFENSE FORCE U.S. M1, MARKED "N.P." AND "J" FOR JAPAN.** THIS IS A STANDARD U.S. M1 GARAND BAYONET WHICH WAS MANUFACTURED FOR THE JAPANESE AND IS STAMPED "N.P." FOR NATIONAL POLICE. THESE HAVE BEEN OBSERVED FOR YEARS AT GUN SHOWS IN A DE-MILLED CONDITION; HOWEVER, SARCO APPARENTLY IMPORTED THESE BAYONETS IN 1985.

NOTE: JAPAN CURRENTLY USES THE TYPE 64 ASSAULT RIFLE.

① JAPANESE POLE
MUKDEN

WATTS & WHITE #479

② JAPANESE POLE
JINSEN

WATTS & WHITE #478
HONEYCUTT PG. 222

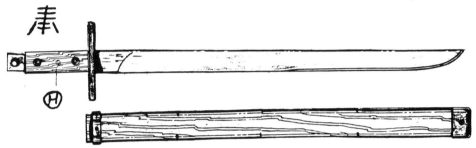

③ JAPANESE TYPE 30
MODIFIED U.S. ENFIELD

HONEYCUTT PG. 219

④ JAPANESE GARAND
S.D.F. 1950

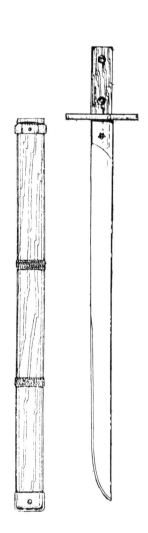

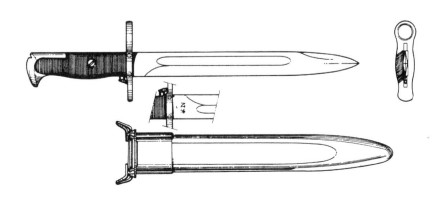

No. 1.   **KOREAN MODEL 1842 - FRENCH WITH KOREAN MARKING.**
This piece is a model 1842 French bayonet with
Korean markings (it is German manufactured, how-
ever, note beehive mark of Samuel Hoppe on blade).

No. 2.   **NORTH KOREAN 1950 - ARISAKA COPY.** This is a North
Korean copy of the Arisaka type 30 bayonet, prob-
ably of the Korean conflict era. This identification is based on characteristics which include a
black enamel finish and a sharpened blade.

No. 3.   **NORTH KOREAN 1950 - ARISAKA COPY.** This is another
Korean copy with the grips held by wood screws on
one side.

① KOREAN M. 1842

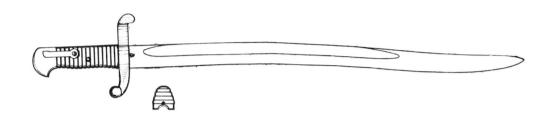

② NORTH KOREAN ARISAKA COPY

WALTER & HUGHES #210

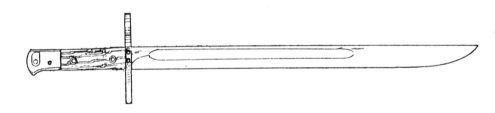

③ NORTH KOREAN ARISAKA COPY

CARTER & WALTER PG. 82

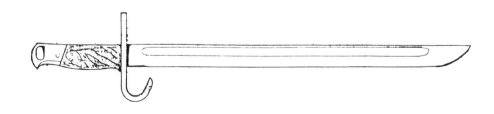

No. 1. **SOUTH KOREAN 1951 - ARISAKA.** THESE BAYONETS ACCOMPANIED THE 133,000 ARISAKA TYPE 99 RIFLES WHICH WERE RECHAMBERED TO U.S. 30-06 FOR USE BY THE REPUBLIC OF KOREA. THE MODIFICATION WAS PERFORMED BY THE TOKYO ARSENAL UNDER U.S. ORDNANCE SUPERVISION BETWEEN JUNE 1951 AND JULY 1952. THE BAYONETS ARE NOT CHANGED, HOWEVER, THE ARISAKA SCABBARD WAS INGENIOUSLY MADE TO FIT THE U.S.-TYPE WEB BELTS.

No. 2. **SOUTH KOREAN M7.** THIS BAYONET IS A KOREAN COPY OF THE U.S. M7 AND IS A VERY HIGH QUALITY WEAPON. IT IS IDENTICAL TO THE U.S. VERSION EXCEPT FOR MARKINGS INCLUDING THE SCABBARD WHICH IS MARKED "KM8AI". THESE PIECES WERE AVAILABLE IN THE U.S. IN THE 1984-85 TIME FRAME, HENCE, WERE PRESUMABLY MANUFACTURED IN THE EARLY 80s.

No. 3. **NORTH KOREAN AK47.** I AM NOT SURE OF THIS DESIGNATION; HOWEVER, R. D C. EVANS, ON PAGE 163 OF THE BAYONET INDICATES THESE WERE MANUFACTURED BY NORTH KOREA. IT IS A VERY UNUSUAL PIECE AND IS A CROSS BETWEEN AN AK, AN AKM AND EARLIER COMMUNIST BLOCK MODELS.

① SOUTH KOREAN ARISAKA

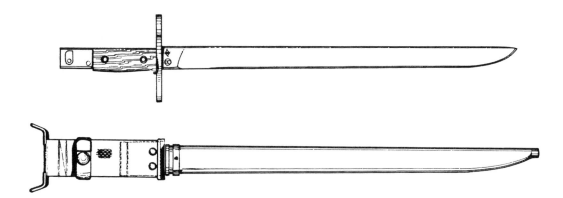

② SOUTH KOREAN M-7

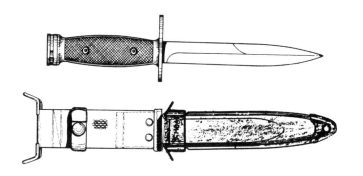

③ NORTH KOREAN AK·47

R.D.C. EVANS PG. 163

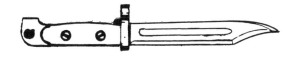

No. 1. **MEXICAN MODEL 1899.** THIS BAYONET IS DEFINITELY OF MEXICAN ISSUE AND HAS "REPUBLIC OF MEXICO" STAMPED ON THE SIDE OF THE CROSSGUARD. IT IS A SHORT REMINGTON VERSION MANUFACTURED FOR THE ROLLING BLOCK RIFLE AND HAS THE REMINGTON ARMS COMPANY DESIGNATION STAMPED ON THE FULLER OF THE BLADE. THE BAYONET HAS A HOOKED QUILLON AND COMES WITH A STEEL MOUNTED LEATHER SCABBARD.

No. 2. **MEXICAN MODEL 1899.** THIS BAYONET IS IDENTICAL TO No. 1 EXCEPT THAT IT HAS NO IDENTIFYING MEXICAN MARKINGS AND COMES WITH A STEEL SCABBARD WITH AN INTEGRAL LEATHER FROG, WHICH HAS THE COAT OF ARMS OF MEXICO STAMPED ON THE BLACK LEATHER FROG (FACING THE FRONT OF THE SCABBARD). IT IS A VERY INTERESTING STAMP, AS IT IS VERY LARGE AND TAKES UP ALMOST THE ENTIRE FROG.

No. 3. **MEXICAN MODEL 1899.** THIS IS IDENTICAL TO THE PREVIOUS TWO BAYONETS, HOWEVER, IT HAS NO MARKINGS, EITHER MEXICAN OR REMINGTON, ON EITHER THE BAYONET OR SCABBARD. ALL THE LITERATURE I HAVE READ IDENTIFIES THESE AS MEXICAN, HOWEVER, IT IS POSSIBLE THESE BAYONETS WERE PRODUCED FOR EXPORT TO A NUMBER OF COUNTRIES, INCLUDING FRANCE.

NOTE: THIS BAYONET ALSO ACCOMPANIED THE BLAKE RIFLE WHICH LOST OUT TO THE KRAG RIFLE IN TESTS CONDUCTED BY THE U.S. ARMY BOARD OF MAGAZINE ARMS IN 1893.

① MEXICAN M.1899
KIESLING VOL. I #53

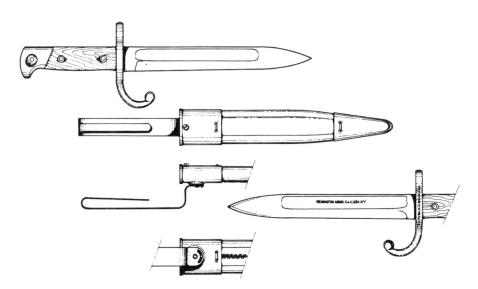

② MEXICAN M.1899
KIESLING VOL. I #51

③ MEXICAN M.1899
KIESLING VOL. I # 52

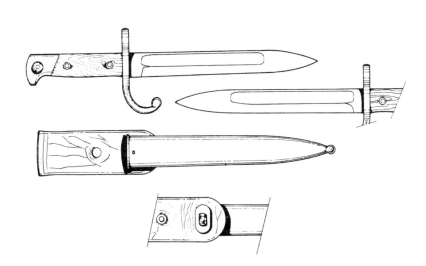

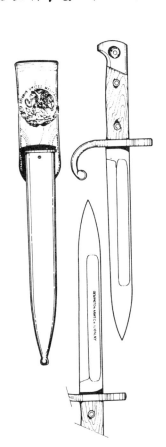

No. 1. **MEXICAN MODEL 1910.** THIS BAYONET IS GERMAN PRODUCED (SIMPSON) AND IS DIMENSIONALLY VERY CLOSE TO THE SPANISH 1893. IT HAS "RM" AND THE MEXICAN CREST STAMPED ON THE CROSSGUARD WHICH, BASED ON THE QUALITY OF THE STAMPING, WAS PROBABLY PERFORMED IN MEXICO. THESE "RM" MARKED VERSIONS ARE A BIT SCARCE.

No. 2. **MEXICAN MODEL 1910.** THIS BAYONET WAS PRODUCED BY CZECHOSLOVAKIA, AS IT HAS A SMALL "Z" IN THE CIRCLE ON THE BLADE. IT IS A VERY WELL MANUFACTURED ARM WITH A HOLLOW GROUND CUTTING EDGE AND WOOD GRIPS HELD BY TWO ROUNDED STEEL PINS. THE POMMEL IS ROUNDED AND HAS A SERIAL NUMBER STAMPED ON THE SIDE. THESE PIECES WERE APPARENTLY EXPORTED TO A NUMBER OF COUNTRIES BY THE CZECHS AND WERE APPARENTLY USED BY MEXICO AS REPLACEMENT BAYONETS FOR THE MAUSER RIFLE.

No. 3. **MEXICAN MODEL 1936.** THIS PIECE IS SCARCE FOR SOME REASON AND WAS THE LAST BAYONET PRODUCED FOR A MEXICAN MAUSER. IT IS ALMOST IDENTICAL TO 143-1 EXCEPT HAS A LONGER BLADE (15.125") AND IS HEAVILY BLUED. IT IS AVAILABLE WITH TWO DISTINCT BLADE VARIATIONS (ROUGH FINISH AND LONG FULLERS VS. GOOD FINISH AND SHORTER FULLERS). IT WAS ALSO USED ON THE LATER M-1954 MAUSER. (MOST AUTHORS ATTRIBUTE THE MANUFACTURE OF THESE PIECES TO THE MEXICANS, HOWEVER, BOTH EXAMPLES IN MY COLLECTION ARE STAMPED WITH A "Z" IN A CIRCLE WHICH NORMALLY DENOTES CZECH MANUFACTURE.)

NOTE: SEE NO. 3 ON PAGE 12 FOR THE AUSTRIAN EXPORT BAYONET UTILIZED BY MEXICO AND CALLED THE MEXICAN MODEL 1912.

143 - MEXICO

① MEXICAN M. 1910
WATTS & WHITE #484

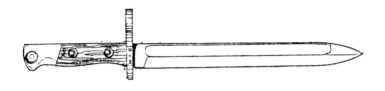

② MEXICAN M. 1910
KIESLING VOL I #154

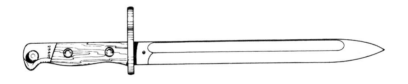

③ MEXICAN M. 1936
KIESLING VOL. III #631

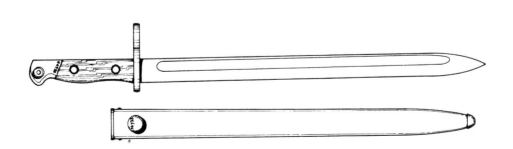

No. 1. **NEPALESE PATTERN 1770.** THIS BAYONET IS VERY INTERESTING IN THAT IT HAS A KUKRI-SHAPED BLADE WITH A BROWN BESS SOCKET. IT IS BELIEVED THAT THESE WEAPONS WERE ISSUED TO NEPALESE TROOPS SERVING WITH THE BRITISH ARMY IN THE 1800S AND THERE HAS BEEN A GREAT DEAL OF SPECULATION AMONG COLLECTORS AS TO THE AUTHENTICITY OF THESE PIECES. THE BAYONET IN MY COLLECTION IS NOTED IN DAN ERNST'S BOOK AND CAME FROM A COLLECTION WHICH WAS PUT TOGETHER IN THE 1940S; HENCE, I DO NOT FEEL IT IS A REPRODUCTION.

No. 2. **NEPALESE PATTERN 1770.** THIS PIECE IS ILLUSTRATED IN THE WORLD'S GUNS ON PAGE 232. THIS PUBLICATION WAS PRODUCED BY GOLDEN STATE ARMS IN THE 1950S; THEREFORE, IF THIS IS A REPRODUCTION, IT IS A VERY EARLY ONE.

No. 3. **NEPALESE PATTERN 1850 - BRUNSWICK.** THIS PIECE IS A NEPALESE-PRODUCED BAYONET APPARENTLY FOR THE NEPALESE BRUNSWICK. IT IS CRUDELY PRODUCED AND CAME FROM EITHER INDIA OR NEPAL.

No. 4. **NEPALESE PATTERN 1850 - BRUNSWICK.** THIS BAYONET, LIKE THE PREVIOUS ONE, WAS DEVELOPED ON THE BAKER RIFLE BAYONET PATTERN AND FITS THE BRUNSWICK RIFLE. IT IS ALSO A CRUDELY PRODUCED WEAPON.

① NEPALESE P. 1770 BROWN BESS

② NEPALESE P. 1770 BROWN BESS

③ NEPALESE P. 1850 BRUNSWICK

KIESLING VOL. IV # 960

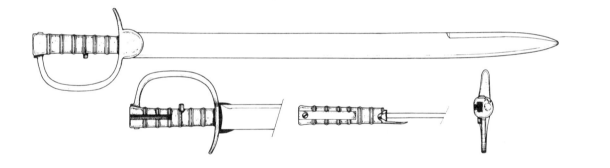

④ NEPALESE P. 1850 BRUNSWICK

KIESLING VOL IV #962

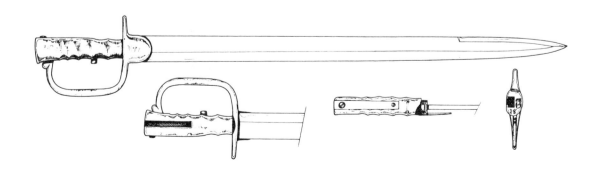

No. 1. **DUTCH MODEL 1871 - FIRST PATTERN.** THIS BAYONET WAS PRODUCED FOR THE DE BEAUMONT RIFLE WITH THE CHARACTERISTIC DUTCH FASCINATION FOR COMPLEXITY. IT IS A QUADRANGULAR BAYONET AND HAS A LOCKING RING WITH TWO ADJUSTING (OR TIGHTENING) SCREWS. I HAVE IN THE PAST POSSESSED THIS RIFLE AND CAN SEE NO PRACTICAL REASON FOR A LOCKING RING OF THIS DESIGN; HOWEVER, THIS UNIQUE ARRANGEMENT DOES MAKE THE PIECE VERY EASY TO IDENTIFY.

No. 2. **DUTCH MODEL 1871 - SECOND PATTERN.** THIS PIECE IS IDENTICAL TO NO. 1, HOWEVER, POSSESSES A MORE CONVENTIONAL LOCKING RING. I SUSPECT THIS WAS DONE WHEN THE DE BEAUMONT RIFLE WAS CONVERTED TO A REPEATING RIFLE IN 1888.

No. 3. **DUTCH MODEL 1873 - FIRST PATTERN CONVERTED TO SECOND PATTERN.** THIS IS ALMOST IDENTICAL TO THE FRENCH MODEL 1866 SABRE BAYONET AND WAS PRODUCED FOR THE DE BEAUMONT NAVY RIFLE. THE CONVERSION IS INTERESTING BECAUSE THE SHORT SPRING OF THE FIRST PATTERN WAS REPLACED BY A LONG SPRING AND THE OLD HOLES CAREFULLY FILLED WITH SOLID BRASS. THESE WERE NOT PRODUCED IN LARGE NUMBERS.

① DUTCH M.1871 FIRST PATTERN

KIESLING VOL. II #348

② DUTCH M.1871 SECOND PATT.

KIESLING VOL. II #349

③ DUTCH M.1873

KIESLING VOL. II #470

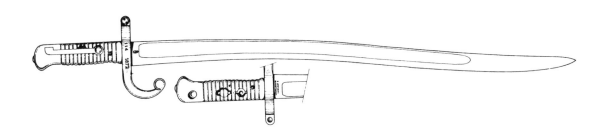

No. 1. DUTCH MODEL 1895 – MANNLICHER CARBINE. THIS BAYONET CAN BE FOUND IN TWO DISTINCT VERSIONS. THE FIRST, AS SHOWN WITH A STRAIGHT CROSSGUARD AND, THE SECOND, WITH A HOOKED QUILLON. THESE PIECES HAVE A DOUBLE EDGED BLADE, A VERY UNUSUAL BULBOUS POMMEL AND ARE RELATIVELY DIFFICULT TO OBTAIN. ONE REASON FOR THIS MIGHT BE THAT THE BLADES WERE USED BY THE JAPANESE FOR ERSATZ BAYONETS IN WORLD WAR II (SEE 137-1). THE DUTCH SCABBARDS ARE UNIQUE TO HOLLAND AND ARE OF ALL LEATHER CONSTRUCTION, AS ILLUSTRATED. THESE BAYONETS WERE ISSUED TO THE CAVALRY AND HORSE ARTILLERY.

No. 2. DUTCH MODEL 1895 – MANNLICHER CARBINE. THIS BAYONET HAS A POMMEL SIMILAR TO NO. 1, HOWEVER, IS EQUIPPED WITH A LONG T-BACKED BLADE. IT WAS ISSUED TO THE FORTIFICATION ARTILLERY, ENGINEERS AND TORPEDOMEN. A VARIATION WITH A HOOKED QUILLON WAS ALSO PRODUCED.

No. 3. DUTCH MODEL 1895 – MANNLICHER CARBINE (2ND VARIATION). THIS BAYONET HAS A BLADE IDENTICAL TO NO. 1, HOWEVER, WAS DESIGNED TO FIT A DIFFERENT RIFLE THAN THE TWO PREVIOUSLY DISCUSSED. IT WAS ALSO ISSUED TO THE CAVALRY AND HORSE ARTILLERY UNITS. THE SCABBARDS FOR THESE BAYONETS ARE ALSO OF A DIFFERENT DESIGN.

① DUTCH M. 1895 CAVALRY

KIESLING VOL. I #100

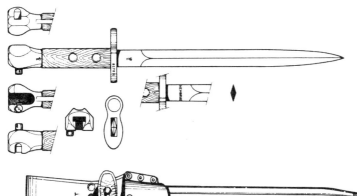

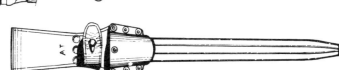

② DUTCH M. 1895 ARTILLERY

KIESLING VOL II #392

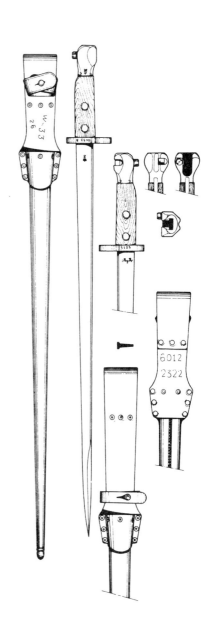

③ DUTCH M. 1895 CAVALRY

KIESLING VOL. I #101

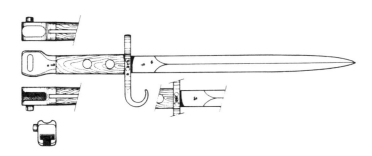

No. 1. DUTCH MODEL 1895 - MANNLICHER. THIS BAYONET WAS DESIGNED FOR THE MODEL 1895 INFANTRY RIFLE AND HAS THE HOOKED CROSSGUARD. THE EARLIER BAYONETS CONTRACTED WITH AUSTRIA AND GERMANY WERE MANUFACTURED WITH HOOKED CROSSGUARDS. IT HAS A T-BACKED BLADE AND THE MORE CONVENTIONAL PRESS STUD ARRANGEMENT AND ALL LEATHER SCABBARD. THE VERSION WITH THE HOOKED CROSSGUARD IS SOMEWHAT SCARCE. THIS PIECE, LIKE THOSE PREVIOUSLY DISCUSSED, IS EQUIPPED WITH THE TYPICAL DUTCH LEATHER SCABBARD.

No. 2. DUTCH MODEL 1895 - MANNLICHER. THIS BAYONET IS A LATER VERSION OF No. 1. THE HOOKS ON THE AUSTRIAN AND GERMAN MANUFACTURED VERSIONS WERE REMOVED WHILE THE LATER ONES MANUFACTURED AT HEMBRUG WERE PRODUCED WITHOUT THE HOOK.

No. 3. MANNLICHER MODEL 1895. THIS BAYONET IS SIMILAR TO THE INFANTRY VERSION EXCEPT THAT THE GRIP FASTENING DEVICE IS A UNIQUE SCREW AND PLATE ARRANGEMENT FOR TROPICAL CONDITIONS AND THE CROSSGUARD HAS A HOOK. THESE BAYONETS WERE ISSUED TO THE MARINES AND ARE SOMEWHAT SCARCE.

① DUTCH M. 1895 INFANTRY

KIESLING VOL. I #237

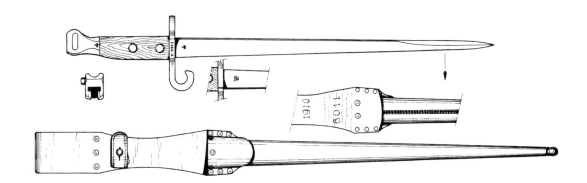

② DUTCH M. 1895 INFANTRY

KIESLING VOL. I #238

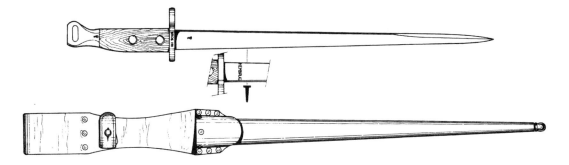

③ DUTCH M. 1895 MARINES

KIESLING VOL. I #239

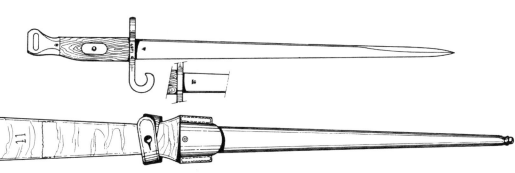

No. 1. **DUTCH M4.** THIS BAYONET WAS PRODUCED BY HORSTER FOR DUTCH USE ON THE M1 CARBINE AND IS DIMENSIONALLY VIRTUALLY IDENTICAL TO THE U.S. MODEL, HOWEVER, THE DUTCH VERSION IS A MUCH HIGHER QUALITY WEAPON INCORPORATING A SHAPED CROSSGUARD, SOLID PLASTIC HANDLE AND BETTER FINISH. THE SCABBARD IS IDENTICAL TO THE U.S. MODEL EXCEPT, AS IN THE CASE OF THE BAYONET, REFLECTS HIGHER QUALITY MANUFACTURING STANDARDS.

No. 2. **DUTCH MODEL AR10.** THESE BAYONETS WERE FOR THE DUTCH-PRODUCED AR10 RIFLE AND WERE VIRTUALLY UNOBTAINABLE FOR YEARS. U.S. IMPORTERS RECENTLY PURCHASED QUANTITIES OF THESE WEAPONS FROM SUDAN. THE BAYONETS REFLECT U.S. INFLUENCE, HOWEVER, HAVE WOOD GRIPS AND A SLIGHTLY DIFFERENT BLADE FORM. THEY COME IN TWO DISTINCT VERSIONS, THE PRIMARY DIFFERENCE BEING THE POMMEL DIMENSIONS. THE ONE ILLUSTRATED HERE IS THE VARIATION WITH THE SMALL POMMEL.

NOTE: THE STONER EXPORT SERIES ILLUSTRATED IN THE GERMAN SECTION ON PAGE 109 ARE USED IN THE NETHERLANDS WHERE THEY ARE DESIGNATED THE KCB-70 BAYONET SERIES.

① DUTCH M·4
KIESLING VOL. I #31

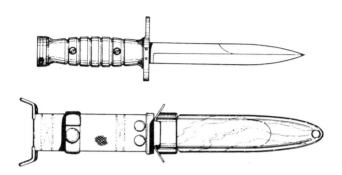

② DUTCH AR·10
KIESLING VOL. I #39

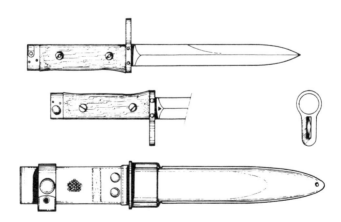

No. 1.   NEW ZEALAND No. 4 MK II. THIS BAYONET IS IDENTICAL
         TO THE BRITISH No. 4 SPIKE BAYONET, HOWEVER, HAS
         NEW ZEALAND MARKINGS ON THE SIDE OF THE SOCKET
         WHICH WERE APPLIED WITH A MARKING TOOL AND CONSIST
         OF A "N Z".

NOTE: NEW ZEALAND UTILIZED THE FULL RANGE OF COMMONWEALTH
         BAYONETS; HOWEVER, I HAVE SEEN FEW WITH MARKINGS.
         THE EARLY WORLD WAR II PHOTOGRAPH SHOWS COMMON-
         WEALTH TROOPS WITH TWO TYPES OF BAYONETS IN USE.
         NOTE THE RETAINING STRAP ON THE SPIKE BAYONET SCAB-
         BARD.

① *NEW ZEALAND*
NO. 4, MK. II

KIESLING VOL I #4

N↑Z

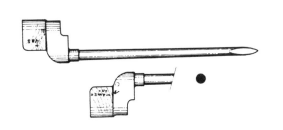

ASSOCIATED PRESS

149

No. 1.   NORWEGIAN MODEL 1855 - JARMAN.   THIS BAYONET IS
         UNUSUAL AND I AM NOT AT ALL SURE OF THIS IDENTIFI-
         CATION.   IT HAS THE CROSSGUARD AND HILT OF THE 1871
         GERMAN MARINE BAYONET, HOWEVER, HAS A YATAGHAN-TYPE
         BLADE AND MODIFIED SLOT.   THE BLACKENED WOOD GRIPS
         ARE HELD IN PLACE BY RIVETS AND THE PIECE HAS ABSO-
         LUTELY NO MARKINGS.

No. 2.   NORWEGIAN MODEL 1860 - REMINGTON.   THIS BAYONET WAS
         DESIGNED FOR THE REMINGTON ROLLING BLOCK AND HAS A
         BRASS POMMEL AND CROSSGUARD WITH A HOLE THROUGH THE
         TOP OF THE POMMEL.   IT IS A BEAUTIFULLY MADE BAYO-
         NET AND QUITE SCARCE.

① NORWEGIAN M. 1855

KIESLING VOL IV. # 966

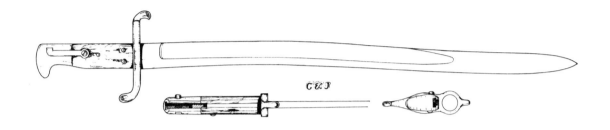

② NORWEGIAN M. 1860

KIESLING VOL. II. # 482

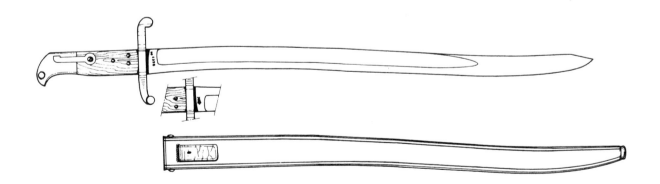

No. 1. **NORWEGIAN MODEL 1894 - KRAG JORGENSEN.** THIS IS THE FIRST VERSION OF THE KRAG JORGENSEN SERIES AND WAS MADE FOR THE M1894 ARMY RIFLE AS WELL AS FOR SOME M1912 CARBINES AND SOME SNIPER'S RIFLES M25. IT WAS FIRST MANUFACTURED AT STEYR AND NUMBERED WITH THE M1894 STEYR RIFLES FROM 1 TO 20,000 AND FROM 30,001 TO 39,000. STEYR BAYONETS ARE MARKED WITH THE LETTERS "OE" OVER "W.G.". IN 1894-95, HUSQVARNA, SWEDEN MADE 2,000 BAYONETS OF THIS TYPE IN THE 20,001 TO 30,000 SERIAL NUMBER RANGE, BUT THE EXACT NUMBERS ARE UNKNOWN. THEY ARE MARKED WITH A CROWNED H. THE REMAINING 8,000 BAYONETS IN THIS SERIAL RANGE, AS WELL AS THE ONES NUMBERED 39,001 TO 121,000 WERE MADE AT KONGSBERG, AND ARE MARKED WITH A CROWNED K.

No. 2. **NORWEGIAN MODEL 1894/1912 - KRAG JORGENSEN.** THIS IS THE SECOND VERSION OF THE LONG KRAG JORGENSEN SERIES OF BAYONETS (THE FIRST MODEL 1912 HAD TWO FULLERS) AND CAN BE IDENTIFIED BY A LONG FULLER WHICH RUNS THE FULL LENGTH OF THE BLADE AND A SCABBARD WHICH HAS A LEATHER BODY AND INTEGRAL FROG. THESE PIECES WERE PRODUCED IN SMALL NUMBERS (PROBABLY LESS THAN 3,000) AND ARE RARELY SEEN, PARTICULARLY WITH THE BAYONET MATCHED TO THE SCABBARD.

No. 3. **NORWEGIAN MODEL 1894/1914 - KRAG JORGENSEN.** THIS IS THE THIRD VARIATION OF THE LONG KRAG JORGENSEN BAYONETS AND HAS A COMPLETELY DIFFERENT BLADE FORM WITH A SHORTER FULLER AND FALSE EDGE. THE SCABBARD IS ALL METAL AND INCORPORATED A DETACHABLE FROG.

① NORWEGIAN M.1894

KIESLING VOL I #60

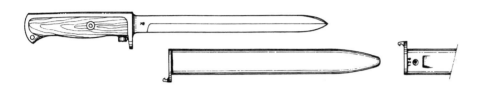

② NORWEGIAN M.1894/12

KIESLING VOL I #246

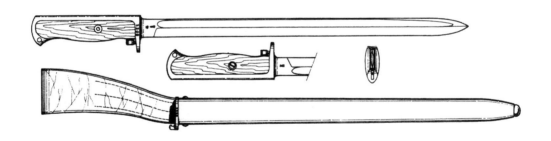

③ NORWEGIAN M.1894/14

KIESLING VOL. I #247

No. 1.   **NORWEGIAN MODEL 1894/14 - SHORTENED.**   THESE PIECES ARE CONVERSIONS OF THE LONG MODELS DISCUSSED ON PAGE 151 WITH MODIFICATIONS PERFORMED DURING GERMAN OCCUPATION OF NORWAY IN WORLD WAR II.   FOR SOME REASON, THE MODIFICATION OF THE FULLERED BAYONETS IS NOT COMMON.   THE EXAMPLE IN MY COLLECTION IS HEAVILY BLUED.

No. 2.   **NORWEGIAN MODIFICATION - FOR THE U.S. M1 CARBINE.**   THIS PIECE REFLECTS AN INTERESTING INNOVATION PER- FORMED BY THE NORWEGIANS TO ALLOW THE MODEL 1894 BAYONETS TO FIT THE M1 CARBINE.   THIS MODIFICATION WHICH I HAVE READ OCCURRED IN 1956 INCORPORATES AN EXTENSION TO THE CROSSGUARD, WHICH ALLOWS THESE PIECES TO FIT THE M1 CARBINE.   THIS MODIFICATION IS VERY WELL DONE.

① NORWEGIAN M.1894/14 SHORTENED

KIESLING VOL. I # 61

② NORWEGIAN M-1 MODIFICATION OF M.1894

KIESLING VOL. III # 527

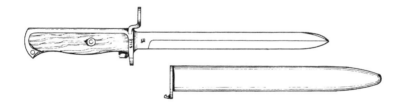

No. 1.   **Norwegian M1 - Garand.** The Norwegians utilized the U.S. M1 Garand and bayonet. The only modification I can see to the U.S. bayonet is the addition of a serial number of the crossguard. Unlike the crude numbering performed on South American Garand bayonets, the Norwegian numbers are very uniform.

No. 2.   **Norwegian Modification - For the M1 Garand.** This modification which apparently occurred in 1957 involved the German 84/98 bayonets and incorporated another bit of innovative engineering by the Norwegians whereby the bayonet was modified to allow an effective connection of the bayonet to the rifle through the use of the gas plug screw slot on the Garand. I suspect this concept was copied from the U.S. development of the M5 bayonet (see Page 229). In addition, the scabbard was modified to utilize the U.S. type web belt. I have also seen the scabbard modification without the bayonet modification which would indicate that the Norwegians apparently also utilized the German rifles and unmodified bayonets.

① NORWEGIAN M·1 GARAND

KIESLING VOL. I #90

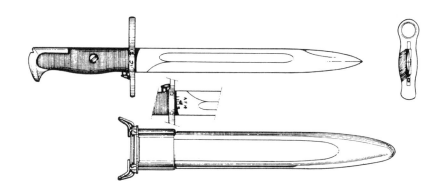

② NORWEGIAN M·1 MODIFIED GERMAN 84/98

KIESLING VOL IV #816

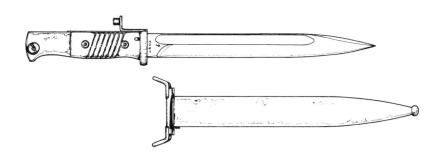

No. 1. **NORWEGIAN AG3 - CETME.** THIS PIECE LOOKS VERY MUCH LIKE THE U.S. CARBINE SERIES OF BAYONETS, HOWEVER, IT INCORPORATES AN UNUSUAL HANDLE OF A ROUGH GREEN FINISH. ALSO, I HAVE AN IDENTICAL VERSION WITH A ROUGH BLACK HANDLE WHICH WAS ISSUED TO CADETS. R.D.C. EVANS SAYS THESE ARE REHILTED VERSIONS OF THE U.S. M4 BAYONET. THE SCABBARDS FOR BOTH THE ISSUE AND CADET VERSIONS ARE ILLUSTRATED. THE CADET SCABBARD IS BLACK WITH A BLACK LEATHER INTEGRAL FROG.

No. 2. **NORWEGIAN AG3 MODEL 1978.** THIS BAYONET IS CURRENTLY ISSUED TO THE NORWEGIAN ARMED FORCES AS WELL AS BEING EXPORTED TO OTHER COUNTRIES. IT UTILIZES THE CARBINE-STYLE BLADE WITH A DARK MOLDED PLASTIC GRIP AND IS RELATIVELY SIMILAR TO OTHER BAYONETS OF THE G3 SERIES. IT ALSO UTILIZES A NEWLY MADE SCABBARD WHICH IS VERY SIMILAR TO THE U.S. CARBINE SERIES EXCEPT THAT IT HAS A WOOD GRAINED PLASTIC BODY.

① NORWEGIAN AG·3 CETME

KIESLING VOL IV # 749

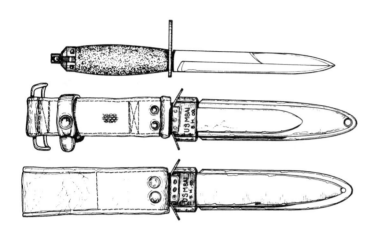

② NORWEGIAN AG·3

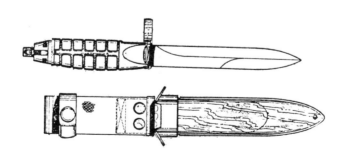

No. 1. **PAKISTANI MODEL 1954 - GARAND.** THE IDENTIFICATION OF THIS PIECE IS PURELY SPECULATIVE SINCE I HAVE NO DATA SUPPORTING THIS IDENTIFICATION EXCEPT THAT THE BAYONET WAS OBTAINED FROM AN IMPORTER WHO WAS ADVERTISING OTHER PAKISTAN BAYONETS AT THE SAME TIME, AND SINCE THE BLADE WAS SHORTENED AND TIPPED VERY SIMILAR TO THE BRITISH "L" SERIES OF BAYONETS. I SPECULATE THAT THE PAKISTAN MILITARY MODIFIED THE GARAND BAYONETS FROM THE STANDPOINT OF UNIFORMITY. THIS BAYONET WILL FIT IN THE BRITISH "L" SERIES SCABBARDS WITH THE RING REMOVED. I HAVE SEEN SEVERAL SCABBARD EXAMPLES SO MODIFIED.

No. 2. **PAKISTANI NO. 9 MARK I.** THIS PIECE IS PAKISTANI ISSUE AND MARKED WITH THEIR SERIAL NUMBERS. BRITISH ENFIELDS HAVE BEEN IN WIDESPREAD USE IN PAKISTAN AND OTHER MOSLEM COUNTRIES FOR A NUMBER OF YEARS AND APPARENTLY THE NO. 9 BAYONET WAS THE LAST OF THE BRITISH BAYONETS TO BE UTILIZED OFFICIALLY.

No. 3. **PAKISTANI G3.** THIS BAYONET IS THE PAKISTANI VERSION OF THE G3 AND IS NUMBERED SIMILAR TO NO. 2. THESE PIECES ARE QUITE COMMON AND HAVE BEEN DUMPED ON THE U.S. MARKET, OBVIOUSLY BY THE THOUSANDS. WITH THE EXCEPTION OF THE BOWIE TIP, THEY RESEMBLE THE G3 SERIES OF BAYONETS UTILIZED BY EUROPEAN ARMIES.

① *PAKISTANI M-1*
  GARAND

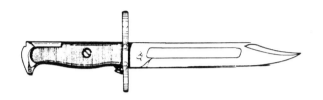

② *PAKISTANI NO.9*
  MK. I

KIESLING VOL. I #6

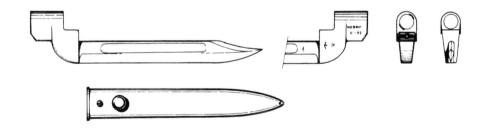

③ *PAKISTANI G-3*

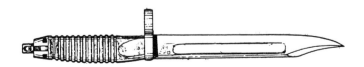

No. 1. PERUVIAN MODEL 1909. THESE BAYONETS ARE IDENTICAL TO THE GERMAN SECOND MODEL 98S AND HAVE BEEN DESIGNATED AS PERUVIAN MODEL 1909S BY SOME COLLECTORS. THE ONLY DIFFERENCE BETWEEN THE GERMAN AND PERUVIAN MODELS IS THAT THERE IS A SERIAL NUMBER STAMPED ON THE CROSSGUARD AND THE PERUVIAN CREST IN A CIRCLE STAMPED ON THE END OF THE POMMEL, AS ILLUSTRATED. I HAVE TWO EXAMPLES IN MY COLLECTION; ONE MANUFACTURED BY SIMPSON AND ONE BY P. D. LUNESCHLOSS.

No. 2. PERUVIAN MODEL 1909 - DRESS. THIS IS THE PERUVIAN MODEL 1909 DISCUSSED PREVIOUSLY; HOWEVER, IT HAS BEEN SHORTENED AND THE CROSSGUARD AND POMMEL BRASS-PLATED, ALONG WITH THE GRIP SCREWS. IN ADDITION, HARD POLISHED MICARTA GRIPS HAVE BEEN FITTED TO THE WEAPON, THE PRESS STUD REMOVED AND THE HOLES FILLED. THIS IS CLEARLY NOT AN OFFICIAL MODIFICATION; HOWEVER, I HAVE NOTED STANDARD PERUVIAN BAYONETS SHORTENED TO THIS LENGTH WHICH MAY BE OFFICIAL.

No. 3. PERUVIAN MODEL 1949 - INGRAM SUBMACHINE GUN. THIS ROD-TYPE BAYONET WAS ISSUED TO THE PERUVIAN NAVY WITH THE U.S.-PRODUCED INGRAM SMG.

NOTE: THE PERUVIAN AIR FORCE UTILIZED THE U.S. GARAND RIFLE AND SHORT MODEL 1905 BAYONET. THESE CAN BE IDENTIFIED BY A CRUDE SERIAL NUMBER STAMPED ON THE CROSSGUARD.

① PERUVIAN M. 1909
KIESLING VOL. II # 424

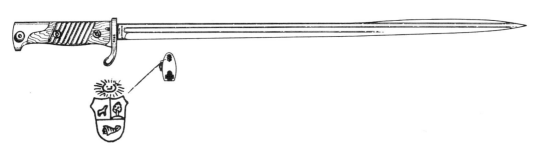

② PERUVIAN M. 1909
SHORTENED DRESS

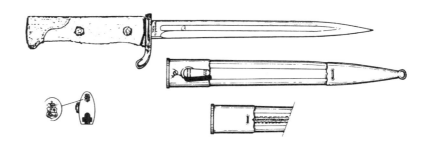

③ PERUVIAN M. 1949
INGRAM SMG

No. 1. **PORTUGUESE MODEL 1885.** THESE PIECES WERE IMPORTED TO THE U.S. SEVERAL YEARS AGO ALONG WITH THE KROPATSCHEK RIFLES THEY WERE MANUFACTURED TO FIT. THESE ARMS ARE VERY WELL MADE HAVING A LONG YATAGHAN BLADE AND BLACKENED HANDLES WITH THE AUSTRIAN MANUFACTURER "STEYR" AND THE DATE MARKED ON THE BACK OF THE BLADE, SIMILAR TO THE FRENCH BAYONETS. THESE PIECES WERE ACTUALLY DESIGNED FOR THE GUEDES-CASTRO RIFLE; HOWEVER, THE PORTUGUESE GOVERNMENT ASKED STEYR TO CHANGE AN EARLIER CONTRACT FROM THE SINGLE-SHOT GUEDES RIFLE TO THE KROPATSCHEK REPEATING RIFLE AND UTILIZE THE SAME BAYONET.

No. 2. **PORTUGUESE MODEL 1904.** THIS BAYONET IS OF STANDARD EUROPEAN DESIGN AND WAS MANUFACTURED IN GERMANY TO FIT THE VERGUERO RIFLE. THESE BAYONETS HAVE RECENTLY (1984) BECOME AVAILABLE ON THE SURPLUS MARKET.

No. 3. **PORTUGUESE MODEL 1934.** THIS BAYONET WAS MANUFACTURED TO FIT THE STEYR SOLOTHURN SUBMACHINE GUN. IT IS AN INTERESTING PIECE IN THAT IT HAS A STANDARD LENGTH BLADE SIMILAR TO THE 1904, HOWEVER, A VERY SHORT HANDLE.

① PORTUGUESE M.1885 KROPATSCHEK

KIESLING VOL II # 373

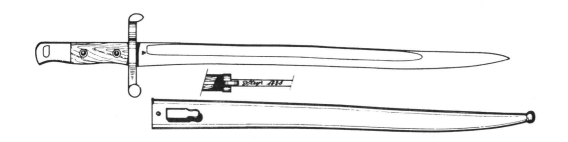

② PORTUGUESE M.1904 VERGUERO

KIESLING VOL III # 573

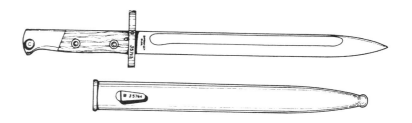

③ PORTUGUESE M.1934 STEYR SOLOTHURN S.M.G.

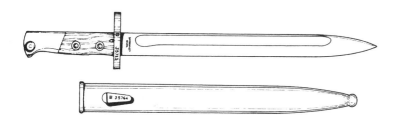

No. 1. **PORTUGUESE MODEL 1937.** THIS BAYONET IS THE STANDARD GERMAN 84/98 WHICH WAS UTILIZED BY PORTUGAL. IT IS HEAVILY BLUED AND MARKED WITH PORTUGUESE SERIAL NUMBERS ON THE POMMEL. THE PORTUGUESE HAD TWO CONTRACTS WITH GERMANY; ONE IN 1937 AND THE OTHER IN 1939. THE ONLY DIFFERENCE BETWEEN THE TWO CONTRACTS IS QUALITY OF FINISH (THE 1937 CONTRACT IS SUPERIOR IN FINISH).

No. 2. **PORTUGUESE MODEL 1948 FBP - SUBMACHINE GUN.** THIS BAYONET, UNTIL RECENT YEARS, WAS SCARCE AND IS A SMALL DOUBLE-EDGED KNIFE BAYONET WITH EXCELLENT PROPORTIONS. THESE DO NOT APPEAR TO HAVE BEEN RELEASED IN LARGE QUANTITIES AND, IN MY OPINION, WERE NOT PRODUCED IN GREAT NUMBERS. IT IS MARKED WITH A PORTUGUESE SERIAL NUMBER.

No. 3. **PORTUGUESE FN FAL.** THIS BAYONET IS A BELGIAN FABRIQUE NATIONALE TYPE "A" BAYONET PURCHASED BY PORTUGAL FOR TRIALS IN 1965. IT HAS RIBBED PLASTIC GRIPS.

① PORTUGUESE M. 1937

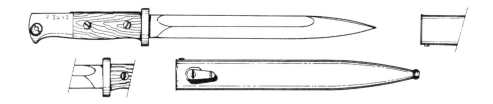

② PORTUGUESE M. 1948
F B P SUB·MACHINE GUN

③ PORTUGUESE F.N. FAL

KIESLING, VOL. IV # 765
RDC EVANS PG. 165

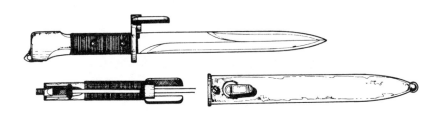

No. 1. POLISH WZ 98. THIS PIECE IS A POLISH REWORK OF A GERMAN MODEL 98/05 WITH THE PRIMARY MODIFICATION BEING THE ADDITION OF SMOOTH GRIPS AND THE STAMPING OF "WZ98" ON THE POMMEL ("WZ" IS THE POLISH ABBREVIATION FOR "MODEL"). IN ADDITION, THERE IS A SERIAL NUMBER STAMPED ON THE CROSSGUARD.

No. 2. POLISH WZ 98. THIS IS ALSO A POLISH MODIFIED GERMAN BAYONET, HOWEVER, THIS IS A VERSION WHICH EITHER THE GERMANS OR THE POLES REMOVED THE SAW BACK FROM THE BAYONET. IT IS MY UNDERSTANDING THAT THESE BAYONETS WERE RECEIVED BY POLAND AS REPARATIONS FROM WORLD WAR I.

POLISH FEMALE TROOPS ARMED WITH MOSIN-NAGANTS IN THE LATER STAGES OF WORLD WAR II.

① *POLISH WZ 98*

KIESLING VOL. III #629

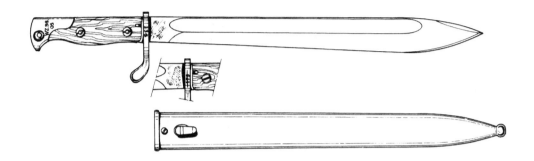

② *POLISH WZ 98*
GROUND

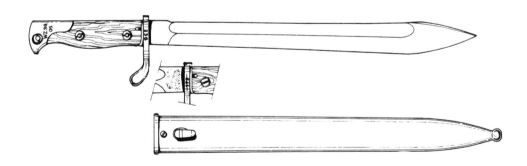

No. 1. **POLISH MODEL 1922 (WZ22).** THIS BAYONET WAS MANUFACTURED AT RADOM AND IS AN EARLY POLISH MAUSER VERSION. IT HAS A CROSS-GUARD WITH A FULL MUZZLE RING AND IS FINISHED BRIGHT.

No. 2. **POLISH MODEL 1922 (WZ22).** THIS PIECE IS MANUFACTURED BY PERKUN AND HAS NO MUZZLE RING. IT IS IDENTICAL TO 160-1 EXCEPT FOR THE MUZZLE RING MODIFICATION. THE RADOM VERSIONS WERE ALTERED AFTER THE GERMAN OCCUPATION; HOWEVER, THE WAFFENAMPT STAMPS WERE NOT ADDED AS IN CZECHOSLOVAKIA.

No. 3. **POLISH MODEL 1924 (WZ24).** THIS IS THE SECOND VERSION OF THE POLISH MAUSER BAYONET AND CONTAINS A FLASHGUARD. IT WAS MANU-FACTURED WITHOUT THE MUZZLE RING, IN MY OPINION, AND HAS A MUCH THICKER CROSSGUARD THAN THE PREVIOUSLY DISCUSSED BAYONETS. ALL POLISH MANUFACTURED BAYONETS ARE WELL MARKED AND HAVE A SERIAL NUMBER ON THE RICASSO OF THE BLADE.

No. 4. **POLISH MODEL 1939 (WZ39).** THIS IS A BAYONET WHICH WAS PRODUCED FOR THE RARE SEMI-AUTOMATIC MAROZEK RIFLE THAT THE POLES HAD JUST STARTED ISSUING WHEN INVADED. IT HAS A "MUSTY" BLUE FINISH VERY SIMILAR TO PARKERIZING AND IS DATED 1939 ON THE RICASSO.

NOTE: JACK SCHRADER NOTED A PATTERN TO THE POLISH WZ 22/24 SERIES AS FOLLOWS:

- ALL RADOM PRODUCED PIECES WERE MANUFACTURED WITH MUZZLE RINGS (MANY WERE REMOVED SUBSEQUENTLY BY THE GERMANS) AND WITHOUT FLASH GUARDS.
- ALL PERKUN PRODUCED BAYONETS WERE MANUFACTURED WITHOUT MUZZLE RINGS AND WITH FLASHGUARDS.

160 - POLAND

① POLISH M.1922
WZ 22

KIESLING VOL I #130

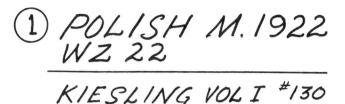

② POLISH M.1922
WZ 22

KIESLING VOL. I #132

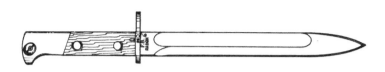

③ POLISH M.1924
WZ 24

KIESLING VOL I #131

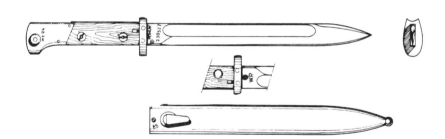

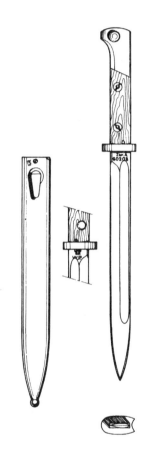

④ POLISH M.1939
WZ 39

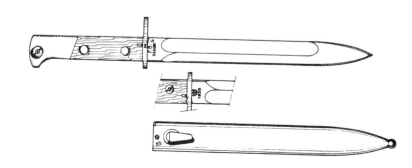

No. 1. **POLISH LEBEL C. 1915-1925.** THIS BAYONET IS A FRENCH MODEL 1886/91/16/35 WHICH WAS ISSUED TO POLISH ARMY UNITS ALONG WITH THE LEBEL RIFLES TO FIGHT THE BOLSHEVIKS FOR THE TERRITORY NOT RETURNED TO POLAND IN THE VERSAILLE TREATY. THE FRENCH ALSO SUPPLIED THE POLES WITH M-1892 CARBINES. THE EFFORT WAS SUCCESSFUL AND POLAND REGAINED THE ORIGINAL BORDERS.

No. 2. **POLISH P.M.K.M. (AKM) MODEL 1978.** THIS PIECE IS LIKE THE RUSSIAN AKM EXCEPT IT HAS NO SERRATED EDGE. THE POLISH VERSIONS HAVE MILKY-ORANGE PLASTIC GRIPS WHILE THE IDENTICAL BAYONET USED BY SOUTH AFRICA HAS BLOOD RED PLASTIC GRIPS.

POLISH AIRBORNE TROOPS WITH MODEL 1978 BAYONET.

① POLISH WZ 86/93 LEBEL

KIESLING VOL. I #224

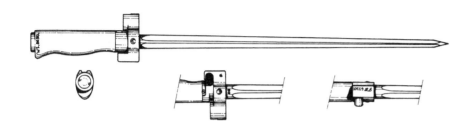

② POLISH PMKM KALASHNIKOV

R.D.C EVANS PG. 170

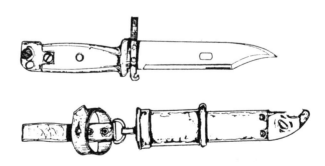

No. 1. **RUMANIAN MODEL 1879 - PEABODY-MARTINI.** THIS IS A GRAS-STYLE OF BAYONET AND HAS A STEYR CREST ON THE BLADE. R. D. C. EVANS SAYS THIS BAYONET WAS USED BY BOTH RUMANIA AND THE VATICAN; HOWEVER, THE EXAMPLE IN MY COLLECTION HAS SIAMESE NUMBERS ON THE CROSSGUARD.

No. 2. **RUMANIAN MODEL 1904 - MANNLICHER.** THIS BAYONET WAS PRODUCED BY AUSTRIA AND HAS A STEP IN THE BACK OF THE HANDLE SIMILAR TO THE GERMAN M-1871. IT IS FINISHED BRIGHT AND HAS THE RUMANIAN "PHOENIX" STAMPED ON THE POMMEL (SEE ILLUSTRATION). THE SCABBARD IS OF THE STANDARD AUSTRIAN DESIGN. THIS BAYONET IS SOMETIMES CALLED AN "IRISH MANNLICHER".

No. 3. **RUMANIAN AKM.** THIS BAYONET IS TYPICAL OF THE COMMUNIST BLOCK BAYONET SERIES FOR THE SOVIET-DESIGNED AKM. THE RUMANIAN VERSION, HOWEVER, HAS A BUFF-COLOR RUBBER INSULATOR AND A LEATHER FROG. IN ALL OTHER WAYS, THE BAYONET IS IDENTICAL TO THE RUSSIAN M.1968 (SEE 167-3).

① RUMANIAN M. 1879

KIESLING VOL. III #693

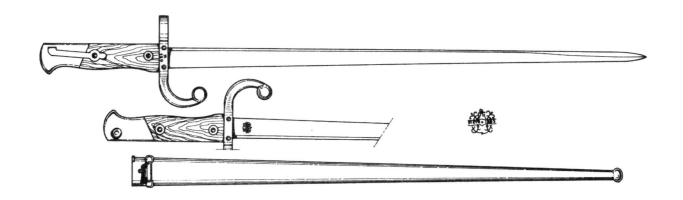

② RUMANIAN M. 1895

KIESLING VOL. III #545

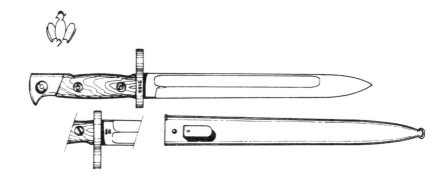

③ RUMANIAN AKM

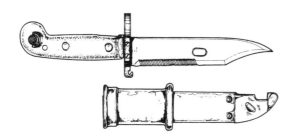

No. 1. **RUSSIAN MODEL 1869 - BERDAN I.** THIS BAYONET IS RARE AND WAS PRODUCED IN THE UNITED STATES IN VERY LIMITED QUANTITIES. IT IS UNIQUE IN THAT IT HAS A VERY SHORT SHANK, HOWEVER, IT IS CHARACTERISTICALLY RUSSIAN IN THAT IT HAS A SCREWDRIVER TIP AND IS HEAVILY BLUED. ACCORDING TO R. D. C. EVANS, 30,000 BERDAN I RIFLES WERE ORDERED BY THE RUSSIANS FROM COLT IN HARTFORD, CONNECTICUT, IN 1868.

No. 2. **RUSSIAN MODEL 1871 - BERDAN II.** THIS BAYONET IS REALLY THE START OF THE QUADRANGULAR SERIES OF RUSSIAN BAYONETS AND, LIKE THE PRECEDING PIECE, INCORPORATES A SCREWDRIVER TIP. THE SOCKET APPEARS TO BE OF VIRTUALLY THE SAME INTERNAL DIMENSIONS AS THE BERDAN I, HOWEVER, THE MORTISE SLOT IS ON THE OPPOSITE SIDE. THESE BAYONETS WERE MANUFACTURED IN RUSSIA AND ARE RELATIVELY SCARCE IN THE UNITED STATES. THE SCABBARDS ARE VERY UNUSUAL IN THAT THEY ARE OF BROWN LEATHER WITH A BRASS FROG STUD ON A SMALL PLATE RIVETED TO THE SIDE AND A BRASS INTERNAL TIP.

① RUSSIAN M.1869 BERDAN I

KIESLING VOL I #347

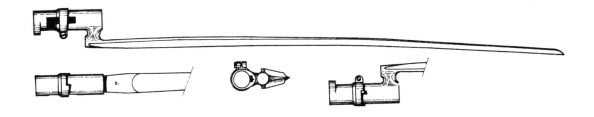

② RUSSIAN M.1871 BERDAN II

KIESLING VOL. II #355

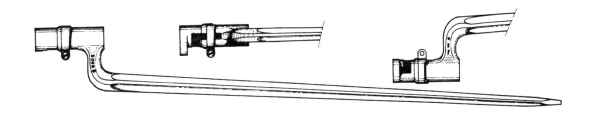

No. 1. **AUSTRIAN MODEL 1891 - MOSIN-NAGANT.** THIS BAYONET IS INCLUDED WITH RUSSIA SINCE IT IS OBVIOUSLY FOR THE MOSIN-NAGANT RIFLE; HOWEVER, THESE WERE AUSTRIAN-PRODUCED FOR USE ON CAPTURED RIFLES. THE EXAMPLE IN MY COLLECTION HAS THE AUSTRIAN CREST ON IT AND AN ARTICLE BY R. D. C. EVANS STATES THESE WERE MANUFACTURED BY AUSTRIA ALONG WITH THE SCABBARDS. THE ONLY UNIQUE ASPECT OF THE BAYONET IS THAT IT HAS A STRAIGHT SLOT RATHER THAN THE OFFSET SLOT OF THE OTHER LOCKING RING EQUIPPED MODEL.

No. 2. **RUSSIAN MODEL 1891 - MOSIN-NAGANT.** THIS BAYONET IS DEFINITELY OF RUSSIAN ISSUE, THOUGH NOT ALL WERE MANUFACTURED IN RUSSIA. I POSSESS SEVERAL VARIATIONS, ONE OF WHICH HAS RUSSIAN MANUFACTURING MARKS (SEE ILLUSTRATION, BOW AND ARROW OF "ISHEVKY"), ONE WHICH WAS MANUFACTURED BY REMINGTON AND SO MARKED ("R" IN CIRCLE) AND A MANUFACTURING BLANK, WHICH WAS DISCARDED BY THE REMINGTON MANUFACTURING PLANT. THESE BAYONETS INCORPORATE A QUADRANGULAR BLADE WITH A SCREWDRIVER TIP AND ARE EQUIPPED WITH A LOCKING RING. THEY WERE INITIALLY ISSUED TO IMPERIAL RUSSIAN FORCES. THESE WERE ALSO MANUFACTURED BY WESTINGHOUSE IN THE U.S. AND CHATELLERAULT IN FRANCE.

No. 3. **RUSSIAN 1891/30 - MOSIN-NAGANT.** THESE PIECES HAVE IDENTICAL BLADE FORMS TO THOSE PREVIOUSLY DISCUSSED, HOWEVER, HAVE INCORPORATED A NEW LOCKING ARRANGEMENT WHICH ELIMINATES THE NEED FOR A LOCKING RING. THESE BAYONETS WERE PRODUCED BY THE THOUSANDS AND WERE PRIMARILY UTILIZED BY COMMUNIST FORCES. THEY WERE NOT ISSUED WITH SCABBARDS, SINCE THEY WERE INTENDED TO REMAIN ON THE RIFLE AND ARE COMPLETELY INTERCHANGEABLE WITH THE EARLIER MOSIN-NAGANT BAYONETS.

① RUSSIAN M 1891
AUSTRIAN ISSUE

WATTS & WHITE #945

② RUSSIAN M. 1891
FIRST PATTERN

KIESLING VOL. I #252

③ RUSSIAN M. 1891/30
SECOND PATTERN

KIESLING VOL. I #253

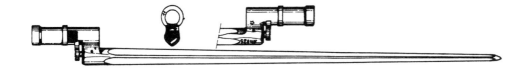

No. 1. **RUSSIAN MODEL 1891/30 - MOSIN-NAGANT.** THIS BAYONET HAS AN IDENTICAL BLADE TO THOSE PREVIOUSLY DISCUSSED, HOWEVER, IS EQUIPPED WITH A SIGHT GUARD, THEREFORE CAN ONLY FIT ON THE NAGANT RIFLES WHICH DO NOT HAVE INTEGRAL SIGHT GUARDS. THESE PIECES WERE ALL OF RUSSIAN MANUFACTURE, HOWEVER, WERE OBVIOUSLY PRODUCED BY TWO DIFFERENT ARSENALS SINCE I HAVE TWO DISTINCT VARIATIONS IN MY COLLECTION. THE VARIATIONS ARE PRIMARILY IN THE DESIGN OF THE FORESIGHT GUARD.

No. 2. **RUSSIAN 1891/30 - MOSIN-NAGANT.** THIS PIECE IS IDENTICAL TO 165-1, HOWEVER, THE FORESIGHT GUARD HAS BEEN REMOVED AND THE SCREWDRIVER TIP MODIFIED BY SHARPENING.

NOTE: THE PROOF MARKING OF THE PROVNAJA KOMISSIJA OR PROOF COMMITTEE IS ILLUSTRATED BELOW NO. 2, ALONG WITH A PHOTOGRAPH OF A "WIRE BREAKER" MANUFACTURED TO FIT THE MOSIN-NAGANT BAYONET.

① *RUSSIAN M. 1891/30 W/FORESIGHT GUARD*

KIESLING VOL I # 254

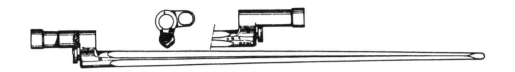

② *RUSSIAN M. 1891/30 W/ GUARD REMOVED*

✳ *WIRE BREAKER ATTACHMENT*

No. 1. **RUSSIAN MODEL 1895 – WINCHESTER.** THIS BAYONET WAS MANUFAC-
TURED FOR THE RUSSIAN CONTRACT OF 1916. WINCHESTER DELIVERED
293,815 M-1895 MUSKETS CHAMBERED FOR THE 7.62MM RUSSIAN CAR-
TRIDGE. THE FIRST 15,000 WERE SUPPLIED WITH THE 8-1/2" KNIFE
BAYONET OF THE TYPE ISSUED WITH THE U.S. M-1895 MUSKET; HOW-
EVER, THE SHORT BLADE WAS NOT WELL RECEIVED BY THE RUSSIANS
AND THE BALANCE OF THE CONTRACT WAS FURNISHED WITH THE ILLUS-
TRATED PIECE (16").

No. 2. **RUSSIAN MODEL 1938G – TOKAREV.** THIS BAYONET IS IDENTICAL TO
166-3, HOWEVER, THE BLADE IS REVERSED. THIS VERSION IS THE
RESULT OF COST REDUCTION EFFORTS ON THE LONGER BLADED MODEL
1938.

No. 3. **RUSSIAN MODEL 1940 – TOKAREV.** THESE ARE THE LATER MANUFAC-
TURED VERSIONS FOR THE TOKAREV RIFLES AND ARE A VERY COM-
PLICATED BAYONET. I HAVE EXAMPLES IN MY COLLECTION WHICH ARE
FINISHED BOTH BRIGHT AND BLUE. THESE PIECES WERE QUITE
SCARCE UNTIL 1985 WHEN A QUANTITY WAS RELEASED BY U.S.
IMPORTERS.

No. 4. **RUSSIAN MODEL 1944 – MOSIN-NAGANT.** THIS BAYONET IS THE FOLD-
ING QUADRANGULAR VERSION WHICH SERVED THE RUSSIANS THROUGH
THE LATTER PART OF WORLD WAR II, WERE LITERALLY PRODUCED BY
THE MILLIONS AND UTILIZED BY THE RED CHINESE ON THEIR CHICOM
RIFLES. I POSSESS BOTH RUSSIAN AND CHICOM VERSIONS AND THEY
ARE IDENTICAL.

① RUSSIAN M. 1895 WINCHESTER

KIESLING VOL. II #282

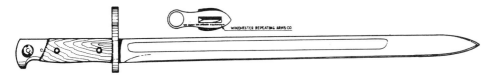

② RUSSIAN M. 1938 G TOKAREV

KIESLING VOL. IV #788

③ RUSSIAN M. 1940 TOKAREV

KIESLING VOL. I #87

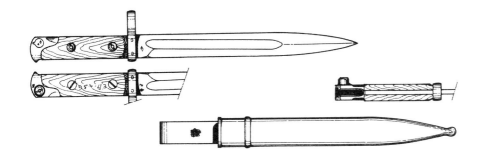

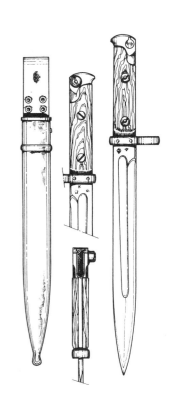

④ RUSSIAN M. 1944 MOSIN NAGANT

KIESLING VOL. I #128

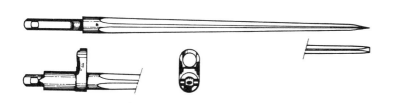

No. 1. **Russian Model AK47.** These bayonets were manufactured in 1947 for the Russian AK series of rifles and are typically complex with a Tokarev-style blade and an extremely unusual pommel.

No. 2. **Russian Model 1949 - Simonov.** The SVS rifle was equipped with a folding blade-type bayonet which utilizes a blade very similar to the AK47 with an improved folding mechanism. A similar version of this bayonet was produced in large quantities by the Chinese Communists.

No. 3. **Russian Model 1968 - SVD.** This bayonet was initially designed for the Dragunov rifle and is a wire-cutter with an oval slot in the blade which engages with a lug in the bottom of the scabbard, such that the bayonet can be used to cut either barbed or electrical wire. The handle and the rubber hand grip on the throat of the scabbard provide insulation for cutting live electrical wires. These are produced in numerous variations and large quantities by Soviet Block countries and come with and without the serrations on the blade edge. These have been released recently (1985) in several variations.

No. 4. **Russian Model 1972 - AKM.** This is the latest version of the Russian wire-cutter bayonet and has a blade very similar to the SVD, however, utilizes a completely redesigned handle of a red, plastic material (note Sestrojevsk mark). It also has a scabbard manufactured of the same material. For some reason, these pieces continue to be a bit scarce. In my opinion, the Russian wire-cutter bayonets were the basis for the entire series of allied wire cutters recently introduced.

① RUSSIAN AK 47
KIESLING VOL. III #517

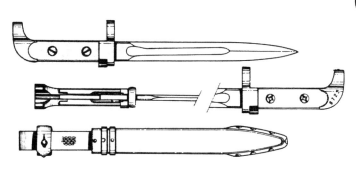

② RUSSIAN M. 1949 SIMONOV
KIESLING VOL. I #45

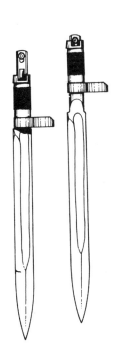

③ RUSSIAN M. 1968 SVD
KIESLING VOL. IV #730

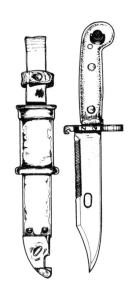

④ RUSSIAN M. 1972 AKM
KIESLING VOL. IV #731

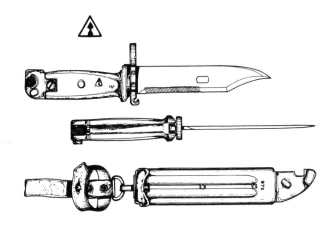

No. 1. **SERBIAN MODEL 1899.** SERBIAN BAYONETS ARE UNIQUE IN THAT THEY HAVE A DOUBLE-EDGED BLADE AND A MAUSER-STYLE HILT, SIMILAR TO THE MEXICAN MODEL 1910. THEY ARE NOT A COMMON BAYONET AND WERE MANUFACTURED, BOTH BY PLUMB IN THE UNITED STATES WITH THE BLADE RICASSO SO MARKED, AND APPARENTLY BY SOME EUROPEAN MANUFACTURER, BECAUSE EXAMPLES EXIST WITH NO MARKS.

NOTE: SERBIA IS PART OF MODERN YUGOSLAVIA. IT PREVIOUSLY WAS UNDER TURKISH INFLUENCE UNTIL 1918, WHEN A KINGDOM OF SLOVENES, CROATS AND SERBS WAS ESTABLISHED UNDER KING ALEXANDER. THE MONARCHY WAS ABOLISHED AFTER WORLD WAR II WHEN THE COMMUNISTS ASSUMED POWER. HENCE, MOST AUTHORS INCLUDE SERBIAN WEAPONS UNDER THE GENERAL HEADING OF YUGOSLAVIA.

① SERBIAN M. 1899

KIESLING VOL. I #96

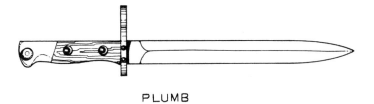

PLUMB

No. 1. **Siamese Model 1903.** This bayonet is identical to the Austrian Model 1888; however, it is known in Siam as a "46th year type bayonet". The pieces utilized by Siam have a Roman Numeral type stamp on the blade ricasso (which may mean they were surplused from Rumania), and handles which show evidence of having been replaced numerous times. The bayonets can be found both with Siamese numerals and with Austrian serial numbers.

No. 2. **Siamese Arisaka Model 1903 - NCO.** This is also identical to its Austrian counterpart and has Siamese numerals stamped on the butt of the hilt. Apparently the Siamese also utilized bayonets to denote rank.

No. 3. **Siamese Model 1908.** This bayonet looks like a short Japanese Arisaka, however, fits a Mauser rifle, and the examples in my collection have no marks. I do possess several of these bayonets, all with different types of grip fastenings. The various grip fastening devices include the oblong screw washer combination used by the Japanese, round screws, and rivets. These pieces were known as the "51st Year Type" and used by the Siamese in the 1908-1910 time frame.

① SIAMESE M.1903
46TH YEAR TYPE
KIESLING VOL. III #546, 547

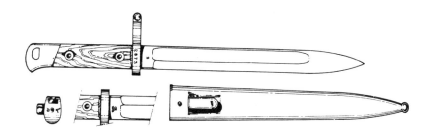

② SIAMESE M.1903
NCO
KIESLING VOL. I # 112

③ SIAMESE M.1908
51ST YEAR TYPE
KIESLING VOL. I #157

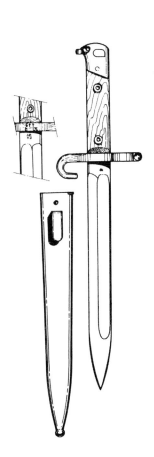

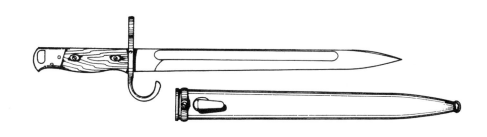

No. 1. JAPANESE TYPE 30 – ARISAKA. THIS BAYONET IS THE EARLY JAPANESE TYPE 30 WITH SIAMESE NUMERALS STAMPED ON THE HILT. IT IS HEAVILY BLUED AND HAS THE TOKYO ARSENAL MARK ON THE BLADE RICASSO.

No. 2. SIAMESE TYPE 30 – ARISAKA. THIS IS AN ARISAKA BAYONET WHICH HAS BEEN ASSEMBLED BY THE SIAMESE APPARENTLY UTILIZING JAPANESE PARTS TO PROVIDE A VARIATION THAT IS UNLIKE KNOWN JAPANESE CONFIGURATIONS. THE PIECE IS SIAMESE MARKED AND HAS A VERY GOOD FINISH.

No. 3. SIAMESE TYPE 30 – ARISAKA. THIS BAYONET, IN MY OPINION, WAS MANUFACTURED BY SIAM TO FIT THEIR ARISAKA RIFLES AND BEARS A STRONG RESEMBLANCE TO THE JAPANESE BAYONET, HOWEVER, REFLECTS TOTALLY DIFFERENT MANUFACTURING OPERATIONS, ROUNDED CORNERS ON THE PARTS, THE ADDITION OF A MAUSER-TYPE FROG STUD TO THE ARISAKA SCABBARD AND AN ARISAKA-TYPE BLADE WITH SIAMESE MARKINGS ON THE RICASSO. SOME COLLECTORS FEEL THESE BAYONETS WERE JAPANESE PRODUCED, HOWEVER, I DISAGREE WITH THIS CONTENTION DUE TO THE OBVIOUS DIFFERENCES IN FINISH AND CONFIGURATION.

① *SIAMESE TYPE 30*

KIESLING VOL. I #262

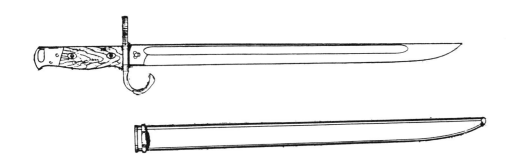

② *SIAMESE TYPE 30*

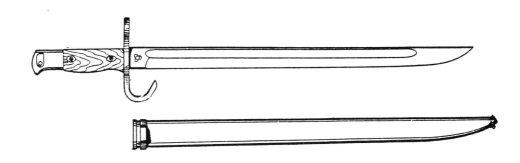

③ *SIAMESE TYPE 30*

ERNST VOL. II PG. #49

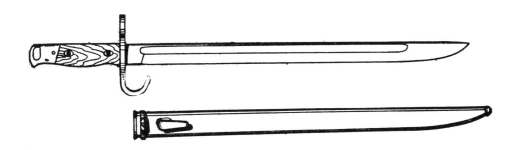

No. 1. SIAMESE MODEL 1888. THIS BAYONET WAS UTILIZED BY SIAM AND CHINA AND HAS A MANNLICHER-TYPE HANDLE AND A DOUBLE-EDGE BLADE; HOWEVER, IT FITS A GERMAN MODEL 88 RIFLE. I POSSESS TWO VARIATIONS; ONE WITH THE GRIPS FASTENED BY RIVETS WITHOUT WASHERS AND HEAVILY BLUED, AND THE OTHER WITH WASHERS BEHIND THE RIVETS AND FINISHED BRIGHT. I ALSO HAVE A TRANSITIONAL MODEL WITH AN AUSTRIAN (TYPE 51) BLADE AND A T-O SLOT, PRESUMABLY FOR A MAUSER.

No. 2. SIAMESE MODEL 1896 - MAUSER. THIS BAYONET IS MANUFACTURED FOR THE SIAMESE MAUSER RIFLE WHICH WAS PRODUCED FOR SIAM BY THE JAPANESE. THIS PIECE COMES IN TWO VARIETIES; THE FIRST OF WHICH HAS THE GRIPS FASTENED WITH THE OBLONG-TYPE OF SCREW-WASHER ARRANGEMENT COMMON ON JAPANESE BAYONETS AND ILLUSTRATED HERE, AND THE SECOND WITH THE ROUND WASHER-SCREW ATTACHMENT SYSTEM.

No. 3. SIAMESE MODEL 1896 - MAUSER. THIS BAYONET IS IDENTICAL IN ALL RESPECTS TO 171-2, HOWEVER, THE GRIPS HAVE BEEN FASTENED USING RIVETS AND WASHERS.

No. 4. SIAMESE MODEL 1896 - MAUSER. THIS BAYONET IS IDENTICAL TO 171-2 AND 171-3, HOWEVER, IT HAS BEEN RE-GRIPPED USING RIVETS AND GRIPS WITH AN OIL HOLE.

① SIAMESE M. 1888
KIESLING VOL. I # 115

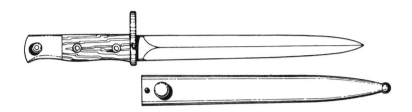

② SIAMESE M. 1896
KIESLING VOL. I # 97

③ SIAMESE M. 1896
KIESLING VOL. I # 98

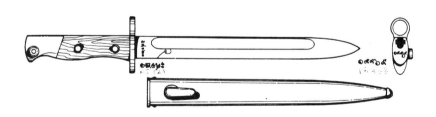

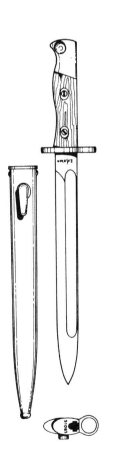

④ SIAMESE M. 1896
REGRIPPED

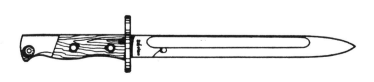

No. 1. SIAMESE MODEL 1920 - ENFIELD. THIS BAYONET IS IDENTICAL TO THE BRITISH PATTERN 1907 BAYONET, HOWEVER, WAS INTENDED SPECIFICALLY FOR SIAM AND HAS A SIAMESE TIGER FACE ON THE RICASSO OF THE BLADE. THESE PIECES WERE REFURBISHED IN 1920 FOR THE WILD TIGER CORPS OF KING RAMA VI AND MANY INCORPORATE A VERY UNIQUE SCABBARD WHEREBY THE STANDARD ENFIELD SCABBARD HAS BEEN MODIFIED BY REMOVING THE LEATHER AND REPLACING IT WITH STEEL. OTHERS ARE FOUND IN THE STANDARD ENFIELD-MARKED STEEL-MOUNTED LEATHER SCABBARD. THESE BAYONETS ARE RELATIVELY COMMON, HOWEVER, ACCORDING TO R.D.C. EVANS IN AN ARTICLE IN GUNS, WEAPONS AND MILITARIA, ONLY 10,000 WERE ORDERED BY RAMA VI FROM B.S.A. (BIRMINGHAM SMALL ARMS COMPANY). THEY ARE FREQUENTLY CALLED "PUSSY CAT" BAYONETS.

NOTE: THE RUMANIAN MODEL 1879 ILLUSTRATED ON PAGE 162 (ITEM NO. 1) HAS BEEN IMPORTED TO THE UNITED STATES WITH SIAMESE NUMBERS ON THE CROSSGUARD.

① SIAMESE M. 1920 ENFIELD

KIESLING VOL. III #648

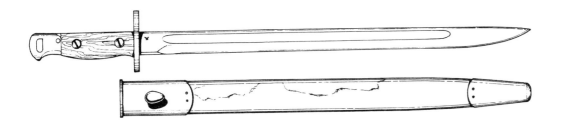

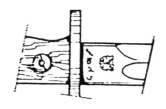

RAMA VI 2642

No. 1. **SOUTH AFRICAN PATTERN 1907.** THIS BAYONET IS THE STANDARD BRITISH PATTERN 1907 BAYONET (SEE 57-3) WITH THE SOUTH AFRICAN ACCEPTANCE MARK, WHICH CONSISTS OF A "U" WITH AN ARROW IN THE MIDDLE. IN ALL OTHER RESPECTS, IT IS IDENTICAL TO THE BRITISH PIECE. THE SOUTH AFRICANS ALSO UTILIZED THE No. 4 RIFLE AND SPIKE BAYONET.

* **TRENCH MIRROR.** THIS IS AN INTERESTING RELIC OF WORLD WAR I USED NOT ONLY BY SOUTH AFRICAN TROOPS BUT BY ALL ALLIED FORCES. THE DESIGN OF THE MIRROR WAS SUCH THAT WHEN ATTACHED TO THE BAYONET, IT COULD BE RAISED ABOVE THE TRENCH TO ALLOW THE SOLDIER TO HAVE A CLEAR (IF LIMITED) VIEW WITHOUT RAISING HIS HEAD ABOVE THE TOP. THESE WERE INVENTED BY THE FRENCH, HOWEVER, WERE PRODUCED BY BOTH ENGLAND AND THE UNITED STATES.

NOTE: SOUTH AFRICA CURRENTLY UTILIZES THE (5.56 x 45) R4 ASSAULT RIFLE WHICH HAS NO PROVISION FOR A BAYONET. THE R2 AND R3 ASSAULT RIFLES UTILIZED THE BELGIUM FAL TUBULAR BAYONETS (SEE PG. 21). THE SOUTH AFRICANS ALSO UTILIZE THE UZ1 SUBMACHINE GUN AND BAYONET (117-2) AND I HAVE BEEN TOLD THAT SPECIAL OPERATION'S TROOPS UTILIZE THE AKM.

① SOUTH AFRICAN P.1907
S. A. ACCEPTANCE
KIESLING VOL. II # 318

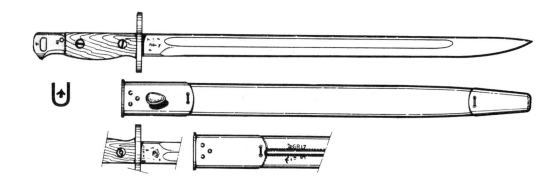

✳ TRENCH MIRROR

No. 1. SPANISH MODEL 1858 - ARTILLERIA. THIS BAYONET IS A
VERY BEAUTIFUL AND UNIQUE WEAPON. IT INCORPORATES
A BRASS HILT WITH A SOCKET-TYPE CROSSGUARD AND A
HEAVY BOWIE-STYLE BLADE. THESE BAYONETS ARE QUITE
RARE AND WERE OBVIOUSLY NOT PRODUCED IN LARGE NUM-
BERS.

No. 2. SPANISH MODEL 1858 - REMINGTON. THE IDENTIFICATION
OF THIS BAYONET IS PURELY A GUESS AND IS BASED ON
SOME BOOKS PUBLISHED IN SPANISH BY CALVO. IN MANY
WAYS, IT RESEMBLES THE U.S. MODEL 1855, HOWEVER,
HAS A BRASS HANDLE CUT FOR THE REMINGTON ROLLING
BLOCK RIFLE.

No. 3. SPANISH MODEL 1859 - SNIDER. THIS PIECE IS UNIQUE
IN THAT IT HAS A VERY LONG CROSSGUARD, A MACHETE-
STYLE BLADE TIP AND BRASS GRIPS. THE BAYONET WAS
UTILIZED WITH THE "ZUAVAS" VERSION OF THE SNIDER
CONVERSION WHICH CALVO DESIGNATES AS "LA
AZPEITIANA".

No. 4. SPANISH MODEL 1871 - REMINGTON. THIS SOCKET BAYO-
NET IS ONE OF THE FEW REMINGTON EXPORT BAYONETS
WHICH CAN BE READILY IDENTIFIED AND IS TYPICAL OF
THE ROLLING BLOCK SOCKET BAYONETS. THE SPANISH
VERSIONS HAVE A HEAVILY BLUED SOCKET WITH A SERIAL
NUMBER AT THE BACK OF THE SOCKET AND LONG, TRIAN-
GULAR-SHAPED BLADES. THESE BAYONETS ARE RELATIVELY
COMMON.

① SPANISH M. 1858 ARTILLERIA

KIESLING VOL. II #344

② SPANISH M. 1858 REMINGTON

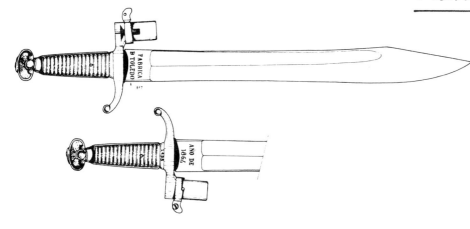

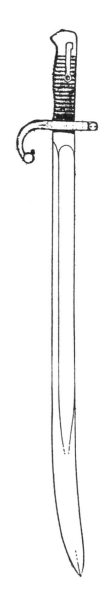

③ SPANISH M. 1859 SNIDER

CALVO LA' MINA 7
KIESLING VOL. IV 932

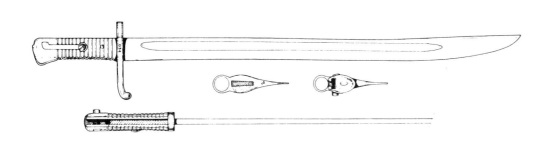

④ SPANISH M. 1871 REMINGTON

KIESLING VOL. II #395

DIMENSIONS	
BLADE LENGTH	21 3/8
BLADE WIDTH	3/4
SOCKET LENGTH	3 "
SOCKET O.D.	45/64
SOCKET I.D.	43/64
SHANK LENGTH	1 1/8

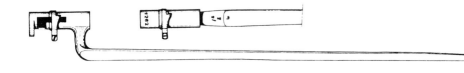

No. 1. **SPANISH MODEL 1893 - MAUSER.** THE SHORT BAYONETS ARE ALSO QUITE COMMON AND COME IN THREE VARIETIES. THE FIRST IS A HUMP-BACKED MODEL VERY SIMILAR TO THE GERMAN MODEL 84; HOWEVER, IT HAS A HIGHER MUZZLE RING. THE INITIAL QUANTITIES OF THESE BAYONETS WERE MANUFACTURED IN GERMANY AND SO MARKED. THE SECOND VARIATION OF THESE PIECES WERE SPANISH COPIES OF THE GERMAN BAYONET (INITIALLY UTILIZING GERMAN BLADES). THE THIRD VARIATION MANUFACTURED IN SPAIN IS A TOTALLY DIFFERENT BAYONET IN THAT THE "HUMP" HAS BEEN REMOVED FROM THE HANDLE AND THE BAYONET HAS BEEN FITTED WITH A THICKER CROSSGUARD. THE FINAL VARIATION HAS A REFINED BLADE FORM. THESE PIECES REFLECT EXCELLENT MANUFACTURING QUALITY. THERE ARE TWO SCABBARD TYPES; ONE BRASS-MOUNTED LEATHER, AND THE OTHER STEEL-MOUNTED LEATHER.

No. 2. **SPANISH MODEL 1913 - MAUSER.** THIS BAYONET IS THE LONG RIFLE MODEL WHICH WAS MADE TO COMPENSATE FOR THE SHORTER LENGTH OF THE RIFLES MANUFACTURED IN SPAIN. IT HAS A CHECKERED WOOD HANDLE AND A STEEL-MOUNTED, LEATHER SCABBARD. THE PIECE IS FINISHED BRIGHT AND MANY HAVE A SPANISH "ARTILLERIA" STAMP ON THE BLADE RICASSO. BOTH CALVO AND RUBI CALL THIS A MODEL 1913.

NOTE: THE STAMP ON THE BLADE IS AN INDICATOR OF PRODUCTION YEARS. THE DATE WAS UTILIZED UNTIL 1906 AT WHICH TIME AN UPDATED "ARTILLERIA" STAMP WAS INTRODUCED. THIS STAMP WAS CHANGED AGAIN IN 1920.

① *SPANISH M. 1893 SHORT*

KIESLING VOL. I #103,104,105,106

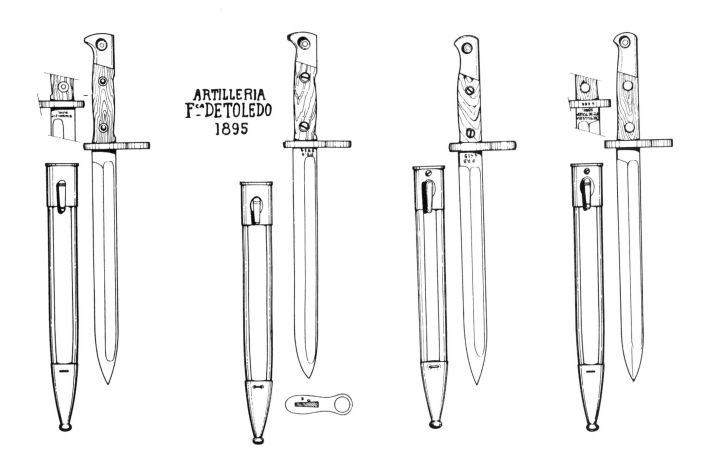

ARTILLERIA
Fᶜᵃ DE TOLEDO
1895

② *SPANISH M. 1893/13 LONG*

KIESLING VOL. II # 291

ARTILLERIA
Fᶜᵃ NACIONAL
TOLEDO

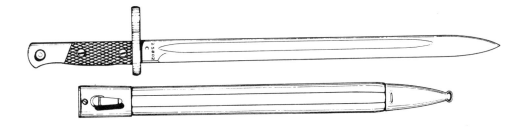

No. 1.   SPANISH MODEL 1936 - MAUSER.   THIS BAYONET WAS MANUFACTURED FOR THE SPANISH MAUSER RIFLES INCORPORATING THE GERMAN-TYPE OF BAYONET LUG AND MANY HAVE THE SPANISH MARKS ON THE RICASSO, AS ILLUSTRATED.   IN ADDITION, MANY EXAMPLES HAVE A RATHER CRUDE SERIAL NUMBER STAMPED ON THE RICASSO.

No. 2.   SPANISH MODEL 1943 - MAUSER.   THIS PIECE IS IDENTICAL TO THE GERMAN 84/98 SERIES OF BAYONETS AND WAS ACTUALLY PRODUCED IN GERMANY; HOWEVER, IT IS MARKED "P.R.S." ON THE CROSSGUARD AND FINISHED DARK "RED".   THE SCABBARD IS BLUED.

No. 3.   SPANISH MODEL 1943 - MAUSER.   THIS BAYONET IS A SPANISH COPY OF THE PREVIOUSLY DISCUSSED GERMAN BAYONET AND HAS WOODEN GRIPS.   IT CAN BE DISTINGUISHED FROM THE GERMAN MODELS BY THE BLADES WHICH ARE MUCH LIGHTER AND BY THE FINISH WHICH IS ROUGH.

No. 4.   SPANISH MODEL 1943 - MAUSER.   THIS IS IDENTICAL TO 176-2; HOWEVER, IT HAS BEEN FITTED WITH RED PLASTIC GRIPS.   THE SCABBARDS FOR THESE BAYONETS LOOK MUCH LIKE THE GERMAN SCABBARDS; HOWEVER, DO NOT HAVE A THROAT.

① SPANISH M. 1936
KIESLING VOL. I #149

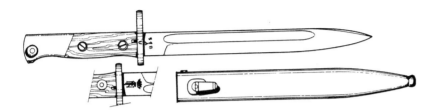

② SPANISH M. 1943
KIESLING VOL. I #148

③ SPANISH M. 1943
KIESLING VOL. I #147

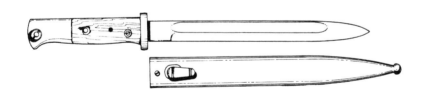

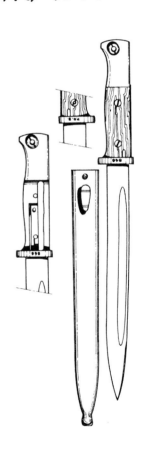

④ SPANISH M. 1943
PLASTIC GRIPS

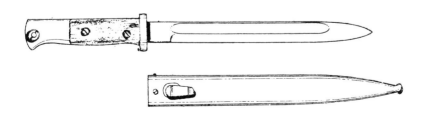

No. 1. **SPANISH MODEL 1941 - MAUSER.** THIS BAYONET WAS EX-TREMELY SCARCE FOR YEARS AND WAS RELEASED IN VERY LARGE QUANTITIES APPROXIMATELY FIVE YEARS AGO. IT HAS A BOLO-TYPE BLADE, A FINAL ON THE CROSSGUARD, AND A RELATIVELY HEAVY HILT, SUCH THAT IT CAN BE USED AS A BOLO. I HAVE TWO VARIATIONS IN MY COL-LECTION; ONE WITH WOOD GRIPS AND ONE WITH CHECKERED PLASTIC GRIPS. THE SCABBARD IS OF THE STANDARD STEEL DESIGN, HOWEVER, HAS A ROUND FROG STUD.

No. 2. **SPANISH MODEL 1969 - CETME.** THIS BAYONET IS FOR THE MODEL 58 ASSAULT RIFLE CURRENTLY USED BY SPAIN AND IS SIMILAR TO THE MODEL 1941. IT IS HEAVILY BLUED, HAS CHECKERED PLASTIC GRIPS AND, LIKE OTHER SPANISH BAYONETS, IS UNIQUE IN SHAPE AND DESIGN. THESE BAYONETS HAVE NOT BEEN RELEASED, THUS, ARE A BIT SCARCE AT THE PRESENT.

① *SPANISH M.1941*

KIESLING VOL. I #107
KIESLING VOL. IV #805

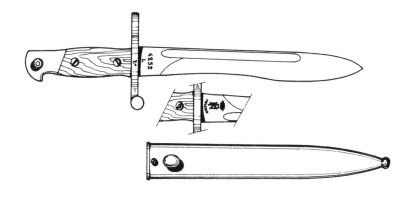

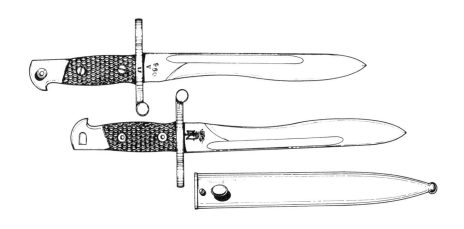

② *SPANISH M.1969*
CETME

KIESLING VOL. IV # 776

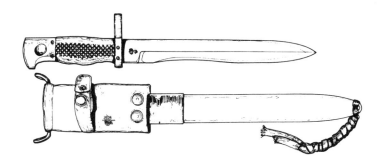

No. 1. **SUDANESE MODEL 1959.** THIS BAYONET WAS PRODUCED IN GERMANY BY INTERARMCO FOR THE U.S.-DESIGNED DUTCH-PRODUCED SUDANESE AR10 AND IS A SOUGHT-AFTER PIECE BECAUSE IT WAS COPIED AFTER THE GERMAN EXPERIMENTAL MODEL (SEE 101-3) PRODUCED AT THE END OF WORLD WAR II, HAVING A REMOVABLE TOOL KIT MOUNTED IN THE HANDLE. THE BLADE IS DOUBLE EDGED AND HEAVILY BLUED. THE HANDLES ARE OF A DARK PLASTIC MATERIAL, AS IS THE SCABBARD. THESE PIECES ARE BECOMING RELATIVELY SCARCE.

NOTE: THE SUDANESE ALSO USED QUANTITIES OF THE AUSTRIAN MODEL 1895 BAYONETS (SEE PG. 9) WHICH WERE REFURBISHED PRIOR TO RECEIPT. I SUSPECT THESE WERE RECENTLY PLACED ON THE WORLD MARKET AS SURPLUS.

① SUDANESE M. 1959
AR·10

KIESLING VOL. I #56

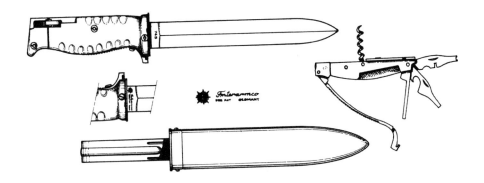

No. 1. **Swedish Model 1867 - Remington.** This bayonet was issued on a limited basis and is very similar to the Norwegian M-1859. It has a brass pommel with a hole in the tip and the blade is marked with a crown over an anchor on the ricasso.

No. 2. **Swedish Model 1867 - Remington.** This bayonet is for the Remington single-shot rifle which Sweden adopted in 1867. This bayonet, which has a cruciform blade and a central locking ring is heavily blued with a very sharp tip. The example in my collection is manufactured by Husqvarna.

No. 3. **Swedish Model 1867-89 - Remington.** This bayonet is an example of the diversity of locking mechanisms utilized by Sweden and is the only socket bayonet that I am aware of with an internal coil spring. It has a cruciform (or quadrangular) blade very similar to 179-2, however, was manufactured by Carl Gustav. This piece was issued with a newer model Remington rifle which was chambered for the 8mm cartridge.

① SWEDISH M. 1867

WATTS & WHITE #585

② SWEDISH M. 1867
SOCKET

LISSMARK PG. 47
KIESLING VOL. IV #888

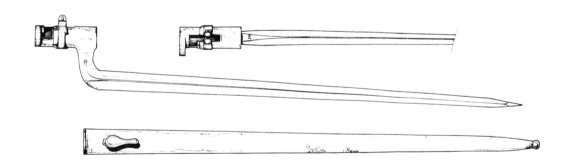

③ SWEDISH M. 1867/89

LISSMARK PG. 49
KIESLING VOL. III #645

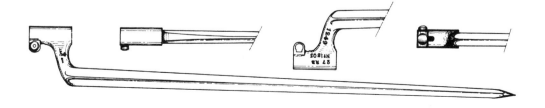

No. 1. **SWEDISH MODEL 1896.** THIS BAYONET IS AN INTERESTING AND WELL DESIGNED ARM AND, IN MY OPINION, MUCH AHEAD OF ITS TIME. IT IS AN ALL METAL BAYONET WITH A DOUBLE-EDGED, VERY HIGH QUALITY BLADE, A KNURLED HANDLE AND A UNIQUE LOCKING MECHANISM. AT ONE TIME, THESE PIECES WERE SCARCE, HOWEVER, HAVE NOW BEEN RELEASED IN LARGE QUANTITIES IN THE UNITED STATES AND ARE COMMON. I POSSESS SEVERAL EXAMPLES: ONE EQUIPPED WITH A CLIP (SEE ILLUSTRATION) WHICH WAS UTILIZED TO HOLD THE SCABBARD ON THE BAYONET FOR BAYONET PRACTICE AND A SECOND ONE WITH THE EARLY MODEL CATCH WHICH IS OF A SLIGHTLY DIFFERENT FORM. (I HAVE AN EXAMPLE OF THIS PIECE WITH SERIAL NO. 001).

① SWEDISH M. 1896

KIESLING VOL. I #59

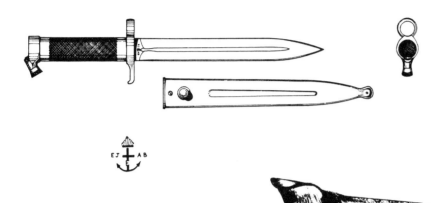

BAYONET PRACTICE
RETAINING CLIP

No. 1. **SWEDISH MODEL 1913.** THIS BAYONET IS A WELL MADE PIECE WITH A DOUBLE-EDGED BLADE, WOODEN HANDLE AND SCABBARD OF THE SAME BASIC DESIGN USED WITH THE M-1896. THE POMMEL AND CROSSGUARD ARE BLUED AND THE BLADE POLISHED BRIGHT. THE M-1913 HAS A <u>ROUND PRESS STUD</u> AND IS SCARCE.

No. 2. **SWEDISH MODEL 1914.** THIS PIECE IS IDENTICAL TO 181-1 WITH THE EXCEPTION THAT AN <u>OBLONG PRESS STUD</u> IS UTILIZED. THE MODEL 1914 BAYONETS ARE MUCH MORE COMMON THAN THE MODEL 1913, AND ON CLOSE INSPECTION REFLECT OTHER MINOR DIFFERENCES.

No. 3. **SWEDISH MODEL 1915.** THIS BAYONET WAS ISSUED TO THE NAVY TO FIT THE SAME CARBINE AS THE PREVIOUS PIECES DISCUSSED. IT, HOWEVER, HAS A LONG BLADE WITH A VERY THIN FULLER AND A HILT IDENTICAL TO THE 1914. THESE PIECES ARE SCARCE.

① SWEDISH M. 1913

BAJONETTEN DA TILL NU #297

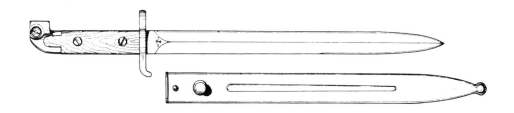

② SWEDISH M. 1914

KIESLING VOL. I #227

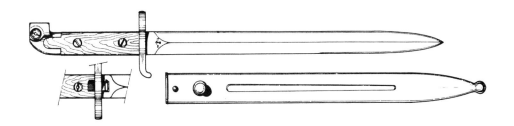

③ SWEDISH M. 1915

KIESLING VOL. III #675

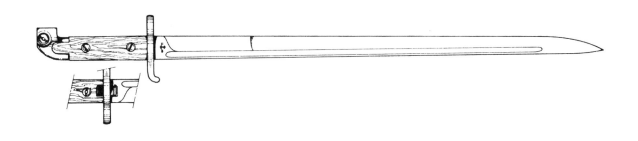

No. 1. Swedish Model 1965 - AK4. This is the current (1985) issue bayonet and is typical of the G3 series of bayonets, with a blade similar to the U.S. carbine series and a handle of a plastic-type material molded in a pattern to facilitate grip. I also have a parade version which is plated. It is illustrated in Bajonetten Da Till Nu #274.

① SWEDISH M. 1965
AK 4

KIESLING VOL. III #523

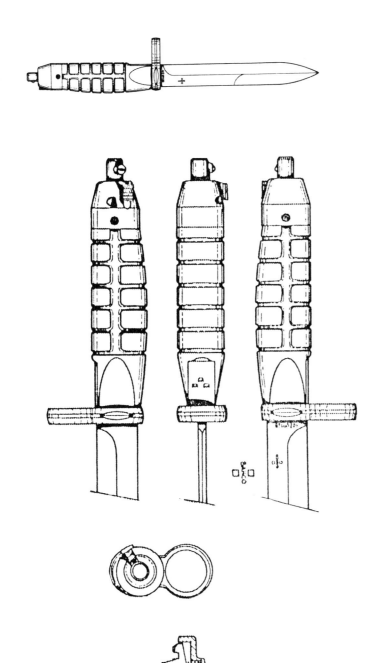

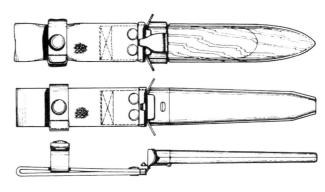

No. 1.   SWISS MODEL 1851 - FEDERAL. THESE BAYONETS DO NOT HAVE SOCKETS AND ARE DESIGNED TO FIT ON SPECIAL BARREL BRACKETS. THERE DOES NOT APPEAR TO BE A REAL MEASURE OF STANDARDIZATION IN THE FEDERAL RIFLE BAYONETS AND I POSSESS SEVERAL VARIATIONS.

No. 2.   SWISS MODEL 1851-1864 - FEDERAL. THIS BAYONET IS ANOTHER EXAMPLE OF THE FEDERAL RIFLE VARIATIONS, THIS ONE UTILIZING A KNURLED LOCKING SCREW.

No. 3.   SWISS MODEL 1867 - "SHARPSHOOTERS". THIS PIECE IS BEAUTIFULLY MADE WITH A BRASS POMMEL AND CROSS-GUARD, YATAGHAN BLADE AND GRIPS OF BLACK CHECKERED LEATHER. IT IS UNIQUE IN THAT THE LOCKING SPRING WORKS ON A PIVOT SYSTEM AND HAS THE PRESS STUD IN THE MIDDLE OF THE GRIPS. THESE ARE NOT COMMON.

① SWISS M. 1851
FEDERAL

WATTS & WHITE #596

② SWISS M. 1851/64
FEDERAL

WATTS & WHITE #595

③ SWISS M. 1867
SHARPSHOOTERS

KIESLING VOL IV #954
WATTS & WHITE #598

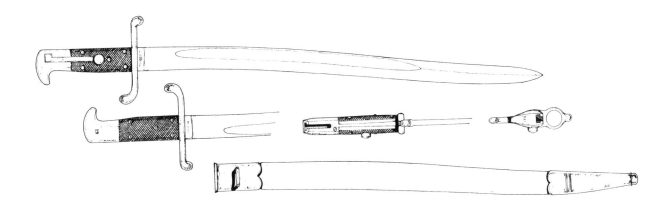

No. 1. **SWISS MODEL 1863.** THIS BAYONET WAS DESIGNED FOR THE PEABODY RIFLE AND IS A QUADRANGULAR SOCKET BAYONET OF LIGHTER CONSTRUCTION THAN THE SUBSEQUENT VETTERLI VERSION.

No. 2. **SWISS MODEL 1871.** THIS BAYONET IS THE QUADRANGULAR SOCKET VERSION UTILIZED ON THE VETTERLI RIFLE AND IS OF NOTICEABLY LARGER DIMENSIONS THAN THE PEABODY VERSION PREVIOUSLY DISCUSSED. THE UNIQUE FEATURE OF THE SWISS SOCKET BAYONETS IS THAT THE SIGHT APERTURE AT THE BACK OF THE BAYONET HAS A SMALL TRIANGULAR INDENTATION TO ALLOW THE PIECE TO CLEAR THE HIGH SIGHT.

NOTE: I ALSO HAVE A TRIANGULAR SOCKET BAYONET WITH THE BLADE CLIPPED WHICH HAS THE SAME SIGHT APERTURE FEATURE MENTIONED IN 184-2, WHICH MAKES ME SUSPECT IT IS ALSO OF SWISS EXTRACTION.

① SWISS M. 1863
KIESLING VOL II #315

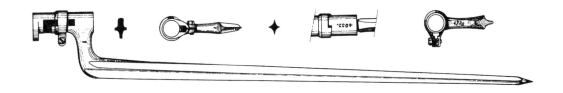

② SWISS M. 1871
KIESLING VOL I #244

No. 1. SWISS MODEL 1878 - PIONEER. THIS BAYONET IS THE EARLIEST OF THE SAWBACKED VERSIONS UTILIZED ON THE VETTERLI AND SCHMIDT-RUBIN RIFLES. AS WITH ALL SWISS WEAPONS, THE MANUFACTURING STANDARDS ARE HIGH AND THE BAYONET HAS A LONG STRAIGHT BLADE WITH SAW-TEETH AND LEATHER CHECKERED HANDLES OF A RATHER BROWNISH COLOR. IT UTILIZES A STEEL-MOUNTED LEATHER SCABBARD. THE MODEL 1878 CAN BE RECOGNIZED BY THE FACT THAT THE HANDLE IS FASTENED BY THREE RIVETS.

No. 2. SWISS MODEL 1887 - PIONEER. THE M-1878 IS FULLERED ON ONE SIDE ONLY AND THE M-1887 IS FULLERED ON BOTH SIDES. THE GRIPS ARE FASTENED BY FOUR RIVETS AND THE EXAMPLE IN MY COLLECTION HAS BLACK GRIPS.

No. 3. SWISS MODEL 1911 - PIONEER. THIS BAYONET IS DESIGNED FOR THE SCHMIDT-RUBIN CARBINE AND IS OF HEAVIER DIMENSIONS THAN THOSE USED ON THE VETTERLI. IT HAS A LONG POMMEL WITH SHORT WOODEN GRIPS AND A SWELLED TIP ON THE BLADE, AS ILLUS-TRATED. THESE BAYONETS WERE APPARENTLY PRODUCED IN LARGE QUANTITIES AND ARE COMMON, THOUGH VERY POPU-LAR.

NOTE: THERE IS A TRANSITION PIECE DESIGNATED MODEL 1906 WHICH HAS THE VETTERLI BLADE (NOS. 1 AND 2) AND THE SCHMIDT-RUBIN HANDLE (NO. 3).

① *SWISS M. 1878 PIONEER*

KIESLING VOL. II #371

② *SWISS M. 1887 PIONEER*

KIESLING VOL. II #372

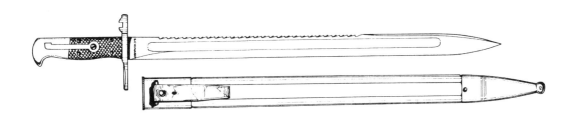

③ *SWISS M. 1911 PIONEER*

KIESLING VOL II #389

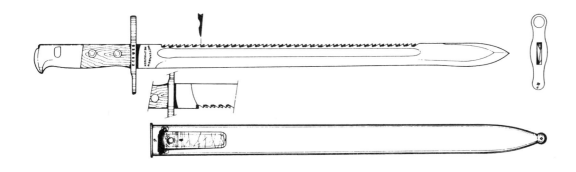

No. 1.   SWISS MODEL 1889 - SCHMIDT-RUBIN. THIS BAYONET IS THE FIRST OF THE BEAUTIFULLY MADE SERIES OF SWISS KNIFE BAYONETS AND LOOKS VERY MUCH LIKE THE U.S. KRAG M1892 FOR WHICH IT WAS A PROTOTYPE. IT HAS WOODEN GRIPS, AND A PLAIN FULLERED BLADE.

No. 2.   SWISS MODEL 1889/99 - SCHMIDT-RUBIN. THIS BAYONET IS IDENTICAL TO 186-1, HOWEVER, IT HAS A RIVET IN THE TOP OF THE BLADE FULLER TO FACILITATE HOLDING THE PIECE IN THE SCABBARD. I ALSO POSSESS A LATER VERSION WITH A LARGER RIVET HEAD FABRICATED TO THE BLADE UTILIZING A DIFFERENT TECHNIQUE.

No. 3.   SWISS MODEL 1889/11 - SCHMIDT-RUBIN. THIS BAYONET WAS THE LAST OF MODEL 1889 SCHMIDT-RUBIN SERIES OF KNIFE BAYONETS AND HAS A SCABBARD LOCKING BAR ACTUALLY MACHINED INTO THE FULLER OF THE BLADE, AS ILLUSTRATED. I POSSESS TWO VARIATIONS OF THIS PIECE; ONE IS POLISHED AND THE SECOND IS PLATED. AN EXPLANATION FOR THE PLATING WAS PROVIDED BY R. D. C. EVANS ON PAGE 186 OF THE BAYONET WHERE HE STATES THAT "SWISS SOLDIERS ARMED WITH THE M-1889 BAYONETS WERE ALLOWED TO HAVE INDIVIDUAL BAYONETS PLATED, IF DESIRED, TO ENHANCE THEIR APPEARANCE."

① *SWISS M. 1889*
KIESLING VOL. I #168

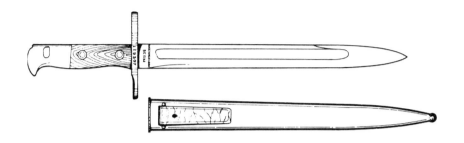

② *SWISS M. 1889/99*
KIESLING VOL. I #169

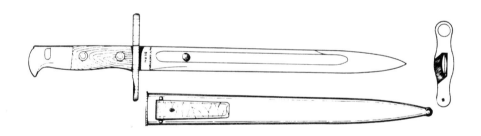

③ *SWISS M. 1889/11*
KIESLING VOL. I #170

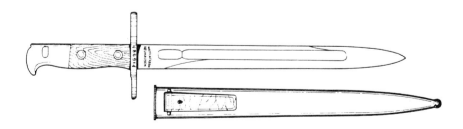

No. 1. SWISS MODEL 1918 - SCHMIDT-RUBIN. THIS BAYONET WAS DESIGNED FOR THE M-1911 AND M-1931 SCHMIDT-RUBIN SHORT RIFLES AND UTILIZES A DOUBLE-EDGED BLADE WITH A POMMEL SLIGHTLY LONGER THAN THE M-1889 BAYONET. IT IS FINISHED BRIGHT AS WAS THE PREVIOUS SERIES. THIS PIECE WAS ALSO USED WITH THE SIG AK53 ASSAULT RIFLE AND A SERIES OF SUBMACHINE GUNS.

No. 2. SWISS MODEL 1900 - SCHMIDT-RUBIN. THIS IS AN ALL STEEL BAYONET WHICH WAS MANUFACTURED UTILIZING AN OLD SOCKET BLADE. IT IS HEAVILY BLUED AND IS A VERY SCARCE PIECE. (WATTS & WHITE DESIGNATE THIS BAYONET AS MODEL 1892).

No. 3. SWISS MODEL 1953 - FAVOR SUBMACHINE GUN. THIS BAYONET WAS DESIGNED FOR THE REXIM FV4 SUBMACHINE GUN AND LOOKS AND FUNCTIONS VERY MUCH LIKE THE FRENCH MAS BAYONETS. WHEN NOT IN USE, THE BAYONET IS REVERSED IN THE SLOT AS ILLUSTRATED ON THE MUZZLE BRAKE. I UNDERSTAND THIS WEAPON WAS NOT UTILIZED BY THE SWISS ARMY.

① SWISS M. 1918
KIESLING VOL I #199

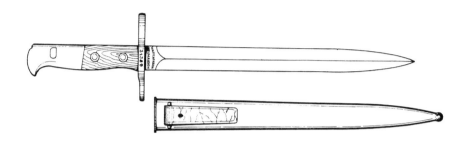

② SWISS M. 1900
KIESLING VOL II #260

③ SWISS M. 1953
FAVOR S. M. G.
KIESLING VOL. I #17

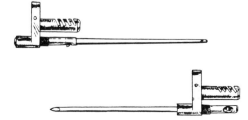

No. 1. SWISS MODEL 1957 - SIG EXPORT. THIS BAYONET IS ONE
        OF TWO VARIATIONS I POSSESS WITH BLACK RIBBED PLAS-
        TIC GRIPS AND DOUBLE-EDGED BLADES. THIS PARTICULAR
        VARIATION WAS EXPORTED TO CHILE FOR USE BY THEIR
        ARMED FORCES.

No. 2. SWISS MODEL 1957 - SIG-AMT. THIS BAYONET IS VERY
        SIMILAR TO 188-1, HOWEVER, IS OF STAINLESS STEEL
        CONSTRUCTION WITH A SHAPED CROSSGUARD. THIS BAYO-
        NET IS STILL UTILIZED BY SWISS RESERVE UNITS.

No. 3. SWISS E.W. 1970. THIS BAYONET WAS APPARENTLY PRO-
        DUCED FOR EXPORT WITH THE SIG ASSAULT RIFLES. IT
        HAS BEEN CONSTRUCTED IN A MANNER SIMILAR TO U.S.
        BAYONETS WITH A DARKENED CARBINE-TYPE BLADE,
        STAMPED CROSSGUARD AND BLACK PLASTIC HILT.

No. 4. SWISS E.W. 1970. THIS BAYONET IS A WIRE-CUTTER
        VERSION OF THE PREVIOUSLY DISCUSSED BAYONET PRO-
        DUCED FOR EXPORT. IT IS BASICALLY THE SIG VERSION
        OF THE STONER SERIES OF BAYONETS ILLUSTRATED IN THE
        GERMAN SECTION.

① SWISS M.1957
SIG EXPORT

KIESLING VOL III #544

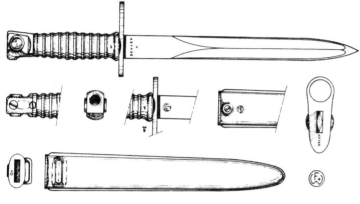

② SWISS M.1957
SIG

KIESLING VOL. I #84

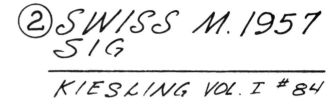

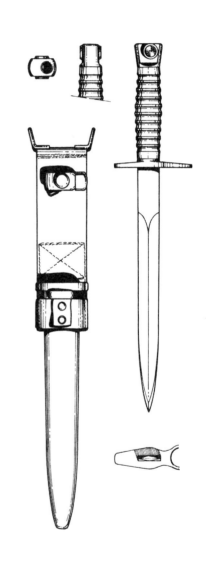

③ SWISS E.W. 70
SIG

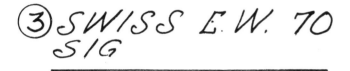

④ SWISS E.W. 70
SIG

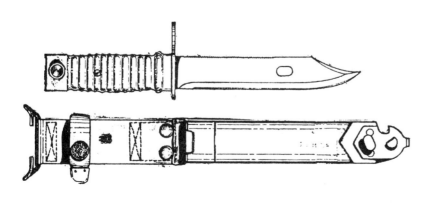

No. 1. **TRANSVAAL (OVS) 1896.** THIS BAYONET WAS PRODUCED FOR THE BOERS FOR USE IN THEIR WAR WITH THE BRITISH. IT WAS MY UNDERSTANDING, HOWEVER, THAT THESE PIECES NEVER REACHED THEIR DESTINATION. IT WAS OBVIOUSLY PRODUCED UTILIZING COMPONENTS FROM THE 1871 GERMAN BAYONETS AND UTILIZES A VERY UNIQUE UPSWEPT QUILLON. MANY COLLECTORS FEEL THESE PIECES ARE TURKISH BECAUSE OF TURKISH MARKINGS; HOWEVER, THE PIECE IN MY COLLECTION WAS OBTAINED AS PART OF A SET WHICH HAS A BUCKLE WITH SOUTH AFRICAN MARKINGS (SEE PHOTOGRAPH), THOUGH IT IS APPARENT THAT MANY OF THE BAYONETS DID IN FACT END UP IN TURKEY AND WERE UTILIZED ON THEIR M-1890 RIFLES.

① TRANSVAAL 1896
KIESLING VOL IV #924

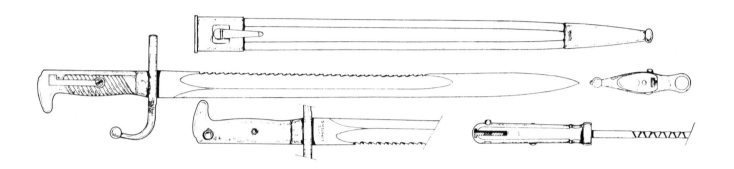

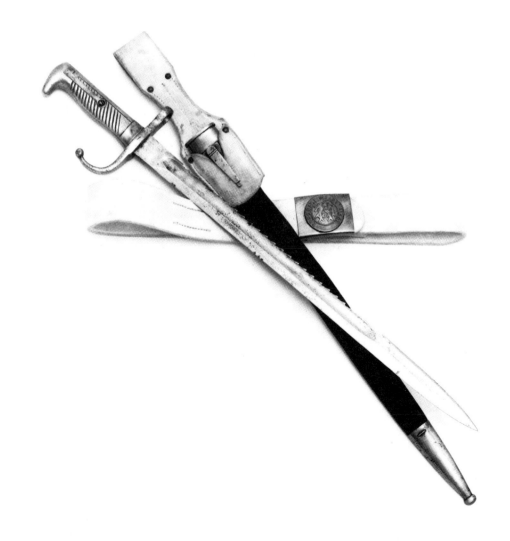

No. 1. **TURKISH MODEL 1874 - PEABODY.** THIS CRUCIFORM-BLADED SOCKET BAYONET ACCOMPANIED THE U.S. MANUFACTURED .45 CAL. PEABODY RIFLE WHICH WAS CONTRACTED BY THE TURKS IN 1873 FROM THE PROVIDENCE TOOL COMPANY. THE EXAMPLES I HAVE SEEN ARE UNMARKED AND CAN BE IDENTIFIED BY THE OFFSET SOCKET, AS ILLUSTRATED. THE EXAMPLE IN MY COLLECTION IS IN VERY GOOD CONDITION AS ARE MOST OF THESE BAYONETS I HAVE OBSERVED, WHICH LEADS ME TO BELIEVE THIS BAYONET AND RIFLE WERE ALSO EXPORTED TO OTHER GOVERNMENTS.

No. 2. **TURKISH MODEL 1874 - PEABODY.** THIS HEAVY YATAGHAN-BLADED BAYONET WAS OBVIOUSLY INSPIRED BY THE BRITISH BAYONETS OF THE PERIOD AND WAS MANUFACTURED IN THE UNITED STATES ALONG WITH THE RIFLES AS PART OF THE 600,000-RIFLE CONTRACT DISCUSSED IN 190-1. THE EXAMPLES I HAVE IN MY COLLECTION ARE OF TWO TYPES; ONE WITH BLACK LEATHER GRIPS WHICH HAVE BEEN CHECKERED (ISSUE) AND THE OTHER WITH WOODEN GRIPS WHICH I SUSPECT WERE REPLACEMENT GRIPS AND WHICH I HAVE BEEN TOLD WERE UTILIZED ON THESE BAYONETS WHEN THEY WERE RELEGATED TO "SIDE ARM" STATUS. THESE PIECES WERE ISSUED WITH A BEAUTIFUL STEEL-MOUNTED LEATHER SCABBARD AND APPEAR TO ME TO BE TOO HEAVY TO BE VERY FUNCTIONAL AS A BAYONET. JACK SCHRADER HAS AN EXAMPLE WITH BRASS GRIPS, WHICH WAS SUPPOSEDLY CAPTURED AND UTILIZED BY THE RUSSIANS.

① TURKISH M. 1874
PEABODY·SOCKET

KIESLING VOL. II #362

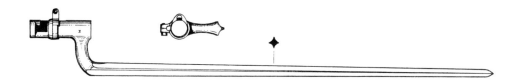

② TURKISH M. 1874
PEABODY·SABER

KIESLING VOL III #701

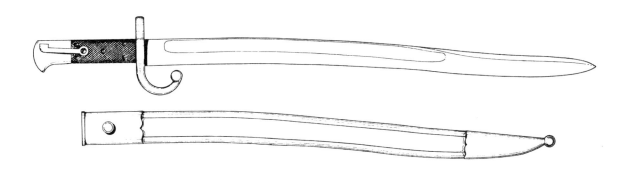

PEABOBY-MARTINI MILITARY RIFLE. (Turkish Model.)

With Quadrangular and Sabre Bayonets.

Entire Length of Peabody-Martini Military Rifle,	49 inches.	Weight of Quadrangular Bayonet,	15 ounces.
Length of Barrel,	32½ "	Entire Length of Sabre Bayonet,	28¹⁄₂ inches.
Weight, without Bayonet,	8½ pounds.	Length of Blade of Sabre Bayonet,	22¹⁄₈ "
Length of Quadrangular Bayonet,	25½ inches.	Weight of Sabre Bayonet,	2 pounds.
Length of Blade of Quadranglar Bayonet,	20½ "	Calibre,	.45 inch.

CARTRIDGE FOR PEABODY-MARTINI MILITARY RIFLE. (Turkish Model.)

Calibre, .45 inch. Powder, 85 grains. Bullet, smooth-patched; weight, 480 grains. Lubricating disc in shell

No. 1. **TURKISH MODEL 1887.** THESE BAYONETS WERE PRODUCED FOR TURKEY BY THE GERMANS AND HAVE THE FIRM NAME OF "SIMPSON AND COMPANY" ON THE RICASSO OF THE BLADE IN ARABIC. IN ADDITION, THE TOUGHRA, OR TURKISH RULER'S MARK, IS STAMPED ON THE POMMEL. THESE PIECES ARE FINISHED BRIGHT AND COME IN A STEEL-MOUNTED LEATHER SCABBARD THAT IS VERY SIMILAR TO THE JAPANESE TYPE 18 SCABBARD AND IS, IN FACT, INTERCHANGEABLE WITH SLIGHT MODIFICATION. SINCE THESE WERE ONLY ISSUED FOR TWO YEARS, THEY ARE SOMEWHAT SCARCE.

No. 2. **TURKISH MODEL 1890.** THIS BAYONET IS IDENTICAL TO THE MODEL 1887; HOWEVER, THE MUZZLE RING IS SET FURTHER BACK FROM THE BACK STRAP. THESE PIECES WERE OBVIOUSLY PRODUCED IN QUANTITY AND ARE COMMON.

No. 3. **TURKISH MODEL 1890 - SHORTENED.** THIS BAYONET IS IDENTICAL TO THE PREVIOUS PIECE, HOWEVER, THE BLADE HAS BEEN SHORTENED TO APPROXIMATELY 9-1/2" AND THE ENTIRE BAYONET BLUED. THIS MODIFICATION WAS APPARENTLY PERFORMED SOMETIME DURING THE 1914-1918 TIME FRAME.

No. 4. **TURKISH MODEL 1890 - SHORTENED.** THIS BAYONET IS IDENTICAL TO 191-2 EXCEPT THAT THE HOOKED QUILLON HAS BEEN REMOVED AND ARABIC SERIAL NUMBERS ARE STAMPED ON THE SIDE OF THE CROSS-GUARD. THIS MODIFICATION MAY HAVE BEEN PERFORMED IN THE LATE 30s, ACCORDING TO CARTER.

① TURKISH M. 1887
KIESLING VOL. III #662

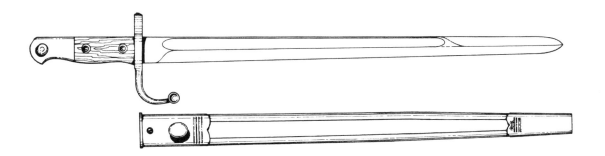

② TURKISH M. 1890
KIESLING VOL. III #663

③ TURKISH M. 1890 SHORTENED
KIESLING VOL. IV #807

④ TURKISH M. 1890 SHORTENED
KIESLING VOL. I #158

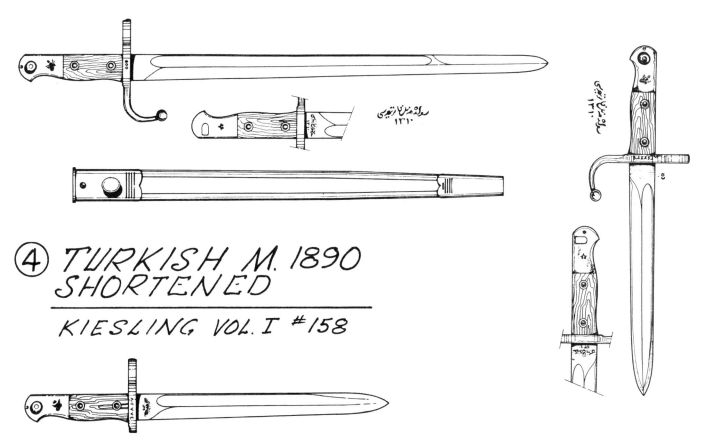

No. 1. TURKISH MODEL 1903. THIS BAYONET IS VERY UNUSUAL AND INCORPORATES THE BLADE OF THE GERMAN SG98 WITH A HILT AND CROSSGUARD SIMILAR TO EARLIER TURKISH MODEL 1890. THESE PIECES ARE SOMEWHAT SCARCE IN UNALTERED CONDITION. THE SCABBARD IS IDENTICAL TO THE GERMAN SCABBARD FOR THE SG98.

No. 2. TURKISH MODEL 1903 - SHORTENED. THIS BAYONET IS IDENTICAL TO 192-1, HOWEVER, THE BLADE HAS BEEN SHORTENED TO APPROXIMATELY 9-3/4" AND THE EXAMPLE IN MY COLLECTION HAS AN ALL-STEEL SCABBARD.

No. 3. TURKISH MODEL 1903 - SHORT. THIS BAYONET IS A SHORT VERSION FOR THE MODEL 1903 RIFLE AND IS NOT A MODIFICATION OF 192-1. IT HAS BEEN PRODUCED WITH A SHORT BLADE SIMILAR IN WIDTH TO THE EARLIER MODEL.

① TURKISH M.1903
KIESLING VOL. II # 423

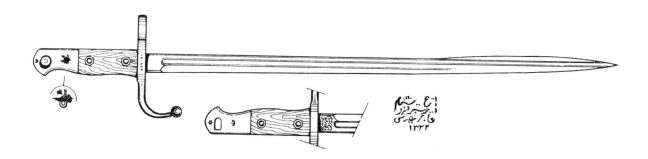

② TURKISH M.1903 SHORTENED
KIESLING VOL. IV #798

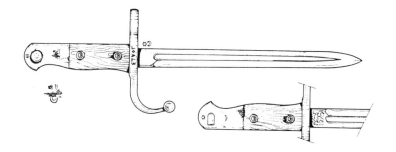

③ TURKISH M.1903 SHORT
KIESLING VOL. III # 548

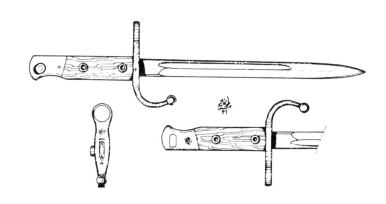

"TUGHRA" OF SULTAN
ABDUL HAMID II

No. 1.   **Turkish Ersatz Model 1916.** This bayonet is a well made, all steel ersatz bayonet for the Turkish Model 1903 rifle. The bayonet comes in two varieties; one with a straight crossguard and the other with a slight step at the muzzle ring. These pieces were scarce for some years, however, have recently (1985) been released in quantity.

No. 2.   **Turkish Ersatz Circa 1917 - Re-Weld.** This bayonet is a standard German ersatz pattern which the Turks have modified by shortening the handle. The purpose of this modification is not known nor do I have any proof it was actually performed by Turkey; however, these pieces were imported with other Turkish weapons to the United States.

No. 3.   **Turkish Ersatz Circa 1917.** This bayonet is another German ersatz which has been modified by extending the crossguard to fit the Turkish Mauser. These can be readily identified by the serial number on the crossguard.

No. 4.   **Turkish Ersatz Circa 1917.** This bayonet is the fullered variation of 193-3 with the extended crossguard.

① TURKISH M.1916 ERSATZ

KIESLING, VOL. IV #808

② TURKISH C.1917 RE·WELD

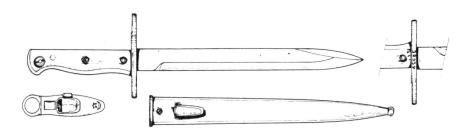

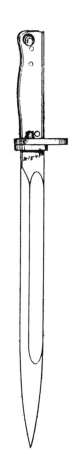

③ TURKISH C.1917 ERSATZ

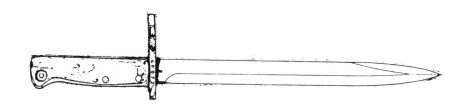

④ TURKISH C.1917 ERSATZ

CARTER VOL. I #89

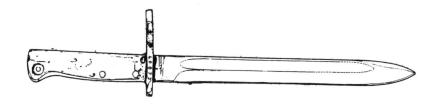

No. 1. **Turkish Ersatz Circa 1917.** This bayonet is a modified World War I Bavarian ersatz which has received a new crossguard so that it can fit the Turkish Mausers.

No. 2. **Turkish Ersatz Circa 1917.** This bayonet is a more unique modification of the standard German ersatz and has the crossguard moved up on the handle as opposed to actually shortening the handle.

No. 3. **Turkish Ersatz Circa 1917.** This bayonet is another German ersatz variation which has had the handle modified to accept the lengthened Turkish crossguard. On this particular piece, however, the blade has also been shortened to conform with some type of Turkish length standard, which must have existed. I base this contention on the fact that numerous bayonets known to be of Turkish issue have had the blade length modified.

NOTE: Turkey utilized virtually every ersatz pattern shown in the German section, pages 89 through 94, and even some of the trench knife versions on page 95. Anthony Carter, in the July 1977 issue of Guns Review, verified that some German ersatz bayonets have been further modified by the Turks for use on their FN FAL rifles.

① TURKISH C. 1917
ERSATZ

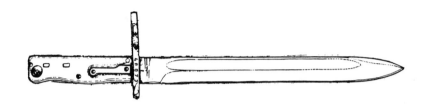

② TURKISH C. 1917
ERSATZ

CARTER VOL. I #88

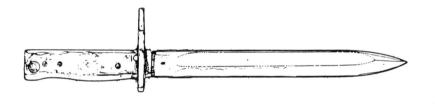

③ TURKISH C. 1917
ERSATZ

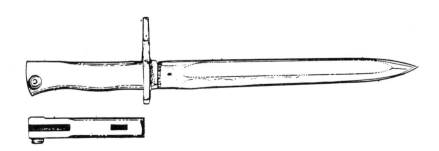

No. 1. TURKISH MODEL 1935. THIS BAYONET IS ONE OF NUMEROUS MODIFICATIONS OF FOREIGN BAYONETS PERFORMED BY TURKEY TO FIT THEIR 1935 RIFLE. THE PIECE ILLUSTRATED WAS ORIGINALLY A PERUVIAN M-1909 WHICH HAS BEEN SHORTENED AND A NEW CROSSGUARD ADDED (SEE PAGE 156 FOR THE UNMODIFIED BAYONET).

No. 2. TURKISH MODEL 1935. THIS IS ANOTHER MODIFICATION OF THE PERUVIAN M-1909, HOWEVER, THIS TIME A NEW BLADE HAS BEEN UTILIZED IN ADDITION TO A NEW CROSSGUARD.

No. 3. TURKISH MODEL 1935. THIS BAYONET IS A MODIFIED ROMANIAN MANNLICHER BAYONET AND HAS BEEN FITTED WITH A NEW CROSSGUARD TO ALLOW USE ON THE MODEL 1935 RIFLE. IT HAS THE INITIALS "AS.FR" STAMPED ON THE POMMEL, WHICH IS AN ABBREVIATION FOR "MILITARY FACTORY".

① *TURKISH M. 1935 CONVERSION*

KIESLING VOL. IV #796

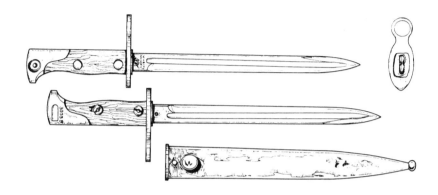

② *TURKISH M. 1935 CONVERSION*

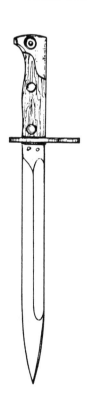

③ *TURKISH M. 1935 CONVERSION*

KIESLING VOL. IV #795

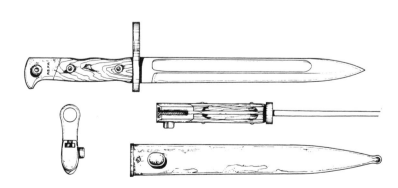

No. 1.   TURKISH MODEL 1935.   THIS BAYONET IS ANOTHER MODI-
FICATION OF FOREIGN BAYONETS PERFORMED BY TURKEY TO
FIT THEIR MODEL 1935 RIFLE.   THIS PARTICULAR PIECE
IS A BRITISH 1907 WHICH HAS HAD THE BLADE SHORTENED
AND IS FITTED WITH A NEW CROSSGUARD.   THESE BRITISH
BLADES WERE PROBABLY CAPTURED AT GALLIPOLI.   ALL OF
THESE BAYONETS ARE EQUIPPED WITH STEEL SCABBARDS.

No. 2.   TURKISH MODEL 1935.   THIS BAYONET, IS NEWLY MANU-
FACTURED FOR THE MODEL 1935 RIFLE AND HAS A HILT
SIMILAR TO THE MODEL 1890 WITH WOODEN GRIPS, A
THICK CROSSGUARD AND A 9-1/2" BLADE.

No. 3.   TURKISH MODEL 1935.   THIS PIECE IS AN INTERESTING
VARIATION OF THE M-1935 SERIES IN THAT IT STILL
UTILIZES A LEAF SPRING.   THIS BAYONET IS ALSO NEWLY
MANUFACTURED AND THE STEEL SCABBARD HAS RETAINED
THE OBLONG FROG STUD IN LIEU OF THE ROUND FROG STUD
UTILIZED ON MOST OF THE 1935 BAYONET SCABBARDS.

No. 4.   TURKISH MODEL 1955 - BRITISH No. 4 RIFLE.   THIS IS
THE ISSUE PATTERN BRITISH No. 9 MK I BAYONET (SEE
61-4); HOWEVER, IT IS HEAVILY BLUED AND MARKED WITH
A STAR AND CRESCENT.

① TURKISH M.1935 CONVERSION

KIESLING VOL IV #792

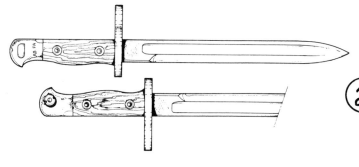

② TURKISH M.1935

KIESLING VOL. IV #793

③ TURKISH M.1935

KIESLING VOL. IV #794

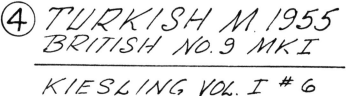

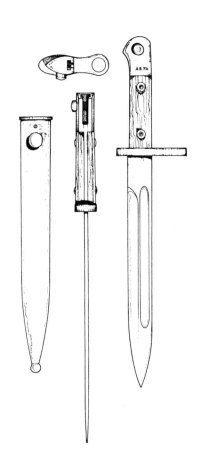

④ TURKISH M.1955 BRITISH NO. 9 MK I

KIESLING VOL. I #6

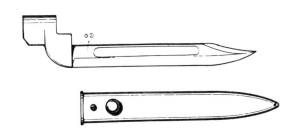

NOTES ON U.S. BAYONETS:

The U.S. section is arranged by type of bayonet in much the same way that Hardin's book is organized. The <u>SOCKET</u> bayonets start below followed by the <u>SABER</u> bayonets starting on page 206, the <u>RAMROD</u> bayonets starting on page 213, the <u>ENTRENCHING</u> bayonets on page 215, the <u>KNIFE</u> bayonets starting on page 216, the training bayonets starting on page 235 and, finally, the <u>MISCELLANEOUS</u> bayonets on page 239. This will allow the section to be tabbed for easier use.

No. 1.   U.S. Revolutionary War - A Committee of Safety Type Socket Bayonet. This was part of the first group made for the Minute Men. They were reasonably uniform and well finished, as they had to pass certain standards set by the Committee of Safety.

No. 2.   U.S. Musket Model 1795 - Socket. This has a wider blade than the previous piece and is based on the French M-1763 Musket with "L" shaped mortise. The gun was a faithful copy of the Charleville musket, manufactured until 1808, according to Bannerman. Three variations of the bayonet are illustrated reflecting increasing quality of manufacture. The first two are made of heavy iron (they weigh over one-half pound) and were blacksmith produced. The third version illustrated was probably arsenal produced and has a top flute running back from the point. All of the examples in my collection have a "brown" finish.

① *U.S. SOCKET C. 1775*
HARDIN #1

DIMENSIONS	
BLADE LENGTH	14 1/4 "
BLADE WIDTH	7/8 "
SOCKET LENGTH	2 3/8 "
SOCKET O.D.	15/16 "
SOCKET I.D.	7/8 "
SHANK LENGTH	1 3/16 "

② *U.S. MUSKET M. 1795*
HARDIN #2

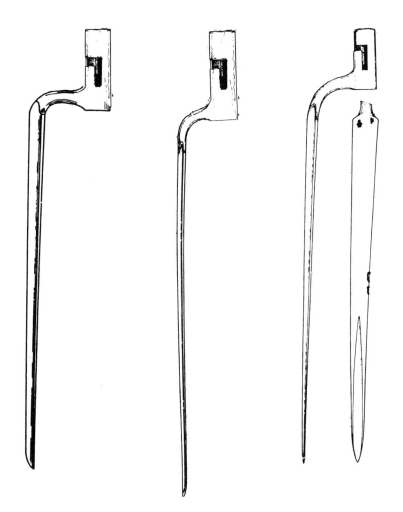

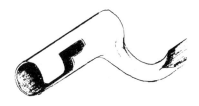

DIMENSIONS	
BLADE LENGTH	12 TO 15 7/8 "
BLADE WIDTH	15/16 TO 1 5/8 "
SOCKET LENGTH	2 1/2 TO 3 11/32 "
SOCKET O.D.	15/16 TO 1 "
SOCKET I.D.	7/8 TO 15/16 "
SHANK LENGTH	1 3/32 TO 1 5/32 "

197

No. 1. **U.S. MUSKET MODEL 1795/1808 - SOCKET.** HARDIN CALLS THESE M-1795/1808 BAYONETS (THERE IS NO SUCH THING AS A 1795/1808 MUSKET) TRANSITIONAL MODELS WHEREAS DONALD WEBSTER (IN <u>AMERICAN SOCKET BAYONETS 1717-1823</u>) CALLS THEM A DEFINITE M-1808. IN ANY CASE THE CHANGE IS VERY SLIGHT; A THINNER BLADE AND THE LENGTHS OF BOTH SOCKET AND BLADE INCREASED.

No. 2. **U.S. MUSKET MODEL 1816 - SOCKET.** THIS MODEL STARTED THE STANDARDIZATION OF ARMS IN THE U.S. ARMY. THE BAYONET HAS A FLUTE STARTING AT THE POINT AND IS ABOUT NINE INCHES LONG. THE REMAINDER OF THE TOP IS FLAT. THE MORTISE HAS A "T" CUT, WITH THE ADDITION OF A "BRIDGE".

No. 3. **U.S. RIFLE MODEL 1819 - SOCKET (HALL).** THIS BAYONET ACCOMPANIES THE FIRST BREECH LOADING MILITARY ARM MANUFACTURED IN THE UNITED STATES. THIS PIECE IS RARE AND CAN BE RECOGNIZED BY THE UNIQUE OPENING IN THE BRIDGE SLOT (ILLUSTRATED) WHICH HAS AN OFFSET TO ALLOW PASSAGE OF THE SOCKET OVER THE ECCENTRIC FRONT SIGHT. IT IS FINISHED BRIGHT.

No. 4. **U.S. MUSKET MODEL 1835/42 - SOCKET.** THE M-1835/40 MUSKET (THE LAST U.S. FLINTLOCK) REFLECTS THE "CROSSOVER" TO THE M-1842 (THE FIRST PERCUSSION MUSKET) FROM FLINTLOCK TO PERCUSSION. THE BAYONET'S IDENTIFYING FEATURE IS ITS RATHER DISTINCTIVE SHANK. IT IS ALSO THE FIRST U.S. BAYONET TO UTILIZE THE CLASP RING AND IS BASED ON THE EARLIER FRENCH M-1777.

① *U.S. MUSKET M. 1795/1808*

HARDIN #3

DIMENSIONS	
BLADE LENGTH	15 7/8"
BLADE WIDTH	15/16"
SOCKET LENGTH	3"
SOCKET O.D.	15/16"
SOCKET I.D.	7/8"
SHANK LENGTH	1 1/16"

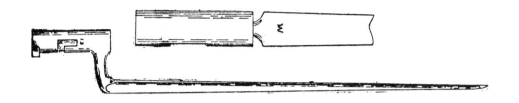

② *U.S. MUSKET M. 1816*

HARDIN #6

DIMENSIONS	
BLADE LENGTH	16 1/2"
BLADE WIDTH	7/8"
SOCKET LENGTH	3"
SOCKET O.D.	1 1/16"
SOCKET I.D.	13/16"
SHANK LENGTH	1 7/32"

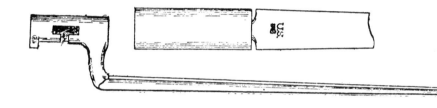
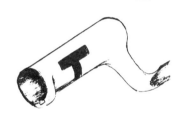

③ *U.S. RIFLE M. 1819*
HALL RIFLE

HARDIN #8

DIMENSIONS	
BLADE LENGTH	16"
BLADE WIDTH	7/8"
SOCKET LENGTH	2 15/16"
SOCKET O.D.	13/16"
SOCKET I.D.	25/32"
SHANK LENGTH	1 1/8"

④ *U.S. MUSKET M. 1835/42*

HARDIN #10

DIMENSIONS	
BLADE LENGTH	18"
BLADE WIDTH	7/8"
SOCKET LENGTH	2 5/8"
SOCKET O.D.	31/32"
SOCKET I.D.	27/32"
SHANK LENGTH	1 1/2"

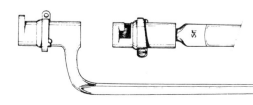

No. 1. **U.S. RIFLE MODEL 1841 - SOCKET- (MISSISSIPPI).** THE M-1841 RIFLE, WHEN ORIGINALLY MADE, HAD NO PROVISION FOR A BAYONET, HENCE THE RIFLE REQUIRED MODIFICATION OF THE FRONT SIGHT AND REDUCTION OF THE MUZZLE DIAMETER TO ALLOW THIS BAYONET TO BE ATTACHED.

No. 2. **U.S. MUSKETOON MODEL 1847 - SOCKET.** THESE BAYONETS SEEM TO BE PRIMARILY M-1842'S THAT HAVE BEEN SHORTENED TO FIFTEEN INCHES. THE SOCKET HAS THE "L" PATTERN MORTISE WITH A CLASP RING AND AN ALMOST VERTICAL SHANK.

No. 3. **U.S. CADET MUSKET MODEL 1851 - SOCKET.** THIS BAYONET HAS A MOST DISTINCTIVE CLASP RING WHICH IMMEDIATELY IDENTIFIES IT. THE RING IS SPLIT TO ACCOMMODATE THE STOP PIN. OTHER-WISE, IT IS LIKE THE M-1842 MUSKET. IT IS STAMPED "U.S." ACROSS THE TOP FLAT RICASSO.

No. 4. **U.S. MUSKET MODEL 1854 - SOCKET (REMINGTON CONVERSION).** BASICALLY THIS BAYONET HAS THE M-1816 "T" SLOT PATTERN SOCKET WITH THE ADDITION OF A SLIMMER BLADE AND THE CORNERS TAPERED. IT HAS NO CLASP RING, WHICH GIVES THE ARM AN OVER-ALL "SLICK" LOOK.

① *U.S. RIFLE M. 1841*
MISSISSIPPI

HARDIN #13

DIMENSIONS	
BLADE LENGTH	19 7/8 "
BLADE WIDTH	27/32 "
SOCKET LENGTH	3 "
SOCKET O.D.	63/64 "
SOCKET I.D.	61/64 "
SHANK LENGTH	1 3/16 "

② *U.S. MUSKETOON M. 1847*

HARDIN #14

DIMENSIONS	
BLADE LENGTH	15 1/8 "
BLADE WIDTH	3/4 "
SOCKET LENGTH	2 5/8 "
SOCKET O.D.	27/32 "
SOCKET I.D.	53/64 "
SHANK LENGTH	1 7/16 "

③ *U.S. MUSKET M. 1851*
CADET

HARDIN #15

DIMENSIONS	
BLADE LENGTH	14 1/2 "
BLADE WIDTH	13/16 "
SOCKET LENGTH	2 21/32 "
SOCKET O.D.	13/16 "
SOCKET I.D.	11/16 "
SHANK LENGTH	1 7/16 "

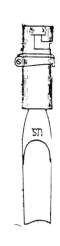

④ *U.S. MUSKET M. 1854*
REMINGTON CONVERSION

HARDIN #16

DIMENSIONS	
BLADE LENGTH	16 1/8 "
BLADE WIDTH	3/4 "
SOCKET LENGTH	3 "
SOCKET O.D.	1 "
SOCKET I.D.	27/32 "
SHANK LENGTH	1 3/16 "

No. 1. **COLT REVOLVING RIFLE MODEL 1855 - SOCKET TYPE 1.** THIS BAYO-
NET IS IDENTICAL TO THE BRITISH M-1853 ENFIELD. IT WAS USED
EXCLUSIVELY ON THE COLT RIFLE. IT HAS THE TYPICAL BRITISH
BLADE STOP AT THE SHANK AND IS VOID OF MARKINGS. THE TYPE 2
BAYONET RESEMBLES THE U.S. M-1855/70 DISCUSSED BELOW. A PART
OF AN 1860 ADVERTISEMENT IS ILLUSTRATED SHOWING THE TYPE 1
BAYONET.

No. 2. **U.S. MUSKET MODEL 1855/70 - SOCKET.** THIS BAYONET WAS PROB-
ABLY THE MOST WIDELY MADE AND UTILIZED SOCKET IN THE U.S. DUE
TO ITS USE BY BOTH SIDES IN THE CIVIL WAR. WITH AN "L" MOR-
TISE CUT AND RING CLAMP, IT IS A VERY SMOOTH LOOKING BAYONET
AND WAS COPIED ON SUBSEQUENT MODELS.

No. 3. **U.S. MUSKET MODEL 1861 - SOCKET.** ACCORDING TO BANNERMAN, THE
U.S. (NORTH) MANUFACTURED 801,997 AND PURCHASED 670,617 RIFLE
MUSKETS WITH BAYONETS DURING THE CIVIL WAR YEARS, ATTESTING
TO THE WIDE USE OF THIS BAYONET BY THE NORTH. THIS MODEL IS
A STURDIER VERSION THAN THE M-1855/70 AND HAS AN "L" MORTISE
CUT AND HAS THE RING CLASP.

① *U.S. RIFLE M. 1855*
COLT REVOLVING RIFLE

HARDIN #34

DIMENSIONS	
BLADE LENGTH	18"
BLADE WIDTH	13/16"
SOCKET LENGTH	3"
SOCKET O.D.	15/16"
SOCKET I.D.	23/32"
SHANK LENGTH	1"

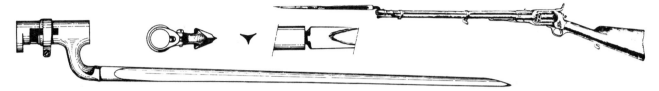

② *U.S. RIFLE-MUSKET M. 1855/70*

HARDIN #17
KIESLING VOL II #305

DIMENSIONS	
BLADE LENGTH	18"
BLADE WIDTH	3/4"
SOCKET LENGTH	3"
SOCKET O.D.	29/32"
SOCKET I.D.	25/32"
SHANK LENGTH	1 3/16"

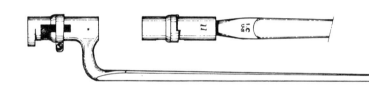

③ *U.S. MUSKET M. 1861*

HARDIN #20

DIMENSIONS	
BLADE LENGTH	17 7/8"
BLADE WIDTH	7/8"
SOCKET LENGTH	2 5/8"
SOCKET O.D.	27/32"
SOCKET I.D.	53/64"
SHANK LENGTH	1 7/16"

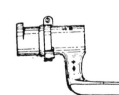

No. 1. U..S. MUSKET MODEL 1862 - SOCKET (H&P CONVERSION). THIS HEWES AND PHILLIPS CONVERSION IS QUITE SIMILAR TO THE M-1854 REMINGTON CONVERSION. IT HAS NO RING CLASP AND HAS A "T" MORTISE CUT IN THE THREE INCH SOCKET. THE BLADE, HOWEVER, IS ONE INCH LONGER AND THE SHANK IS .25 INCH LONGER THAN ITS M-1854 COUNTERPART.

No. 2. PEABODY MODEL 1867 - SOCKET. THE RIFLE WAS A MILITIA GUN AND WAS NEVER OFFICIALLY ADOPTED BY THE U.S. GOVERNMENT. ACCORDING TO BANNERMAN, IT WAS ADOPTED BY THE CONNECTICUT MILITIA IN 1871. THE OVERALL LOOK OF THE BAYONET IS VERY MUCH LIKE THE M-1855, EXCEPT FOR THE PEABODY'S LONGER BLADE.

No. 3. J. D. GREENE - SOCKET. THE BOLT ACTION J. D. GREENE RIFLE WITH ITS UNDERBARREL HAMMER IS NOT A WELL KNOWN GUN AND THE BAYONET EVEN LESS. THE BAYONET WAS PATTERNED AFTER THE FRENCH M-1763 WITH THE CLASP RING BUTTING UP AGAINST THE REAR REINFORCING RING ON THE THREE-INCH SOCKET. "J.D.G." IS STAMPED ON THE UPPER FLAT.

No. 4. CONFEDERATE HALL RIFLE - SOCKET. THESE BLADES ARE QUITE RARE WITH "T" MORTISE CUTS AND THREE-INCH SOCKETS. THEY ARE NOT UNLIKE THEIR M-1816 PREDECESSORS, EXCEPT FOR THE FACE FLUTE BEING TWO INCHES SHORTER AND THE BLADE .50 INCH SHORTER.

① U.S. MUSKET M. 1862

HARDIN # 23

DIMENSIONS	
BLADE LENGTH	18"
BLADE WIDTH	7/8"
SOCKET LENGTH	3"
SOCKET O.D.	25/32"
SOCKET I.D.	13/16"
SHANK LENGTH	1 7/16"

② PEABODY RIFLE M. 1867

WEBSTER PG. 41
HULL PG. 30

DIMENSIONS	
BLADE LENGTH	21"
BLADE WIDTH	3/4"
SOCKET LENGTH	2 5/8"
SOCKET O.D.	27/32"
SOCKET I.D.	25/32"
SHANK LENGTH	1 3/16"

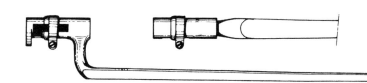

③ J.D. GREENE C. 1857

HARDIN # 39

DIMENSIONS	
BLADE LENGTH	18"
BLADE WIDTH	13/16"
SOCKET LENGTH	3"
SOCKET O.D.	29/32"
SOCKET I.D.	25/32"
SHANK LENGTH	1 15/16"

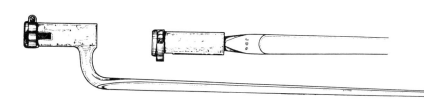

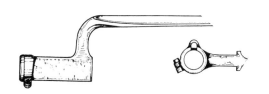

④ CONFEDERATE HALL RIFLE

HARDIN # 37

DIMENSIONS	
BLADE LENGTH	15 3/4"
BLADE WIDTH	27/32"
SOCKET LENGTH	3"
SOCKET O.D.	7/8"
SOCKET I.D.	25/32"
SHANK LENGTH	1 1/8"

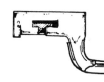

No. 1. **WINCHESTER MODEL 1866 - SOCKET.** THE DISTINCTIVE PART OF THIS BAYONET IS THE VERY SHORT SHANK. THIS IS AN EXTREMELY WELL MADE BAYONET WITH "L" SHAPED MORTISE AND CAN BE FOUND WITH BRIGHT OR BLUE FINISH.

No. 2. **REMINGTON RIFLE MODEL 1866/71 - SOCKET-SHORT.** THE .50 CALIBER REMINGTON BREECH LOADER WAS USED BY BOTH THE ARMY AND THE NAVY AND LATER ON BY THE MILITIA FOR MANY YEARS (I HAVE A NATIONAL GUARD MARKED PIECE). THE SOCKET BAYONET DESIGNED FOR IT WAS MANUFACTURED IN MANY VARIATIONS. IT IS FINISHED BRIGHT.

No. 3. **REMINGTON RIFLE MODEL 1866/71 - SOCKET-LONG.** THESE BAYONETS REFLECT THE MANY REMINGTON VARIATIONS AND ARE MOST PROBABLY EXPORT PIECES. AS NOTED IN 202-2, REMINGTON PRODUCED MANY TYPES OF BAYONETS FOR THE ROLLING BLOCK RIFLE.

① WINCHESTER M. 1866

HARDIN #42
KIESLING VOL. IV #849

DIMENSIONS	
BLADE LENGTH	15 1/8"
BLADE WIDTH	11/16"
SOCKET LENGTH	2 21/32"
SOCKET O.D.	43/64"
SOCKET I.D.	5/8"
SHANK LENGTH	17/32"

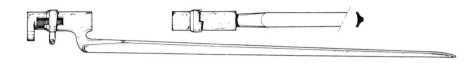

② REMINGTON M. 1866/71 SHORT

KIESLING VOL II #289

DIMENSIONS	
BLADE LENGTH	18"
BLADE WIDTH	3/4"
SOCKET LENGTH	3"
SOCKET O.D.	45/64"
SOCKET I.D.	43/64"
SHANK LENGTH	1 3/8"

③ REMINGTON M. 1866/71 LONG

KIESLING VOL III #673. #674

DIMENSIONS	
BLADE LENGTH	21 To 21 3/8"
BLADE WIDTH	3/4"
SOCKET LENGTH	3"
SOCKET O.D.	43/64"
SOCKET I.D.	43/64"
SHANK LENGTH	1 1/8"

202

No. 1.   **U.S. Cadet Rifle Model 1868/69 - Socket.** It is not really known whether the Cadet model did officially exist. There is the possibility that it might just be the M-1855/70 cut down to the Cadet size. The fullers, edges and marks all conform to the M-1855/70.

No. 2.   **U.S. Rifle Model 1871 - Socket.** This bayonet has the typical "L" mortise slot and ring clasp as the earlier U.S. models made at Fayetteville and in Mississippi. Only 10,000 were made.

No. 3.   **U.S. Rifle Model 1873 - Socket.** These are very similar to the Civil War period sockets, many are M-1855/70 bayonets "cold-pressed" to reduce the socket diameter for the new .45-70 "Trapdoor" Springfield rifle. This model is the first U.S. bayonet to be blued. Several of the scabbard variations are illustrated.

① U.S. CADET RIFLE M. 1868/69

HARDIN #24

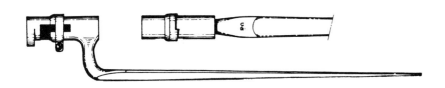

DIMENSIONS	
BLADE LENGTH	14"
BLADE WIDTH	25/32"
SOCKET LENGTH	3"
SOCKET O.D.	29/32"
SOCKET I.D.	25/32"
SHANK LENGTH	1 3/16"

② U.S. RIFLE M. 1871

HARDIN #25

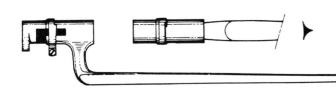

DIMENSIONS	
BLADE LENGTH	18 5/16"
BLADE WIDTH	53/64"
SOCKET LENGTH	2 15/16"
SOCKET O.D.	53/64"
SOCKET I.D.	51/64"
SHANK LENGTH	1 9/32"

③ U.S. RIFLE M. 1873

HARDIN #26
KIESLING VOL. II #308

DIMENSIONS	
BLADE LENGTH	18"
BLADE WIDTH	3/4"
SOCKET LENGTH	3"
SOCKET O.D.	13/16"
SOCKET I.D.	47/64"
SHANK LENGTH	1 3/16"

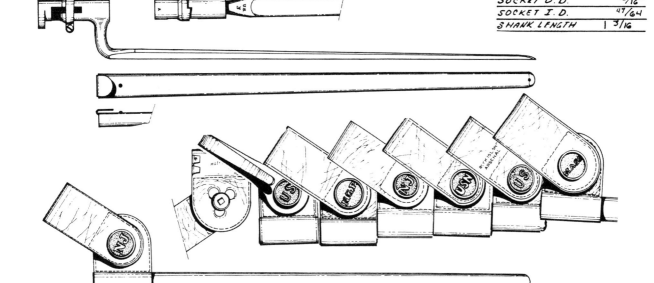

No. 1.   U.S. CADET RIFLE MODEL 1873 - SOCKET.   THIS WAS THE LAST CADET SOCKET BAYONET ISSUED TO THE UNITED STATES ARMY CADET CORPS.   IT IS A SCALED-DOWN VERSION OF THE M-1873.

No. 2.   WINCHESTER REPEATING RIFLE MODEL 1873 - SOCKET.   THIS PIECE, AS THE WINCHESTER M-1866, HAS A SHANK LENGTH OF ONLY .75 INCH.   HOWEVER, AN UNUSUAL ASPECT OF THE M-1873 IS THE BRIDGE ON THE OBVERSE OF THE SOCKET.   IT IS ALSO FINISHED BRIGHT.

No. 3.   U.S. SCOUT CIRCA 1873 - SOCKET.   THIS "SCOUT" SOCKET HAS A LONG VERTICAL SHANK SIMILAR TO THE EARLY MUSKET M-1835/42. HOWEVER, THE BRIDGE IS ON THE OBVERSE OF THE SOCKET.   THE BLADE IS FINISHED BRIGHT WITH "U.S." STAMPED ON THE TOP FACE AT THE RICASSO.   IN MY OPINION, THESE BAYONETS WERE USED ON AN EARLY WINCHESTER CARBINE WITH THE SHORT MAGAZINE.

① U.S. CADET RIFLE M.1873

HARDIN #27

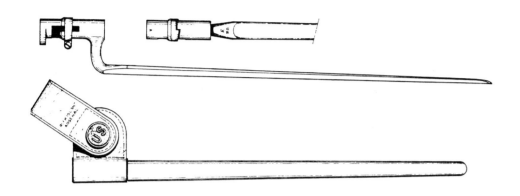

DIMENSIONS	
BLADE LENGTH	16 1/4 "
BLADE WIDTH	11/16 "
SOCKET LENGTH	3 "
SOCKET O.D.	13/16 "
SOCKET I.D.	47/64 "
SHANK LENGTH	1 1/4 "

② WINCHESTER M.1873

HARDIN #43
KIESLING VOL. IV #882

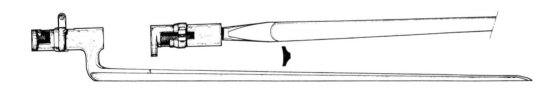

DIMENSIONS	
BLADE LENGTH	17 7/8 "
BLADE WIDTH	3/4 "
SOCKET LENGTH	3 "
SOCKET O.D.	11/16 "
SOCKET I.D.	21/32 "
SHANK LENGTH	3/4 "

③ U.S. SCOUT C. 1873

KIESLING VOL. IV #876

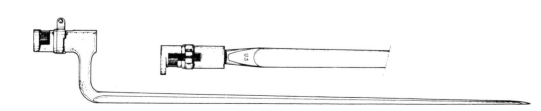

DIMENSIONS	
BLADE LENGTH	18 "
BLADE WIDTH	7/16 "
SOCKET LENGTH	2 5/8 "
SOCKET O.D.	55/64 "
SOCKET I.D.	23/32 "
SHANK LENGTH	1 3/4 "

No. 1. U.S. RIFLE MODEL 1882 - SOCKET (LEE). THE MOST STRIKING FEATURE OF THIS BAYONET IS THE BLADE LENGTH - 21.44 INCHES. ALTHOUGH THIS GUN WAS A BOLT-ACTION .45 CALIBER WITH FIVE RAPID SHOTS, IT WOULD BE TEN YEARS TO THE ADOPTION OF THE M-1892 KRAG BOLT-ACTION. THE LEE WAS PRINCIPALLY A NAVY RIFLE, WHICH MAY BE THE REASON FOR THE LENGTH OF THE BLADE WHICH, WHEN ATTACHED TO A RIFLE, BECAME A FORMIDABLE REPELLING PIKE.

No. 2. MOSIN-NAGANT MODEL 1891. THIS IS THE STANDARD RUSSIAN MODEL 1891 BAYONET; HOWEVER, IT IS STAMPED WITH A U.S. ORDNANCE BOMB AND WAS PROBABLY USED BY THE NATIONAL GUARD. HARDIN SAYS THE U.S. PURCHASED 280,049 RUSSIAN RIFLES WHICH WERE DISTRIBUTED TO THE VARIOUS STATE GUARD ORGANIZATIONS. I AM CURIOUS TO KNOW HOW THE U.S. COPED WITH THE FACT THAT THESE PIECES WERE NOT FURNISHED WITH SCABBARDS (SEE 164-2 FOR THE RUSSIAN ISSUE).

No. 3. JOHNSON SEMI-AUTOMATIC RIFLE MODEL 1941. THIS BAYONET COULD REALLY BE CALLED A "SPIKE". IT HAD TO BE VERY LIGHT DUE TO THE FACT THAT THE BARREL RECOILED AND A HEAVY BAYONET COULD CAUSE THE RIFLE TO GET OUT OF PHASE WITH THE RECOIL ACTION. THE RIFLE WAS NOT POPULAR WITH THE TROOPS. IT WAS ISSUED WITH AN ALL LEATHER SCABBARD.

No. 4. BLOW GUN BAYONET - C.1983. I INCLUDED THIS PIECE FOR "KICKS" AS IT WAS FURNISHED WITH A COMMERCIAL BLOW GUN IN THE 1983 TIME FRAME. IT WAS OBVIOUSLY INSPIRED BY THE HOWARD MUSKET BAYONET, A LITTLE KNOWN ARM PRODUCED IN 1866.

① U.S. RIFLE M. 1882 LEE

HARDIN #28
KIESLING VOL. II #297

DIMENSIONS	
BLADE LENGTH	21 3/8"
BLADE WIDTH	3/4"
SOCKET LENGTH	2 5/8"
SOCKET O.D.	3/4"
SOCKET I.D.	23/32
SHANK LENGTH	1 1/4"

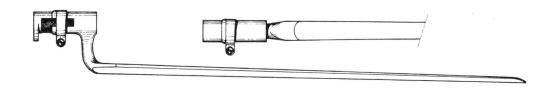

② MOSIN NAGANT M. 1891

HARDIN #45
KIESLING VOL I #252

③ JOHNSON RIFLE M. 1941

HARDIN #46
KIESLING VOL. I #37

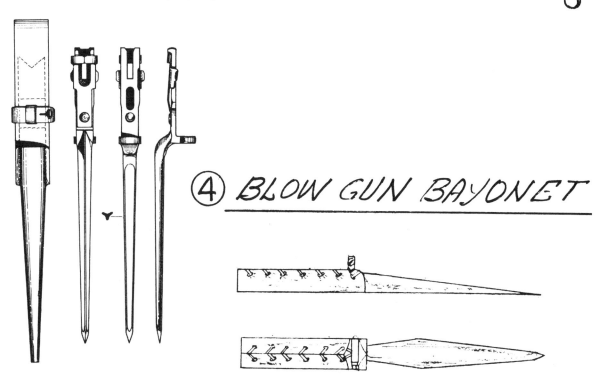

④ BLOW GUN BAYONET

No. 1.   HORSTMAN AND SONS CIRCA 1835 – SOCKET/SWORD COMBINATION. IT
         IS NOT REALLY KNOWN TO WHICH RIFLE THIS BELONGS. AN UNUSUAL
         TYPE, THE BRASS SECTION IS A SINGLE CASTING.   THE WIDE
         FULLERED BLADE RESEMBLES A SHORT SWORD MORE THAN A BAYONET.
         THESE PIECES WERE PROBABLY UTILIZED FOR PARADE USE ONLY.

No. 2.   U.S. RIFLE MODEL 1841 – TYPE I. THIS BRASS-GRIPPED, SLIGHTLY
         YATAGHAN-BLADED BAYONET WAS MADE TO FIT AN ALREADY EXISTING
         RIFLE. A RING WAS ATTACHED TO THE POMMEL AND A TWIST THUMB
         SCREW AFFIXED TO THE OBVERSE OF THE GUARD. IT IS COMMONLY
         REFERRED TO AS THE SNELL-VERSION BAYONET. IT WAS ISSUED WITH
         A BLACK LEATHER SCABBARD WITH BRASS MOUNTS.

No. 3.   U.S. RIFLE MODEL 1841 – TYPE II. THIS BAYONET HAS A MORE
         CONVENTIONAL ATTACHMENT, DUE TO A STUD BAND, CLAMPED TO THE
         MISSISSIPPI RIFLE BARREL INTO WHICH THE GRIP SLOT FITS. THIS
         BAYONET DIFFERS FROM TYPE I IN THAT THE BLADE HAS A MORE
         PRONOUNCED CURVE. THE BRASS HANDLE IS ALMOST IDENTICAL TO
         TYPE I. THE SCABBARD DIFFERS FROM TYPE I IN THAT IT HAS A
         FROG STUD BUTTON.

No. 4.   U.S. MUSKETOON MODEL 1847 – SAPPERS & MINERS. THIS BAYONET
         WAS DESIGNED BY N. P. AMES, JR. IN 1846 AND SUBMITTED AS A
         PROTOTYPE. THE ORDNANCE DEPARTMENT ORDERED 500 PIECES. THE
         PRICE WAS BASED ON THE FIRST 200 BAYONETS PRODUCED, AT WHICH
         TIME AMES REQUESTED THE BLADE FULLER BE ELIMINATED. THE
         ORDNANCE DEPARTMENT AGREED, SO THE LAST 300 BAYONETS WERE
         PRODUCED WITHOUT THE FULLER. THIS TYPE IS ILLUSTRATED.

① HORSTMAN & SONS C. 1835

HARDIN # 76

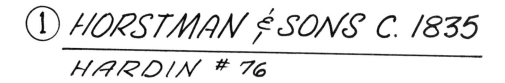

② U.S. RIFLE M.1841
TYPE I · SNELL

HARDIN #67
KIESLING VOL. IV # 976

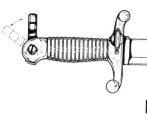
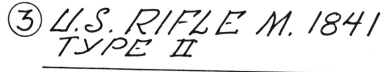

③ U.S. RIFLE M. 1841
TYPE II

HARDIN #67

④ U.S. MUSKETOON M.1847
SAPPERS & MINERS

HARDIN # 68
KIESLING VOL. IV # 969

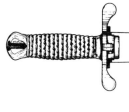
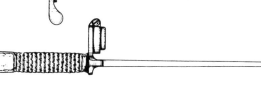

206

No. 1.   **U.S. RIFLE MODEL 1855.** ANOTHER BRASS-GRIPPED BAYONET, MANU-
FACTURED TO FIT THE NEW .58 CALIBER RIFLE. THE BLADE TAKES
AN UPWARD SWEEP NEAR THE POINT BUT IS NOT CONSIDERED TO BE OF
YATAGHAN STYLE. THIS MODEL SIGNALS THE BEGINNING OF
SWORD/SABER BAYONETS IN THE U.S. ARSENAL. IT UTILIZES A
BLACK LEATHER SCABBARD WITH BRASS MOUNTS, SIMILAR TO THE M-
1841.

No. 2.   **COLT REVOLVING RIFLE MODEL 1855.** THIS BAYONET IS SOMEWHAT
CONTROVERSIAL IN THAT COLLECTORS HAVE DIFFERING VIEWS ON THE
ACTUAL BAYONET ISSUED WITH THE COLT REVOLVING RIFLE. THIS
PIECE MATCHES HARDIN'S DESCRIPTION. THE BLADE IS YATAGHAN
WITH A BRASS GRIP. THE STEEL GUARD HAS THE "COCK'S COMB" ON
TOP OF THE MUZZLE RING. THE SCABBARD IS BLACK LEATHER WITH
BRASS MOUNTS.

No. 3.   **SPENCER NAVY RIFLE MODEL 1861.** THIS BAYONET ACCOMPANIED THE
SPENCER RIFLE SOLD TO THE NAVY DURING THE CIVIL WAR AND WHILE
THE PIECE LOOKS MUCH LIKE THE SHARPS BAYONET, IT IS NOT
INTERCHANGEABLE. THE MARKINGS INDICATE MANUFACTURE BY THE
AMES MFG. CO. AND I IDENTIFIED THE PIECE BY THE .875 MUZZLE
RING DIAMETER WHICH IS MUCH LARGER THAN EITHER THE SHARPS
CARBINE OR RIFLE. HARDIN DATES THIS PIECE AS 1863; HOWEVER,
THE BLADE IS MARKED 1861.

No. 4.   **U.S. NAVY RIFLE MODEL 1861 - PLYMOUTH/WHITNEYVILLE.** ALSO
KNOWN AS THE "PLYMOUTH RIFLE BAYONET", THIS IS ANOTHER BRASS-
GRIPPED YATAGHAN BLADED SWORD BAYONET. THESE WERE MADE FOR
THE PLYMOUTH NAVY RIFLE AND WERE DESIGNED BY ADMIRAL J. A.
DAHLGREN. (SEE 216-1 FOR ANOTHER DAHLGREN DESIGN.)

① U.S. RIFLE M. 1855

HARDIN #69
KIESLING VOL. II #436

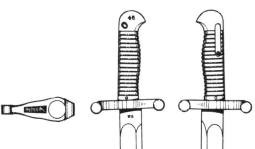

② COLT REVOLVING RIFLE M. 1855

HARDIN #81
KIESLING VOL IV #933

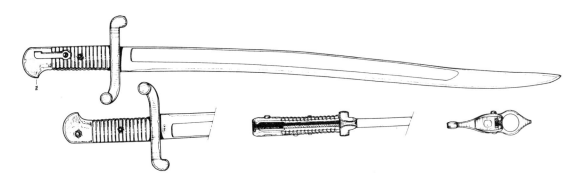

③ SPENCER NAVY RIFLE M. 1861

HARDIN #98

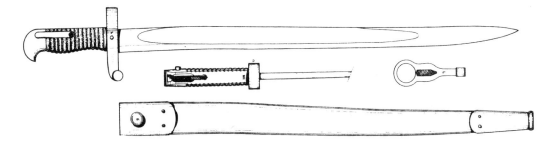

④ U.S. NAVY RIFLE M. 1861

HARDIN #70

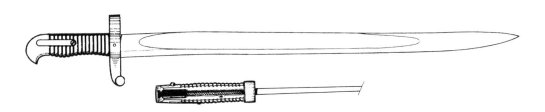

No. 1. **A. Rein Rifle Circa 1861.** A number of gunsmiths accommodated their customers with a bayonet that could be attached to special rifles and this is one example. The brass grip has cast into it the words "Bahn-Frei", which in German is loosely translated as "Paid in advance (of goods transported by rail)". It could also be interpreted as "Open road" and I have seen it translated as "Born free". The blade is an elongated "Bowie-type" with a long false edge and clipped point.

No. 2. **U.S. Rifle Model 1862 - Remington "Zouave".** This model is a direct descendant of the Models 1841 and 1855. It has the usual ribbed-brass grip and yataghan blade with black leather scabbard with brass mounts. This is one of the most popular of the sword bayonets.

No. 3. **Merrill Navy Rifle Model 1862.** This bayonet has had many arguments, pro and con, as to which gun it fits (it could fit the Model 1841). The ungainly blade is 25.50 inches long and, attached to a rifle, is in reality a pike, ready to repel boarders. It has the typical brass grip with an extremely long yataghan blade. According to Bannerman, this rifle first saw service in 1858 in .54 caliber.

① A. REIN RIFLE C. 1861

HARDIN #91

② U.S. RIFLE M. 1862 ZOUAVE

HARDIN #74
KIESLING VOL. III #678

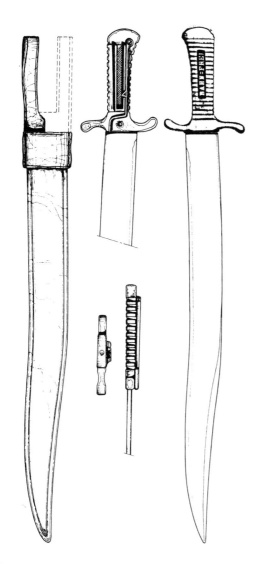

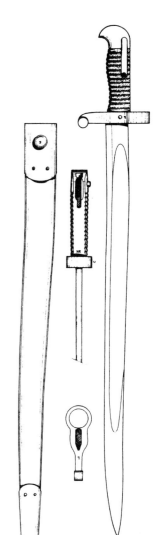

③ MERRILL NAVY RIFLE M. 1862

HARDIN #97
KIESLING VOL III #704

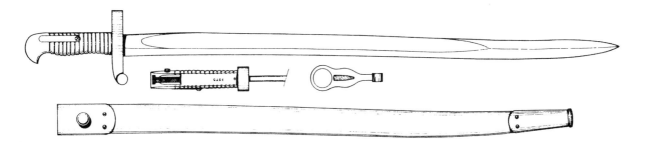

No. 1. **J. Henry and Son - Circa 1862.** This bayonet was identified by Rollin V. Davis, Jr. for a percussion muzzle-loading rifle issued under a militia contract.

No. 2. **Import English Sea Service Enfield.** This bayonet has also been attributed to the Colt revolving rifle and, according to Kiesling, never saw service in the British Navy. I have seen it "snapped on" a Belgian contract musket with Liege proofs. In any event, it was made in Germany for the U.S. and, with its brass grip and long fullered blade (24 inches), it fits right in with the rest of the U.S. sword bayonets.

No. 3. **U.S. Navy Rifle Model 1870.** This bayonet has a most unusual attachment system. The back of the feathered brass grip has a high, flat ridge that attaches to the gun. This, therefore, makes the contour of the grip quite unique. The pommel has the Board of Naval Ordnance monogram cast into it and has a bird's beak pommel. The blade is straight with a central fuller. The Ames Mfg. Company produced 10,000 of these bayonets. There also exists a variant which has a yataghan blade and is quite scarce. The scabbard is black leather with brass mounts.

① J. HENRY & SON C. 1862

ROLLIN DAVIS PG. 35 # XVII

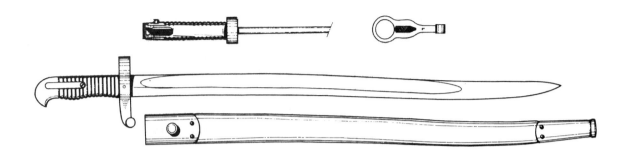

② ENGLISH SEA SERVICE ENFIELD (?)

HARDIN #80
KIESLING VOL. II #487

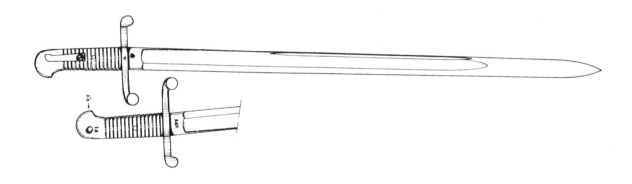

③ U.S. NAVY RIFLE M. 1870

HARDIN # 75
KIESLING VOL. III #679

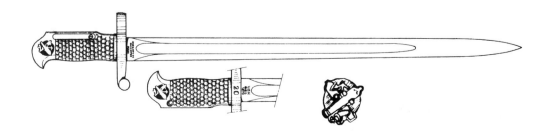

No. 1. **WINCHESTER MODEL 1873.** IN 1873, WINCHESTER REPLACED THEIR FAMOUS BRASS RECEIVER RIFLE WITH A CASE-HARDENED ONE. THE BAYONET MADE FOR IT HAD A WELL MADE YATAGHAN BLADE AND A FEATHERED PATTERN BRASS GRIP. THE SCABBARD IS TYPICALLY BLACK LEATHER WITH BRASS MOUNTS. (AS A NOTE OF INTEREST, THE ONLY MODEL 1866 SABER BAYONET I HAVE OBSERVED <u>ALSO</u> HAS THE CUT-OUT ON THE MUZZLE RING.)

No. 2. **WINCHESTER MODEL 1873 - EXPORT.** THIS PIECE IS LISTED BY HARDIN AS UNKNOWN. HOWEVER, I HAVE SEEN THESE BAYONETS AFFIXED TO WINCHESTER RIFLES REPORTED TO BE OF SOUTH AMERICAN ORIGIN. I ALSO SUSPECT THESE WERE USED BY TURKEY.

No. 3. **UNKNOWN.** THIS BAYONET LOOKS MUCH LIKE A "ZOUAVE" (U.S. M-1862), HOWEVER, HAS A SMALLER MUZZLE RING AND MUCH LIGHTER BLADE. I HAVE MORE "ODD BALLS" SUCH AS THIS AND WOULD SPECULATE THESE TYPES MAY BE USED ON LATER WEAPONS SUCH AS THE PEABODY-MARTINI MILITARY MODELS. SIMILAR BAYONETS ARE ILLUSTRATED IN THE 1878 PEABODY CATALOG.

① *WINCHESTER M.1873*

HARDIN #104

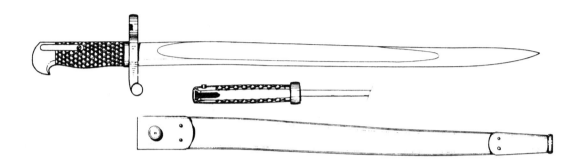

② *WINCHESTER M. 1873*
EXPORT

HARDIN #126

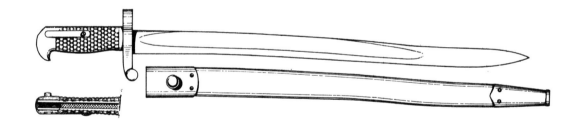

③ *U.S. UNKNOWN*

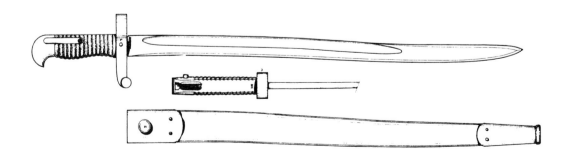

No. 1. BOYLE, GAMBLE & MACFEE, C.1861. These are an interesting series of bayonets and the history of the firm is vague; however, it is suggested by Hardin that Messrs. Boyle, Gamble and Macfee utilized a brass adapter to fit their bayonets to virtually any kind of rifle <u>and</u> also utilized many types of blades (Hardin illustrates three and Kiesling illustrates two). I would guess the bayonets are matched to a particular production run of adapters and so marked. The example in my collection has a number prominently stamped on the crossguard.

No. 2. COOK & BROTHER, C.1861. This firm initiated operations in New Orleans early in the U.S. Civil War and produced arms for the Confederate states through most of the war although forced to move twice. The most notable characteristic of the Cook & Brother bayonets is the stud spring which is dumbbell-shaped with a <u>circular</u> end. Hardin feels these pieces reflect strong English influence. The piece in my collection has been cut down and repointed.

No. 3. UNKNOWN CONFEDERATE, C.1861. These Confederate bayonets are most sought after. This one has an unusual diamond cross-sectioned blade with a ribbed brass cylindrical grip and a brass stud bolster. The scabbard was obviously brass mounted leather because the leather shell was with the piece.

① *BOYLE, GAMBLE & MACFEE*

HARDIN #71
KIESLING VOL. IV #936

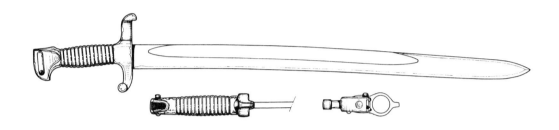

② *COOK & BROTHER*

HARDIN #72

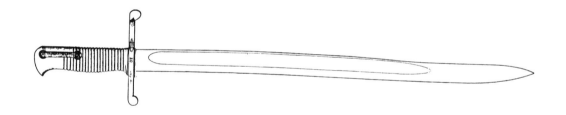

③ *CONFEDERATE UNKNOWN*

HARDIN #115, TYPE II

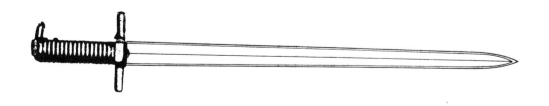

A number of foreign saber bayonets were utilized in the U.S.
Civil War by both sides. These were also fitted to U.S. weapons
and include the following:

A.   Joslyn Rifle - See 68-3 (except German export)

B.   English Short Rifle P1856 - See 50-1

C.   English Navy Rifle P1859 - See 52-2

D.   Mendenhall Jones & Gardner - See 49-4

E.   British P1837 Brunswick - See 49-1

The first two were used in large quantities while the remainder
saw limited use.

Confederate soldier with
English P1856 bayonet (collection of James C. Frasca)

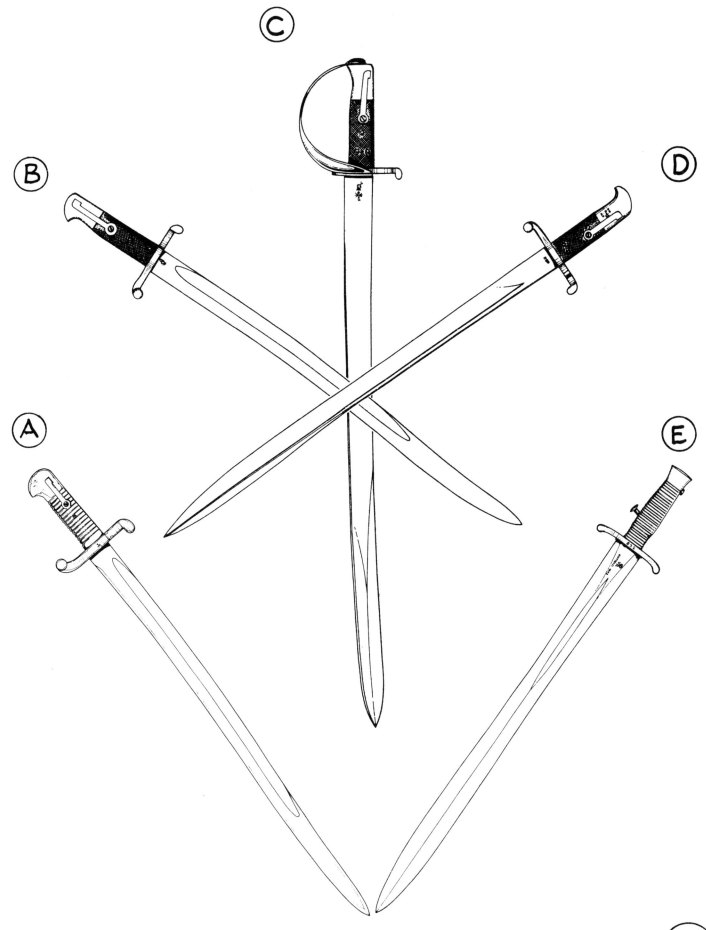

C

B

D

A

E

212

No. 1.   **U.S. Short Rifle Model 1882 – Ramrod.**   By this time everyone has heard of Teddy Roosevelt's dictum on rod bayonets; however, they were popular in America having first started in use in 1833 for the North Hall M-1833 musketoon; triangular in cross section. The M-1882 was little different from the previous M-1880 except in length. They are blued with no fullers and held to the rifle by a transverse locking key.

No. 2.   **U.S. Rifle Model 1884 – Ramrod.**   A lot more work was encompassed in this model as compared to the M-1882. It is round in cross section with a knurled section just behind the point which is shallowly scalloped in three sections. The rod tapers toward the tail and it is held in the rifle by notches cut into the body at various lengths which fit a spring loaded locking plate.

① U.S. RIFLE M. 1882
RAMROD

HARDIN #57
KIESLING VOL III #716

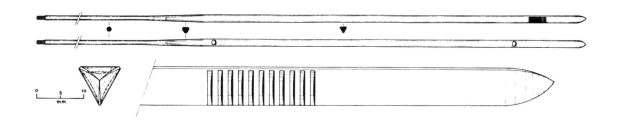

② U.S. RIFLE M. 1884
RAMROD

HARDIN #58
KIESLING VOL. III #715

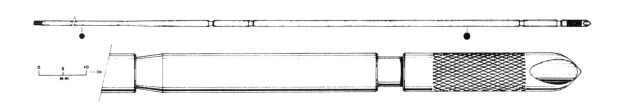

No. 1. U.S. RIFLE MODEL 1889 - RAMROD. ONLY MINOR MODIFI-
CATIONS SEPARATE THIS MODEL FROM THE M-1884. THE
LOCKING CANNELURES WERE REDESIGNED AND THE LOCK WAS
IMPROVED. THE ONLY WAY TO TELL THEM APART IS THE
DIFFERENT DISTANCES OF THE UPPER CANNELURES FROM
THE POINT.

No. 2. U.S. RIFLE MODEL 1903 - RAMROD. THE LAST OF THE
RAMROD BAYONETS, THE MODEL 1903 ROD BAYONET HAD THE
DISTINCTION OF BEING SNAPPED IN TWO BY PRESIDENT
TEDDY ROOSEVELT USING A KRAG MODEL 1892, WHICH WAS
THE DEATH GURGLE OF THE ROD BAYONET IN THE UNITED
STATES. BY THIS TIME, THE KNURLED FINGER GRIP HAD
DISAPPEARED AND A WASP-WAISTED CANNELURE SUBSTI-
TUTED. IT HAD ONLY TWO LOCKING GROOVES AND DID NOT
TAPER TOWARDS THE TAIL.

① U.S. RIFLE M. 1889 RAMROD

HARDIN #59
KIESLING VOL. III #717

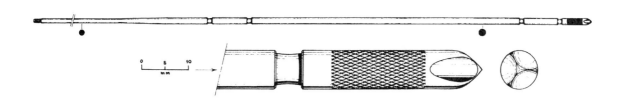

② U.S. RIFLE M. 1903 RAMROD

HARDIN #61
KIESLING VOL. III #712

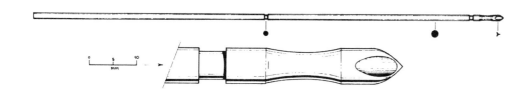

No. 1. U.S. Rifle Model 1871 – Trowel Model 1868. This was the first of many U.S. trowel bayonet designs. Lt. Rice had an international patent issued on November 17, 1868. They were made in 1871 and issued for field trials which were unfavorable. Approximately 700 were made. This bayonet was virtually flat on the top surface and had a ring fashioned to the shank to allow a "finger through" for added control while digging. They were brightly finished. The brass-mounted leather scabbard had a 90^0 curved belt hook that was too stiff for the soldiers' likes and was partially responsible for its nonacceptance.

No. 2. U.S. Rifle Model 1873 – Trowel Model 1873. This Model 1873 trowel was the distillation of a series of previous trowel designers, including Col. Edmund Rice, Ira Merrill, 2nd Lt. Henry Metcalf and Felix Chillingworth. It had a beautifully designed spade body with a reinforcing spine down the back. A wooden dowel attachment was issued to aid in the grip of the socket and also to prevent dirt entering the socket bore. They were blued and had a brass-mounted black leather scabbard with a belt loop. (The M.1873 scabbards are currently (1987) being reproduced in India.)

① U.S. RIFLE M.1871
TROWEL M.1868

HARDIN #164
KIESLING VOL. IV #768

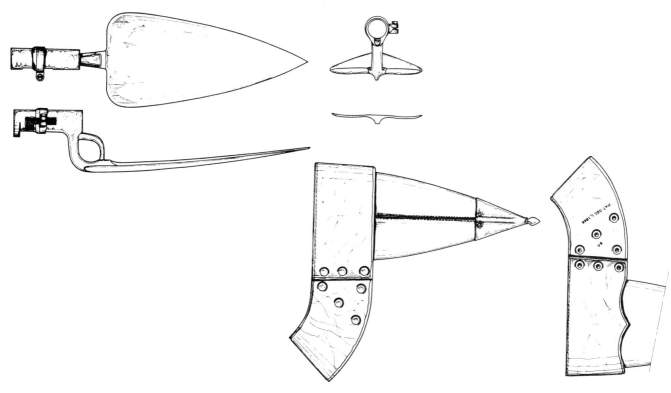

② U.S. RIFLE M.1873
TROWEL M.1873

HARDIN #167
KIESLING VOL. I #88

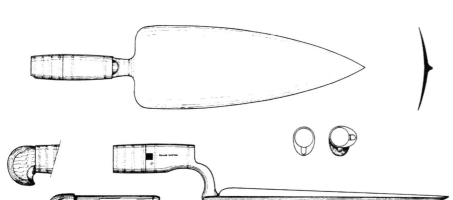

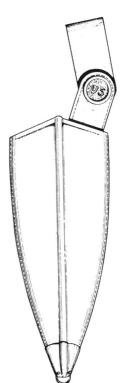

215

No. 1.   U.S. Navy Model 1861 - Dahlgren. This bayonet, designed by the famous weapons designer Admiral John A. Dahlgren, has the distinction of being the first U.S. knife bayonet. It was used on the Model 1861 Plymouth/Whitneyville '69 Cal. short musket rifle. It is a massive and spectacular bayonet. It has a strangely made heavy blade with brass guard and backstrap/pommel and a one-piece wooden grip. It weighs over two pounds and has a brass mounted black leather scabbard. According to Hardin, this piece was produced in four distinct variations. I have two of these represented in my collection: the first variation which has the grip fastened by three copper pins passing vertically through the hilt (see photograph) and is marked only with a small 1861 <u>AND</u> the variation illustrated which has the grip secured by a single screw passing through the hilt. The remaining two variations differ only in markings. The "USN" marked example in my collection is a Japanese-produced replica which was released in the 1970s.

1 U.S. NAVY RIFLE M. 1861 DAHLGREN

HARDIN #129
KIESLING VOL. I #173

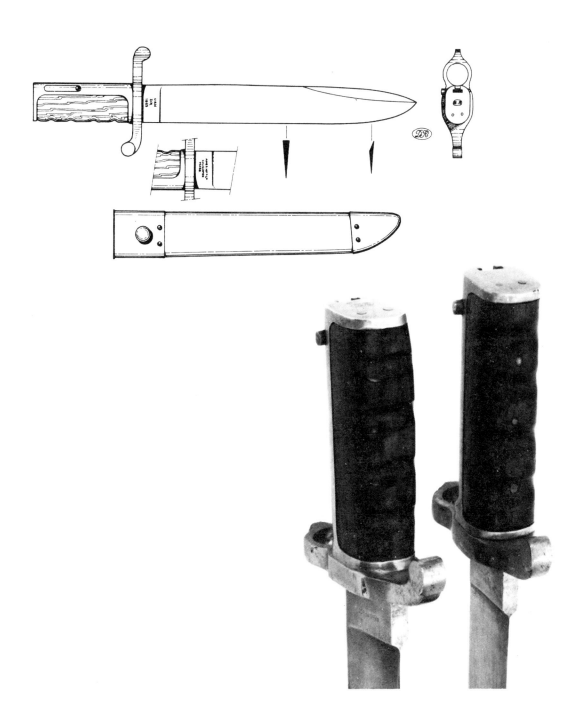

No. 1. **U.S. RIFLE MODEL 1892 - KRAG JORGENSEN.** FIRST U.S. KNIFE BAYONET SINCE 1861, IT HAD A SINGLE-EDGED, FULLERED BLADE MARKED "U.S." AND YEAR OF MANUFACTURE, WITH WOOD GRIPS AND FLUSH RIVETS. THE RIVETS CHANGED IN NOVEMBER OF 1899 WHEN THEY WERE ROUNDED. WHEN FIRST ISSUED IN 1894, THE BLADES WERE BLUED. BLUING STOPPED IN APRIL OF THE FOLLOWING YEAR. THE METAL SCABBARDS WENT THROUGH FOUR CHANGES, MAINLY THE HOOK-TYPE SWIVEL ARM.

No. 2. **U.S. RIFLE MODEL 1898 - KRAG BOLO.** AN EXPERIMENTAL BAYONET TO AID THE TROOPS IN THE PHILLIPINES. THIS COMBO TOOL/BAYONET MAY BE THE SCARCEST OF ALL, ACCORDING TO LT. COL. WILLIAM S. BROPHY, IN HIS BOOK THE KRAG RIFLE. THE SPRINGFIELD ARMORY STATES ONLY SIX WERE MADE. IT HAS A CONVENTIONAL BOLO BLADE WITH THE TYPICAL 1900 ROUNDED RIVETS WITH WOOD GRIPS. ACCORDING TO BROPHY, ALL BOLOS ARE STAMPED "1902". BANNERMAN OFFERED THESE BOLOS FOR $8.95 WITH SCABBARDS AND MENTIONED HE HAD ONLY SIX IN STOCK. I SUSPECT THE PIECE IN MY COLLECTION IS BOGUS.

No. 3. **U.S. RIFLE MODEL 1898 - KRAG BOWIE.** ALSO AN EXPERIMENTAL BAYONET FOR THE KRAG IN THE FORM OF THE BOWIE KNIFE, AND ALSO A "BUST" AS A COMBO TOOL/BAYONET. IT WAS ACTUALLY LIGHTER IN WEIGHT THAN THE BAYONET IT WAS MEANT TO REPLACE. THE BLADE WAS FINISHED BRIGHT AND STAMPED "U.S." AND "1900". THESE ARE SCARCE.

NOTE: THE 1892 KRAG BAYONET WAS ALSO USED ON THE COMMERCIALLY MARKETED WINCHESTER 07 POLICE RIFLE, WHICH WAS ANNOUNCED IN SEPTEMBER, 1935. THE WEAPON APPEARED IN COMPANY LITERATURE ONLY IN THE YEARS 1935, 1936 AND 1937, ACCORDING TO RICHARD RATTENBURY IN AN ARTICLE IN THE SEPTEMBER/OCTOBER 1983 MAN AT ARMS (SEE ILLUSTRATION).

① U.S. RIFLE M.1892
KRAG JORGENSEN

HARDIN #130
KIESLING VOL. I #155

1935 PARTS LIST

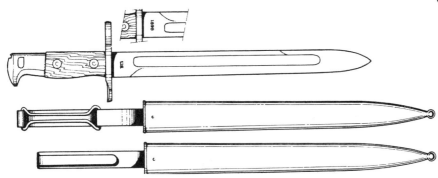

② U.S. RIFLE M.1898
KRAG · BOLO

HARDIN #175
KIESLING VOL. III #558

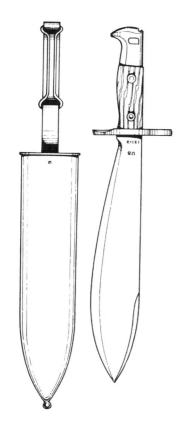

③ U.S. RIFLE M.1898
KRAG · BOWIE

HARDIN #133
KIESLING VOL. III #533

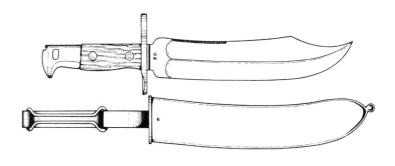

No. 1. **U.S. Cadet Model 1896 - Krag-Jorgensen.** Perhaps one of the most sought after bayonets by U.S. collectors is the Krag Cadet. These are not shortened Model 1892 Krags, but were made with an 8.6 inch blade and 6 inch fullers. These were used by the Corps of Cadets at West Point until 1963 when replaced by the M6 bayonet. There were five variant scabbards used with the bayonet throughout its history at West Point.

No. 2. **U.S. Cadet Model 1896 - Krag-Joregensen.** A nickle-plated full-length Krag bayonet was also employed when the Corps of Cadets exceeded the supply of short blades. The full-length version has a rounded tip and was apparently issued in at least two variations (the difference being the grip fastening). The scabbard used was the Model 1903 with a waist belt adapter, as shown.

No. 3. **U.S. Rifle Model 1898 - Cut Down.** Many bayonets in their short history have been, at one time or another, adapted by soldiers in the field for close proximity fighting. This almost completes the circle, for knives adapted for use as a plug bayonet, then the reverse. By shortening the blade, removing the muzzle ring and either grinding the pommel button or filling the removed button area with lead, in many cases, this resulted in a nicely balanced fighting knife.

NOTE: A slightly modified version of the Krag bayonet was offered as an accessory to the Thompson military Model 1921 submachine gun.

① U.S. CADET M. 1896
KRAG JORGENSEN

HARDIN #132 TYPE I
KIESLING VOL. III #526

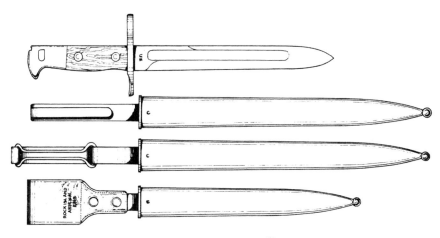

② U.S. CADET M. 1896
KRAG JORGENSEN

HARDIN #132 TYPE II

WAIST BELT ADAPTER
USED WITH SCABBARD

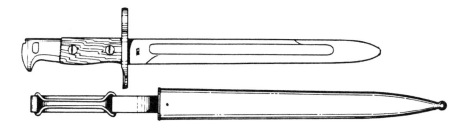

③ U.S. FIGHTING KNIFE
CUT DOWN KRAG

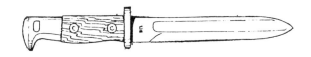

No. 1. **REMINGTON MODEL 1889.** THIS BAYONET IS THE STANDARD REMINGTON ROLLING BLOCK EXPORT BAYONET IDENTICAL TO THOSE USED BY MEXICO, EXCEPT IT IS STAMPED "UNITED STATES NAVY" ON THE FULLER OF THE BLADE IN A MANNER WHICH LOOKS OFFICIAL TO ME. SO . . ., THE NAVY MAY HAVE USED THESE PIECES. JACK SCHRADER HAS A MID-LENGTH VERSION (452MM) OF THIS BAYONET WHICH IS ILLUSTRATED IN KIESLING VOL. IV, #852, AND WAS USED BY SOME STATE MILITIA UNITS.

No. 2. **LEE NAVY MODEL 1895.** THE 6MM. LEE STRAIGHT-PULL RIFLE HAD A SHORT LIFE SPAN IN THE U.S. NAVY, FROM 1896 TO 1900. THIS, OF COURSE, MAKES THE BAYONET THAT MUCH MORE SCARCE, AS ONLY ABOUT 150,000 RIFLES WERE MADE BY WINCHESTER. REMINGTON ARMS CO. MADE THE BAYONETS AND THEY ARE USUALLY SO MARKED IN THE REVERSE FULLER. ALL METAL SURFACES ARE BRIGHT.

No. 3. **WINCHESTER MODEL 1895.** THIS WAS ANOTHER EXPERIMENTAL BAYONET FOR TRIALS IN THE PHILLIPINES. VERY SIMILAR TO THE MODEL 1895 LEE, BUT ONE CAN DIFFERENTIATE BY OBSERVING "WINCHESTER REPEATING ARMS CO." STAMPED UNDER THE GUARD. THE SCABBARD IS IDENTICAL TO THE FIRST LEE MODEL 1895 WITH ATTACHED FROG. HARDIN STATES THAT ONLY 100 WERE ISSUED.

① REMINGTON M. 1889
KIESLING VOL I #51

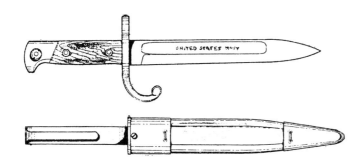

② LEE NAVY M. 1895
HARDIN #131
KIESLING VOL. I #48

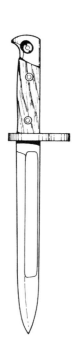

③ WINCHESTER M. 1895
HARDIN #144
KIESLING VOL. III #524

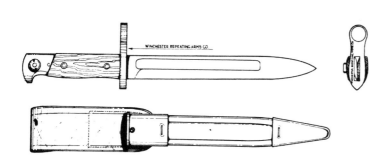

No. 1.   **WINCHESTER MODEL 1895/05 – MODIFIED.** THIS PIECE IS A REAL HYBRID IN THAT IT HAS THE POMMEL AND CROSS-GUARD OF A WINCHESTER M-1895, THE BLADE OF A U.S. M-1905 AND THE GRIPS OF THE U.S. M-1917. THE SLOT IS NOT FUNCTIONAL, WHICH PLACES IT IN THE "WHO KNOWS" CATEGORY.

No. 2.   **U.S. MODEL 1905 – 1ST TYPE.** THIS RARE BAYONET WAS ANOTHER EXPERIMENTAL PIECE, TRYING TO USE THE KRAG LOCKING SYSTEM WITH THE NEW PATTERN 1903 RIFLE. THE BRIGHT, 16 INCH BLADE IS STAMPED "U.S." ON THE OBVERSE AND "1905" ON THE REVERSE RICASSOS (SEE CLOSE-UP); THE GRIPS ARE WOOD FASTENED BY TWO EARLY-TYPE KRAG FLUSH RIVETS. THE SHEATH IS AN EXTENDED BLUED METAL KRAG-TYPE SCABBARD WITH METAL SWIVEL ARM.

① *WINCHESTER M.1895/05*
MODIFIED, HYBRID

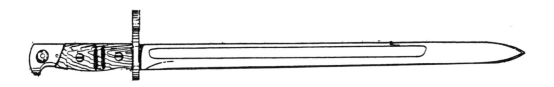

② *U.S. MODEL 1905*
FIRST TYPE

M.H. COLE PG. 30
D. ERNST VOL. II PG. 80

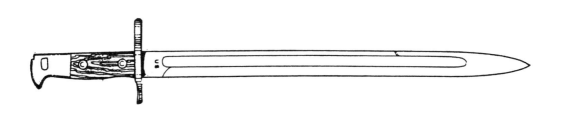

No. 1. **U.S. MODEL 1905 "FIELD TRIAL".** I HAVE BEEN TOLD THESE WERE THE INITIAL MANUFACTURING LOT OF U.S. M-1905 BAYONETS (DISCUSSED BELOW) WHICH ROCK ISLAND ARSENAL PRODUCED FOR FIELD TRIAL PURPOSES. THE BLADES <u>DO NOT</u> HAVE A SERIAL NUMBER.

No. 2. **U.S. MODEL 1905.** AFTER A HEATED LETTER FROM PRESIDENT THEODORE ROOSEVELT, AS EARLIER MENTIONED, A NEW BLADE BAYONET WAS ADOPTED UTILIZING A LONGER BLADE THAN THE KRAG TO COMPENSATE FOR A SHORTER RIFLE. THE SCABBARD AND RIFLE LOCKING DEVICE WAS ADAPTED FROM THE NORWEGIAN MODEL 1894 KRAG. THE CORRUGATED WOOD GRIPS WERE HELD BY SCREW BOLTS. THE HILT AND PART OF THE BLADE RICASSO WERE BLUED. THE OBSERVED DATES ON THE M-1905 SERIES BY ARSENAL ARE:

> RIA 1906 THROUGH 1913, AND 1917 THROUGH 1919
> S.A. 1906 THROUGH 1922

SEVERAL SCABBARD TYPES ARE ILLUSTRATED.

No. 3. **U.S. MODEL 1905/42.** DURING WORLD WAR II, MANY ORIGINAL MODELS WITH PARKERIZED OR BLUED BLADES HAD THEIR WOODEN GRIPS REPLACED WITH BLACK RIBBED PLASTIC. THIS THEN MADE THEM A U.S. MODEL 1905/42 DESIGNATION; HOWEVER, THEY WERE REFERRED TO AS BAYONET MODEL 1942. THE SCABBARD WAS THE GREEN PLASTIC MODEL WITH THE U.S. ORDNANCE BOMB AND THE WIRE BELT ATTACHMENT.

NOTE: THE U.S. MODEL 1905 WAS ALSO OFFERED AS AN ACCESSORY WITH THE THOMPSON MILITARY MODEL 1923 SUBMACHINE GUN.

① *U.S. MODEL 1905*
FIELD TRIAL

M.H COLE PG. 30

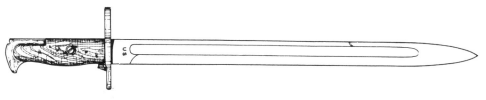

② *U.S. MODEL 1905*

HARDIN #134
KIESLING VOL. II #292

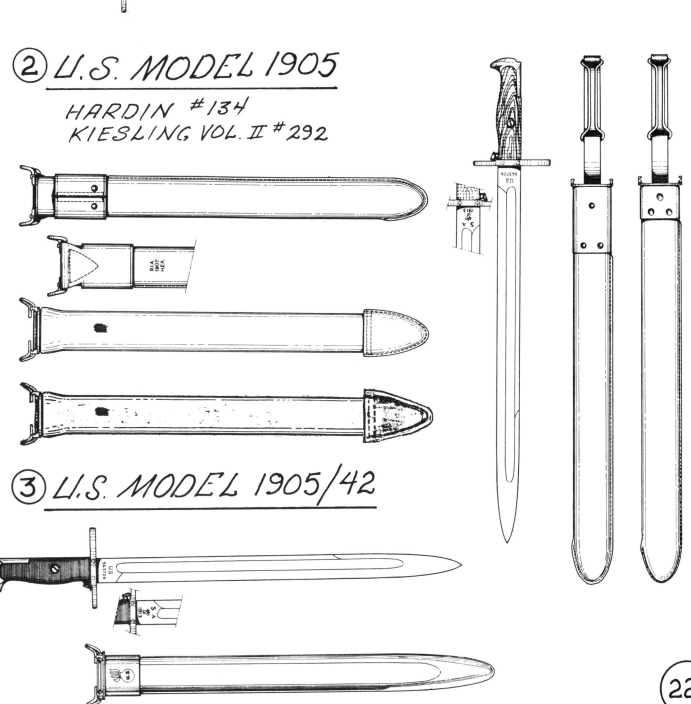

③ *U.S. MODEL 1905/42*

No. 1. **U.S. Ross Rifle Model 1905/10.** The Canadian Ross Model 1905/1910 was used with the Ross rifle for training U.S. troops during World War I. The Ross had been declared obsolete, not being able to withstand the rigors of trench warfare in Europe. Hence, the U.S. purchased 20,000 of the rifles for training and home guard use. Both bayonet and leather scabbard were stamped with the ordnance bomb and "U.S.". Both Evans and Kiesling conclude that the <u>correct</u> year for the first Ross is 1908; however, I have used the more common designation.

NOTE: The British also contracted for Canadian Ross bayonets with Hugh Carson Limited of Ottawa. It, like the U.S. example, is easily identified being a MK II of the "hatchet" point design with a dull mat-gray finished blade and blued hilt. The British examples <u>do not</u> have the "MK" and date of production on the left-hand side of the pommel, as the U.S. and Canadian versions.

① U.S. ROSS RIFLE M.1905/10

HARDIN #146
KIESLING VOL. I #109

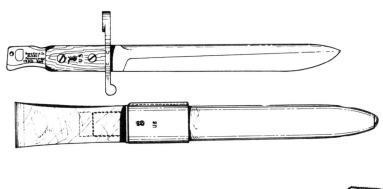

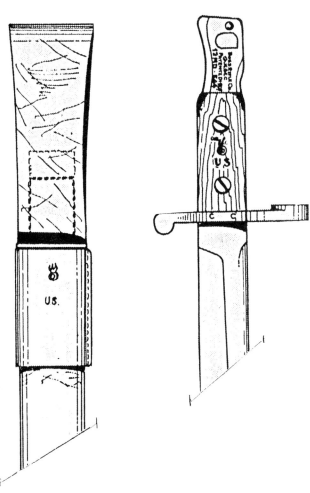

US.

No. 1. **U.S. Model 1913/17 – English Enfield.** This bayonet was made under British contract by Remington and Winchester for the British Pattern 1914 rifle. However, after the American entry into the war, all production was diverted to the U.S. and any British marks were overstamped with U.S. marks. Early P-1913 examples sent to Britain were made with the oil cleaning holes in the pommels, although the two deep grooves in the grips were retained to differentiate between the P-1907 and the P-1913.

No. 2. **U.S. Model 1917.** This bayonet is known as an "U.S. Enfield" or "Eddystone" and was manufactured by both Remington and Winchester. It will also fit the service issue riot shotguns. These pieces are common and have seen service in both world wars and numerous police departments. A second scabbard variation is illustrated.

No. 3. **U.S. Model 1917.** This bayonet is identical to 223-2 except that it has <u>NO OIL HOLE</u> in the pommel. The scabbard illustrated is the later plastic version. Most of these pieces have the manufacturer and the date "1917" on the blade ricasso; however, some are dated 1918.

NOTE: In Denmark, Item No. 3 is known as Bajonet M.53/17.

223 - UNITED STATES - KNIFE

① U.S. MODEL 1913/17

HARDIN #135
KIESLING VOL. II #321

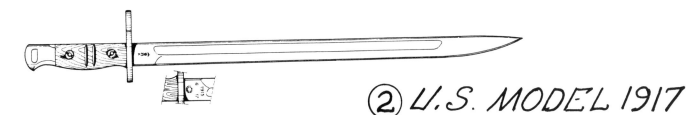

② U.S. MODEL 1917

HARDIN #135
KIESLING VOL II #322

③ U.S. MODEL 1917
W/O OIL HOLE

KIESLING VOL. II #

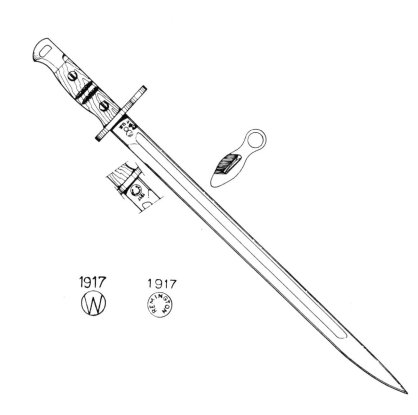

1917
Ⓦ

1917
REMINGTON

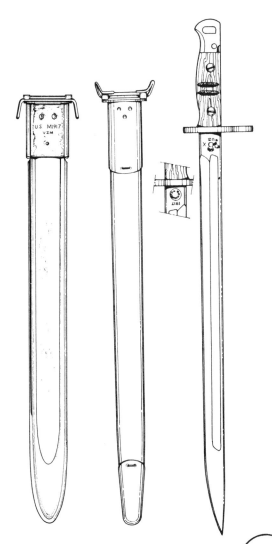

No. 1. **U.S. Model 1917 - Service Issue Shot Gun.** According-ing to M. H. Cole, this bayonet was manufactured in the 1960's (Vietnam) for shotguns to be used for guard and riot duty. They were produced in Canada by General Cutlery.

No. 2. **U.S. Model 1942 - Springfield.** This bayonet was introduced during World War II and, but for minor modifications, is the same as the M-1905. The blade finish is not of the quality of the 1905 and the grips are of a black or redish-brown ribbed plastic construction. These pieces are dated 1942 or 1943 and were manufactured by the following contractors:

Oneida Ltd. - OL
Union Fork & Hoe - UFH
Pal Blade Co. - PAL
Wilde Tool - WT
American Fork & Hoe - AFH
Utica Cutlery Co. - U.C.

① U.S. MODEL 1917 SHOTGUN

KIESLING VOL. IV #892
M.H. COLE PG. 34

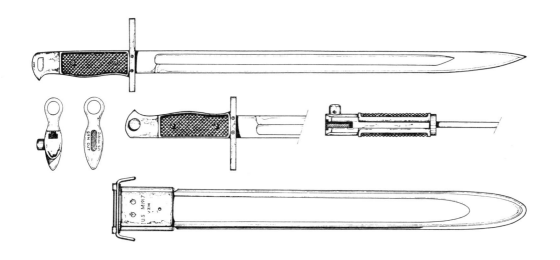

② U.S. MODEL 1942

HARDIN #136
KIESLING VOL. II #293
M.H. COLE PG. 32

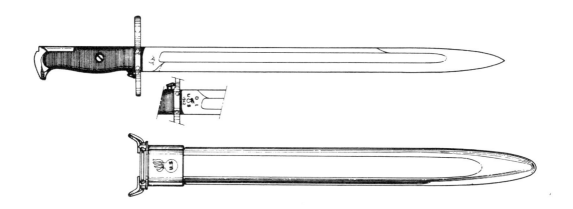

224

No. 1. **U.S. MODEL 1905 E1.** THIS WAS NOTHING MORE THAN A SHORTENED M-1942 OR 1905 WITH EITHER THE ORIGINAL WOOD OR RIBBED BLACK PLASTIC GRIPS. NOTE THE FULLER RUNNING THROUGH THE POINT. ISSUED WITH THE GREEN PLASTIC M7 SCABBARD.

No. 2. **U.S. MODEL 1905 E1 - VARIANT.** THIS BLADE WAS CUT DOWN FROM THE ORIGINAL BY GRINDING APPROXIMATELY 6" FROM THE POINT. THIS PARTICULAR BLADE WOUND UP WITH A WEDGE SHAPE (MANUFACTURED BY UFH, PAL, AFH, UC, OL).

No. 3. **U.S. MODEL 1905 - VARIANT.** HERE IS ANOTHER VARIANT WITH THE BLADE SHORTENED TO 10" AND GROUND WITH A BOWIE-TYPE POINT. (THIS MAY BE A POST-WAR JOB, DONE BY INDIA OR PAKISTAN FOR THE SURPLUS GARANDS BOUGHT FROM THE U.S.)

No. 4. **U.S. BAYONET M1 - GARAND.** THE BLADE WAS APPROXIMATELY 10" LONG AND THE FULLER APPROXIMATELY 7". THESE FIT THE GARAND RIFLE. THEY HAD THE SAME BLACK PLASTIC GRIPS AS THE M-1942 AND WERE ISSUED WITH THE M7 SCABBARD.

NOTE: I POSSESS SEVERAL INTERESTING VARIATIONS OF THE M1 BAYONET SERIES AS FOLLOWS:

225-1 WITH BLUED BLADE AND SMOOTH WOOD GRIPS MARKED WITH ANCHOR ON ONE SIDE AND "USS HELENA CL 50" ON THE OTHER, WITH A GRAY SCABBARD

225-3 WITH ROUNDED TIP AND "9" ETCHED ON RICASSO (A TRAINING PIECE, I ASSUME)

225-3 WITH SERIAL NUMBER STAMPED ON THE CROSSGUARD

225 - UNITED STATES - KNIFE

① U.S. MODEL 1905 E1

HARDIN #137
KIESLING VOL. I #89
M.H. COLE. PG. 32

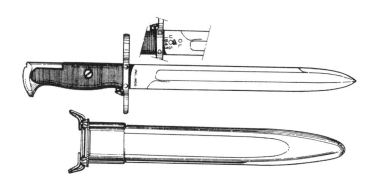

④ U.S. RIFLE M1

HARDIN #137
KIESLING VOL I #90
M.H. COLE PG. 33

② U.S. MODEL 1905 E1

KIESLING VOL. III #539
M.H. COLE PG. 32

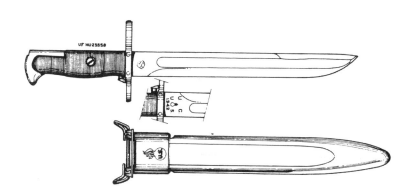

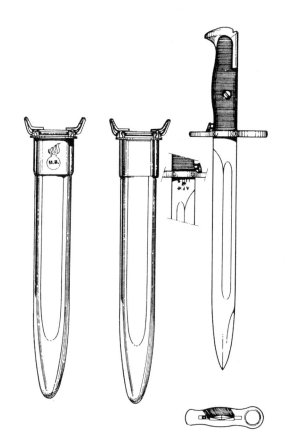

③ U.S. MODEL 1905 SHORTENED

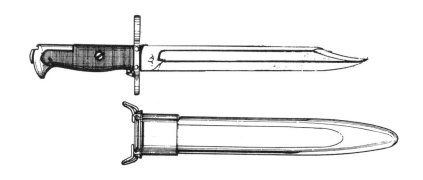

No. 1. **U.S. FIGHTING KNIFE.** THIS KNIFE WAS CUT DOWN FROM A M-1942 OR M1 BAYONET. THE BLADE IS 6-3/4" IN LENGTH AND THE SCABBARD IS OF RIVETED LEATHER CONSTRUCTION. THESE PIECES MAY HAVE SOME OFFICIAL STATUS AS I HAVE SEEN SEVERAL IDENTICAL EXAMPLES AT GUN SHOWS AND COLE REPORTS A WORLD WAR II COMBAT PICTURE SHOWING THE KNIVES BEING WORN.

No. 2. **KUTMASTER KNIFE.** THESE KNIVES WERE PRODUCED BY UTICA CUTLERY CO. FOR SALE TO THE COMMERCIAL MARKET FROM M1 BAYONET PARTS. I POSSESS TWO VERSIONS, ONE PLATED WITH NO CUT OUT FOR THE BAYONET LUG AND THE OTHER POLISHED WITH THE ORIGINAL LUG SLOT INTACT. BOTH ARE STAMPED "KUTMASTER UTICA N.Y. USA" ON THE BLADE. THE BLACK RIBBED PLASTIC GRIPS OF THE BAYONET ARE RETAINED, HOWEVER, THE SCABBARDS ARE OF LEATHER CONSTRUCTION.

NOTE: I ALSO HAVE A MODEL 1905 CUT TO THE 6-3/4" LENGTH WITH A WEDGE SHAPE LIKE THE "KUTMASTER" VERSIONS.

① *U.S. FIGHTING KNIFE*

M.H. COLE PG. 189

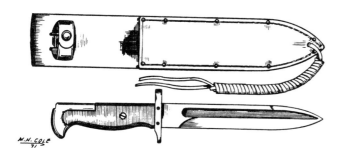

② *KUTMASTER KNIFE*

M. H. COLE PG. 198

<u>No. 1 ALL METAL CHROME PLATED</u>

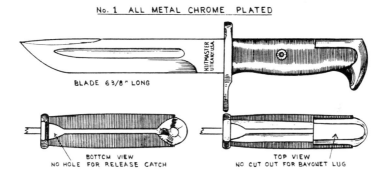

BLADE 6 3/8" LONG

KUTMASTER UTICA N.Y. U.S.A

BOTTOM VIEW
NO HOLE FOR RELEASE CATCH

TOP VIEW
NO CUT OUT FOR BAYONET LUG

<u>No. 2 ALL METAL FINISHED BRIGHT</u>

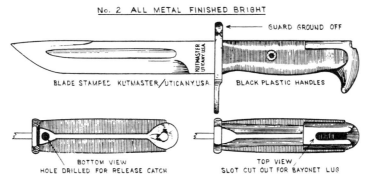

GUARD GROUND OFF

KUTMASTER UTICA N.Y. U.S.A

BLADE STAMPED KUTMASTER/UTICA N.Y. U.S.A

BLACK PLASTIC HANDLES

BOTTOM VIEW
HOLE DRILLED FOR RELEASE CATCH

TOP VIEW
SLOT CUT OUT FOR BAYONET LUG

No. 1. **U.S. Trench Knife M3.** This knife was the basis for the adaption of the M4 Carbine bayonet. A beautifully balanced weapon, without fullers, it was much stronger than its British counterpart, the Sykes-Fairbairn Commando knife. The grooved leather washers provided a firm, non-slip grip. It had a leather scabbard with metal reinforcements termed the M6.

No. 2. **U.S. fighting knife M3/M4.** This hybrid is an M4 bayonet with the hilt of an M3 trench knife, looks official, however, may have been made up of parts after the war.

No. 3. **U.S. Bayonet M1 - Carbine.** This bayonet has a blade marked "U.S. M3 Case" which means that it was one of the early M4 bayonets which utilized the blades of the M3 trench knives. (The M3 was manufactured in 1943 while the M4 was manufactured in 1944.) This was confirmed by M. H. Cole in his book.

No. 4. **U.S. Bayonet M4 - Leather Grip.** The M1 carbine was originally manufactured without provision for a bayonet. The demand became so heavy for some form of bayonet that by 1944 a new small blade bayonet, based on the M3 fighting knife, was issued. A revolutionary form of attachment with two spring-loaded locking catches was designed and the M4 has become one of the most copied bayonets in the world today. A green plastic scabbard with a webbed attachment was termed the M8 and later the M8A1. This bayonet was manufactured by the following contractors: Case, Aerial Cutlery Co. (ACC), Camillus, Imperial, Pal, Utica, Kinfolks Inc. (K.I.), Kiffe (Japan).

① U.S. TRENCH KNIFE M3

M.H. COLE PG. 95

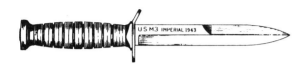

U.S M3 IMPERIAL 1943

② U.S. FIGHTING KNIFE M3/M4

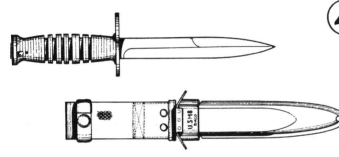

U.S M8
B.M.C.O

④ U.S. BAYONET M4

HARDIN # 138
KIESLING VOL. I # 22
M.H. COLE PG 107

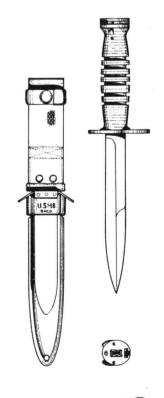

U.S M8
B.M.C.O

U.S. CASE

③ U.S. BAYONET M4

M.H. COLE PG. 102

U.S.M3 CASE

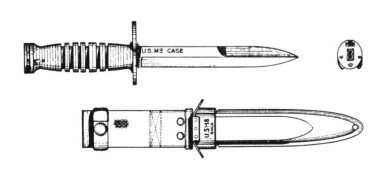

U.S M8
B.M.C.O

No. 1. **U.S. BAYONET M4 - RUBBER GRIP.** DUE TO THE EXTREME HUMIDITY IN THE SOUTH PACIFIC, MANY OF THE LEATHER GRIPS DETERIORATED BADLY AND MANY DIFFERENT MATERIALS WERE SUBSTITUTED. THIS PARTICULAR ONE IS RUBBER GRIPPED. ALL OTHER PARTS WERE AS ISSUED. (I WAS TOLD THAT A PLATED VERSION OF THIS VARIANT WAS USED BY DOUGLAS MACARTHUR'S MILITARY POLICE UNITS IN POST-WAR JAPAN.)

No. 2. **U.S. BAYONET M4 - WOOD GRIP.** THIS EXAMPLE HAS CRUDELY CROSS-HATCHED WOODEN GRIPS. NONE OF THESE MODIFICATIONS WERE OFFICIAL AND WERE PROBABLY DONE IN FORWARD AREAS OF COMBAT.

No. 3. **U.S. BAYONET M4 - PLASTIC GRIPS.** IN 1956, BLACK, CHECKERED PLASTIC GRIPS WERE ADOPTED. THESE WERE MOLDED IN TWO PIECES AND HELD BY TWO MACHINE SCREWS AND BOLTS. THIS WAS THE FINAL SOLUTION TO MILDEW FOR THE M4 BAYONET. THE CONTRACTORS WHO MANUFACTURED THESE BAYONETS ARE TURNER (TMN), IMPERIAL, CONETTA AND BREN-DAN. ALSO, I HAVE CASE AND PAL EXAMPLES, HOWEVER, SUSPECT THEY ARE WORLD WAR II BAYONETS WITH THE HANDLES REPLACED.

No. 4. **U.S. BAYONET M4 - LONG VERSION.** THIS BAYONET MAY POSSIBLY BE A PROTOTYPE, AS IT IS A WELL MANUFACTURED DUPLICATE OF THE M4 WITH A 9-5/8" BLADE. HOWEVER, IT IS ALSO LIKELY IT WAS FABRICATED FOR AN UNSUSPECTING COLLECTOR, LIKE MYSELF. I HAVE NO INFORMATION ON ITS DERIVATION.

① U.S. BAYONET M4
RUBBER GRIP

KIESLING VOL. I #24
M.H. COLE PG. 108

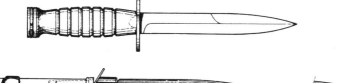

② U.S. BAYONET M4
WOODEN GRIP

KIESLING VOL. I #25
M.H. COLE PG. 109

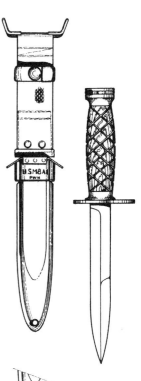

③ U.S. BAYONET M4
PLASTIC GRIPS

HARDIN #138
KIESLING VOL. I #23
M.H. COLE PG. 110

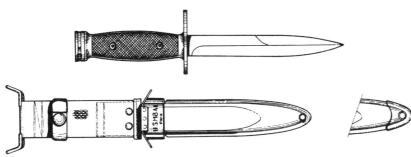

④ U.S. BAYONET M4
LONG BLADE

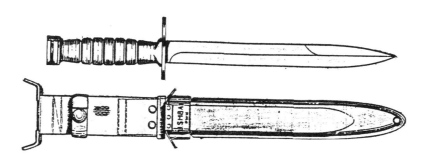

No. 1.   U.S. BAYONET M5 - M1 GARAND.   THE FINAL BAYONET ISSUED FOR THE GARAND WAS THE M5 SERIES.   IT COULD FIT ONLY THE GARAND RIFLE DUE TO THE REAR-FACING BUTTON WHICH FIT INTO THE GAS CYLINDER PLUG ON THE RIFLE.   THE BLADE IS SIMILAR TO THE M4; HOWEVER, THE RELEASE MECHANISM WAS A STAMPED, STEEL METAL PIECE THAT OPERATED WITH A GLOVED HAND IN WINTER.   THE GRIP IS OF CHECKERED, BLACK PLASTIC.   (MANUFACTURED BY AERIAL, IMPERIAL, UTICA AND J & D TOOL CO.).

No. 2.   U.S. BAYONET M5-1 - M1 GARAND.   THIS BAYONET HAD AN IMPROVED RELEASE LATCHING LEVER, OTHERWISE, IT IS IDENTICAL TO THE M5.   THESE PIECES WERE PRODUCED BY AERIAL AND J & D TOOL AND ARE CURRENTLY MANUFACTURED BY EICKHORN IN GERMANY.

No. 3.   U.S. BAYONET M5A1 - M1 GARAND.   THIS BAYONET WAS THE FINAL VERSION OF THE M5 SERIES.   IT HAS A REFINED BLADE FORM AND MINOR CHANGES TO THE LOCKING MECHANISM, HOWEVER, IS VIRTUALLY INDISTINGUISHABLE FROM THE M5 AND M5-1.   THESE WERE MANUFAC-TURED BY IMPERIAL AND MILPAR.

No. 4.   U.S. BAYONET M6 - M14 RIFLE.   THIS BAYONET WAS DEVELOPED FOR THE M14 RIFLE IN 1957.   IT HAS BASICALLY THE M5 GRIP, HOW-EVER, THE GUARD WAS REDESIGNED WITH A MUZZLE RING AND THE BLADE IS CLOSER TO THE ORIGINAL M4.   IT TAKES THE M8A1 SCAB-BARD.   THE KNOWN CONTRACTORS FOR THE M6 ARE AERIAL, IMPERIAL, MILPAR AND "AN" (I REALLY DON'T KNOW WHAT COMPANY "AN" DENOTES).

① U.S BAYONET M5
M1 GARAND

HARDIN #139
KIESLING VOL I #26
M.H. COLE PG. 112

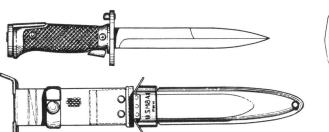

② U.S. BAYONET M5-1
M1 GARAND

KIESLING VOL I #26
M.H. COLE PG. 112

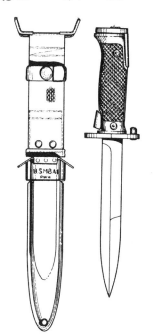

③ U.S. BAYONET M5A1
M1 GARAND

KIESLING VOL I #26
M.H. COLE PG. 112

④ U.S. BAYONET M6
M14 RIFLE

HARDIN #140
KIESLING VOL.I #27
M.H. COLE PG 113

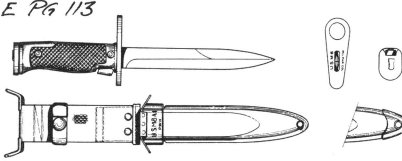

No. 1. U.S. BAYONET M7 - COLT, TYPE I. THIS BAYONET WAS PRODUCED BY COLT FOR THEIR AR15 RIFLES AND IS A MUCH HIGHER QUALITY BAYONET THAN 230-2, IN THAT IT HAS A SOLID, OLIVE-DRAB PLASTIC HANDLE, A MUCH BETTER FINISH, AND CARRIES EITHER THE SINGLE-LINE COLT DESIGNATION OR THE COLT RAMPANT STALLION LOGO ON THE BLADE. I HAVE SEEN THESE BAYONETS WITH SOLID BLUE PLASTIC HANDLES.

No. 2. U.S. BAYONET M7 - M16 RIFLE, TYPE II. THIS BAYONET IS THE ISSUE U.S. BAYONET FOR THE M16 AND AR15 RIFLES. IT WAS PRODUCED BY SEVERAL U.S. MANUFACTURERS, SOME OF WHICH ARE ILLUSTRATED. IT IS TYPICAL OF THE CARBINE SERIES OF BAYONETS IN THAT IT IS A VERY UTILITARIAN WEAPON AND COMES IN A STANDARD U.S. PLASTIC SCABBARD.

No. 3. U.S. BAYONET M7 - EXPERIMENTAL BAYONET. THESE PIECES WERE APPARENTLY PRODUCED ON AN EXPERIMENTAL BASIS IN 1974 FROM ALTERED NAVY MARK 2 KNIVES. THE PIECE IN MY COLLECTION HAS, IN MY OPINION, BEEN PUT TOGETHER IN RECENT YEARS, AS I HAVE SEEN A NUMBER OF THEM AT GUN SHOWS AND ALWAYS FROM THE SAME DEALER.

No. 4. U.S. BAYONET M7 - SECOND PATTERN. THIS BAYONET IS PART OF THE FIRST BATCH OF BAYONETS TO BE PRODUCED BY CARL EICKHORN FOR COLT INDUSTRIES TO BE SOLD WITH THE HECKLER & KOCH G3 RIFLES. THE REASON FOR THE ABSENCE OF A LOWER QUILLON IS THAT THE BAYONET ON THE G3 RIFLE FITS ABOVE THE BARREL AND THE LONG QUILLON OF THE ORIGINAL M7 DESIGN WOULD BLOCK THE LINE OF SIGHT WHEN THE BAYONET IS FIXED IN THE UPSIDE-DOWN POSITION. FOR SOME REASON, THESE PIECES ARE RELATIVELY SCARCE. (NOTE THE CONSTRUCTION DIFFERENCE WITH 230-2.)

230 - UNITED STATES - KNIFE

① U.S. BAYONET M7
COLT, TYPE I

HARDIN #141 TYPE I
KIESLING VOL I #28
M.H. COLE PG. 114

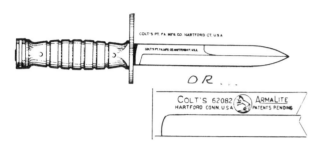

O R . . .

② U.S. BAYONET M7
M16 RIFLE, TYPE II

HARDIN #141. TYPE II
KIESLING VOL I #29
M.H. COLE PG. 115

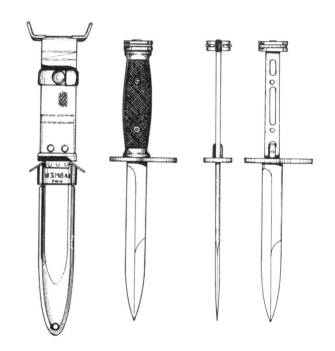

③ U.S. BAYONET M7
EXPERIMENTAL

M.H. COLE PG. 119
D. ERNST VOL. II #46

④ U.S. BAYONET M7
SECOND PATTERN

KIESLING VOL. IV #746
M.H. COLE PG. 118

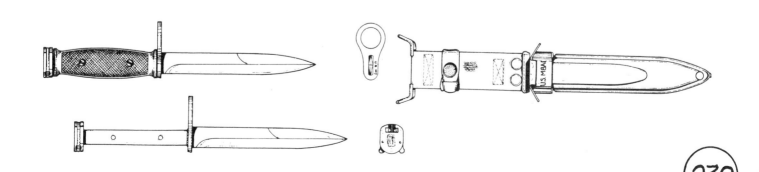

No. 1. **U.S. BAYONET M7 – COLT AR15.** THIS BAYONET IS ONE OF A SERIES OF CONTRACTS PRODUCED BY CARL EICKHORN FOR COLT INDUSTRIES FOR SALE WITH COMMERCIAL ARMALITE AR15 RIFLES. IT IS IDENTICAL TO THE U.S. PRODUCED M7 EXCEPT IT HAS THE COLT RAMPANT STALLION AND IS MARKED "MADE IN GERMANY" ON THE BLADE, AS ILLUSTRATED.

No. 2. **U.S. BAYONET M7 – COLT AR15.** THIS BAYONET IS IDENTICAL TO 231-1 EXCEPT THAT THE "MADE IN GERMANY" DOES NOT ACCOMPANY THE COLT LOGO ON THE BLADE.

No. 3. **U.S. BAYONET M7 – COMMEMORATIVE.** THIS BAYONET SERIES WAS MANUFACTURED BY THE AMERICAN HISTORICAL FOUNDATION IN 1985/86 TO COMMEMORATE THE VIETNAM WAR. IT HAS A PLATED POMMEL AND CROSSGUARD WITH A BEAUTIFULLY ENGRAVED BLADE. A GRIP MEDALLION HAS BEEN INSET IN THE STANDARD BLACK PLASTIC GRIPS AND THE PIECE COMES IN FOUR VARIATIONS: U.S. ARMY, U.S. AIR FORCE, U.S. MARINES, AND U.S. NAVY. THE COMMEMORATIVE SERIES WAS PRODUCED BY THE IMPERIAL KNIFE COMPANY IN RELATIVELY SMALL QUANTITIES (2,000 EACH) AND EACH BAYONET IS SERIAL NUMBERED.

① U.S. BAYONET M7
COLT AR 15

M. H. COLE PG. 117
RDC EVANS PG. 174

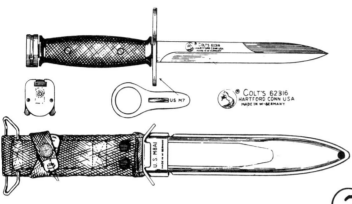

② U.S. BAYONET M7
COLT AR 15

M. H. COLE PG. 115

③ U.S. BAYONET M7
COMMEMORATIVE

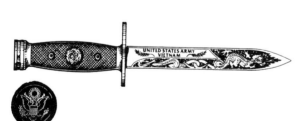

No. 1. **U.S. BAYONET M7 – GERMAN MANUFACTURE.** THIS BAYONET WAS APPARENTLY MADE UP OF PARTS AVAILABLE AT THE CARL EICKHORN FACTORY AT THE TIME OF THE FIRM'S BANKRUPTCY IN 1976. IT IS AN INTERESTING PIECE WITH A DOUBLE-EDGED BLADE AND VERY UNUSUAL PLASTIC GRIPS. (SEE 108-1 FOR VERY SIMILAR G-3 VERSION.)

No. 2. **U.S. BAYONET M7 – GERMAN MANUFACTURE.** ACCORDING TO R.D.C. EVANS, THIS M7 BAYONET WAS MANUFACTURED BY EICKHORN AFTER THE FIRM'S REORGANIZATION. THESE HAVE A REDESIGNED ONE-PIECE DULL, PLASTIC GRIP WITH A REMOVABLE POMMEL AND UTILIZE A DOUBLE-EDGED BLADE VERY SIMILAR TO 232-1.

No. 3. **U.S. BAYONET M7 – WIRE CUTTER, GERMAN MANUFACTURE.** THIS BAYONET IS ANOTHER EICKHORN DERIVATIVE AND IS EQUIPPED WITH THE ONE-PIECE HANDLE, REMOVABLE POMMEL AND IS MODIFIED TO ALLOW USE AS A WIRE CUTTER, AS ILLUSTRATED.

No. 4. **U.S. BAYONET M7 – GERMAN MANUFACTURE.** THIS BAYONET IS IDENTICAL TO 232-3 EXCEPT THAT IT HAS <u>NOT</u> BEEN MODIFIED AS A WIRE CUTTER. THE BAYONETS IN THIS SERIES ARE ALL EQUIPPED WITH A U.S.-STYLED SHEATH WITH A SOMEWHAT BETTER FINISH.

① U.S. BAYONET M7
GERMAN EXPORT

R.D.C. EVANS PG. 174

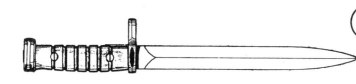

② U.S. BAYONET M7
GERMAN EXPORT

R.D.C. EVANS PG. 175

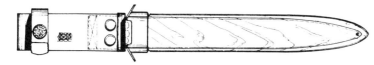

③ U.S. BAYONET M7
WIRE CUTTER

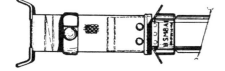

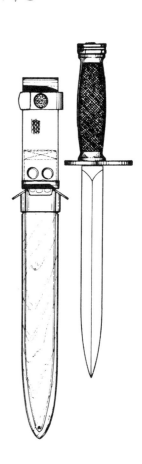

④ U.S. BAYONET M7
GERMAN EXPORT

R.D.C. EVANS PG. 175

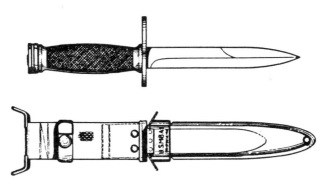

232

No. 1. COMMERCIAL BAYONET - RUGER 10/22. THIS BAYONET IS THE RESULT OF PERCEIVED DEMAND BY RUGER OWNERS TO MAKE THEIR RIFLES APPEAR MORE MILITARY. THIS RATHER CRUDE PIECE WAS MANUFACTURED BY PIONEER FIREARMS IN 1982 AND INCORPORATES A COMMERCIAL SURVIVAL KNIFE WITH A MACHINED METAL ATTACHMENT TO THE HANDLE, WHICH ALLOWS THE BAYONET TO BE AFFIXED TO A STANDARD RUGER 10/22.

No. 2. COMMERCIAL BAYONET - RUGER MINI-14. THIS BAYONET IS VERY SIMILAR TO 233-1 EXCEPT IT HAS BEEN MANUFACTURED TO FIT THE RUGER MINI-14 AND THE SURVIVAL KNIFE UTILIZED BY THE MANUFACTURER DOES NOT HAVE A SERRATED EDGE AS ILLUSTRATED IN 233-1. THESE PIECES ARE VERY CRUDELY PRODUCED AND APPARENTLY ENJOYED LIMITED SUCCESS.

No. 3. U.S. KNIFE - M6. THIS PIECE IS NOT A FUNCTIONAL BAYONET AND HAS BEEN ASSEMBLED FROM U.S. M6 BAYONET PARTS TO A KNIFE CONFIGURATION. IT IS VERY POORLY MANUFACTURED AND APPARENTLY AIMED AT THE COMMERCIAL MARKET.

No. 4. KUTMASTER KNIFE. THIS KNIFE WAS ALTERED FOR THE BLADE HUNGRY AMERICAN PUBLIC AFTER WORLD WAR II. IT WAS PRODUCED BY UTICA CUTLERY COMPANY FROM BAYONET OR TRENCH KNIFE COMPONENTS.

① RUGER MODEL 10/22

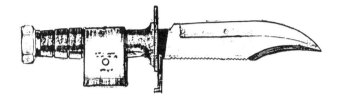

② RUGER MINI 14

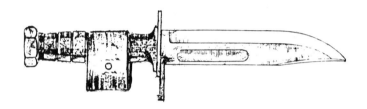

③ U.S. KNIFE M6

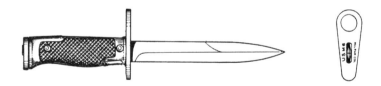

④ KUTMASTER KNIFE

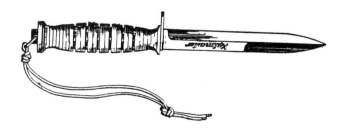

U.S. BAYONET M9. THIS BAYONET IS NOT IN MY COLLECTION; HOWEVER, TO MAKE THIS BOOK AS COMPLETE AS POSSIBLE, I WANTED TO PROVIDE THE INFORMATION AVAILABLE AT THE TIME OF THIS WRITING CONCERNING THE CURRENT U.S. OFFERING. THE BAYONET WAS DEVELOPED IN RESPONSE TO U.S. SOLDIERS CARRYING THEIR OWN SURVIVAL KNIVES TO THE FIELD.

THE ARMY FIRST SPELLED OUT WHAT IT WANTED IN A NEW BAYONET IN DECEMBER, 1985, ULTIMATELY SOLICITING BIDS FROM 49 CONTRACTORS. THE SERVICE ENDED UP TESTING SIX PROTOTYPES AND RECEIVING EIGHT BIDS, BUT FOUND ONLY ONE DESIGN THAT IT REALLY LIKED. EARLY IN OCTOBER, 1986, THE OCEANSIDE, CALIFORNIA, COMPANY OF PHROBIS III LTD. RECEIVED A $15.6 MILLION TO PRODUCE 315,600 OF THE NEW BAYONETS. THE BAYONETS AND ACCOMPANYING SCABBARDS, WHICH TOGETHER WEIGH SLIGHTLY LESS THAN 1.8 POUNDS, ARE SCHEDULED FOR DELIVERY BY OCTOBER, 1989. THE PURCHASE PRICE OF $49.60 PER BAYONET IS ALMOST THREE TIMES THE COST OF THE BAYONET THE ARMY HAS BEEN USING FOR THE PAST 25 YEARS.

THE ARMY'S BIGGEST COMPLAINT ABOUT THE ISSUE M7 IS THAT IT DOES NOT HOLD AN EDGE AND IS POORLY BALANCED FOR HAND-TO-HAND COMBAT WHEN NOT ATTACHED TO THE END OF A RIFLE. (PHOTO COURTESY OF U.S. ARMY INFANTRY CENTER, FORT BENNING, GEORGIA.)

① *U.S. BAYONET M9*

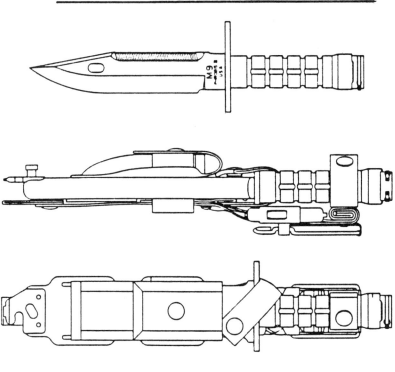

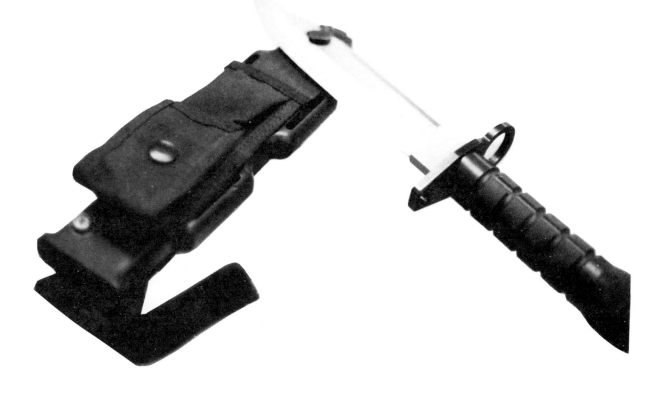

No. 1. **U.S. FENCING MODEL 1858.** THIS BAYONET IS DESIGNED SPECIFICALLY FOR PRACTICE AND CONSISTS OF A STEEL SOCKET (FABRICATED FROM A BAYONET?) WITH A WHALE-BONE EXTENSION AFFIXED BY A HAND SCREW. A VERY LIGHT LEATHER COVERED BALL IS FASTENED TO THE TIP OF THE WHALEBONE. THE STEEL SOCKETS ARE RELATIVELY PLENTIFUL, HOWEVER, THE WHALEBONE EXTENSIONS ARE VERY RARE. THE REASON IS ATTRIBUTED BY SOME TO THE STORAGE OF THE BAYONETS ON BANNERMAN ISLAND WHERE THE WHALEBONE WAS DESTROYED BY RATS.

No. 2. **U.S. FENCING MODEL CIRCA 1906.** THIS DATE IS VERY APPROXIMATE AND BASED ON DATES STAMPED ON THE LEATHER COVER. THESE PIECES WERE FABRICATED FROM 1855 SOCKET BAYONETS AND INVOLVED EXTENSIVE GRIND-ING AND RETEMPERING OF THE BLADE. THE BLADES WERE THEN COVERED WITH LEATHER. THIS WORK WAS PERFORMED AT ROCK ISLAND ARSENAL.

No. 3. **U.S. FENCING MODEL CIRCA 1906.** THIS BAYONET WAS PROBABLY FABRICATED DURING THE SAME PERIOD AS 235-2 AND WAS DESIGNED TO FIT A SPECIALLY FABRICATED TRAINING RIFLE. I HAVE EXAMINED TRAINING RIFLES OF THIS TYPE AND SUSPECT THEY WERE UTILIZED ONLY FOR BAYONET TRAINING BECAUSE OF THE ABSENCE OF FUNC-TIONING PARTS.

① U.S. FENCING M. 1858

HARDIN #157
KIESLING VOL. IV #894

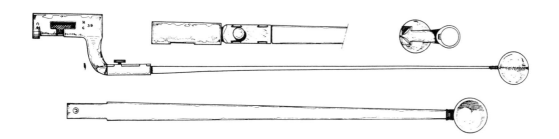

② U.S. FENCING C. 1906

HARDIN #158
KIESLING VOL. IV #884

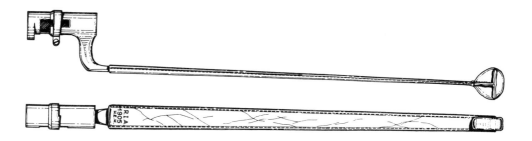

③ U.S. FENCING C. 1906

HARDIN #159
KIESLING VOL II #243

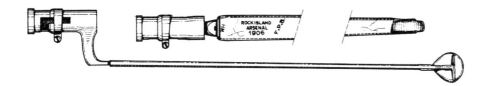

No. 1. **U.S. FENCING MODEL 1909.** THIS PIECE WAS FABRICATED SPECIFICALLY FOR TRAINING AND CONSISTS OF A SPRING EXTENSION, BENT INTO A CIRCLE AND COVERED WITH LEATHER AT THE TIP. THIS BAYONET WAS DESIGNED FOR USE WITH A SPECIAL TRAINING RIFLE.

No. 2. **U.S. FENCING MODEL 1912.** THIS BAYONET IS IDENTICAL TO 236-1 EXCEPT THAT THE ENTIRE EXTENSION IS COVERED WITH LEATHER. THE ARMED SERVICES DEVOTED MUCH TIME TO FENCING IN THE PRE-WORLD WAR I ERA AND ROCK ISLAND ARSENAL WAS EQUIPPED WITH EXTENSIVE LEATHER MANUFACTURING CAPABILITY FOR THE COVERING OF THESE BAYONETS.

① U.S. FENCING M. 1909
HARDIN #161

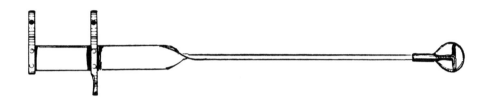

② U.S. FENCING M. 1912
HARDIN #162
KIESLING VOL. III #620

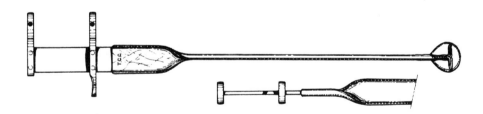

No. 1. **BANNERMAN CADET BAYONET - QUAKER RIFLE.** THIS CRUDE CAST PIECE WAS MANUFACTURED FOR USE ON A WOODEN BARRELED RIFLE SOLD IN THE EARLY BANNERMAN CATALOGS (FOR EXAMPLE, THE RIFLE AND BAYONET ARE ILLUSTRATED ON PAGE 81 OF THE 1925 CATALOG). THE MARKET FOR SUCH WEAPONS WAS VERY GOOD IN THE EARLY 1900s.

No. 2. **BANNERMAN CADET BAYONET.** THIS IS ANOTHER SMALL CADET SOCKET BAYONET WHICH I THINK WAS ISSUED WITH BANNERMAN CADET RIFLES. I AM NOT AT ALL SURE OF THIS IDENTIFICATION. THE PIECE IS WELL MANUFACTURED AND IS EQUIPPED WITH A HGH QUALITY LEATHER SCABBARD WHICH LOOKS LIKE THE TYPES USED IN THE UNITED STATES CIVIL WAR.

No. 3. **CADET BAYONET - QUAKER RIFLE.** THIS SOCKET BAYONET IS ANOTHER CRUDELY FABRICATED PIECE PROBABLY DESIGNED FOR USE ON A WOODEN BARRELED (OR QUAKER) GUN. THIS BAYONET IS PLATED.

No. 4. **DAISY AIR RIFLE - No. 40 BB GUN.** THIS SOCKET BAYONET IS INTERESTING AND WAS MANUFACTURED FOR USE ON THE DAISY No. 40 BB GUN. ALTHOUGH FABRICATED FROM SHEET STEEL, THE PIECE IS VERY WELL MADE. IT IS BLUED AND EQUIPPED WITH A RUBBER TIP. THIS BAYONET WAS PRODUCED IN SMALL NUMBERS AND IS RELATIVELY SCARCE. ALSO ILLUSTRATED IS AN AD FROM THE 1917 SEARS, ROEBUCK AND CO. CATALOG 133 WHERE THIS BAYONET IS SHOWN ON THEIR MARKHAM-PRODUCED "NEW KING ARMY RIFLE". MARKHAM WAS ACQUIRED BY DAISY SOMETIME AFTER THE TURN OF THE CENTURY.

① BANNERMAN CADET

KIESLING VOL III #529
BANNERMAN 1903 PG. 11

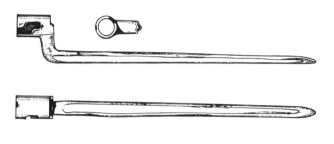

③ UNKNOWN CADET

KIESLING VOL II #839

② BANNERMAN CADET

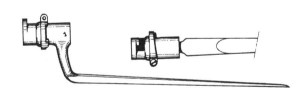

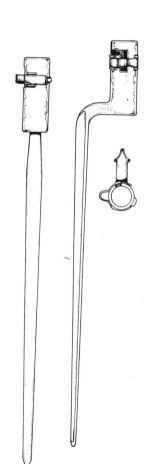

④ DAISY AIR RIFLE

R.D.C. EVANS PG. 225

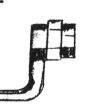

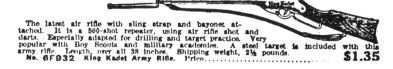
237

No. 1. **REMINGTON MILITARY MODEL No. 1913.** THIS BAYONET WAS MANUFACTURED TO ACCOMPANY THE REMINGTON No. 4S MODEL 1913 BOYS' RIFLE. THE PIECE IS RATHER CRUDELY MANUFACTURED WITH A HOLLOW CAST HANDLE, TOP RELEASE AND UNFULLERED STEEL BLADE. THE SCABBARD IS MANUFACTURED OF LEATHER AND IS OF HIGH QUALITY. BOTH THE BAYONET AND RIFLE ARE OF REDUCED DIMENSIONS AND THE BAYONET LUG ON THE BARREL LOOKS LIKE A NAIL. THIS IS A RARE BAYONET, AS ONLY 1,000 WERE MANUFACTURED. AN AD FROM THE 1918 CATALOG IS ILLUSTRATED.

No. 2. **USN Mk I - TRAINING BAYONET.** THIS PIECE WAS PRODUCED IN THE 1940S FOR USE BY THE NAVY. IT HAS A METAL TANG AND A BLACK PLASTIC BLADE. THOUGH CALLED A TRAINING BAYONET, I FEEL IT WAS USED FOR GUARD DUTY AND OTHER NON-COMBAT FUNCTIONS. THE USN MK I WAS ISSUED WITH TWO SCABBARDS; THE USN MK I AS ILLUSTRATED AND AN ALL CANVAS VERSION EQUIPPED WITH A BELT HOOK. THIS BAYONET IS MARKED ON THE RICASSO OF THE BLADE "USN MK I" ON ONE SIDE AND HAS THE MANUFACTURER ON THE OTHER SIDE WHICH WILL BE EITHER "B. M. CO" OR "P. B. CO", PLUS AN ALPHA NUMERIC CODE.

① *REMINGTON MODEL 1913*

R.D.C. EVANS PG. 225

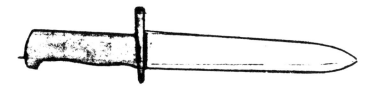

Remington UMC No. 4S "Military Model" .22 Cal. Single Shot Rifle

(Formerly called "Boy Scout" Rifle)

No. 4S "Military Model," Solid Frame. { With bayonet . . . List, $15.50
{ Without bayonet . . List, 13.00

Specifications—Single shot rifle, chambered for .22 Short and Long cartridges. Stock and fore-end are of oil-finished selected walnut, barrel of Remington steel, accurately rifled and sighted, 28 inches in length. Length over all, 43 inches. Weight, 5 lbs. Equipped with oak-leather sling straps, bayonet, scabbard, stacking swivel, etc.

The Remington UMC "Military Model" rifle is designed to meet the demand for an attractive and durable .22 cal. military Arm of light weight for the younger generation.

Its extreme accuracy and splendid handling qualities recommend it particularly for drill and target work. These features have caused it to be adopted by a number of the leading boys military organizations throughout the country.

② *U.S. NAVY MK I*

HARDIN # 163
KIESLING VOL II # 295

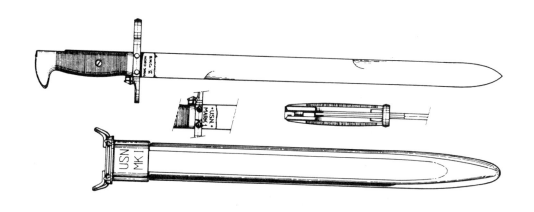

No. 1. **Ingram Model M-6 - Submachine Gun.** This bayonet was commercially produced by Ingram for some of their compact submachine guns (frequently called machine pistols). It is my understanding the M-6 is utilized in some South American countries.

No. 2. **Miniature Bayonets.** The United States also enjoyed a fascination with small bayonets and the examples shown reflect "trench art" as well as recent replicas of the M.1892 Krag.

① INGRAM M-6
SUBMACHINE GUN

WATTS & WHITE #940

② MINIATURE BAYONETS

No. 1.   URUGUAYAN MODEL 1895 - MAUSER.   THIS BAYONET WAS COPIED FROM THE BELGIUM M-1889 MAUSER BAYONETS AND WAS PRODUCED BY FN IN BELGIUM.   THE MAJOR DIFFERENCE FROM THE BELGIUM CIVIL GUARD BAYONET IS A SMALLER (15MM) MUZZLE RING.   IT WAS IMPORTED TO THE UNITED STATES IN 1985 WITH OTHER URUGUAYAN ARMS.

No. 2.   URUGUAYAN MODEL 1895 - MAUSER.   THIS BAYONET WAS FABRICATED FROM A BAVARIAN WERDER BY URUGUAY FOR THEIR ARTILLERYMAN.   THE WERDER BAYONET WAS MODI-FIED BY THE ADDITION OF A BRASS CROSSGUARD WITH A RATHER CRUDE DOWN-SWEPT HOOK.

No. 3.   URUGUAYAN MODEL 1900 - MAUSER.   THIS BAYONET HAS A CRUCIFORM BLADE SIMILAR TO A FRENCH LEBEL, A STEEL CROSSGUARD WITH A HOOKED QUILLON AND AN ALL BRASS HANDLE.   THE PIECE IS WELL MADE AND MAY HAVE BEEN FABRICATED IN EUROPE.

No. 4.   URUGUAYAN MODEL 1908 - MAUSER.   THIS BAYONET IS A STANDARD MAUSER DESIGN WITH A SHORT SLOT AND IS IDENTIFIED AS URUGUAYAN SIMPLY BECAUSE THE IMPORTER IDENTIFIED IT AS SUCH.   THIS PIECE IS IDENTICAL TO THE BRAZILIAN MODEL 1908; HOWEVER, IT WAS MANUFAC-TURED WITHOUT THE HOOKED QUILLION.

① URUGUAYAN M.1894

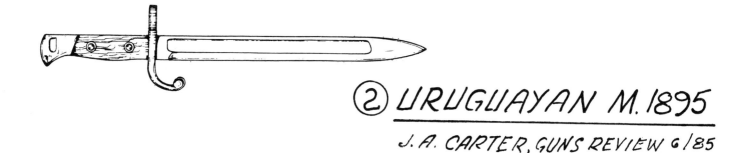

② URUGUAYAN M.1895

J.A. CARTER, GUNS REVIEW 6/85

③ URUGUAYAN M.1900

KIESLING VOL. III # 681

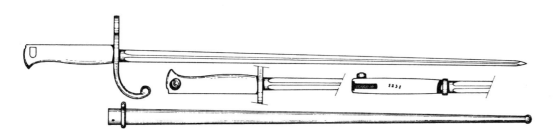

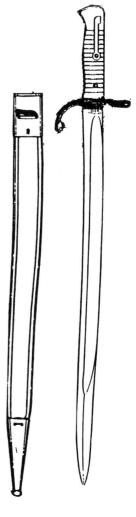

④ URUGUAYAN M.1908

No. 1. **VENEZUELAN C. 1900 - MAUSER.** THESE BAYONETS WERE IMPORTED TO THE UNITED STATES IN QUANTITY SOMETIME DURING 1984 OR 1985 AND LOOK MUCH LIKE THE BELGIUM MAUSER, HOWEVER, WERE MANUFACTURED TO FIT A GERMAN MODEL 1871/84 MAUSER AND WERE APPARENTLY MADE UNDER A CONTRACT FOR VENEZUELA. THEY ARE BEAUTIFUL PIECES IN MINT CONDITION AND HAVE HOOKED QUILLONS, SPANNER SCREWS IN THE GRIPS AND AN ALL METAL SCABBARD. THERE ARE NO MARKINGS ON THE PIECES I HAVE SEEN.

No. 2. **VENEZUELAN C. 1900 - MAUSER.** THIS BAYONET IS IDENTICAL TO 241-1, HOWEVER, THE QUILLON HAS BEEN REMOVED AND ALL OF THE EXAMPLES EXAMINED HAVE SEEN USE. THESE PIECES HAVE A SERIAL NUMBER STAMPED ON THE CROSSGUARD AND ONE IMPORTER TOLD ME HE HAD OBTAINED THE PIECES FROM VENEZUELA.

No. 3. **VENEZUELAN MODEL 1949 - ABL.** THESE PIECES ARE IDENTICAL TO THE LONG M-1924 BELGIUM MAUSER BAYONETS, HOWEVER, HAVE BEEN EQUIPPED WITH A MUCH LARGER MUZZLE RING WHICH ALLOWS THEM TO FIT THE BELGIUM ABL 49 RIFLE. MANY EXAMPLES I HAVE EXAMINED HAVE LARGE NUMBERS STAMPED ON THE GRIPS. THE LONG STEEL SCABBARD IS IDENTICAL TO THAT USED ON THE M-1924 MAUSER.

① *VENEZUELAN M.1900*

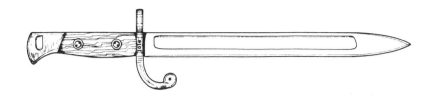

② *VENEZUELAN M.1900 MODIFIED*

KIESLING VOL. IV #831

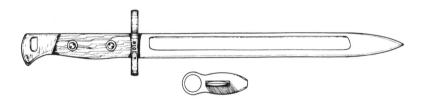

③ *VENEZUELAN M.1949 F.N. EXPORT PATTERN*

KIESLING VOL. I # 278

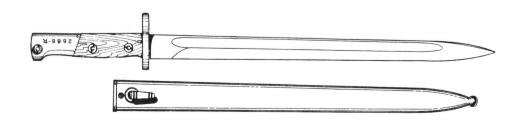

No. 1. YUGOSLAVIAN CONVERSION OF AUSTRIAN MODEL 1895. THIS BAYONET IS IDENTICAL TO THE AUSTRIAN MODEL 1895, HOWEVER, HAS THE KRAGIYERVAC ARSENAL STAMP (B.T.3 IN A TRIANGLE) ON THE BLADE, AS ILLUSTRATED.

No. 2. YUGOSLAVIAN CONVERSION OF AUSTRIAN MODEL 1895M. THIS PIECE IS A COMBINATION OF A MANNLICHER AND MAUSER BAYONET AND I HAVE TWO EXAMPLES; ONE WITH AN AUSTRIAN EAGLE ON THE BLADE AND SPANNER BOLTS IN THE GRIPS, AND THE OTHER WITH NO MARKS AND RIVETED GRIPS, AS ILLUSTRATED. MY IDENTIFICATION IS SPECULATIVE AND THE PIECES MAY BE FOR AN AUSTRIAN TRANSITIONAL RIFLE OF SOME TYPE.

No. 3. YUGOSLAVIAN CONVERSION OF AUSTRIAN MODEL 1895. THIS BAYONET IS DEFINITELY YUGOSLAVIAN BECAUSE OF THE KRAGIYERVAC MARKINGS; HOWEVER, IT IS ONCE AGAIN A COMBINATION OF MANNLICHER AND MAUSER CHARACTERISTICS AND HAS A LONG MAUSER-STYLE BLADE SIMILAR TO THE M-1924.

No. 4. YUGOSLAVIAN MODEL 1924. THIS PIECE IS THE STANDARD LONG PATTERN MODEL 1924 BAYONET, HOWEVER, HAS THE KRAGIYERVAC ARSENAL MARKINGS AND SPANNER-TYPE GRIP FASTENERS. THESE BAYONETS ARE NUMBERED ON THE CROSSGUARD AND SCABBARD STUD, AS ILLUSTRATED. THE YUGOSLAVIAN SCABBARDS ALSO HAVE THE KRAGIYERVAC STAMP AND ARE SLIGHTLY MORE TAPERED THAN THE BELGIUM VERSIONS.

① YUGOSLAVIAN CONV.

KIESLING VOL. I # 67
WATTS & WHITE # 960

② YUGOSLAVIAN CONV.

KIESLING VOL. I #114

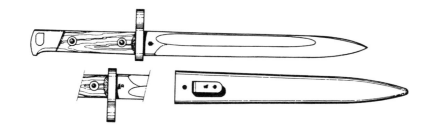

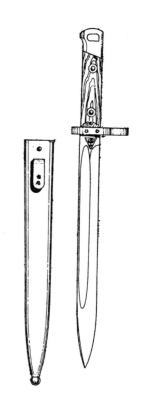

③ YUGOSLAVIAN CONV. LONG

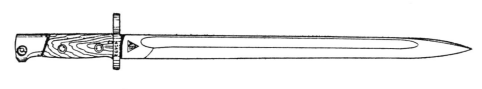

④ YUGOSLAVIAN M.1924

KIESLING VOL. II # 280

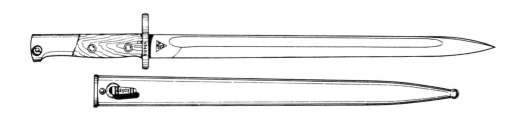

No. 1. **YUGOSLAVIAN MODEL 1924 - SHORT.** THE BAYONET ON THE LEFT IS IDENTICAL TO 242-4; HOWEVER, THE BLADE HAS BEEN SHORTENED AND THE ENTIRE PIECE BLUED. THE SCABBARD HAS ALSO BEEN SHORTENED. I ALSO POSSESS TWO VERSIONS OF THIS BAYONET WHICH WERE MANUFACTURED SHORT (THE PIECE ILLUSTRATED ON THE RIGHT). ONE VERSION HAS NO MAKER MARKS, THE OTHER IS CYRYLIC MARKED WITH THE NUMBER "44"; HOWEVER, BOTH ARE SERIAL NUMBERED ON THE CROSSGUARD. A SIMILAR PIECE IS ILLUSTRATED IN WATTS & WHITE NO. 970 AND I HAVE BEEN TOLD THEY WERE USED BY SYRIA.

No. 2. **YUGOSLAVIAN MODEL 1924.** THIS BAYONET IS IDENTICAL TO 242-4; HOWEVER, THE MUZZLE RING HAS BEEN REMOVED, AS ILLUSTRATED. THIS PIECE IS FINISHED BRIGHT AND HAS THE STANDARD M-1924 SCABBARD.

No. 3. **YUGOSLAVIAN MODEL 1924B.** THESE PIECES ARE REWORKS OF IMPERIAL GERMAN BAYONETS AND ARE INTERESTING BECAUSE OF THE EXTENSIVE MODIFICATIONS. THE GRIPS HAVE BEEN REPLACED WITH A SLIGHTLY DIFFERENT VERSION AND THE SCABBARDS ARE ALL METAL. I HAVE SEEN ALL TYPES OF GERMAN WORLD WAR I BAYONETS MODIFIED BY THE YUGOSLAVS. THESE INCLUDE THE 98/05, AS ILLUSTRATED; THE SEITENGEWEHR 98 SHORTENED; AND THE SEITENGEWEHR 98 WITH SAWBACK UNSHORTENED, THOUGH EQUIPPED WITH A METAL SCABBARD.

No. 4. **YUGOSLAVIAN MODEL 1956 - SUBMACHINE GUN.** THIS IS AN INTERESTING BAYONET WITH A BLACK FINISH AND BLACK PLASTIC HANDLES. IT IS 11" LONG WITH A VERY SMALL MUZZLE RING.

NOTE: YUGOSLAVIA CURRENTLY UTILIZES THE AKM WITH AN ALL-BLACK VERSION OF THE RUSSIAN M.1972 (SEE 167-4).

243 - YUGOSLAVIA

① YUGOSLAVIAN M.1924
SHORT

KIESLING VOL I # 203
KIESLING VOL I # 126

② YUGOSLAVIAN M.1924
MODIFIED

KIESLING VOL.II #279

③ YUGOSLAVIAN M.24b

KIESLING VOL.III # 624

④ YUGOSLAVIAN M.1956
SUB·MACHINE GUN

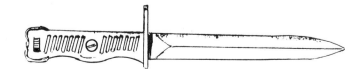
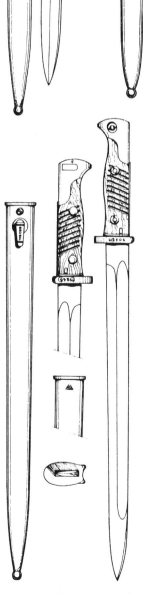

243

No. 1. UNIDENTIFIED SOCKET. THIS BAYONET IS A VERY INTERESTING PIECE AS IT WILL SNAP RIGHT ON TO A GERMAN M-1871 MAUSER, HOWEVER, IS BRITISH-MARKED WITH BRITISH CHARACTERISTICS. A PROMINENT JAPANESE COLLECTOR HAS A JAPANESE-MARKED M-1871 MAUSER WITH THIS BAYONET. IT IS VERY EASY TO IDENTIFY BECAUSE OF THE SHORT SOCKET AND THE FACT THAT IT HAS NO CLASP SCREW.

No. 2. UNIDENTIFIED SOCKET. THIS PIECE MAY BE BAVARIAN BECAUSE THE SOCKET DIMENSIONS ARE IDENTICAL TO THE BAVARIAN M-1858 (13-1); HOWEVER, THE BLADE IS QUADRANGULAR AND FEW MARKINGS ARE EVIDENT.

No. 3. UNIDENTIFIED SOCKETS. THESE SOCKET BAYONETS ARE ALL READILY DISTINGUISHABLE FROM THE SOCKET DETAIL PROVIDED ON THE PHOTOGRAPH. THEY ARE PIECES ACQUIRED THROUGH 15 YEARS OF COLLECTING WHICH HAVE DEFIED MY RESEARCH. ANY READER INPUT WOULD BE VERY MUCH APPRECIATED.

No. 4. UNIDENTIFIED SABRE. THIS IS AN EXAMPLE IN MY COLLECTION OF WHAT I THINK IS A BAYONET PRODUCED BY INDIAN SMITHS FOR QUASI-INDEPENDENT INDIAN RULERS DURING THE "HEYDAY" OF THE YATAGHAN BAYONET. IT IS ONE OF SEVERAL RATHER CRUDE COPIES OF THE BRITISH PATTERN 1856 BAYONETS I HAVE SEEN. THEY ALL HAVE WOOD GRIPS, HOWEVER, VARY AS TO BLADE FORM AND M/R DIAMETER. AMERICAN DEALERS LIKE TO CALL THESE CONFEDERATE.

DIMENSIONS	
BLADE LENGTH	17 1/2"
BLADE WIDTH	25/32"
SOCKET LENGTH	2 1/8"
SOCKET O.D.	30/32"
SOCKET I.D.	23/32"
SHANK LENGTH	15/16"

DIMENSIONS	
BLADE LENGTH	18 3/4"
BLADE WIDTH	26/32"
SOCKET LENGTH	3 3/16"
SOCKET O.D.	29/32"
SOCKET I.D.	25/32"
SHANK LENGTH	1 23/32"

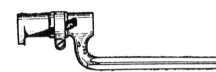

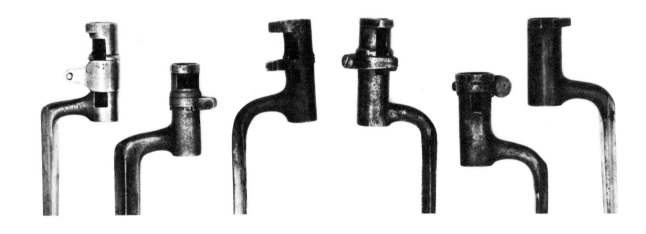

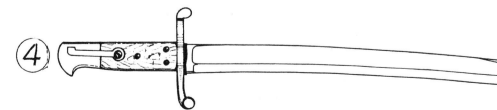

BIBLIOGRAPHY

BAYONETS - DEFINITIVE REFERENCE WORKS

P. KIESLING. BAYONETS OF THE WORLD. 4 VOLS. MILITARY COLLECTORS SERVICE. HOLLAND 1973

J. WATTS AND P. WHITE. THE BAYONET BOOK. PRIVATELY PUBLISHED. BIRMINGHAM, ENGLAND 1975

J. A. CARTER AND J. WALTER. THE BAYONET 1850-1970. ARMS AND ARMOUR PRESS. LONDON, ENGLAND 1974.

R. D. C. EVANS AND F. J. STEPHENS. THE BAYONET. MILITARIA PUBLICATIONS. BUCKINGHAMSHIRE, ENGLAND 1985

BAYONETS - GENERAL

F. J. STEPHENS. BAYONETS. ARMS AND ARMOUR PRESS. LONDON, ENGLAND 1968

F. J. STEPHENS. THE COLLECTOR'S PICTORIAL BOOK OF BAYONETS. A & A PRESS. LONDON, ENGLAND 1971

_____ BAJONETTEN DA TILL NU. SVENSKA VAPENSTIFTELSEN. SWEDEN 1976

J. A. CARTER. ALLIED BAYONETS OF WORLD WAR 2. ARMS AND ARMOUR PRESS. LONDON, ENGLAND 1969

J. L. HAYDEN. THE SOCKET BAYONET. CROMPTON PRESS. LETCHWORTH, HERTS, ENGLAND 1978

R. J. WILKINSON LATHAM. PICTORIAL HISTORY OF SWORDS & BAYO-
NETS. IAN ALLEN. LONDON, ENGLAND 1973

G. HUGHES & C. FOX. A COMPENDIUM OF BRITISH AND GERMAN REGI-
MENTAL MARKINGS. PRIVATE PUBLICATION. BRIGHTON, ENGLAND
1975

J. WALTER & G. HUGHES. A PRIMER OF WORLD BAYONETS. PARTS 1 &
2. PRIVATE PUBLICATION. BRIGHTON, ENGLAND 1969

B. WALSH. BAYONETS ILLUSTRATED. BASHEL EAVES. DUBLIN, IRELAND
1970

I. D. DAVIDSON. BAYONET MARKINGS. PRIVATELY PUBLISHED,
ENGLAND 1973

H. A. MAEURER. MILITARY EDGED WEAPONS OF THE WORLD. PRIVATELY
PUB. NEW YORK, USA 1970

D. ERNST. GUIDE TO FOREIGN & U.S. BAYONETS & MISC. EDGED
WEAPONS. PRIVATE PUB. IOWA, USA 1970

D. ERNST. POCKET GUIDE TO BAYONETS AND MISC. EDGED WEAPONS.
OMAR PRINTING CO. LECLAIRE, IOWA, USA 1978

J. A. CARTER. BAYONET BELT FROGS. PARTS 1 & 2. THARSTON
PRESS. NORWICH, NORFOLK, ENGLAND 1983

J. A. CARTER. WORLD BAYONETS 1800 - PRESENT. ARMS & ARMOUR
PRESS. LONDON, ENGLAND 1984

BAYONETS - INDIVIDUAL NATIONS

BRITAIN AND COLONIES

R. J. WILKINSON LATHAM. BRITISH MILITARY BAYONETS. HUTCHINSON. LONDON, ENGLAND 1967

C. FFOULKES & E. C. HOPKINSON. SWORD LANCE & BAYONET. CAMB. UNIV. PRESS, ENGLAND 1938. A&A PRESS REPRINT

R. B. MANAREY. THE CANADIAN BAYONET. CENTURY PRESS. EDMONTON, ALBERTA, CANADA 1971

R. B. MANAREY. HANDBOOK OF IDENTIFICATION MARKS ON CANADIAN ARMS. CENTURY PRESS. EDMONTON, ALBERTA, CANADA 1973

I. D. SKENNERTON. AUSTRALIAN SERVICE BAYONETS. PRIVATE PUB. MARGATE, AUSTRALIA 1976

R. J. WILKINSON LATHAM. SWORD BAYONET PATTERN 1888. MILITARIA PUBS. LTD. SOUTHEND, ENGLAND 1970

I. D. SKENNERTON. THE BRITISH SPIKE BAYONET. PRIVATE PUB. MARGATE, AUSTRALIA 1982

G. PRIEST. THE BROWN BESS BAYONET 1720-1860, THARSTON PRESS, NORWICH, NORFOLK, ENGLAND 1986

GERMANY

M. WELSER. REICHSWEHR AND WEHRMACHT BAYONETS 1920 - 1945. ESCONDIDO, CALIFORNIA, USA 1985

J. WALTER. THE GERMAN BAYONET. ARMS AND ARMOUR PRESS. LONDON, ENGLAND 1976

J. WALTER. THE SWORD & BAYONET MAKERS OF IMPERIAL GERMANY. LYON PRESS. BRIGHTON, ENGLAND 1973

_____ GEW. 98 GERMAN MAUSER RIFLE. BANNERMAN. NEW YORK, USA 1921

C. DANGRE'. BAYONETTES ERSATZ ALLEMANDES. ARTICLES IN CARNET DE LA FOURRAGERE. BRUSSELS, BELGIUM 1925-31

J. A. CARTER. GERMAN ERSATZ BAYONETS. VOL. 1. LYON PRESS. BRIGHTON, ENGLAND 1976

J. A. CARTER. GERMAN BAYONETS S.98-02 & S.98-05. THARSTON PRESS. NORWICH, NORFOLK, ENGLAND 1984

G. L. WALKER AND R. J. WEINAND. GERMAN CLAMSHELLS AND OTHER BAYONETS. QUINCY, ILLINOIS, USA 1985

G. WINDHIEL. IMPERIAL GERMAN EDGED WEAPON CATALOGUE AND PRICE GUIDE. PRIVATE PUBLICATION. ZIEGLERVILLE, PA., USA 1985

R. FRANZ, EIN LEITFADEN FUR DEN BLANK WAFFEN SAMMLER. JOURNAL-VERLAG GERMANY 1979

JAPAN

L. JOHNSON. JAPANESE BAYONETS. PRIVATE PUBLICATION. BROKEN ARROW, OKLAHOMA, USA 1987

F. L. HONEYCUTT, JR. AND F. P. ANTHONY. MILITARY RIFLES OF JAPAN. PRIVATE PUBLICATION. LAKE PARK, FLORIDA, USA 1977

MEXICO

J. B. HUGHES, JR. MEXICAN MILITARY ARMS, THE CARTRIDGE PERIOD 1866-1967. DEEP RIVER ARMORY, INC. HOUSTON, TEXAS, USA 1968

SPAIN

J. L. CALVO' PASCUAL. BAYONETAS DEL EJERCITO ESPANOL. PRIVATE PUB. BARCELONA, SPAIN 1971

B. BARCELO RUBI'. ARMAMENTO PORTAIL ESPANOL 1764-1939. LIBERIA EDITORIAL. SAN MARTIN, MADRID, SPAIN 1976

FRANCE

J. P. PITOUS. LES BAIONNETTES REGLEMENTAIRES FRANCAISES. CREPIN-LEBLOND. PARIS, FRANCE 1973

RUSSIA

R. KARHA. RUSSIAN & SOVIET BAYONETS. PRIVATE PUB. HELSINKI, FINLAND 1975

SWEDEN

B. LISSMARK. SVENSKA BAJONETTER. VAPENLITTERATURFORLAGET. KARLSKRONA, SWEDEN 1974

U.S.A.

A. N. HARDIN. THE AMERICAN BAYONET. RILING AND LENTZ. PHILADELPHIA, U.S.A. 1964

D. B. WEBSTER. AMERICAN SOCKET BAYONETS. MUSEUM RESTORATION SERVICE. OTTAWA, CANADA 1964

R. G. HICKOX. COLLECTORS' GUIDE TO AMES U.S. CONTRACT MILITARY EDGED WEAPONS: 1832-1906. PRIVATE PUBLICATION. BRANDON, FL., USA 1984.

R. V. DAVIS. U.S. SWORD BAYONETS 1847-65. PRIVATE PUB. PITTSBURG, PA. U.S.A. 1963

M. H. COLE. U.S. MILITARY KNIVES BAYONETS MACHETES. BOOK 3. B'HAM, ALABAMA, U.S.A. 1979

G. C. NEUMANN. SWORDS & BLADES OF THE AMERICAN REVOLUTION. STACKPOLE. HARRISBURG, PA., USA 1973

B. WEST. REMINGTON ARMS & HISTORY. PRIVATE PUBLICATION. AZUSA, CAL., USA 1970

E. A. HULL. PROVIDENCE TOOL COMPANY MILITARY ARMS. PRIVATE PUBLICATION. MILTON, FL., USA 1978.

W. S. BROPHY. THE KRAG RIFLE. BEINFELD PUBLISHING, INC., USA 1980

GEORGE MADIS. THE WINCHESTER BOOK. ART & REFERENCE HOUSE. BROWNSBORO, TEXAS, USA

W. A. ALBAUGH II. CONFEDERATE EDGED WEAPONS. HARPER & BROTHERS. PUBLISHED BY BONANZA BOOKS, USA 1960

GERMAN THIRD REICH DRESS BAYONETS

J. P. ATWOOD. THE DAGGERS & EDGED WEAPONS OF HITLER'S GERMANY. PRIVATE PUB. BERLIN, GERMANY 1965

F. J. STEPHENS.   A GUIDE TO NAZI DAGGERS SWORDS & BAYONETS. PRIVATE PUB. BURY, LANCS 1965

F. J. STEPHENS. EDGED WEAPONS OF THE THIRD REICH. ALMARK. NEW MALDEN, SURREY, ENGLAND 1972

T. M. JOHNSON. COLLECTING THE EDGED WEAPONS OF THE THIRD REICH. 5 VOLS. PRIVATE PUB. U.S.A. 1977-85

F. J. STEPHENS. REPRODUCTION RECOGNITION! PRIVATE PUB. MILTON KEYNES, BUCKS 1976; 2ND ED. MILITARIA COLLECTOR INC. CALIFORNIA, USA 1981

PERIODICALS WITH BAYONET ARTICLES

J. PHILLIP LANGELLIER, BRUCE N. CANFIELD, ROBERT M. REILLY, DAVID MORRISON, A. MOWBRAY – <u>MAN AT ARMS</u>

FRED SLATON, RICHARD MUNNO – <u>THE GUN REPORT</u>

FRED WEBER – <u>AMERICAN RIFLEMAN</u>

J. A. CARTER, GRAHAM PRIEST – "BAYONETS" IN <u>GUNS REVIEW</u>

DEREK V. COMBLIN, KENNETH L. COPE, ROBERT J. DYNES, R. A. PICKERING, FRANK J. DUPUIS, DANNY J. FAREK, JOHN A. BELTON – <u>THE CANADIAN JOURNAL OF ARMS COLLECTING</u>

PETER WHITE, ERIC OVESEN – <u>WABENHISTORISK TDSSKRIFT, THE JOURNAL OF THE DANISH ARMS & ARMOUR SOCIETY</u>

WOLFGANG SEEL, MARTIN BEHRENS – <u>DEUTSCHES WAFFEN JOURNAL</u>

R. D. C. EVANS, G. PRIEST, "STONEWALL" - <u>GUNS, WEAPONS & MILITARIA</u>

J. A. CARTER, C. BROWN - <u>KAISERZEIT</u>

LEON WINN, WILLIAM EASTERLY, FRANK KNAPP, GEORGE TAYLOR, LARRY JOHNSON - <u>BANZAI</u>

AVE ATQUE VALE

WELL, THAT'S IT – MY COLLECTION AND EVERYTHING I KNOW ABOUT IT; ALSO, HOPEFULLY, SUFFICIENT INFORMATION AS TO THE REAL EXPERTS. IN THIS REGARD, WE CAN LOOK FORWARD TO FORTHCOMING BOOKS ON ASSAULT RIFLE BAYONETS BY HOMER BRETT, U.S. SOCKET BAYONETS BY ROBERT REILLY, JAPANESE BAYONETS BY LARRY JOHNSON AND, HOPEFULLY, MORE OFFERINGS FROM ANTHONY CARTER.

THIS EFFORT HAS BEEN ENJOYABLE AND I HOPE YOU FIND IT OF USE. I WOULD BE VERY HAPPY TO HEAR FROM ANY OF YOU AND WOULD ENTERTAIN THE POSSIBILITY OF UPDATING THIS BOOK AS WE ALL LEARN MORE. YOU CAN WRITE ME AT P.O. BOX 2863, TULSA, OK 74101.

BAYONETS

FROM JANZEN'S NOTEBOOK

Order Form ░░░░░░░░░░░░░░░░░░░░░

JERRY JANZEN
POST OFFICE BOX 2863
TULSA, OK 74101

Dear Jerry:

Please send _____ copies of Bayonets from Janzen's Notebook to:

_____
Name

_____
Company

_____
Street Address   Apt.

_____
City   State   Zip Code

___ PLEASE PLACE MY NAME ON YOUR MAILING LIST.

Enclosed is my payment for:

_____ Books @ $20.00 ....$_____

BAYONETS

FROM JANZEN'S NOTEBOOK

Order Form ░░░░░░░░░░░░░░░░░░░░░

JERRY JANZEN
POST OFFICE BOX 2863
TULSA, OK 74101

Dear Jerry:

Please send _____ copies of Bayonets from Janzen's Notebook to:

_____
Name

_____
Company

_____
Street Address   Apt.

_____
City   State   Zip Code

___ PLEASE PLACE MY NAME ON YOUR MAILING LIST.

Enclosed is my payment for:

_____ Books @ $20.00 ....$_____

Order Form □□□□□□□□□□□□□□□□□□□□□□□

JERRY JANZEN
POST OFFICE BOX 2863
TULSA, OK 74101

Dear Jerry:

Please send _____ copies of Bayonets from Janzen's Notebook to:

_____
Name

_____
Company

_____
Street Address   Apt.

_____
City   State   Zip Code

___ PLEASE PLACE MY NAME ON YOUR MAILING LIST.

Enclosed is my payment for:

_____ Books @ $20.00 ....$_____

Order Form □□□□□□□□□□□□□□□□□□□□□□□

JERRY JANZEN
POST OFFICE BOX 2863
TULSA, OK 74101

Dear Jerry:

Please send _____ copies of Bayonets from Janzen's Notebook to:

_____
Name

_____
Company

_____
Street Address   Apt.

_____
City   State   Zip Code

___ PLEASE PLACE MY NAME ON YOUR MAILING LIST.

Enclosed is my payment for:

_____ Books @ $20.00 ....$_____